A Flight of Parsons

A Flight of Parsons

The Divinity Diaspora of Trinity College Dublin

Edited by THOMAS P. POWER

☙PICKWICK *Publications* · Eugene, Oregon

A FLIGHT OF PARSONS
The Divinity Diaspora of Trinity College Dublin

Copyright © 2018 Wipf and Stock Publishers. All rights reserved. Except for brief quotations in critical publications or reviews, no part of this book may be reproduced in any manner without prior written permission from the publisher. Write: Permissions, Wipf and Stock Publishers, 199 W. 8th Ave., Suite 3, Eugene, OR 97401.

Pickwick Publications
An Imprint of Wipf and Stock Publishers
199 W. 8th Ave., Suite 3
Eugene, OR 97401

www.wipfandstock.com

PAPERBACK ISBN: 978-1-5326-0909-1
HARDCOVER ISBN: 978-1-5326-0911-4
EBOOK ISBN: 978-1-5326-0910-7

Cataloguing-in-Publication data:

Names: Power, Thomas P., editor.

Title: A flight of parsons : the divinity diaspora of Trinity College Dublin / edited by Thomas P. Power.

Description: Eugene, OR : Pickwick Publications, 2018 | Includes bibliographical references and index.

Identifiers: ISBN 978-1-5326-0909-1 (paperback) | ISBN 978-1-5326-0911-4 (hardcover) | ISBN 978-1-5326-0910-7 (ebook)

Subjects: LCSH: Trinity College (Dublin, Ireland)—History.

Classification: LF915 .F55 2018 (paperback) | LF915 .F55 (ebook)

Manufactured in the U.S.A.   07/24/18

Front Cover Illustration
"A Flight of Parsons" from the Robinson Collection of Caricatures (Digital No. OLS-CARI-ROB0051), Department of Early Printed Books, Trinity College Library is reproduced with the permission of The Board of Trinity College Dublin.

Contents

Contributors | vii
Acknowledgments | ix
Abbreviations | x

1 Introduction | 1

2 Trinity College, Dublin, and the Making of Irish Evangelicalism, 1790–1850 | 13
   —Alan R. Acheson

3 The Formation of a Seceder: John Nelson Darby at Trinity College, 1815–1819 | 41
   —Timothy C. F. Stunt

4 "An Awful Mystery": William Magee on the Atonement | 60
   —Ephraim Radner

5 A Question of Possession—Who Owned the Church of Ireland's History? | 80
   —James Blake Knox

6 James Henthorn Todd, an Irish High Churchman and Early Tractarian at Trinity College, Dublin | 102
   —Patricia McKee

7 The Role of Bible Societies in Identity Formation, 1800–1850 | 129
   —Miriam Moffitt

8 "That Ultra-Protestant Nursery": Trinity College, Dublin, and the Supply of Anglican Clergy to England, 1830s–1880s | 143
   —Ann McCormack

9 "A Zealous, Well-educated, and Well-informed Body of Clergy": Trinity College, Dublin, and the Church in Upper Canada in the 1830s | 162
   —Thomas P. Power

10 Samuel Blake's Projects and Ministries: A Canadian's Church of Ireland Vision | 201
  —ALAN L. HAYES

11 Anglican Deaconesses in Canada 1889–1969: Two Operational Models of a Gendered Order of Ministry | 226
  —ALAN L. HAYES

12 From Trinity College, Dublin, to *Terra Australis*: Trinity-educated Clergymen in Colonial Australia | 276
  —MICHAEL GLADWIN

13 The Word of God is Seed: John Wyclif's Evangelical Theology and the Naming of Wycliffe College | 297
  —SEAN OTTO

Index | 319

Contributors

Alan R. Acheson has a PhD from Queen's University, Belfast. His publications include *A History of the Church of Ireland1691–2002* (2nd ed. 2002), *Bishop John Jebb and the Nineteenth Century Anglican Renaissance* (2013), and *The Shaping of Northern Ireland: A Historical Perspective*. He lives in Cobourg, Ontario, Canada.

James Blake Knox recently completed his PhD at Trinity College, Dublin, entitled *Fact or Fiction? The Church of Ireland's Writing of Irish Church History, 1838–1870*.

Michael Gladwin is Lecturer in History at St. Mark's National Theological Centre in the School of Theology, Charles Sturt University, Canberra, Australia. He is the author of *Anglican Clergy in Australia, 1788–1850: Building a British World* (2015).

Alan L. Hayes is Bishops Frederick and Heber Wilkinson Professor of the History of Christianity at Wycliffe College, University of Toronto, and Director of the Toronto School of Theology. He has published broadly in Anglican studies and Canadian church history. He is a priest of the Anglican Church of Canada in the diocese of Niagara.

Ann McCormack is a local historian based in Berkshire, England. She is a former nurse and administrator. As a mature student, she undertook a BA in History at the University of Reading and an MA in Modern History at Royal Holloway, University of London. She has published items on local history and contributes to history tours and lectures in Berkshire. Her interests include Irish migration and church history.

Patricia McKee is a scholar, academic, Anglican priest, and former chaplain. While studying for her BD (Hons), she developed an interest in the outworkings of the Oxford Movement in Ireland. She published her initial findings on the leading Irish Tractarian, James Henthorn Todd, in *Search:*

A Church of Ireland Journal (2006), followed by a longer essay on Todd, his family and antiquarian networks in Romantic Ireland *From Tone to Gonne: Fresh Perspectives on Nineteenth Century Ireland*, (2013), and then completed her PhD thesis at Trinity College, Dublin: *James Henthorn Todd, A Tractarian at Trinity: Making Ireland in the Mid-Nineteenth Century* (2015). Her current interests include writing historical biography and memoir in literature, history and theology.

Miriam Moffitt lectures in church history in St. Patrick's College, Maynooth, Ireland. Her publications include *Soupers and Jumpers, the Protestant Missions in Connemara, 1848–1937* (2008) and *The Society for Irish Church Missions to the Roman Catholics, 1849–1950* (2010). She is a contributor to and co-editor of *The Church of Ireland and its Past* (2017).

Sean Otto is assistant registrar and adjunct professor of church history, Wycliffe College, University of Toronto. His research interests include medieval theology, preaching, and heresy. He is the author of several articles on the theology and sermons of John Wyclif, and is currently completing a monograph on Wyclif's anti-fraternal preaching.

Thomas P. Power is adjunct professor of church history, Wycliffe College, University of Toronto. Most recently he is the author of *Ministers and Mines: Religious Conflict in an Irish Mining Community, 1847–1858* (2014), editor of *Change and Transformation: Essays in Anglican History* (2013), and contributor to and co-editor of *Reformation Worlds: Antecedents and Legacies in the Anglican Tradition* (2016).

Ephraim Radner is Professor of Historical Theology, Wycliffe College, University of Toronto. An Anglican priest, he is author, most recently, of *Time and the Word: Figural Reading of the Christian Scriptures* (2016) and *A Time to Keep: Theology, Mortality, and the Shape of a Human Life* (2016).

Timothy C. F. Stunt has taught history in Switzerland, Britain, and the United States. His books include *From Awakening to Secession: Radical Evangelicals in Switzerland and Britain 1815–35* (2000) and *The Elusive Quest of the Spiritual Malcontent: Some Early Nineteenth-century Ecclesiastical Mavericks* (2015). He contributed numerous articles to *The Dictionary of National Biography* (Oxford University Press), including biographies of J. N. Darby, Francis W. Newman and Archbishop Power Trench.

Acknowledgments

ACKNOWLEDGEMENT IS MADE TO the editor of the *Journal of the Canadian Church Historical Society* 53.1–2 (2015) 40–66, where the essay by Alan Hayes on Samuel Blake first appeared.

My grateful thanks to Rachel Lott of Wycliffe College for her diligent work formatting the manuscript for submission, her stellar work on the bibliographic apparatus, and for useful suggestions.

Thomas P. Power

Abbreviations

ACC   Anglican Church of Canada
AO   Archives of Ontario
AWTC   Anglican Women's Training College
CCSS   Colonial Church and School Society
CIHM   Canadian Institute of Historical Micro-reproductions
CMS   Church Missionary Society
DCB   *Dictionary of Canadian Biography.* 15 vols. Toronto: University of Toronto Press, 1966–2005.
DEB   *Dictionary of Evangelical Biography, 1730–1860.* 2 vols. Edited by Donald M. Lewis. Oxford: Blackwell, 1995.
DNB   *Oxford Dictionary of National Biography.* Edited by H. G. C. Matthew and Brian Harrison. Oxford: Oxford University Press, 2004.
DUM   *Dublin University Magazine.* Dublin: Curry, 1833–77.
GSA   General Synod Archives, Anglican Church of Canada
HBS   Hibernian Bible Society
HCMS   Hibernian Church Missionary Society
JCCHS   *Journal of the Canadian Church Historical Society*
LPL   Lambeth Palace Library
NLI   National Library of Ireland
RCBL   Representative Church Body Library
SPCK   Society for the Promotion of Christian Knowledge
SPG   Society for the Promotion of the Gospel
TCD   Trinity College, Dublin
WCA   Wycliffe College Archives

1

Introduction

RECENT PUBLICATIONS HAVE HIGHLIGHTED the contributions of the Irish of different denominations in the creation of a global religious diaspora.[1] As one dimension to this movement, this volume of essays examines the experience of Irish Anglicans in the nineteenth century, particularly clergy who were graduates of Trinity College, Dublin (TCD), and their lay associates, the formative influences on them, and the varied contributions they made and legacies they left in Britain, Canada, and Australia.

Irish Anglican clergymen played an important role in the creation of a nineteenth-century "Greater Ireland," which denotes a diasporic movement in which the Irish transformed into a global people, actively participating in British imperial expansion and colonial nation-building. These essays address the formative influences and circumstances that informed the mental world and disposition of Irish Anglicans, particularly their clergy, in the early decades of the nineteenth century, and how these emanated in the colonial church and their legacy there.

In the course of the early nineteenth century, movement outward was triggered because of a number of developments that challenged the dominant position of the Established Church in Ireland. Foundational in this respect was the historic minority status of its adherents. In Ireland, although Anglicans constituted the largest Protestant denomination, they were in a minority in relation to the majority Catholic population. Around 1840, the ethnic-religious breakdown of the Irish population was 80 percent Roman Catholic, 12 percent Anglican, and the Ulster-Scots at 8 percent, who

1. Barr and Carey, *Religion and Greater Ireland*.

were mostly Presbyterian.[2] Their position as a minority served, on the one hand, to sharpen their sense of self-identity, and on the other, gave them a missionary purpose. While its embattled minority status emanated in an evangelical and missionary upsurge in the 1820s, this was not enough to propel the church into a majority position. Rather there were additional circumstances that further undermined its status in Irish society.

That status was based on the fact that the Church of Ireland, though a minority denomination, was the established, official state church, which gave it a position of authority and influence beyond its numbers. Such influence extended through its parishes which were units of local government, its ecclesiastical courts, its bishops and clergy (some of whom held official positions in the government, local and central), and its churches as places of worship. While a series of reforms since 1800 addressed some of the more serious abuses like non-residence, pluralism, and political interference, and while the number of churches increased by about one-third, and better financial practices were introduced, the church was still in a precarious position for the wider historical context was not auspicious.

All the indicators were that the government of the day was intent on dismantling its privileged position. Increased mobilization by Catholics resulted in significant concessions, notably the act of 1829, which conceded the right of Catholics—if elected—to sit in parliament, which was a major dent to Anglican dominance of the political system. For many Protestants the victory of the Catholic Association under Daniel O'Connell held out the prospect of a radical restructuring of Irish society, one that suggested Catholic hegemony. To exacerbate the situation, in 1831 the introduction by the Whig government of a national system of nondenominational education was seen as an attack on a sector seen by many Anglicans as their prerogative.

Further, the Church Temporalities Act (3 and 4 Will. IV, c.37) of 1833 was a landmark piece of legislation, for it signaled direct government intervention in the institutional structure of the church. The act reduced the number of archbishoprics in Ireland from four to two, the number of bishops by ten, and appointed commissioners with powers to divide livings, suspend appointments, and allocate revenues. Given the administrative downsizing it mandated, the act was wide-ranging in its impact, for since episcopal patronage was the main source of clerical recruitment in Ireland, the act reduced and made more competitive the opportunities for advancement by clergy and caused them to seek out openings elsewhere.[3] In fact, the

---

2. Wilson, *Irish in Canada*, 8; Vaudry, *Anglicans and the Atlantic World*, 48.
3. Trollope, *Clergymen of the Church of England*, 111, where it is noted that livings

act was the direct cause of many Irish clergy emigrating, most immediately to pursue openings in England.[4] As Gladwin shows, among the Irish-born clergy who served in Australia, only seven migrated to Australia before the passing of the Church Temporalities Act, while forty-one clergymen (85 percent of all Irish Australian clergymen) migrated during 1833–50.[5] Already many Irish clergy had gone to Canada prior to the act's passage and the exodus was to accelerate thereafter.[6]

Added to all this was the collapse of the economic boom generated by the Napoleonic wars. After 1815 depression set in and continued into the 1820s and was exacerbated by a severe cholera outbreak in 1832–33. Further, as the 1830s progressed, recurrent agrarian violence was to coalesce around the unresolved issue of tithe, the main source of clerical income.[7] The clergy who emigrated in the first few decades of the nineteenth century were the inheritors of a long experience of their class in dealing with tithe. It had become one of contention increasingly in the second half of the eighteenth century and was to continue into the 1830s.[8] Although the tithe amounts collected in individual cases were not (in the words of one rector) "enormous," being on average a net sum of £324.9s.10d. (or even as low as £250), and, although the tax had the sanction of law, it lacked equity as it was not only payable by adherents to the Church of Ireland but was also demanded of Roman Catholics and non-conformists, and resisted by them on the basis that no desired service was provided in return for payment, nor was it sought.[9] Change was therefore inevitable, especially in trying economic times.

Resistance to tithe gathered into a crescendo in the early 1830s, resulting in a widespread refusal by Catholics to pay a legal demand. Arrears of tithe payments mounted, those in the diocese of Ferns and Leighlin, for instance, in 1833 being £40,777 and £34,986 respectively.[10] Although an act (3 and 4 Will. IV, c.100) provided relief for tithe owners who could

---

in Ireland were more generally in the gift of the bishops compared to England and were given on the basis of merit.

4. Haig, *Victorian Clergy*, 32, 119, 123, 194–95.

5. Gladwin, "Mindful of Her St. Columbas," 301. The Irish famine appears to be a major factor: twenty-four clergymen (half of all Irish clergymen) arrived in Australia.

6. Talman, *Authentic Letters from Upper Canada*, 119–20.

7. Two-thirds of clerical incomes derived from rectorial tithes: Refaussé, *Church of Ireland Records*, 32.

8. For the eighteenth-century background on tithes, see Power, *Land, Politics, and Society*, 196–210.

9. Townsend, *Facts and Circumstances*, 87–89; "State of the Irish Clergy," 734–35.

10. Thomas [Elrington], Ferns to the primate, 26 Apr. 1833 (RCBL Ms 183/1/22).

demonstrate the scale of their arrears, the days of tithe exactions were numbered, and continued popular unrest precipitated further legislation (1 and 2 Vict., c.56) which converted tithe into a rent charge and reduced the amount payable, in effect abolishing the tax. The undermining of tithe as a source of income made the prospect of a clerical life in Ireland less attractive to graduating ordinands. The result was that many existing and aspirant clergy were led to entertain the prospect of emigration.

Political and ecclesiastical changes precipitated new configurations and identities within Irish Protestantism. One expression of this was the growth of Irish sympathies for high churchmanship and their development into an orientation towards Tractarianism and the Oxford movement, with J. H. Todd of TCD being a key figure. As Patricia McKee elucidates, although always a minority voice, high church devotional, liturgical, and church practices were incorporated over time into the Church of Ireland, and as such constitute an important development of this period. In the realm of historical reconstruction, Irish high churchmen advanced a convincing narrative to demonstrate the bona fides of the Church of Ireland as an authentic Irish institution. The result, as James BlakeKnox demonstrates, was that the respective writings of Richard Mant and Charles Richard Elrington, the Regius Professor of Divinity at TCD (1829–50), served as a defense in light of external criticism of the Church of Ireland, as a disavowal to the low church faction within the church, and as a counter to Presbyterian and Roman Catholic interpretations of the church's past. The historical interpretation advanced by Mant and Elrington influenced the perceptions and understanding of generations of Irish clergymen, including John Travers Lewis, the first bishop of Ontario, who acknowledged the mentorship role Elrington had played in his own formation.

Adding to theological diversity, at the other extreme from high churchmanship there was unease among Anglicans over a growing number of secessionist laity and clergy.[11] These included Irish clergy such as Thomas Kelly, John Walker, and John Nelson Darby, all TCD graduates who drifted into non-conformity, as well as laity such as Lady Theodosia Powerscourt. Such seceders became Plymouth Brethren, and Kelly and Walker established their own denominational following. The most notable and influential was John Nelson Darby, who by the early 1830s was speaking at prophecy conferences near Dublin, out of which the embryonic Plymouth Brethren denomination was to emerge with Darby advancing its

---

11. Carter, *Anglican Evangelicals*, appendix (399–403) lists about 170 seceders in the period c.1730–1900.

dispensationalist distinctives.¹² Darby in particular drew with him members from such prominent Church of Ireland families as Synge and Digby. Such secession was a source of turbulence and disunity in the church at a time when it was under assault from without on a number of sides. Nevertheless, the incidence of secession and the rise of high churchmanship indicate that there was significant theological diversity among Trinity College graduates, including clergy, in that they were not universally ultra-Protestant in their theological commitments. In Canada, while Benjamin Cronyn was firmly in the evangelical camp and John Travers Lewis was of a high church orientation, yet both were keen to promote church growth in a frontier setting.

The cumulative effect of attacks on the church was that they fed into a rising sense among Protestants as a whole of an apocalyptic end times. Apocalyptic fervor had been growing since the French Revolution. Significantly, the majority of early nineteenth-century writers on biblical prophecy were Anglicans; and a disproportionately large number of these, including futurists like John Nelson Darby, were educated at TCD. In this regard, it is notable that the college curriculum stressed, in the study of the books of Isaiah, Jeremiah, Daniel, Micah, Zechariah, and Malachi, the "omitting [of] such chapters as do not contain direct prophecies of the Messiah."¹³ Irish Anglicans were particularly apprehensive because of the prophecy of Signor Pastorini, the pseudonym for Charles Walmesley, a Catholic bishop, whose work *General History of the Christian Church*, first published in 1771 and reprinted many times, predicted the end of Protestantism and particularly the destruction by God in 1825 of the Church of Ireland. The prophecies were disseminated extensively and were particularly influential among rural agitators to whose cause the prophecies gave a sectarian purpose.¹⁴ The Trinity constituency was concerned about the dissemination of such predictions, evidenced in an anonymous pamphlet by one of its graduates, its title indicating that its concern was deemed of broader imperial import than merely domestically in Ireland.¹⁵ That the college was aware of events around the country is exemplified by the receipt by Rev. Charles Boyton of TCD, an Orangeman, in 1831, of reports of outrages against Protestants, one of which expressed the probability of "expel[l]ing Protestants by an im-

12. Akenson, *Discovering the End of Time*.
13. *Dublin University Calendar* (1838), 3.
14. Donnelly, *Captain Rock*, 119–49 traces the overt sectarian element.
15. *The Prophecies of Pastorini, analyzed and refuted, and the powerful tendency of inflammatory predictions to excite insurrection, satisfactorily demonstrated, from incontrovertible historical records, with a cursory view of the dangerous state of Ireland, from an exclusively Popish conspiracy. Humbly submitted to the consideration of the Protestants of the British Empire. By a Graduate of Trinity College* (1823).

mediate and systematic rebellion."[16] In addition, attacks on clergy, attacks on churches, bible burnings, and the expulsion of congregations are recorded for the period.[17] Such outrages against Protestants and the expectancy around 1825 caused many to emigrate.[18] Further, the coinciding of the year 1825 with the growing political aspirations of Irish Catholics and recurrent rural unrest only added to Protestant fears of a repetition of the massacres of 1641 and 1798. While nothing came of these specific predictions of annihilation, Protestants realized that something ominous was in the air and that their position was no longer secure. It comes as no surprise to note that an association for the relief of distressed Protestants was founded in 1836.[19] Nor does it come as a surprise that the cumulative set of circumstances nurtured an anti-Catholic bias among Anglican emigrants, which they brought to the new world.

In the 1820s and 1830s, therefore, the prospects for the Church of Ireland and its adherents, including its existing and aspirant clergy, were not propitious. As described by one emigrant, conditions in Ireland by c.1830 had become "irksome, unprofitable, and insecure," and as described by another, for Protestants Ireland was "growing too hot."[20] An Irish peer addressing the House of Lords in 1827 referred to Protestants being "persecuted and proscribed in Ireland and would be forced out of the country or annihilated."[21] Political upheaval in the form of Catholic emancipation, the decimation of tithe as an income source, the sundering of a monopoly on education, the reduction in the number of bishoprics, a detrimental economic environment coupled with secessionism, and rising apocalyptic fervor informed the mental world of Irish Anglicans. Such circumstances coalesced to push large numbers from Ireland.

Pivotal in the formation of attitudes among the Irish Anglican élite was the education received at Trinity College, Dublin. It was the gathering point for Anglicans of different backgrounds, and as such acted as a great leveler and formative center where laity and aspirant clergy were educated together under a common curriculum. As Stunt outlines, the latter

---

16. Robert Crawford, Castlecomer to Rev. Charles Boyton, TCD, 5 Jan. 1831 (NLI Ms 18,609 [2]).

17. "State of the Irish Clergy," 727–32. It tabulates fifty outrages against clergy in the period 1834–37: ibid., 730. For a similar situation of outrages against Protestants in the 1680s: Power, "Lapsed Member and Penitent Convert," 111–13.

18. Phelan and O'Sullivan, *A Digest of the Evidence*, i, 36–37, 39, 42.

19. RCBL Ms 485 Association for the Relief of Distressed Protestants. It contains minutes, accounts, inventories, and reports dating from 1836 in twenty-two volumes.

20. Talman, *Authentic Letters*, xxii, 99.

21. Quoted in Akenson, *Discovering the End of Time*, 243.

was unspecialized and provided the average student with a basic classical grounding. Yet, as Power demonstrates, those studying for the BA degree were obliged to take lectures in divinity, irrespective of whether they were intended for holy orders or not. This meant that graduates had a foundation in biblical knowledge and an oral articulation of the faith.

So far as divinity education specifically is concerned, prior to 1833 there existed no further professional education beyond the BA degree for those wishing to enter the church. Basic education at the undergraduate level was deemed sufficient, for the arts curriculum was formative for divinity studies. In it, study of the Bible was central, there was an emphasis on catechetical instruction, and an expectation of regular attendance at the college chapel. Reforms introduced in 1833 inaugurated a two-year graduate degree in divinity, thereby providing a concentration and raising the standard. The result was that clergy graduates who came to the new world possessed a classically-based education supplemented with a strong biblical literacy, a catechetical facility, and a grounding in apologetics.

In such an education particular texts were influential. One such was by William Magee, entitled *Discourses on the Scriptural Doctrines of Atonement and Sacrifice*, based on two sermons delivered at Trinity College and later published as *Discourses and Dissertations*. As Radner demonstrates, such a text could be impactful on generations of students who were formed at TCD and subsequently went out to serve in the church, or appealed to the reading public. Its inclusion in the curriculum at Trinity for several decades assured its influence in the Irish church and beyond. Because the work was a defence of orthodoxy against Unitarians and Catholics in particular, not only was it useful in domestic contexts but in colonial situations as well.

Situating the prevailing piety of TCD as deriving in part from the eighteenth-century culture of reason and in part from the Romantic movement, Stunt depicts the faculty of the college as possessing a wide range of political and religious temperaments, though the prevailing one by the 1820s was evangelical. In fact TCD was at the center of Irish evangelical life, as evinced by the numbers of scholarly and evangelical clergy it produced. As Acheson documents, its graduates, lay and clerical, had a wide impact domestically and internationally, notably in the fields of law, literature, politics, and the church. In the evangelical advance, the relationship between Trinity College and the Bethesda Chapel was of strategic value, with the ministry of Benjamin Mathias proving attractive to students, and with John Walker and Thomas Kelly, the seceders, among its champions. Another key figure was Rev. Joseph H. Singer, who from his base in TCD influenced other facets of the evangelical cause in the church at large. Beyond Dublin, clerical graduates maintained a collectivist sense through clerical associations, that under Peter Roe in Ossory being the most notable.

In terms of wider influence, the most immediate context being the Church of England, until 1870 TCD provided more graduate clergy for the church in England than anywhere outside Oxford and Cambridge. As McCormack demonstrates, urban growth in England was the pull factor which occasioned a steady stream of TCD-trained clergy to the newly industrialized areas, including most prominently Lancashire, where in its parishes a prominent cohort of Trinity evangelicals was to be found. Between 1840 and 1880, over one hundred Dublin-educated clergymen were active in Liverpool and Birkenhead, while London brought together Irish Tractarians and several TCD evangelicals who operated in the crowded areas of London, where poor Irish Catholics had settled. Internationally, the Society for the Propagation of the Gospel (SPG) sponsored other TCD graduates for service in Australia and Canada, while others served the Church Missionary Society (CMS) in Asia, Africa, and New Zealand.

Central in connecting local, national, and international levels, and also formative in the experience of Irish Anglicans in the early nineteenth century, was involvement in agencies and organizations intent on the dissemination of the Scriptures and scriptural education. Such agencies and organizations, drawing support from those of a low church or evangelical orientation, and through the dissemination of literature, acted to connect local communities and efforts with the wider missionary movement. For instance, Rev. Dominick Edward Blake Sr. (d.1821) (father of Dominick Edward Blake who emigrated to Canada in 1832) as rector of Kiltegan, Co. Wicklow, collected funds locally for the Hibernian CMS.[22] Other clergy associated with the CMS prior to their coming to Canada included Rev. Charles Brough, who by 1826 was a committee member.[23] J. N. Darby was a supporter.[24] The most tangible connection between the CMS and Trinity College was in the person of Rev. Joseph H. Singer, who was one of a number who went on a preaching tour in 1827 to raise funds for the society.[25] Another older society, the Association of Discountenancing Vice (1792), had in its membership nearly all the fellows of TCD.[26] As Moffitt's case study

22. Rev. D. E. Blake, Kiltegan Glebe, Baltinglass to the Society, 26 Mar. 1819: RCBL Ms 315/1 Abstract letter book, 1814–23.

23. RCBL Ms 315/3/1 Abstract letter book, 1814–23; 315/1/1/2, 3, 76, 84; minutes, 1826–37.

24. RCBL Ms 315/1/1/2/10 Minutes 1826–37, where his subscription of £1.1s.0d. is recorded.

25. RCBL Ms 315/1/1/1–3 Minutes 1814–58 sub 1827.

26. Liechty, "Irish Evangelicalism, Trinity College Dublin," 97.

of the Sligo branch of the Hibernian Bible Society indicates, experience of being involved with educational, philanthropic, or scriptural organizations connected local communities with the wider world of missionary activity, and was formative in conveying the realization that local efforts were part of a larger, worldwide movement, with domestic and foreign efforts being complementary. Not only was this context formative in itself but was one in which an early missionary vocation could arise and was particularly relevant for emigrants who were already familiar with a wider world even before they left. All this bears witness to an intertwined, connected, and cohesive world domestically and internationally.

Lay participation in educational, philanthropic, and scriptural societies was critical to the success of such bodies.[27] The many para-church organizations succeeded because their membership was composed of committed ordinary people who subscribed to their goals and who engaged in multiple efforts in their support, including fundraising. Lay involvement and prominence in church affairs was a feature of the old world that was transferred to the new. Anything from the concern of immigrants in having churchmen in accord with their own theological views, to the critical lay vote which gave Benjamin Cronyn victory in the episcopal election in Huron in 1857, to the multiple involvements of Canada's chief Anglican layman, Samuel Hume Blake, in advancing the interests of the church, exemplify the robust nature of lay involvement in the new world.

In common with the Irish as a whole, TCD graduate clergy exerted an influence on colonial life in the religious, cultural, intellectual, and political spheres, out of all proportion to their numbers. While Irish clergymen made up only about a quarter (23 percent) of the 235 Anglican clergymen who served in Australia prior 1850, and while by 1911 Protestants made up a quarter of the Irish-born population there, with their lay confreres they were among the country's leading churchmen, educators, scholars, journalists, and in other sectors vital to public life and institutions. Also Irish Anglicans exhibited a high degree of involvement in public affairs as a natural extension of their worldview and drawing on their experience in Ireland. They were prominent in the legal profession, in politics, and in educational initiatives. As Hayes demonstrates, they were to the fore in their support of educational institutions such as the University of Toronto (an institution initially led by three of their own), social service, and evangelistic associations, including the Deaconess School.

In another contribution, Hayes rehabilitates the neglected and misunderstood ministry of deaconesses, and highlights the often devalued role

---

27. Ibid., 67–69.

they played in the church because of the lack of prestige associated with that ministry. In its genesis, a key individual linking old world and new was Rev. William Pennefather (1816–1873). Born in Dublin and a graduate of TCD (1840), Pennefather's evangelical credentials derived from multiple connections in the Irish evangelical world. He was the nephew of Edward Pennefather (1774–1847), the Irish chief justice, whose wife was the sister of J. N. Darby.[28] Because of his connection with Darby, Pennefather introduced the latter's ideas to a wider audience, including influencing D. L. Moody, whom he invited to England in 1873. Pennefather proceeded into the Anglican ministry with the various churches he served experiencing growth, and in the process becoming a noted preacher, ecumenist, and social reformer in London. He founded the Mildmay Institute (later renamed Mildmay Deaconess House), which included the training of women in that ministry. In Canada, with no bishop willing to assume responsibility for advancing the new ministry, the alumni association and supporters of Wycliffe College championed it with Samuel Blake, its main founder, taking the lead. Through contacts established for training purposes, Mildmay molded the training of deaconesses in the Canadian Church with a few hundred set apart in the eighty years after 1889. Representing them as "collegially organized, mission-minded, professionally skilled women with a heart for the marginalized," Hayes traces how the deaconesses made a significant impact on church life and on wider Canadian society.

The deaconesses are a prime example of the transfer of an agency or service from the old to the new world. Another index of continuities and adaptation is naming practices. Many Irish place names were applied to the settlements where the Irish settled, marking a continuity of identity with the old world. Although the Irish were influential in its formation and ethos, the new theological college founded by Cronyn in 1863 was not named "Ussher College" after Archbishop James Ussher, the seventeenth-century divine associated with the theological ethos of the early decades of Trinity College, Dublin. But rather Cronyn named it Huron College, patterning the name of the new diocese on where it was situated. Frederick O'Meara and Samuel Blake were among the founders of the Protestant and Episcopal Divinity School in 1877, later Wycliffe College, the naming of which is probed by Otto. While the founders chose the fourteenth-century scholar John Wyclif as a highly representative figure of Evangelicalism, a close examination of the distinctive attributes of Evangelicalism indicates the extent to which each aligned with Wyclif's theology and hence his appropriateness

---

28. *DEB*, vol. 2, 871. William Pennefather was seemingly a first cousin of R. T. Pennefather (1830–1865) who served as secretary of Sir Edmund Walker Head, governor general of Upper Canada, from 1854 (Leighton, "Pennefather, Richard Theodore," n.p.).

for naming purposes. The conclusion is that while Wyclif and nineteenth-century Anglican evangelicals lie in the same tradition, there are clear differences between them as well.

Faced with its dismantling in the old world, adherents of the Church of Ireland availed themselves of opportunities for its reconstruction in the new. If efforts to mount a so-called "Second Reformation" in Ireland in the 1820s were stunted, the new world provided an opportunity for its evangelical impulses to be unleashed. The zeal that proved impossible to give full reign to in the 1820s or was constrained because of political shifts and the dismantling of the ecclesiastical apparatus, was given a new, largely untrammeled, expression in a pioneering missionary setting in Australia and Canada.

BIBLIOGRAPHY

Akenson, Donald Harman. *Discovering the End of Time: Irish Evangelicals in the Age of Daniel O'Connell*. Montreal: McGill-Queen's University Press, 2016.

Barr, Colin, and Hilary M. Carey, eds. *Religion and Greater Ireland: Christianity and Irish Global Networks, 1750–1950*. Montreal: McGill-Queen's University Press, 2015.

Carter, Grayson. *Anglican Evangelicals: Protestant Secessions from the Via Media, c.1800–1850*. Oxford: Oxford University Press, 2001.

Donnelly, James S., Jr. *Captain Rock: The Irish Agrarian Rebellion of 1821–1824*. Madison, WI: University of Wisconsin Press, 2009.

The Dublin University Calendar, for the Year 1838. Dublin: Curry, 1838.

Gladwin, Michael. "'Mindful of her St. Columbas and Gaels': Ireland, Empire and Australian Anglicanism, 1788–1850." In *Religion and Greater Ireland*, edited by Colin Barr and Hilary Carey, 297–318. Montreal: McGill-Queen's University Press, 2015.

Haig, A. G. L. *Victorian Clergy: Ancient Profession Under Strain*. London: Croom Helm, 1984.

Leighton, Douglas. "Pennefather, Richard Theodore." In *DCB* 9. Toronto: University of Toronto Press, 2003–. http://www.biographi.ca/en/bio/pennefather_richard_theodore_9E.html.

Liechty, Joseph. "Irish Evangelicalism, Trinity College Dublin, and the Mission of the Church of Ireland at the End of the Eighteenth Century." PhD diss., St Patrick's College, Maynooth, 1987.

Phelan, W., and M. O'Sullivan, *A Digest of the Evidence Taken before the Select Committee of the Two Houses of Parliament Appointed to Inquire into the State of Ireland, 1824–25*. 2 vols. London: Cadell, 1826.

Power, Thomas P. *Land, Politics, and Society in Eighteenth-Century Tipperary*. Oxford: Clarendon, 1993.

———. "Lapsed Member and Penitent Convert: Reformation, Liturgy and Conversion in Ireland in the 1690s." In *Reformation Worlds: Antecedents and Legacies in the*

Anglican Tradition, edited by Thomas P. Power and S. Otto, 111–13. Studies in Church History 13. New York: Lang, 2016.

The Prophecies of Pastorini, Analyzed and Refuted. Dublin: George Bull,1823.

Refaussé, Raymond. *Church of Ireland Records.* Dublin: Four Courts, 2006.

"State of the Irish Clergy." *DUM* 10 (Dec 1837) 727–36.

Talman, James J., ed. *Authentic Letters from Upper Canada Including an Account of Canadian Field Sports by Thomas William Magrath, the Whole Edited by the Rev. Thomas Radcliff.* Toronto: Macmillan, 1953.

Townsend, T. S. *Facts and Circumstances Relating to the Condition of the Irish Clergy of the Established Church.* Dublin: Curry, 1832.

Trollope, Anthony. *Clergymen of the Church of England.* Leicester, UK: Leicester University Press, 1974.

Vaudry, Richard W. *Anglicans and the Atlantic World: High Churchmen, Evangelicals and the Quebec Connection.* Montreal: McGill-Queen's University Press, 2003.

Wilson, David A. *The Irish in Canada.* Ottawa: Canadian Historical Association, 1989.

2

Trinity College, Dublin, and the Making of Irish Evangelicalism, 1790–1850

ALAN R. ACHESON

"THE IRISH ESTABLISHMENT BECAME by far the most evangelical section of the Anglican church."[1] Lecky's observation can be extended to note that, largely out of the strength of that defining tradition of the nineteenth-century Irish Church, a preponderant influence in Anglicanism worldwide was achieved. The curious neglect of the tradition itself, its importance in Ireland, and its impact overseas is a unique failure in both Anglican Church history and Irish history. The Church of England has long been able to read its evangelical history, and continues to publish its biography. The church in Wales is also well briefed about its evangelical heritage. But that of the Church of Ireland is virtually unknown, in virtual defiance of Primate William Alexander's call to his General Synod in 1905, as he embarked on a masterly and moving analysis of that heritage. "But let us note this: the evangelical revival in Ireland was wonderful and it was almost everywhere."[2] The studied neglect of the past century is impoverishing, and not only for Ireland. For through its unique outreach the revival in the Church of Ireland strengthened the growing Anglican churches in the old Commonwealth—Australia, Canada, and New Zealand—enhanced the expanding work of

1. Lecky, *History of England*, vol. 2, 611.
2. Alexander, "President's Address," lxvii.

the Church Missionary Society (CMS) in Africa and India, and provided the Church of England with hundreds of clergy. At home it touched the Presbyterian Church and brought the Bible to the Irish people. A movement seen as distinct from Methodism in 1784, and as the dominant school in the church of 1878, was at once Irish and evangelical. Rooted in the doctrinal principles of the Reformation, it also drew inspiration from the history of Ireland's national church. If its worldwide outreach recalled the heroic mission of the sixth century, its scholarly and saintly character was equally redolent of the early Celtic church. If that heritage, then, has been strangely ignored, so in particular has been the place of Trinity College, Dublin (TCD), as the beating heart of Irish evangelical life and outreach.

From 1756, when A. M. Toplady (author of the hymn "Rock of Ages") entered TCD as a student recently converted in a barn in county Wexford under the preaching of a semiliterate Methodist, evangelicals had been represented in the college. From the 1790s until after disestablishment in 1871, there were always evangelical clergy who had been scholars, tutors, and fellows of TCD; and from the 1840s, evangelical bishops who had been divinity professors or assistant lecturers. Whereas the evangelical revival in England was showing signs of decadence by 1830, in Ireland, by contrast, its vigor, both intellectual and spiritual, was at its height during the half century from 1825. In that year, Edward Hincks, the famed Egyptologist, became rector of Killyleagh in county Down. He epitomized the new genre of Irish clergyman, at once scholarly and evangelical. Most were educated at Trinity College. Its intellectual eminence, conservative theology, and biblical divinity training—the hallmarks of TCD in the nineteenth century—both served and were served by evangelicals. Two learned bishops of Ossory did much to establish and consolidate the evangelical tradition of the Irish Church. Hugh Hamilton (1799-1805), a founder of the Royal Irish Academy, was its first episcopal patron. Of his five sons identified with the tradition, George Hamilton too was an erudite scholar, his publications including *Codex Criticus of the Hebrew Bible* (1821). A bust of Bishop James Thomas O'Brien adorns the Long Room in Trinity College, which he had served with distinction before his appointment to the see of Ossory (1842-1874). His learning informed his episcopal charges, his trenchant analyses of Tractarian principles being especially valued in England and the United States as well as Ireland. With Robert Daly's appointment to the see of Cashel in 1843, two evangelicals had become bishops within two years. As rector of Powerscourt from 1814, Daly's influence among the aristocracy and gentry of county Wicklow was such that Glendalough diocese became a stronghold of the evangelical revival. As Bishop of Cashel (1843-1872),

Daly identified with and encouraged the church's home mission in Dingle and other areas of southwest Munster.

Evangelicals educated in TCD were prominent in the legal profession also. From their ranks came a Lord Chancellor of England, Hugh McCalmont, Earl Cairns, and of Ireland, Sir Joseph Napier; and two chief justices of Ireland—Edward Pennefather and Thomas Lefroy. From 1867, Cairns was Chancellor, and Napier Vice-Chancellor of Dublin University, until 1885 and 1882, respectively; and the provostship of the liberal evangelical Dr. George Salmon lasted until 1902.

LITERARY ASSOCIATIONS

The evangelical revival, as the late Vivian Mercier established, was the background of the literary families of Brontë, Synge, and Yeats, and touched George Bernard Shaw in his boyhood in Dublin. It was linked with the Romantic movement. The author of the tragedy *Bertram*, first performed at Drury Lane in 1816, was C. R. Maturin, curate of St. Peter's, Dublin, who had much influence on French Romanticism. Like another evangelical curate, Charles Wolfe in the diocese of Armagh, best known for his poem *The Burial of Sir John Moore*, Maturin was admired by Byron and Scott. The traditions of Gaelic Ireland held a fascination for evangelicals. Their leader in Kerry, Archdeacon Arthur Rowan, was an authority on the history and antiquities of the county, and published *The Old Countess of Desmond* and other works. Henry Monck Mason, chief librarian of King's Inns (1815–1851), wrote a definitive history of parliaments in Ireland, and on the religion of the ancient Irish saints. Caesar Otway was, however, without peer. The co-founder in 1824 and literary editor of *The Christian Examiner and Church of Ireland Magazine*, he first published (under the pseudonym Wilton) the work of William Carleton, the native authority on the customs and folklore of the Irish peasantry. Otway was renowned also for his sketches of contemporary Irish life and his interest in Celtic Christianity. Primarily to him evangelicals owed their partly romantic, partly realistic devotion to the early Celtic church: for its independence, biblical ethos, hymnody, and missionary spirit. All of the eminent men identified here had Dublin University as their *alma mater*; each merited an entry in the nineteenth-century *Dictionary of National Biography*.[3]

---

3. These biographies were rewritten or revised for the DNB's successor publication, *The Oxford Dictionary of National Biography*. The foregoing sections draw on Acheson, *A True and Lively Faith*, 33–35.

GROWTH AND INFLUENCE

John Wesley made reference to evangelical clergy in England, but not in Ireland. Six years after his death in 1791, the Dublin bookseller Johnston listed the principal names of such clergy in Ireland: twenty-nine in number,[4] reduced by one when Henry Fulton was transported as a convict to Sydney Cove in 1800. Things were much changed by 1840, the *Christian Examiner* doubting that "the forty years' history of any other church presents such a mighty change as has taken place in the Church of Ireland."[5] Contemporaries concurred. William Alexander, born in 1824, commented: "The Evangelical revival had in my boyhood begun to lay a strong hand upon the younger clergy."[6] In his analysis for his clergy in Ossory of their church's recent history, Bishop J. T. O'Brien judged that, as more clergy embraced evangelical doctrines and more ordinands became imbued with them, "at last a great preponderance of the piety, energy and ability in the ministry was on the Evangelical side."[7] Outside observers, at the time and since, pointed to the influence that this Anglican renewal had on other churches. Paul Collins, a historian of Catholicism in Australia, has concluded that the devotional revolution in Irish Catholicism paralleled the evangelical revival in the Church of Ireland: "This devotional change flowed into Catholic religiosity and by the 1830s it had begun to permeate Australian Catholicism."[8] In his evidence to the parliamentary Commission of Education in 1825, Henry Cooke, then in the throes of his epic struggle with Henry Montgomery in the Synod of Ulster, attributed the decline in Arianism in his own church "to a visible and increasing improvement in the Established clergy," particularly those in the north: "Their name, their learning, their influence, have in many cases been thrown into the scale of orthodoxy, as well in the Presbyterian as in the Established Church, and from this co-operating power a great revolution of sentiment seems to have arisen in the Presbyterian body."[9]

A year before, Bishop John Jebb of Limerick had advised the House of Lords of the range and quality of the education that the clergy received in TCD. He had widened the scope of his tribute to his *alma mater* to include its training of members both of the medical profession and of the bar: "I can say that our physicians are skilful, learned, and sagacious; and that our

---

4. Motherwell, *A Memoir of the Late Albert Blest*, 64.
5. *Christian Examiner* (1840) 122–23.
6. Alexander, *Primate Alexander*, 29.
7. O'Brien, *A Charge to the Clergy*, 24.
8. Shiels and Woods, *Churches, Ireland and the Irish*, 246.
9. *Christian Examiner* (1840) 125–26.

school of surgery is confessedly one of the first in Europe." As to the bar, he claimed: "My lords, I do not know, in the community, a more exemplary, a more moral, a more religious body of men, than the Irish bar." That character, he held, contrasted with the infidelity of the bar under Gibbon's influence thirty years before, and was the more valuable in that, since the Union, the bar had become the most influential body that Ireland possessed. "And how were these men formed? My Lords, with few exceptions, they were formed at the Irish University, by the Irish clergy." Jebb drew a contrast between the ample resources of the two English universities and the more modest provision for Dublin. In the former, conjointly, some 3,500 students were educated in forty-one colleges and halls, by forty-one heads of houses and 965 fellows; while Dublin's 1,500 students had one college, one provost, and twenty-five fellows.[10]

If the evangelical tradition in Ireland had lagged behind that in England by half a century, then its rapid advance, once begun, was astonishing. Several factors combined to speed that advance: gentry influenced by John Wesley's preaching during his twenty-one visits to Ireland; aristocrats and general officers of both army and navy returning from war in Europe, imbued with evangelical zeal; and clergy educated at Cambridge and Oxford. Among the last, Viscount Lifford, dean of Armagh, an Oxonian, was the leader of the vigorous evangelical revival in the primatial see that so impressed Daniel Wilson, the future bishop of Calcutta, when as the guest of the deanery he toured the diocese in 1814. In Dromore diocese, Thomas Tighe, formerly fellow of Peterhouse, was regarded as a patriarch among the early evangelical clergy. Under these several influences, every sphere of the ascendancy was affected: banking and commerce, the judiciary, the medical and clerical professions, Dublin Castle, and the army. The exceptions initially were Dublin University and the bench of bishops, with episcopal bans and expulsions by provosts, or derogatory episcopal charges, the order of the day. Such opposition could not nullify the power of the patronage wielded by a sympathetic aristocracy, or the provision of proprietary chapels by committed laity, nor yet survive the evangelical conversion of a bishop, or the awkward truth that some fellows of Trinity College identified as evangelicals and on departure from Dublin influenced the rural church in the college livings to which they retired, many of these in the dioceses of Armagh and Raphoe.

---

10. Jebb, *Practical Theology*, vol. 2, 374–78.

TRINITY COLLEGE AND EVANGELICALISM

TCD and the Bethesda

The relationship, informal but intimate, between Trinity College and the Bethesda Chapel in Dorset Street highlights many of these characteristics.[11] The Bethesda's founder was William Smyth, a wealthy Dublin merchant who had been converted under William Romaine's preaching in London. The chapel was attached, as was the practice with early evangelical philanthropy, to a charity, in this case a female orphanage. It was opened for worship on 28 June 1786, with the church's liturgy and a hymnal compiled by Edward Smyth, the founder's brother and first co-chaplain, as service books. The brothers Smyth were nephews of an archbishop, Arthur Smyth of Dublin, and Edward had been educated at TCD. Bethesda's foundation signalled on the part of William Smyth, a committed churchman, a distinctive evangelical departure, in that it distanced itself from the schismatic tendencies of Methodism. Ironically, it was refused a licence by the Archbishop of Dublin, Robert Fowler, essentially because of its evangelical ethos, and Smyth was obliged to licence it under the Toleration Act. In 1794, for the better governance of the orphanage and of a second charity (the Lock Penitentiary, begun in that year), Smyth made formal release of his foundation. The deed appointed five trustees, all of whom had to be clergy. Two of them were Henry Maturin and John Walker, both fellows of TCD. Within weeks of their appointment, the archbishop inhibited both, and also Thomas Kelly, son of Chief Baron Kelly and a friend of Edmund Burke, the three of the five trustees under his jurisdiction, from preaching in the diocese of Dublin. In response to the inhibition, Maturin and Walker now became chaplains of the Bethesda, but were able to remain trustees as they received no remuneration from Bethesda. They preached to what had become one of the largest and most elite congregations in Dublin, drawn not only from the nearby fashionable Mountjoy and Rutland Squares, but from the business community, the Castle, and Trinity College itself. John Wesley had noted honorable and right honorable persons present among the congregation, perhaps eight hundred strong, when he preached at Bethesda on Easter Sunday 1787.

---

11. The status of Bethesda Chapel as essentially of, but for forty years not formally within, the established church has been subject to factual error and misunderstanding. That status, and Bethesda's significance in evangelical advance in the church, are established in Acheson, "Evangelicals in the Church of Ireland," 29–33, and Appendix A, v–x. This section is sourced throughout in that work and so ultimately in the primary sources that inform it.

Arthur Guinness, related to William Smyth through both his mother and his wife, attended Bethesda chapel without detriment to his status as a parishioner of St. Catherine's parish. He and his brother Benjamin were part of a circle of philanthropists that centered on the Bethesda and involved academics, other professional men, and business leaders like themselves. One was Josiah Smyly, surgeon to the Meath Hospital and vice president of the Royal College of Surgeons of Ireland. Another, perhaps the most illustrious of them all, was Dr. Robert Perceval (1756–1839), the first professor of chemistry in Dublin University. Perceval was a founder and sometime secretary of the Royal Irish Academy, physician general to the armed forces from 1819, and a prime mover in the opening of the Sir Patrick Dun's Hospital. With Henry Monck Mason, he was also a founder of the Prison Discipline Society, which merged later with the Howard Society, and spent much time working with prisoners.

Crisis overtook the Bethesda in 1804. Walker, who had been sole chaplain from 1798 when Henry Maturin "went out on" the Trinity College living of Clondevaddock in county Donegal, pronounced direly, "I must separate myself from all religious connections," so indicating not only dissent from the establishment, but what was known as marked separation.[12] He offered to resign his fellowship in TCD, but was instead expelled by the provost and deans. His attempt to remain chaplain of the Bethesda and to carry it into schism was thwarted by the unequivocal declaration of William Smyth that he had founded a chapel in connection with the Established Church. One of the five trustees, Benjamin Mathias, was appointed as a salaried chaplain in Walker's stead (and resigned as a trustee). Brought up a Presbyterian in Dublin, he had joined the Established Church and, when a scholar of TCD, was influenced by Maturin and Walker in college and by George Maunsell, rector of Drumcree, an early evangelical in Armagh, with whom he spent his summers. His formation for his unique ministry of thirty-five years in Dublin had been as curate for seven years with the wise and saintly Thomas Tighe in Drumgooland. With his rector's support he was a founder of the Dromore Clerical Society. His immediate situation in Dublin was unpropitious: both the Bethesda and its chaplain were unlicensed by the church, Mathias was inhibited from preaching in the diocese, and the chapel was placed under ban to students of TCD by the provost.[13]

Mathias's ministry was of strategic value in the evangelical advance. The earl of Clancarty, a distinguished British diplomat, attended Bethesda

---

12. Acheson, "Evangelicals in the Church of Ireland," 124. Walker's letter to Mathias is in [Mathias], *Brief Memorials of B. W. Mathias*, 90–91.

13. Acheson, "Evangelicals in the Church of Ireland," 25–26, Appendix A vii–ix.

when in Dublin, as did the earl of Roden and other landed proprietors. Despite the provost's ban, so did divinity students from Trinity College. Archbishop Power Trench, a brother of Lord Clancarty, ordained without question those of their number whom Mathias recommended. As secretary of the Hibernian Bible Society, founded in 1806, Mathias became known throughout Ireland when travelling on deputation work. His scholarship found outlet in his *Inquiry into the Doctrines of the Reformation* (1814), an apologetic work that established the pedigree of evangelical principles then denounced by most church authorities. The highest honor in the gift of the evangelical establishment in England was conferred on him in 1820: he preached in London the annual CMS sermon, a remarkable recognition of the gifts and Anglican integrity of an unlicensed Irish chaplain.[14]

TCD and the Irish Church

Bethesda Chapel apart, the burgeoning strength of the evangelical revival might be represented in the influence of an individual, a center of activity, or collective action at a national level. For twenty years Joseph Stopford—fellow (1790), Archbishop King's lecturer in divinity (1801)—enjoyed an unobtrusive influence in Trinity College. He reportedly gave lectures in his chambers on the duties of a clergyman to "candidate divines."[15] His pupil John Jebb, later bishop of Limerick, held him in high regard, corresponded with him, and wrote on his death in 1833 that he died "alike regretted and beloved."[16] Stopford had in 1810, as Maturin before him, taken up a college living in Raphoe diocese, that of Conwall (Letterkenny). Contemporaries such as Dr. Thomas Grace in Aughaval (Westport) and Dr. John Quarry in Shandon exemplified J. C. Beckett's wide-ranging discernment that the leading evangelical clergy who strove to "transform the life of the church and give it a new sense of unity and purpose," were "men of great strength of character, and distinguished for learning as well as zeal."[17]

Another TCD-educated individual of singular influence was William Digby, latest of a clerical dynasty in the Irish church. Archdeacon of Elphin, he was one of only three evangelical clergy there whose doctrines Bishop Power Trench denounced in his visitation sermon in 1816. Nothing daunted, Digby remonstrated with his diocesan, defending his doctrine from St. Paul and the church's Articles of Religion, and asserting boldly that Trench

---

14. Lewis, *Dictionary of Evangelical Biography*, vol. 2, 753–54. (Hereafter *DEB*.)
15. McDowell, *Ireland in the Age of Imperialism*, 205.
16. Acheson, *Bishop John Jebb*, 5, 70.
17. Beckett, *Anglo-Irish Tradition*, 104–7.

was a stranger to saving faith. The archdeacon's letter was the instrument of Bishop Trench's evangelical conversion, and effectively the launch of his leadership of the evangelical revival after he became Archbishop of Tuam (1819–1839). Digby was too, as a gifted preacher, at the heart of the revival in Elphin diocese, described thus in his own words: "The word of God, at this time, increased remarkably in the neighbourhood, and the number of disciples, (especially among the gentry) multiplied . . . and a great company of the parochial clergy became obedient to the faith."[18] Earlier, soon after he had left Trinity College, Digby had separated from the church. His return was influenced, he disclosed, by his discerning that the search for a perfect church was both erroneous in concept and impossible of fulfilment in practice, a conviction that was not shared by his contemporaries John Walker FTCD and John Nelson Darby.

The young clergy in Ossory who founded their Clerical Association in 1800, all of them TCD graduates, developed a distinctive evangelical ethos that was anchored in Reformation doctrines, especially that of justification by faith, and exercised in pastoral faithfulness through home visitation, catechizing, Sunday schools, Bible and prayer groups, and regular celebration of the Eucharist. Of their number, Henry Irwin as the first minister of Sandford Chapel from 1824 would be one of the great preachers of mid-century Dublin. Peter Roe, incumbent of St. Mary's, Kilkenny, restored the observance of saints' days and (with Bishop Hugh Hamilton) the neglected rite of confirmation; and in his personal life was given to fasting and an ascetic lifestyle. John Jebb, a guest at one meeting of the Association, saw the Ossorian clergy as exempt from criticism in England of the prevalent lax Irish clerical standards.[19]

At the national level, in the space of twenty-seven years beginning with the Hibernian Bible Society (1806) and ending with the Island and Coast Society (1833), ten societies were launched in Dublin variously to promote mission in Ireland and overseas. The secretary of the interdenominational Sunday School Society (1809) was the banker J. D. La Touche, who had taken the gold medal in Trinity College at the age of nineteen.[20] The Irish Society (1817), with Bishop Power Trench as president, circulated the Irish Bible, a purpose reinforced when Sergeant (later Chief Justice) Thomas Lefroy founded the Scripture Readers Society (1822). The support enjoyed by all ten agencies bespoke the energy of the revival in the Established Church. The launch in 1814 of CMS's Hibernian auxiliary (HCMS) took place in the

---

18. Sirr, *A Memoir*, 83. The text of Digby's letter is given at 63–69.
19. *DEB*, vol. 2, 951–52; Acheson, *Bishop John Jebb*, 52, 96.
20. Urwick, *Biographic Sketches of James Digges La Touche*, 27–28.

face of opposition from the church's hierarchy. It mattered little: commerce and banking, the judiciary and aristocracy, the Castle and army, were all represented on the platform at the Rotunda and among those elected to office. Lieutenant General Sir Robert King, Viscount Lorton, was elected president, with Dr. Robert Perceval of TCD among many distinguished vice presidents, including General Sir George Hewitt, one of the lords justices, and three other privy councillors. George Maunsell, now Dean of Leighlin, was the sole church dignitary present as such. The Dean of Armagh astutely took his place among his peers as Lord Lifford. Dublin clergy had been warned not to offer their pulpits to the distinguished CMS deputation from London. In the end St. George's in north Dublin was receptive, its rector William Bushe having recently been converted under Mathias's preaching, and also St. Werburgh's, the Castle church, for Dr. Hosea Guinness feared the displeasure of his brothers, Arthur and Benjamin, more than the disapproval of his church.[21] With the exception of the Irish Society on St. Patrick's Day, all the societies held their annual meetings in the Rotunda during the same week in the spring, these April meetings corresponding to those of the English societies in London's Exeter Hall in May. The Regius Professor of Divinity, Richard Graves, attended in the same year as Charles Grant, the Claphamite evangelical who was chief secretary for Ireland (1819–1823).[22] It became established custom for the clergy to meet for breakfast on the Friday, the day that the HCMS held its annual meeting, and this clerical breakfast introduced an annual address, Henry Irwin and Peter Roe being invited speakers in the early years. Soon the clergy were meeting on all four mornings, with advertised subjects for discussion on three of them. Attendance of more than one hundred in the 1830s gave the clergy a sense of *déjà vu* in that divinity classes in TCD were of similar size.

William Magee was sensitive to both the scholarship and pastoral integrity of evangelical clergy. After his illustrious career in TCD and some years as Dean of Cork, his arrival in Raphoe as bishop in 1819 was like a college reunion, with four former fellows resident in college livings in the diocese: Maturin and Stopford had been joined by the brothers John and Henry Ussher, in the livings respectively of Raymochy and Tullyaughnish. Hugh McNeile, a young curate appointed to Stranorlar in 1820, married Magee's daughter Ann. In 1822 Magee succeeded Lord John George Beresford, now the Irish primate, as Archbishop of Dublin. His son-in-law disclosed Magee's mind to George Hamilton, one of the Ossory clergy, who recorded:

---

21. Acheson, *History of the Church of Ireland*, 124–25.

22. This fact was reported sneeringly to John Jebb by the Provost of TCD, Samuel Kyle: Acheson, *Bishop John Jebb*, 54.

"McNeile seems very anxious that those who were objects of the Primate's jealousy should treat the Archbishop with confidence and consult him."[23] The allusion to Mathias and Bethesda Chapel was clear. Beresford had lately rejected the request by J. H. Singer, FTCD, and some eminent laymen to licence Mathias. In 1825 Magee did just that, and also licensed Bethesda and other Dublin proprietary chapels. He encouraged church planting by evangelicals, gave his patronage to their Church Home Mission, and generally integrated their movement and its missionary ethos into the Establishment.[24] With two of the four archbishops—both of them distinguished alumni of Trinity College—now identified with the movement, Trench as champion and Magee as patron, the church evangelicals had moved from rejection to full acceptance and growing influence within the Irish church.

WITHIN TRINITY COLLEGE

Divinity School and Chapel

In pointing out that the Church Missionary Society entered men in Trinity College before its own training institution at Islington was founded, Stuart Piggin comments that in many respects TCD was a more progressive institution than Oxford or Cambridge, and that its theological course was the envy of the older universities.[25] A new divinity curriculum sustained the widely discerned improvement in the clergy. Under the reforming zeal of provost Bartholomew Lloyd, and implemented under Charles R. Elrington, the Regius Professor of Divinity, a systematic two-year course in theology was introduced in the divinity school in 1833. In the first year, which undergraduates could combine with their fourth (senior sophister) year, the Archbishop King's professor (then styled lecturer) lectured for two terms on the evidences of natural and revealed religion, and for one term on the Socinian controversy; and his assistants lectured on the Greek Testament, Pearson's *Exposition of the Creed*, and articles I, II, and VIII of the Thirty-nine Articles. In the second year, Dr. Elrington and his assistants lectured on biblical criticism and exegesis, the liturgy, the Articles in general, and the church controversies. The course thus combined emphasis on the church's Catholic and Reformed tradition with study of the theological fashions

---

23. Acheson, *History of the Church of Ireland*, 137, 157; McNeile's letter dated 11 Jul. 1822 in PRONI (Public Record Office of Northern Ireland): Johnston of Kilmore Papers.
24. Acheson, *History of the Church of Ireland*, 156–57.
25. Piggin, *Making Evangelical Missionaries*, 198, 203–4.

inherited from the previous century. The *Christian Examiner* in 1840 saw the divinity school in TCD as "one of the most fruitful sources of present good," supplying each year "the demand for a spiritual and enlightened ministry."[26]

Before he was appointed bishop of Ossory in 1842, James Thomas O'Brien had himself influenced this advance as Archbishop King's lecturer in divinity from 1833 and as one of the six Dublin University preachers, 1828–1842. In 1839 William Pennefather (TCD 1833–1840) wrote of the influence of both doctors O'Brien and Singer. He was then attending O'Brien's "interesting Divinity lectures. They are highly useful and profitable. Our class is large, a hundred and thirteen attend."[27] Apart from lecturing on the evidences of religion and the Socinian controversy, in 1832 O'Brien preached in Trinity College chapel a series of sermons on faith and published these in 1833, dedicated to the students of Trinity College, Dublin. O'Brien offered it as "An attempt to explain and establish the doctrine of justification by faith only."[28] Ordination candidates were examined on this work for decades. It was adjudged thirty years later "a classic in our theological literature . . . as the fullest and most unanswerable statement of the *articulus stantis vel cadentis ecclesiae*, which has appeared in modern times."[29] In point of weight of authorities, clarity of thought, and essential argument, the work bears comparison with George Salmon's later *Infallibility of the Church*.

Dr. Piggin sees J. H. Singer, an assistant divinity lecturer, as the vital link between the college and CMS. Singer was that and much more. He entered TCD in 1802 as a fellow-commoner, and on his appointment as bishop of Meath in 1852 had completed fifty years in college. He succeeded Joseph Stopford as a fellow in 1810 and took his DD in 1825; he was Donnellan Lecturer in 1835 and 1837, became professor of modern history in 1840, and Regius Professor of Divinity in 1850. Singer's scholarship was less profound, his life less academically detached, than that of the formidable O'Brien. Warm-hearted and of pastoral instinct, his influence was personal and allied to a penchant for university reform. Tributes to him noted that he had not sought eminence in any one branch of learning and that his abilities had been widely applied: *nihil tetigit quod non ornavit*. Maurice F. Day, who would become in 1872 the first bishop to be elected by the

---

26. *Christian Examiner* (1840), 122–23.

27. Braithwaite, *Life and Letters of Rev. William Pennefather*, 83.

28. O'Brien, *Ten Sermons Upon the Nature and Effects of Faith*, title page. This author's copy bears the signature of Samuel Butcher, later Regius Professor of Divinity in TCD.

29. *Christian Examiner* (1862), 282.

post-disestablishment church, said that his college rooms were "the very center of every Christian work."[30] A student whose tutor he was from 1822 wrote: "We liked to see him ascending the chapel pulpit. His sermons were neither original, profound, nor dogmatic, but they were gentle, sound and moderate, and thoroughly fluent."[31] In 1839 William Pennefather found his lectures "very instructive, not dry criticisms of Scripture, but a devout searching into their meaning."[32] In his final years in college, Singer gave voluntary lectures on pastoral theology, so supplementing the formal divinity curriculum—or, as the senior class put it in its farewell tribute to him, supplying "the present deficiency in the University course of Divinity instruction."[33]

From his base in TCD Singer influenced other facets of the burgeoning evangelical advance in the church at large. He was chaplain to the Magdalen Asylum and preached regularly in its chapel. He spoke often at the April meetings in the Rotunda. In 1819 he became the clerical secretary of Hibernian CMS. The enthusiasm aroused by Edward Bickersteth's visits to Ireland for CMS was channelled by Singer into an effective national entity through his extensive travel and capacity for organization. By this effort, and in inculcating in his TCD students a missionary awareness, he was able to claim in 1829, when he preached the annual CMS Sermon in London: "This society has given the Irish Church an impetus, and it now possesses a Missionary character."[34] The evidence was seen in the scores of TCD students who went out to serve the new stations in Africa and India during CMS's period of expansion. In his study of the formation of missionaries to 1858, Dr. Piggin found that Singer's name recurred often in the records of the Irish in India.[35] Singer was also the founding editor in 1825 of *The Christian Examiner* (with Caesar Otway as literary editor). A monthly publication until 1869 with a nationwide readership, its theological and historical depth, its provision of "Religious Intelligence," analysis, and counsel, and its influence on evangelical thought and action, were crucial to the movement's strength and cohesion. Singer gave support to the Established Church Home Mission, founded in 1828 to promote itinerant preaching (by clergy only) in neglected areas of Ireland.

30. *Christian Examiner* (1866), 191–93.
31. Brooke, *Recollections of the Irish Church*, 9.
32. Braithwaite, *Life and Letters of Rev. William Pennefather*, 83.
33. *Christian Examiner* (1852), 321.
34. *CMS Missionary Register* (1829) 246.
35. This fact was given verbally by Dr. Piggin to the author in Menzies College, Sydney NSW, in 1990.

In another initiative relating to Trinity College, Singer and Otway joined with R. J. M'Ghee in founding in 1830 the College Theological Society. Its declared aim was to train ordinands in ecclesiastical history and polemical divinity, in effect supplementing the course taught by the Regius Professor of Divinity on the Roman controversy. Norman Emerson, later Dean of Christ Church Cathedral in Dublin, commented in 1930 in his *A Short History of the Society* that Robert M'Ghee "apparently knew all there was to be known about the teaching of the Church of Rome," and had published both major works of scholarship and popular pamphlets on the subject. In 1841 Singer contributed the preface to the *Brief Memorials* of Mathias, paying tribute to his character and leadership. Versatile and far-ranging as his activity and influence were in the making of Irish evangelicalism, and in encouraging its extension overseas, it was his half century of service to Trinity College that Singer adjudged his paramount work, as he said in reply to the address of the senior class in TCD on his departure to the see of Meath in 1852: "to have assisted in any way in arming and sending forth those who are to contend for Ireland, and Ireland's Church, and Ireland's God, is a high and holy privilege."[36]

Trinity Church

The informal and intimate relationship that Trinity College enjoyed with an Evangelical place of worship in Dublin continued in mid-century, with Trinity Church rather than Bethesda Chapel. John Gregg had succeeded Mathias as the Bethesda's chaplain in 1836. He had heard Mathias preach there when a student in TCD, and "first caught the spark that set my soul on fire." A native of county Clare, Gregg was a fluent Irish speaker and spoke in Irish, wherever it was known, on preaching tours for the Church Home Mission. The Bethesda burned down in the great storm of January 1839. Although it was rebuilt, it had become clear that the chapel could not accommodate all who desired to hear Gregg preach, and, on a site opposite the Custom House, a new church was built for him: Trinity Church, with a parochial district assigned to it from St. Thomas's parish. Here he stayed until he was appointed Bishop of Cork in 1862 by the Earl of Carlisle, who regularly attended Trinity Church, as did J. P. Mahaffy, the future provost of TCD, on occasions. Gregg's preparation of his expository sermons, delivered extempore, was noted by his son, Robert Samuel Gregg, who would succeed him as Bishop of Cork and be elected primate in 1893. He studied books on the art of speaking and the old classic writers on oratory—Homer,

---

36. *Christian Examiner* (1852), 321.

Virgil, and Horace—and the poets Shakespeare, Milton, Gray, Goldsmith, Cowper, Campbell, Wordsworth, and Coleridge. In this way he formed his style, concentrating his mind and "trusting to the general effect of his reading, and the habit of mind thus formed, for the clothing of the rushing thoughts in appropriate language."[37]

Robert Gregg revealed a Sunday morning in Trinity Church. The congregation numbered over two thousand, all but two hundred seated in the pews and on the pulpit steps, and the remainder standing halfway up the aisles, the majority of these students from Trinity College. The liturgy was read and a psalm and hymn sung before John Gregg entered the pulpit. And then: "He has spoken for over an hour. All are rapt in deepest attention, when suddenly his voice again changes, and in tones of wondrous softness, gentle as the whisper of a summer breeze, he speaks in some such words as these"—the peroration thus randomly selected took up more than two pages of Robert Gregg's biography. John Gregg held a young men's class in Trinity Church on Thursday evenings, attended by many divinity students from TCD, with his beloved poets recited and discussed, as well as passages from Burke and other writers. He sometimes devoted his Sunday morning sermon to young men. Robert Gregg published the impressions of John Gregg's discourse to young men left at his early death by John W. Winslow, a student at Trinity College:

> It was the experience of one who had been a young man. He told his feelings then—his want of sympathy—his strength of passion—his struggle to rise—his difficulties and temptations; all this and more, in piercing language, touching the innermost soul, he uttered to hundreds of our college students. May I ever remember it![38]

TRINITY COLLEGE AND THE CHURCH OVERSEAS

Dublin parishes of high church tradition evinced a missionary zeal that took men and women overseas, particularly to India and South Africa. Most were sponsored by the Society for the Propagation of the Gospel (SPG). With the CMS concentrating its work in colonial Africa and the Orient, SPG sponsored both high churchmen and evangelicals for mission in Australia and, more so, in Canada. Irish missionaries served the CMS—in China and India, Sierra Leone, Kenya and Uganda, and New Zealand—not only as

---

37. Gregg, *Memorials of the Life of John Gregg*, 12, 72.
38. Ibid., 75–80, 156.

clergy, but as doctors, linguists and translators, and college principals; and some became early martyrs. Many clergy emigrated to the United States, with TCD-trained evangelicals attracted in particular to the diocese of Ohio under the intrepid Bishop Charles McIlvaine.

Australia

In Australia, Bishop Frederic Barker of Sydney, who had worked with missions in Ireland—his wife and he both had Irish connections—encouraged immigration of clergy from Ireland. He received eighteen TCD-trained Irish clergy as against forty-two trained in Sydney's Moore College.[39] From 1847, the first Bishop of Melbourne, the evangelical Charles Perry, relied much on Irish clergy, among them Hussey Burgh Macartney, formerly curate with William Digby, who had gone out with Perry. He built St. Paul's Cathedral and was Dean of Melbourne until he was ninety-five. The first colonial chaplain in South Australia, Charles Howard, was a TCD graduate, as was James Farrell who succeeded him in Holy Trinity, Adelaide, on his early death, married his widow, and became the first Dean of Adelaide in 1849. The evangelical tradition of the diocese was to be sustained by Sir Richard Graves Macdonnell, educated at TCD and the son of a provost, who was governor of South Australia (1855–1862).[40]

The pioneer in the significant Irish contribution to the church in Australia, however, had been Henry Fulton, who arrived in Sydney Cove in 1800 as a convict on the *SS Minerva* out of Cork. He had entered TCD as a pensioner in 1788 and graduated with a BA in 1792. Out of admiration for Wolfe Tone, he had joined the United Irishmen. Vicar of Monsea in Killaloe diocese during the 1798 rebellion, he was convicted of seditious practices after it, and sentenced to transportation for life. His wife Ann, a sister of John Walker FTCD, sailed in the same ship with their child as free settlers. Fulton was soon pardoned and licensed for ministry in New South Wales, his services sorely needed given the paucity of Anglican clergy in the early years, and the preoccupation of the principal chaplain, Samuel Marsden, with the estate and flocks that he had accumulated.[41] William Knox, formerly Fulton's bishop in Killaloe, procured him a Crown chaplaincy,

---

39. Judd and Cable, *Sydney Anglicans*, 75, 80.

40. Dickey, *Holy Trinity Adelaide*, 23, 29, 45–47. Observing that Farrell was ordained by Bishop Sumner of Chester, Dickey opines (p. 23) that TCD was "a Mecca for Evangelicals planning to enter the Church of England ministry," with Oxford and Cambridge less sympathetic.

41. Cathcart, *Manning Clark's History of Australia*, 22.

and—to Marsden's wrath—a share in the salary of the principal chaplain. Fulton's ministry of forty years included a period on Norfolk Island before he settled in the Napean region. He was incumbent of St. Peter's, Richmond, and founder of St. Stephen's, Penrith. His wife and he evinced a gentle, caring influence amid the harshness of convict settlement and early colonial life, and this Irish characteristic, complementing their personal courage and toughness, made them ideal pioneers.[42]

The Canadas

The Irish were the largest ethnic component in Upper Canada (Ontario) in 1867, as confirmed by the 1871 census; and the ratio of 2:1, Protestant to Roman Catholic, obtained among Irish immigrants to Ontario before and after the Great Famine.[43] Among these were the immigrant Irish clergy, a large and influential group, all of them trained in divinity in Trinity College, their presence all the more valuable in that Bishop Bond of Montreal, a Cornishman, averred that the English were useless as pioneers in the Canadas.[44] As it was, the Irish in 1871 numbered over 40 percent of the Church of England population in the new Dominion of Canada, provided much of its leadership, and determined its predominantly evangelical ethos.

Post-war depression in Ireland after 1815 had precipitated early emigration. This exodus was reinforced for Protestants by the forebodings arising from Catholic Emancipation in 1829 and the concomitant tithe wars that caused such hardship and misery for the parochial clergy in the south and southeast. In its July 1834 number, the *Dublin University Magazine* deemed the emigration of the early 1830s "an evil of awful and tremendous magnitude threatening to leave this island in a few years without any Protestant population whatever."[45]

Talman concluded that "By 1840 no less than twenty and almost certainly twenty-seven [TCD] graduates had served or were serving in Upper Canada." His certain figure of twenty compares with ten from Oxford and thirteen from Cambridge. He found that the TCD men, most of whom arrived after 1830, stayed longer, and that nine of the twenty settled in what would become the diocese of Huron, long known as the Irish diocese.[46] This record was epitomized when the *Anne of Halifax* sailed from Dublin Bay in

42. *DEB*, vol. 1, 416.
43. Akenson, *Being Had*, 82–84.
44. Carrington, *Anglican Church in Canada*, 185.
45. *Dublin University Magazine* (hereafter *DUM*) 4 (Jul–Dec 1834) 2.
46. Talman, "Some Notes on the Clergy," 62.

June 1832. On board were the widow and adult family of Edward Blake, formerly rector of Kiltegan in county Wicklow. William Blake, a law graduate of TCD, would become Chancellor of Upper Canada and first Chancellor of the University of Toronto. His brother Edward Blake and brother-in-law Charles Brough were pioneer clergy, and his sister Frances married Richard Flood, who joined them a year later and became missionary to the Muncey Indians. Flood maintained a painstaking register of births, marriages, and deaths, of both white settlers and Indigenous peoples.[47] Of other TCD-trained clergy with the Blakes on the *Anne of Halifax*, Arthur Palmer became Archdeacon of Toronto, and Benjamin Cronyn, who ministered in London for twenty-five years, was elected the first Bishop of Huron, centered on London. His election in 1857 by both clergy and laity was the first such in Anglican history, after legal standing for such election had been granted in England to Anglican synods overseas.

Cronyn had grown up in St. Mary's, Kilkenny, one of the twenty-two men of the parish whom Peter Roe had influenced to seek ordination. Cronyn, like Edward Blake, had been ordained by Archbishop Power Trench of Tuam, and from 1827 had served the county Longford parish of Kilcommick—in Trench's diocese of Ardagh—before he emigrated. He was one of sixty-seven clergy in Canada, many of them evangelicals like himself, sponsored by SPG. Of Cronyn's episcopate, Philip Carrington wrote: "The diocese of Huron, under its energetic and forceful bishop, became a powerhouse for the whole Canadian Church. He was a great fighter, and a great fisher of men."[48] After his consecration at Lambeth Palace, Cronyn with sure instinct made for Dublin. There he recruited for ordination in Huron three friends from Trinity College who attended Dr. Fleury's Bible class at the Molyneux Chapel: James Carmichael, Edward Sullivan, and John Philip du Moulin. Known in Canada as the three musketeers, they became ministers of large urban churches, and all three bishops in the Canadian Church. The oldest of the three had been born in 1832, the year Cronyn had emigrated.[49]

England

Hundreds of Irish clergy transferred, within the United Church of England and Ireland—brought into being by the act of union, it lasted until disestablishment—to the English church. Many were attracted to the extensive diocese of Chester, in which Liverpool and Manchester were expanding

---

47. Acheson, "Pioneer Clergy in Upper Canada," 133–46.
48. Vaudry, "Cronyn, Benjamin," 271.
49. Carrington, *Anglican Church in Canada*, 118, 129, 131, 135, 143.

rapidly. Its evangelical bishop J. B. Sumner (1828–1848), later Archbishop of Canterbury, welcomed Irishmen, one of whom, Joseph Baylee, formerly of Tuam diocese, founded St. Aidan's College, Birkenhead. Hugh McNeile, who had achieved national notice when rector of Albury in Surrey, was appointed to St. Jude's, Liverpool, in 1834, and made a canon of Chester by Sumner in 1845. His dynamic personality and energetic ministry as pastor and philanthropist yet allowed him scope as a national speaker on the controversial issues of the day. Eugene Stock pronounced him "unquestionably the greatest Evangelical preacher and teacher in the Church of England."[50] Further south, William Pennefather and his wife Catherine saw church growth in affluent English parishes until they moved to the poor area of Mildmay Park, Islington, to minister and press for social reform. They founded a residential deaconess center with its own hospital and training facilities, and a capacious hall for conferences. The best known was the annual Mildmay conference, an early holiness and missionary convention.[51]

TRINITY COLLEGE AND THE IRISH PEOPLE

In Time of Famine

In his speech in the House of Lords on 10 June 1824, in which he defended the Irish church from attacks in England by the misinformed and malicious, Bishop Jebb outlined the role that the much maligned clergy had in Irish society, in point of what he termed their "social and civil services." In county Kerry, "shamefully neglected" by non-resident, rent-deriving landowners, the clergy—whose numbers he increased as Bishop of Ardfert—did the work that resident gentry, parish officers, and overseers of the poor did in England. In many parts of Munster, he averred, the clergy were the main, often the "sole prop and stay": they supported hospitals and almshouses, oversaw prisons, and channelled relief to starving people during famine times. Petitions, he pointed out, "lie upon the table of your Lordships' House, signed by multitudes of Roman Catholics, praying that they may have more Protestant clergy sent to reside among them."[52] The Ireland of which Jebb spoke underwent, in the forty-five years from the union in 1801 to the great famine, a population explosion: the 1841 census, recording more than eight million, is thought to have understated the total. In that period, the combined influences of Westminster's control and largesse, reforming

---

50. Stock, *History of the Church Missionary Society*, 1, 374.
51. *DEB*, vol. 2, 871.
52. Jebb, *Practical Theology*, vol. 2, 400, 416–20.

bishops, and evangelical revival achieved a transformation of the Established Church, with many more resident clergy and hundreds of additional churches. The latter were provided both through the government-funded Board of First Fruits and under the terms of the Chapels of Ease Act, piloted through the Commons by Thomas Lefroy, one of the members for Dublin University. By contrast, the Roman Catholic Church lacked the resources adequately to cope with the huge increase in its population, particularly in Connacht and southwest Munster.

Clergy trained in TCD, imbued with a love for Ireland, and encouraged by voluntary agencies, understood their responsibility to the Irish people as holistic. When the peasantry starved in the many famine years, they provided them with food. When they desired the Scriptures in their own tongue, they supplied them with the Irish Bible. Individual cases illustrate the point. One of the Ossory clergy, Robert Shaw of St. John's, Kilkenny, brought in cartloads of bibles from England and had them distributed through post offices; in January 1814, a month of unprecedented snow, he spent his days dealing out meal to the townspeople. George Seaver as a curate in south Armagh organized the vast soup kitchens that fed thousands during the great famine; as a Belfast rector in 1859, he evinced a like energy and commitment in the Ulster revival.[53] William Pennefather, while still a student at TCD, visited the west of Ireland where the Island and Coast Society (1833) worked, noted the value of the Irish Bible, and wrote of the Aran island of Inisturk that it had neither priest nor Protestant pastor. When the great famine struck, he was incumbent of Mellifont near Drogheda, desperate to find food for his starving people, recording their suffering in harrowing terms.[54] These experiences were formative for the balance that he achieved in his ministry in Islington.

Richard Chenevix Trench, professor of divinity in King's College London and future Archbishop of Dublin, learned about Irish rural life and the vital role of the clergy when he worked in 1847 in soup kitchens set up by his cousin that fed the starving peasantry of west Cork. When Dr. Caulfield, rector of Skibbereen there, was consecrated Bishop of Nassau in Lambeth Palace in 1862, James Freke of Durrus, who gave the sermon, said that he had "laboured in the midst of famine and pestilence with an energy which only great physical power, sustained by great spiritual zeal, could have supplied."[55] Robert Traill, the rector of Schull and uncle of the future provost Anthony Traill of TCD, had as a classical scholar translated Josephus. In 1832 he

53. Acheson, *A History of the Church of Ireland*, 122, 132, 188, 192–93.
54. Braithwaite, *Life and Letters of Rev. William Pennefather*, 86–89, 194–98, 209–10.
55. *Christian Examiner* (1862), 39.

worked tirelessly in his community during the cholera epidemic, and during the great famine was instrumental both in securing relief supplies and drawing national attention to the plight of West Cork, before he succumbed to famine disease.[56] Archer Butler, professor of moral philosophy in TCD, felt the "appalling intensity" of the famine in Donegal and supervised food distribution in his college living of Raymochy. He observed that this vital work by the clergy removed prejudice towards them "on the part of their poorer Roman parishioners." Butler's biographer Thomas Woodward noted the recognition accorded to the "inestimable value of our parochial system, even in a temporary aspect, in districts which could be reached by no other machinery."[57] To feed the starving during famine required two essentials: food supplies and organizing ability, in many places shown by clergy. When it was not available, people died.

The commitment given to the physical and spiritual needs of the Irish people by leaders of the Established Church is epitomized in Archbishop Power Trench of Tuam. His primary concern was to acquire and support clergy who were resident and committed pastors, who preached the gospel, and who were given to relief work during recurring famine and concomitant disease in his province. At a national level, as president of the Irish Society he took a prominent part in establishing the Chair of Irish in Trinity College. During 1822, two contrasting scenarios challenged Trench's leadership. In April he presided at the annual meeting of the Hibernian Bible Society, from which the archbishops of Armagh and Dublin had recently withdrawn their patronage. Trench was on delicate ground. His very presence at the Rotunda dissociated him from the decision of the two primates, and he was bound to justify his stance. He discharged this painful duty with both courage and grace. A distinguished English visitor compared him with Paul before Festus in point of "his whole action, spirit, and deportment."[58] The second challenge was the famine that ravaged the province of Connacht later that spring. Trench became "the mainspring, the regulator, the minute-hand of the whole charitable system" of famine relief, the role ascribed to him in Bishop Jebb's speech in the Lords two years later.[59] From 4:00 a.m. each day he was unsparing of himself in unremitting toil and incessant travel. In collaboration with the London Tavern Committee, he procured relief supplies, required his clergy to organize

---

56. Acheson, *A History of the Church of Ireland*, 189–90.

57. Woodward, *Sermons Doctrinal and Practical*, xxviii–xxix.

58. Carus, *Memoirs of the Life of the Rev. Charles Simeon*, 394. Sirr, *Memoir*, 462–65 gives the text of the archbishop's speech.

59. Acheson, *Bishop John Jebb*, 111.

the food distribution in cooperation with neighboring Roman Catholic priests, and required both to give public notice of their stewardship. He presided himself at meetings of local relief committees as he moved about. The clergy of both churches accepted his authority and obeyed his directions, giving him in effect the status of proconsul for the entire region. Among the tributes paid to him by the province when the crisis was past, the Roman Catholic Warden of Galway, Dr. Edmond Ffrench, hailed his discharge of "a sacred ministry" and his return home with "the benedictions of a grateful and affectionate people." Trench, for his part, said of Dr. Ffrench that relief money "could not be put into more honest, more impartial, more humane hands." Archbishop Trench engaged with all subsequent famines during his lifetime, the most severe of these in 1831. He did not live to see the great famine. For Ireland overpopulated and perilously dependent on the potato crop, the blazing logic of his conclusion in 1822 went unheeded by authority as catastrophe approached: "our case cannot be met by *ordinary* rules or reasonings. If we are not supplied, we must die; if we are promptly supplied, many may yet be saved."[60]

The pejorative term "souperism" was unknown to Archbishop Trench or to clergy in his dioceses (and clergy wives and daughters) who laid down their lives in relief work during the famine of the 1840s. Some who have researched this vexed term, and the concomitant charge of proselytism, have concluded generally that they are invalid: Eoghan Harris with his Abbey Theatre play *Souper Sullivan*, Patrick Hickey in his profile of six parishes in West Cork in 1846–1847,[61] Desmond Bowen with an analysis of the experience of (Trench's dioceses) of Killala and Achonry in 1847. Bowen's conclusion was that the clergy there "were not guilty of either souperism or proselytism during the crisis of 1847."[62] Suggestion is offered by writers of integrity that this myth was rather devised to "distract attention"—the phrase is used by both Harris and Hickey—from the labors and sacrifice of the Protestant clergy.[63]

---

60. Sirr, *Memoir*, 142–59. Trench's graphic plea for relief supplies is at 144.
61. Hickey, "Famine, Mortality, and Emigration," 888, 912.
62. Bowen, *Souperism*, 233.

63. Eoghan Harris comments that at a time when many Roman Catholics "would welcome a progressive evangelical Protestantism," the Church of Ireland is "taking refuge in an empty ecumenism," with clergy inhibited from preaching the gospel by their "fear of proselytism." He urges the church to celebrate and renew her nineteenth-century mission to evangelize Ireland. *Sunday Times* (1 Oct. 2000).

IN MISSION

The home missionary work has been a contentious issue in Irish church history.[64] It derived from a mindset, inculcated at Trinity College as an integral part of clergy training, which consisted in two convictions. The first was that the Roman Catholic Church was in error and must be engaged in "controversy"—a technical term. The College Theological Society from 1830 equipped clergy for it. Leading academics sought the same end: in 1852 Samuel Butcher, the Regius Professor of Divinity in TCD, his successor George Salmon, and Archdeacon Edward Stopford of Meath, launched the journal *Catholic Layman* because they disapproved of "the tone and spirit" of much contemporary controversy. Their aim, they stated in the preface to the first number, was to provide "a knowledge of controversial theology and ecclesiastical history" sufficient to allow "a man of ordinary intelligence" to decide between the rival claims of the Church of England and the Church of Rome. The second conviction was that truth (as distinct from error) must be shared with all Irish people irrespective of their creed. The stated purpose of the Church Home Mission, with three future bishops among its founders, was to bring the gospel to all who were "ignorant and out of the way," that of the Irish Society to make the Irish Bible available to the Irish people. At the society's annual meeting in 1826, resolutions signed by 375 of its masters and scholars in the Kingscourt District were presented to Earl Annesley in the chair. They stated *inter alia*, "we consider that the reading of the Holy Scriptures is our right as men, our duty as Christians, and our privilege as Roman Catholics."[65] An encyclical of Pope Leo XII took a contrary view; and Mathias published in 1827 his scholarly analysis, *Vindiciae Laicae*, of the traditional access to Scripture enjoyed by the laity as a catholic privilege.

The influences of Reformation societies based in England and of an English cleric, Alexander Dallas, in Irish Church Missions from 1848 have attracted a disproportionate attention that obscures the unobtrusive, Indigenous character of the spiritual work that profoundly affected pre-famine Ireland. William Magee saw it as "a spirit that must lead to Protestantism," and a later successor of his as Archbishop of Dublin, William Conyngham, Lord Plunket, established that many of the converts to his church were carried away by the tide of post-famine emigration.[66] For conversions there were sometimes so numerous as to be identified as revival. The revival in Elphin diocese after Bishop Trench's conversion took up nominal Protestants; that

---

64. Space constraints allow only identification of its complex facets. For a fuller analysis, see Acheson, *A History of the Church of Ireland*, 160–64, 196–99.

65. Sirr, *Memoir*, 556–57 gives the text of the Resolutions.

66. Seddall, *Edward Nangle*, xxviii–xxx.

in the Dingle peninsula, Roman Catholics; that in Ulster in 1859, Protestants both churchgoing and unattached. In the minds of those who understood conversion and revival—who, as was said, "tested the spirits whether they be of God"—no distinction of creed obtained in these and like experiences.

THE 1859 REVIVAL IN ULSTER

By the 1850s attendance at the four clerical breakfasts held during the week of April meetings in the Rotunda in Dublin had risen appreciably. The *Christian Examiner* reported that a quarter of the clergy, some five hundred, attended in 1859. Most had been trained in the divinity school in TCD; many were from Ulster parishes. The religious revival that had begun in 1857 in America had been widely reported in the Church of Ireland; amid expectation, revival was the topic studied at the third breakfast: "Spiritual awakenings, the direct result of the work of the Spirit, and how far human means may be used to promote them." The journal noted that "the recent revivals in America were described from personal experience, as well as corroborated from the testimony of men such as Bishop McIlvaine."[67]

Evangelical clergy had long since clarified their thinking on revival. The recovery of their own tradition had been due to biblical preaching and they saw such preaching as essential to revival. The *Christian Examiner* had provided analyses of the history and characteristics of revivals in America and Scotland as early as 1835. Clergy understood both human responsibility and divine sovereignty, recognised that evil intermingled with the good, and insisted that all developments must be sifted by Scripture. Such evaluation had become instinctive to them, both by conviction and through experience. Maurice F. Day of St. Matthias's in Dublin spent time in Ulster parishes appraising the revival. He was relieved to find that God was "not employing any new instrument for the salvation of souls," and that when any had been brought to faith in Christ, however awakened, it had been "still by the truths of God's word applied to their hearts by the mighty power of God the Holy Spirit."[68] In Belfast, the incumbent of St. John's Laganbank, Charles Seaver, recorded that above seventy parishes in the dioceses of Down and Connor had "felt the power of the Holy Ghost": vice and immorality were much decreased, Sunday school attendance nearly doubled, the churches crowded, and communicants greatly increased. At the conference called by Bishop Knox, the vicar of Belfast, Dr. Miller, noted that all the clergy present desired to continue active in the revival work "in a calm and prayerful

---

67. *Christian Examiner* (May 1859), 101–2.
68. *Christian Examiner* (Oct. 1859), 245.

spirit," resolved to embrace every opportunity "to teach and preach Christ." Bishop Robert Knox, who was to be the first primate elected by the Church of Ireland after disestablishment, wrote that he had discerned, after hearing "the report of men of sober mind and sound judgments," a widespread "spirit of knowledge and fear of the Lord," evinced in "strong conviction of sin, prayer for mercy, calling upon Christ for pardon, and the testimony of a reformed life—and who can scoff at such fruits as these?"[69] Perplexed initially by such features as what he called "physical and bodily prostrations," Knox had written to Charles McIlvaine for advice, and then read to his assembled clergy the Bishop of Ohio's response and its encouraging conclusion: "Now, my dear bishop, may the Lord strengthen you and your clergy, and give you all wisdom and grace to carry forward, as His instruments, by His power, this glorious work."[70]

The dark side to the Ulster experience in 1859 tends to be either ignored or misunderstood in some accounts of the revival, both at the time and since. The publications in 1859 of two ministers of the Presbyterian Church highlight the two aspects of the year of revival. The Moderator of the General Assembly, Dr. William Gibson, published *The Year of Grace*; his Belfast colleague, Isaac Nelson, published *The Year of Delusion*. The copious literature from Church of Ireland sources in 1859 distinguished revival from "revivalism" under various figures: wheat and tares, good and evil, the work of God and the counterwork of Satan. The latter is seen to have been active in attempts to induce excitement, to procure prostrations, or, later in the year, visions and stigmata; and in attitudes that either misinterpreted or glorified these phenomena. Bishop McIlvaine warned the Ulster clergy that such were, in his experience and judgment, counterfeit features, to be shunned and opposed. The *Christian Examiner* in the past had concluded the same of seventeenth-century Ulster revivals and in Kentucky more recently.

Those who opposed revivalism in whatever form were at the time, and by undiscerning writers since, adjudged to be opposed to the revival. Edward Hincks is one such. The charge is, however, refuted by the very title of his published sermon, "The devices of Satan as they respect a great work of God which is now going on in this country." Another leading churchman, equally respected for his learning and authority, was Edward Stopford, archdeacon of Meath. He had given a paper on nervous disorders at the opening in 1858 of the Adelaide Hospital in Dublin. In 1859 in Belfast he observed scenes both in inner city churches and in mass open-air gatherings that disturbed him

---

69. Weir, *Ulster Awakening*, 205; Massie, *Revivals in Ireland*, 41; Seaver and M'Cosh, *Religious Revivals in the North of Ireland*, 7–8.

70. Seaver and M'Cosh, *Religious Revivals in the North of Ireland*, 34–35.

and that he analyzed in a voluminous publication.[71] In the parish of Arboe in county Tyrone, a sermon by the rector, later published, warned against what he deemed the popular superstition as to the supernatural character of what he termed the bodily affections. He was none other than Dr. MacNeece, the archbishop King's lecturer in divinity in TCD. He counselled his rural congregation: "These affections are not conversion: for conversion consists in a sinner's repenting of his evil ways, and turning to God 'with all his heart and all his soul,' and bringing forth fruits worthy of repentance."[72] That MacNeece held a college living, and resided and ministered there as his academic commitments allowed, evinces that interaction of Trinity College with Ulster parishes that did much to foster Evangelical strength.

Away from his base in Trinity College, Dr. George Salmon, the future Regius Professor of Divinity and Provost, monitored in person the Ulster experience as it progressed during 1859, commended the good and denounced the evil, and gave encouragement or warning to the clergy as appropriate. His unique authority held the revival under Scripture. He summarized his purpose thus:

> It is then in no spirit of hostility that I have laboured to distinguish from the real work of God those human elements which, in my judgment, disfigure this movement. If the clergy pet and encourage what they ought to suppress, thereby inducing false tests of the presence of God's Spirit, and giving occasion to the enemy to blaspheme, it is a Christian duty to labour to correct those errors.

Salmon's advised conclusion was, however, that when all deductions were made, "much would remain to the praise and glory of the Lord in the day of His appearing."[73]

CONCLUSION

It is the very uniqueness of TCD's evangelical pioneering that in retrospect stands out. Alone among national churches in the British colonial world, TCD trained almost all the clergy and most in the legal and other professions who would be in pre-famine Ireland a resident, humanitarian presence.

This heritage has been in this age not so much neglected as suppressed. Ireland has changed, TCD has adapted, and its divinity school (and its

---

71. Stopford, *The Work and the Counterwork*.
72. MacNeece, *Words of Caution and Counsel*, 21.
73. *Christian Examiner* (Aug. 1859), 177.

successors) have long shed an evangelical ethos. The Church of Ireland is dismissive of this tradition (epitomized in famine relief, philanthropy, and holistic service to the Irish people) in its past. The magisterial scholarship of O'Brien and Salmon is neglected also.

For Canada, the experience, character, and influence of the evangelical century in shaping English Canada have been opened up by Gauvreau, Rawlyk, and Westfall, among others, and the contribution of TCD to this achievement is now being acknowledged. The research of Gladwin on the TCD graduates in Australia has served to recover their contribution there. In sum, the making of evangelicalism worldwide was the more possible because its prototype was Irish-made.

BIBLIOGRAPHY

Acheson, Alan R. *Bishop John Jebb and the Nineteenth-Century Anglican Renaissance*. Toronto: Clements, 2013.

———. "Evangelicals in the Church of Ireland 1784–1859." PhD diss., Queen's University Belfast, 1967.

———. *A History of the Church of Ireland, 1691–2001*. 2nd ed. Dublin: Columba, 2002.

———. "Pioneer Clergy in Upper Canada." In *Reformation Worlds: Antecedents and Legacies in the Anglican Tradition*, edited by Sean Otto and Thomas P. Power, 133–46. New York: Peter Lang, 2016.

———. *A True and Lively Faith: Evangelical Revival in the Church of Ireland*. Belfast: Church of Ireland Evangelical Fellowship, 1992.

Akenson, Donald Harman. *Being Had: Historians, Evidence, and the Irish in North America*. Port Credit, Canada: Meany, 1985.

Alexander, Eleanor, ed. *Primate Alexander: A Memoir*. London: Arnold, 1913.

Alexander, William. "The President's Address." *Journal of the Session of the General Synod Holden in Dublin, Anno Domini 1905*. Dublin, 1905.

Beckett, J. C. *The Anglo-Irish Tradition*. London: Faber, 1976.

Bowen, Desmond. *Souperism: Myth or Reality*. Cork: Mercier, 1970.

Braithwaite, Robert. *The Life and Letters of Rev. William Pennefather*. 2nd ed. London: Shaw, n. d.

Brooke, Richard Sinclair. *Recollections of the Irish Church*. London: Macmillan, 1877.

Carrington, Philip. *The Anglican Church in Canada: A History*. Toronto: Collins, 1963.

Carus, W., ed. *Memoirs of the Life of the Rev. Charles Simeon*. 3rd ed. London: Hatchard, 1848.

Cathcart, Michael, ed. *Manning Clark's History of Australia*. London: Chatto, 1994.

The Christian Examiner and Church of Ireland Magazine. Dublin: Curry, 1840–66.

CMS Missionary Register. London: Seeley, 1829.

Dickey, Brian. *Holy Trinity Adelaide, 1836–1988*. Adelaide, Australia: Trinity Church Trust, 1988.

Gregg, Robert Samuel. *Memorials of the Life of John Gregg*. Dublin: Herbert, 1879.

Hickey, Patrick. "Famine, Mortality and Emigration: A Profile of Six Parishes in the Poor Law Union of Skibbereen, 1846-7." In *Cork History and Society*, edited by

Patrick O'Flanagan and Cornelius G. Buttimer, 873–917. Dublin: Geography Publications, 1993.

Jebb, John. *Practical Theology: Comprizing Discourses on the Liturgy and Principles of the United Church of England and Ireland*. 2 vols. London: Duncan, 1830.

Judd, Stephen and Kenneth Cable. *Sydney Anglicans*. Sydney: The Anglican Information Office, 1987.

Lecky, William Edward Hartpole. *History of England*. 2 vols. London: Longmans, Green, 1878.

Lewis, Donald M., ed. *Dictionary of Evangelical Biography 1730-1860*. 2 vols. Oxford: Blackwell, 1995.

MacNeece, Thomas. *Words of Caution and Counsel*. Belfast: Phillips, 1859.

Massie, James W. *Revivals in Ireland, Facts, Documents, and Correspondence*. London: John Snow, 1859.

[Mathias, Benjamin Williams]. *Brief Memorials of B. W. Mathias*. Dublin: Curry, 1842.

McDowell, Robert Brendan. *Ireland in the Age of Imperialism and Revolution, 1760-1801*. Oxford: Clarendon, 1991.

Motherwell, Maiben Cunningham. *A Memoir of the Late Albert Blest*. Dublin: Curry, 1843.

O'Brien, James Thomas. *A Charge to the Clergy of the United Dioceses of Ossory, Ferns and Leighlin*. Dublin: Macmillan, 1867.

———. *Ten Sermons Upon the Nature and Effects of Faith*. London: Longman, 1833.

Oxford Dictionary of National Biography. Oxford: Oxford University Press, 2004.

Piggin, Stuart. *Making Evangelical Missionaries, 1789-1858: The Social Background, Motives and Training of British Protestant Missionaries to India*. Abingdon,UK: Sutton Courtenay, 1984.

Seaver, Charles, and James M'Cosh. *Religious Revivals in the North of Ireland, as Described and Explained by the Lord Bishop of Down, Connor and Dromore*. Dublin: Dixie Hardy, 1859.

Seddall, Henry. *Edward Nangle: The Apostle of Achill*. London: Hodges Figgis, 1884.

Shiels, William J., and Diana Woods, eds. *The Churches, Ireland and the Irish*. Oxford: Oxford University Press, 1989.

Sirr, Joseph D'Arcy. *A Memoir of the Honorable and Most Reverend Power Le Poer Trench, Last Archbishop of Tuam*. Dublin: Curry, 1845.

Stock, Eugene. *History of the Church Missionary Society*. London: Church Missionary Society, 1899.

Stopford, Edward Adderley. *The Work and the Counterwork*. Dublin: Hodges, Smith, 1859.

Talman, James J. "Some Notes on the Clergy of the Church of England in Upper Canada Prior to 1840." *Transactions of the Royal Society of Canada*, 3 ser., sec. 2, 32 (1938) 62–66.

Urwick, William. *Biographic Sketches of James Digges La Touche*. Dublin: Robertson, 1868.

Vaudry, Richard W. "Cronyn, Benjamin." In *DEB, vol. 1*, edited by Donald M. Lewis, 271. Oxford: Blackwell, 1995.

Weir, John Thomas. *The Ulster Awakening: its Origin, Progress and Fruit*. London: Hall Virtue, 1860.

Woodward, T., ed. *Sermons Doctrinal and Practical by the Rev. William Archer Butler, with a Memoir of the Author's Life*. 3rd ed. Cambridge: Macmillan, 1855.

3

The Formation of a Seceder
John Nelson Darby at Trinity College, 1815–1819

TIMOTHY C. F. STUNT

STUDENTS OF NINETEENTH-CENTURY ECCLESIASTICAL history are far from unanimous in their assessment of John Nelson Darby (1800–1882), but he is generally recognized as an early leader among the Plymouth (and later Exclusive) Brethren, a pioneer expositor of the doctrine of "the Ruin of the Church," and, more controversially, a leading proponent of the dispensationalist hermeneutic.[1] More than once has the question been raised whether the evangelical predilections which supposedly prevailed at Trinity College, Dublin, where Darby studied for four years, may have played a part in the development of his distinctive thinking or in the success with which he promulgated his ideas.[2] Before we can consider such a question, however, we must briefly look at Darby himself and the college to which he was admitted in 1815.

---

1. For basic summaries of Darby's career, see Dickson, "Darby"; Stunt, "Darby." Other sources can be found in Stunt, "John Nelson Darby: Contexts and Perceptions" 83–98; and Akenson, *Discovering the End of Time*, 86–156.

2. Sandeen, *Roots of Fundamentalism*, 90; Hempton, "Evangelicalism and Eschatology," 185. Aspects of the question have been considered in unpublished theses by Liechty, "Irish Evangelicalism, Trinity College Dublin," and Elmore, "A Critical Examination," 64–73. I have not had access to either of these theses, but they are cited by Nebeker, "John Nelson Darby, and Trinity College, Dublin," 87–108.

ADMISSION

Darby's family had been Irish gentry for several generations, but his father John Darby had successfully gone into commerce and settled in London with his wife, Anne, whose father, Samuel Vaughan, owned sugar plantations in Jamaica. Prior to her marriage in 1784, she had lived with her family in Philadelphia. John Nelson Darby, their sixth son, was born in 1800 and attended Westminster School[3] before his admission to Trinity College in 1815.[4]

The University of Dublin was an institution steeped in tradition, but in the early nineteenth century, its composition was changing. The anxieties and tensions arising from the long drawn-out conflict with France were bound to have had some effect on such a bastion of conservatism, especially when we remember that two rebellions at home and developments arising from the act of union at the turn of the century had focused the Irish mind on the dangers or possibilities (depending on one's point of view) of change. However, whether by choice or of necessity, the working and composition of the university was evolving.[5] In addition to significant changes in Trinity College's teaching regulations enacted in 1815, and again almost twenty years later in 1833, the social composition of the college had altered. Not only was the average age of the senior fellows significantly higher, but so also was that of the undergraduates—a matter of some significance with the subject of our enquiry.

John Darby was admitted to Trinity College as a fourteen-year-old fellow commoner on 3 July 1815;[6] but, whereas in the mid-eighteenth century the average age of an undergraduate had been fifteen years old, the admission of a fourteen-year-old like Darby was much more of an exception in 1815. For the previous three years, he had attended Westminster School, where many students of his age would continue for a further four years in the Up-

---

3. Darby was admitted to the Royal College of St. Peter in Westminster (more commonly referred to as Westminster School) on 17 February 1812. See Barker and Stenning, *Record of Old Westminsters*, vol. 1, 245. As an eleven-year-old he would have been in the "Under School." For an excellent (not uncritical) contemporary account of the school see Lewis, "Public Schools of England," 64–82.

4. For further details of his family (particularly on his mother's side) see my "Influences in the Early Development," 122–124.

5. The University of Dublin is effectively synonymous with the College of the Holy and Undivided Trinity, founded by Queen Elizabeth I in 1592. In my understanding of its operations in the early nineteenth century, I have been heavily dependent on an essay in two parts by McDowell and Webb, "Trinity College in 1830." See also McDowell and Webb, *Trinity College, Dublin, 1592–1952*.

6. Burtchaell and Sadleir, *Alumni Dublinenses*, 210.

per School, as had his older brother, Christopher, before matriculating from Christ Church at Oxford.[7] We have no idea why the young John Darby was sent to Trinity at such a tender age; there are no indications that either of his parents accompanied him to Dublin and, more than fifty years later, he recalled his "desolation" on leaving home.[8]

But when Darby arrived at Trinity, the earlier "atmosphere [of the 1750s] of a boarding-school, with the tutors discharging the quasi-paternal functions of house masters"[9] had changed somewhat as there had been a significant increase in the number (as well as the age) of undergraduates. This meant that, although Darby lived in college[10] and his tutor would still have been very much *in loco parentis* for the fourteen-year-old boy, far more of his fellow students were living out in lodgings, and the "school community" atmosphere would have been less prevalent.[11]

The entrance exam that Darby had to take when applying for admission assumed a basic knowledge of Latin and Greek grammar.[12] The applicant was required to be familiar with several books of the *Iliad* and the *Aeneid*, together with some of the *Eclogues* and selections from Horace, Juvenal, and Terence, as well as extracts from Sallust and Livy. As if to emphasize the Protestant roots and piety of this university (in contrast to Oxford and Cambridge), the applicants were also expected to be able to translate some of the Gospels and the Acts of the Apostles, even though many scholars of the day deplored what they regarded as the stylistic poverty of the *koine* Greek of the New Testament.[13] In reality, it appears that the exam was less

---

7. At the age of thirteen, his older brother, Christopher Lovett Darby, had won a position as one of the King's Scholars at Westminster, from where he had proceeded at the age of eighteen to Christ Church, Oxford, in 1811. See Barker and Stenning, *Record of Old Westminsters*, vol. 1, 245.

8. Darby, *Letters of J. N. D.*, vol. 2, 45.

9. McDowell and Webb, "Trinity College in 1830," *Hermathena* 75, 4.

10. Information from Bernard Meehan, Acting Keeper of MSS, Trinity College, in a letter to Max Weremchuk, 24 May 1982; see below, note 15.

11. It is interesting to note that, a few months before Darby, one of his future fellow Plymouth Brethren, John Bellett, was admitted as a pensioner when he was very nearly twenty years old; and although their close friendship originated at Trinity, this is probably only explained by the fact that Bellett's younger brother George was admitted to Trinity on the same day as Darby. George (aged seventeen) was three years younger than his brother and three years older than Darby, so the otherwise significant age disparity was more easily bridged. The university register inaccurately gives John's age as eighteen (Burtchaell and Sadleir, *Alumni Dublinenses*, 57). In fact he was born 19 July 1795 (Bellett, *Recollections of the Late J. G. Bellett*, 7).

12. For the contents of the Entrance Exam, see McDowell and Webb, "Trinity College in 1830," *Hermathena* 76, 7–8.

13. Academic appreciation of the nuances of the *koine* Greek of the Hellenistic

rigorous than one might suppose, and it was rare for more than 2 or 3 percent of the applicants to be refused admission. With a solid grounding from his years at Westminster, Darby probably found the entrance requirements fairly easy, but the next four years could have been challenging for other students whose classical grounding might have been less secure, as will become apparent.

It is evident that Darby was ultimately destined for a legal career. Even before he was enrolled at Trinity, he was admitted as a student of the Society of the King's Inns in Dublin, with his brother-in-law, Edward Pennefather[14], as his sponsor, and throughout his time at Trinity he "kept Commons," which meant dining a required number of times in the Inns' dining hall. On graduating from Trinity he was admitted as a full member and then kept eight terms in London at Lincoln's Inn to be called to the bar in 1822 as a fully qualified barrister.[15] With such a career envisaged, it would be strange if he did not do some preliminary legal reading, but for the next four years at Trinity he was pursuing the standard course of study for the BA degree, which had an unspecialized curriculum and was designed for the average student with a good rudimentary classical grounding. It is true that a significant number of Darby's fellow students would have been studying with a view to subsequent ordination as ministers in the Established Church, but their theological studies would only begin in earnest after graduation, and in any case as an undergraduate, Darby had no plans for ordination.[16] Any theological study in the curriculum was but a part of a wider study of philosophy, a fact that becomes apparent when we examine the curriculum in some detail.[17]

---

period only dates from the late nineteenth century. Moïse-Fréderic Conod, a professor of Greek in the (Protestant) University of Lausanne from 1791 to 1825, quoted from the New Testament only in Latin because he despised the barbaric Greek of the original. Vuilleumier, "La société de Bible," 177.

14. Edward Pennefather (1774–1847), a graduate of Trinity and later Solicitor-General for Ireland (1835) and Chief Justice of Queen's Bench (1841), was married to Darby's sister, Susan.

15. For these details and for a copy of Darby's admission bond at King's Inns, I am indebted to Max Weremchuk, who clarified matters in correspondence with A.M. Brophy when she was a librarian at the Honorable Society of King's Inns in February–March 2003.

16. Some ten years after Darby graduated, divinity students were required in their last undergraduate year to attend a series of divinity lectures delivered by the Archbishop King's Lecturer; see the lengthy footnote on the superior preparation of divinity students at TCD, compared with Oxford and Cambridge, in the anonymous "University of Dublin," 217–218n.

17. This and the following paragraphs are heavily dependent on the summary in ibid. 215, and on some of the observations in McDowell and Webb, "Trinity College in 1830," *Hermathena* 76, 8–10.

UNDERGRADUATE CURRICULUM

In his first year, every undergraduate had to study the compendium of logic originally published in 1759 in Latin by a fellow of the college, Richard Murray[18] (but available since 1805 in an English translation made by a younger fellow of the university, John Walker[19]), together with the *Elements* of Euclid, the first six books of which had been published in 1793 by another fellow of Trinity who in Darby's time would be the provost, Thomas Elrington.[20] These studies in logic and geometry were accompanied by a systematic course of reading in the *Aeneid*, the *Georgics*, and the *Iliad*, together with the works of some minor Greek poets. In the fourth term of the year, they began some historical reading in the writings of Livy and Herodotus.

In their second year, undergraduates completed Euclid and tackled the three-volume edition (1714) of the works of John Locke, beginning with the *Essay on Human Understanding* followed by the *Treatises on Civil Government* and the *Letters on Toleration*. We cannot be sure as to how systematic their study of Locke was, and it is possible that the author's exposition of the writings of St. Paul was neglected. In his day, Locke could claim to be a theologian, but in the early nineteenth century he was a political philosopher *par excellence*. This basic study of Locke was accompanied by a substantial quantity of ancient history in the writings of Livy, Plutarch, Xenophon, and Caesar, laced with a Dialogue of Plato and some of the poetry of Horace.

The third year had a more scientific bent with readings in astronomy, mechanics, hydrostatics, pneumatics, and optics, but the accompanying classical literature was undiminished and included readings from Juvenal, Lucian, Cicero, and some of the Orations of Demosthenes, several of which authors were available in editions by another earlier fellow of Trinity, Joseph Stock (1740–1813), who had been headmaster of Portora Royal School before his elevation to the episcopal bench in 1798.

In the final year, students concentrated on ethics and philosophy, paying special attention to Burlamaqui's *Natural Law*[21] and Conybeare

---

18. Murray, *Artis logicae compendium*. Murray's appointment as Trinity's Provost in 1795 was a significantly non-political appointment.

19. Walker, *A Familiar Commentary*. For the unusual religious development of John Walker, who resigned his Trinity fellowship and seceded from the Establishment in 1804, some ten years before Darby matriculated, see Stunt, "Trinity College, John Darby and the Powerscourt milieu," 50–53.

20. Elrington, *Euclidis Elementorum*. Elrington was appointed Provost in 1811 before being raised to the episcopal bench in 1820.

21. Thomas Nugent's translation of Burlamaqui's *Les Principes du droit naturel* (1747) was regularly published in Dublin in the later eighteenth century.

on *Revealed Religion*,[22] with readings from Tacitus (the *Germania* and the *Annals*) and the playwrights Sophocles, Euripides, Plautus, and Terence. It should be understood that such a program of reading was probably less demanding on the student than it may appear to the twenty-first-century reader. Few of us today are familiar with the routines of classical learning (often mercilessly instilled with no little degree of brutality) that characterized the educational *mores* of two centuries ago. In fact, although the Dublin curriculum was dry and narrow, the recent historians of the university argue that it was more balanced than the Oxford and Cambridge programs, which were obsessed with little more than the classics and mathematics, while it avoided the superficial eclecticism of the Scottish universities.[23] They further remind us that the program at Trinity was "inevitably tempered to the capacity of the weaker pass-man," leaving "the able undergraduate with a fair surplus of time and energy" to devote to professorial lectures and special efforts directed to the award of a gold medal at examination time.

GOLD MEDALIST

The examination gold medals had been instituted in the year of Darby's admission and were only available for students identified in the previous exam lists as *primarii in sua classe*. The students competing for the classical gold medal were examined more searchingly and on a wider ranging course, which included some extra prescribed texts from Aristotle, Aeschylus, Cicero, and Horace. They were also advised to be "prepared in an extensive course of History, and should be well acquainted with the Prosody and other niceties of the Greek language, besides the nature and history of Greek Drama . . . It is also requisite to possess an acquaintance with the classical English poets and to be practiced in Latin composition at the least."[24]

It may be coincidental, but Darby's examiners in the Easter, Trinity, and Michaelmas exams in his last year (1819) were some of the most recently appointed junior fellows. Richard Purdon,[25] a mathematician, had

22. Conybeare, *Defence of Revealed Religion* (1732). Shortly after Darby's time, Conybeare's work was replaced with a combined edition of John Leland's *Advantage and Necessity of the Christian Revelation* (1762) and Bishop Porteus's *Evidences for the Truth and Divine Origin of the Christian Religion* (1800).

23. McDowell and Webb, "Trinity College in 1830," *Hermathena* 76, 10–11.

24. *Discipline of Dublin University*, 25, quoted in McDowell and Webb, "Trinity College in 1830," 12.

25. Richard Francis Purdon (1790?–1828) had written *Theory of Some of the Elementary Operations in Arithmetic and Algebra*, published in Dublin in 1814. The exam for which he was responsible in Easter 1819 covered "Logic, Mathematics, Astronomy,

been appointed in 1813; Thomas Robinson,[26] who would soon be a distinguished astronomer, had been appointed in 1814; and Henry Harte,[27] another mathematician, had been appointed in the year of the exam. Knowing that older teachers are more liable to succumb to "grade inflation," we may be pretty sure that these young scholars were demanding examiners. Faced with the paucity of information available to us relating to Darby's undergraduate years, the few details of his performance in the final exams are valuable. In the Trinity term exam he was in the first division, and one of the seven (out of thirty-six) students endorsed as "*V[alde] B[ene] in omnibus*,"[28] which made clear that he was one of the "*primarii in sua classe*" and therefore in the running for the gold medal awarded to him in the Michaelmas examination. That he won the medal in his fourth year[29] is a significant indication that Darby had definitely been a serious scholar rising to the challenge of the wider range of studies and reading required for the medal.

Nearly forty years later in 1852, Darby observed that although his "education was in my judgment not well *directed*," he reckoned himself to be intellectual and his mind to be cultivated.[30] Whether he was dissatisfied with the content or the method of his education is not clear, nor does he indicate whether Westminster School or Trinity College was the prime target of his criticism, but the continuing intellectual enquiry that characterized the rest of his life suggests that, in this respect, his experience at Trinity College had a lasting effect.[31] This leads us to take our enquiry a step further than just the books and topics that undergraduates were required to study, and to consider the intellectual climate that prevailed in Trinity.

Physics, Greek, Latin and Theology" (Examination Records, IE TCD MUN V 27/5). *Alumni Dublinenses* has a very slender entry for this elusive scholar.

26. Thomas Romney Robinson (1792–1882), who as a boy "displayed exceptional precocity," graduated when he was barely eighteen and was later famed for his astronomical work at the Armagh observatory. See *Alumni Dublinenses* and the *Oxford Dictionary of National Biography*.

27. Henry Hickman Harte (1790–1848) translated and added a supplement to La Place's *Systeme du Monde*, published in Dublin in 1830; see *Alumni Dublinenses* and the *Oxford Dictionary of National Biography*.

28. "Very well in everything."

29. There is a curious discrepancy. According to the printed record in *Dublin University Calendar* (1838) 50, Darby's classical medal was awarded in the Easter term exam 1819, but I have followed the MS Examination Records (1810–1819) in the College Archives (IE TCD MUN V 27/5) which indicate that the award came with the Michaelmas term exam. I am beholden to the editor for obtaining a transcript of this document.

30. Darby, *Letters*, vol. 1, 205.

31. I have briefly considered some aspects of Darby's intellectual curiosity in "John Nelson Darby: The Scholarly Enigma," 70–74.

RATIONALISM

Although Trinity College "was routinely criticized . . . for being wealthy, exclusive, indolent and outmoded,"[32] it was more than a bastion of staunch churchmanship as it enshrined a well-established tradition of Protestant piety. When John Wesley had attended Sunday chapel in 1756, he famously noted in his journal:

> Dr. [James] K[night] preached a plain, practical sermon after which the sacrament was administered. I never saw so much decency at any chapel in Oxford, no not even at Lincoln College. Scarce any person stirred, or coughed, or spit from the beginning to the end of the service.[33]

Although Trinity undoubtedly evolved in the following sixty years, there is no reason to think that this heritage was lost. Protestant piety could take different forms, and a "Trinity piety" is hard to identify—all the more so as there is always the temptation (to which many have succumbed) of projecting the evangelical attitudes of the 1820s and 1830s into the earlier era.

More often than not we are dealing with what is frequently called a high-church piety but what is perhaps better (and less exclusively) referred to as one of exact churchmanship. It was a way of thinking which valued the Anglican liturgy and the sacraments of the episcopal order and was hostile to anything simplistic or emotional, into which category most dissenting religion would fall. It was theologically Arminian, with a tendency to dismiss Calvinism as antinomian. It was more concerned with sanctification than justification, and it emphasized indwelling grace as opposed to imputed righteousness.[34] It took issue with Roman Catholicism not so much over points of doctrine as on historical grounds, asserting the superiority of the Irish church's successional continuity with the primitive church of St. Patrick. This opposition to the Roman Church was declared but was not intolerant as such. Catholics had been allowed to matriculate and receive degrees at Trinity since 1793, and it is perhaps of interest that no fewer than three of the fellows in Darby's day came originally from Roman Catholic families.[35] Although the fellows at Trinity were only rarely Whig in their

32. Farrell, "Dublin University," para. 1.

33. Wesley, *Journals and Diaries*, 48.

34. As, for example, found in Alexander Knox's "Letter to Mr. Parken on Justification"; see Brilioth, *The Anglican Revival*, 279.

35. Henry Griffin (c.1785–1866), appointed a fellow in 1810 and later Bishop of Limerick (1853); Thomas Gannon (c.1779–1837), appointed a fellow in 1813; William Phelan (1789–1830), appointed a fellow in 1817.

politics, there was a significant voice in favor of Catholic Emancipation. We might note in passing that as early as 1809, Richard Nash, another exact churchman, was lecturing at Trinity on the Roman breviary and missal.[36]

In the early nineteenth century, such attitudes characterized the provost Thomas Elrington (1760–1835)[37] and his successor Samuel Kyle (1772–1848)[38] and other influential fellows like William Magee (1766–1831),[39] all of whom eventually found their way to the episcopal bench. Theirs was what might be called a sacramental rationalism. They would have vehemently rejected any suggestion that they were disciples of Voltaire, but within the context of the Irish Protestant tradition, they were unquestionably products of the Enlightenment. The same could be said for the less sacramental and more evangelical piety of fellows like Richard Graves (1763–1829), Whitley Stokes (1763–1845), Joseph Stopford (c. 1765–1833), and John Walker (1768–1833). Their rational and unemotional approach to sacred matters was also unmistakably a product of Enlightenment rationalism. In the four volumes of Richard Graves's *Works*, no fewer than 223 pages are devoted to establishing that the apostles and evangelists were not enthusiasts and cannot be charged with fanaticism because their conduct was rational.[40] The essay is in effect a Protestant reply to the skepticism of Gibbon's account in *The Decline and Fall of the Roman Empire*, where the early church is portrayed as a community of regrettably enthusiastic fanatics. We need not be surprised that the works of John Locke took pride of place in the second year of the undergraduates' reading list, nor indeed that Burlamaqui's *Natural Law* was paired with Conybeare's *Natural Religion* in the final year's reading. On both the sacramental and evangelical wings, the piety of Trinity College was part of an eighteenth-century culture of reason.

TENSION

But we have been considering the older generation of fellows. There were also younger men whose formative years had been overshadowed by the turbulence of the French Revolution and the uncertainties of the Napoleonic wars, not to mention rebellions at home. Historians are rightly cautious in

---

36. Nockles, "Church or Protestant Sect?," 477 n.114. Richard Herbert Nash (1772?–1847), appointed a fellow 1796; Chaplain to the Magdalen Asylum (1810); Rector of Ardstraw (1820).

37. Bishop of Limerick (1820); Bishop of Leighlin and Ferns (1822).

38. Bishop of Cork (1831).

39. Bishop of Raphoe (1819); Archbishop of Dublin (1822).

40. Graves, "Essay on the Character," ccxvii–ccxxxvi.

making generalizations about the so-called "Romantic Movement," but this was a generation that was more at home with emotion and feeling. Such a development was characteristic of the younger evangelicals, many of whom, like Robert Daly,[41] developed an almost aggressive oratory that an earlier generation would have shunned. It was out of this more outgoing and emotional form of evangelicalism that a few years later a number of dissatisfied enthusiasts like Nicholas Armstrong[42] and Henry Dalton[43] would leave the establishment. But even in the early years of the century, this more assertive style was leaving its mark on some of the older generation who were becoming more conscious of their ecclesiastical identity. When the eloquent and charming evangelical Henry Maturin[44] wrote in 1812 to the CMS secretary Josiah Pratt, he expressed his satisfaction that three former fellows of Trinity "are now settled as Parish Ministers in this Diocese [Raphoe], and are not ashamed of the Gospel of Christ—the number of such Ministers in the Establishment is, I think, increasing."[45]

A good example of the outworkings of the less demonstrative form of piety can be found in the case of a Trinity student who graduated in 1802. The arrival of Henry Kearney and his wife in the parish of Kilgobbin, a few miles south of Dublin, in 1817 made an immediate impression on some of his parishioners, who included the Bellett family. Although their father was hostile at first, his sons very soon became seriously devout. Kearney was ready to cooperate with evangelicals and often invited the uncompromising Robert Daly to preach in his parish, but he himself was an exact churchman, who according to George Bellett believed that

> the Sacraments acted in a supernatural way upon the soul in virtue of our Lord's appointment. His style of conversation too, was more after the fashion of the High Church school than of

41. Robert Daly (1783–1872) graduated Trinity (1803); Rector of Powerscourt (1814); Bishop of Cashel (1843). As early as 1820, the Archbishop of Canterbury refused to give Daly a bishopric on the grounds that he was a "fanatic"; see Nockles, "Church or Sect?," 465n49.

42. Nicholas Armstrong (1801–1879) Trinity graduate (1825); Irvingite Apostle (1834).

43. Henry Dalton (1805–1869), Trinity graduate (1827); Wolverhampton (1831); Bridgnorth (1832); Irvingite Apostle (1835).

44. Henry Maturin, appointed a fellow of Trinity (1792); Rector of Clondevadoge (1797); described as "a fluent extempore preacher, and inclining to Calvinistic views; he had words softer than the droppings of oil from a cruet, and singular conversational powers." Brooke, *Recollections of the Irish Church*, 58–59.

45. CMS Archives, quoted in Acheson, *A History of the Church of Ireland*, 130. The other two Trinity fellows in question were John Ussher and Joseph Stopford, both of whom were appointed in 1790.

the Evangelical party,—e.g., I never heard him use the name of our Blessed Lord without an adjunct of reverence, he never talked of a "Gospel Sermon," and his good taste as well as his deep-seated devotional feeling made him averse to the use of the phraseology which was too common. He had also a great delight in many Roman Catholic writers, and used to regard their piety of a much higher cast than that which prevailed among those who adopted the Evangelical system.[46]

The ongoing tension in the early nineteenth century between the older, restrained, and severely rational approach, and the more earnest and emotional frame of mind in the younger generation, is well illustrated in the comments of one of the most interesting observers of Irish religion at this time, Alexander Knox. As one who had a great affection for the memory of John Wesley and yet was a high churchman who appreciated the beauty and order of the Anglican liturgy, Knox's judgment at the turn of the century (1801) is revealing. In correspondence with another high churchman, John Jebb, he agreed that the students who attended the lectures of the evangelical Joseph Stopford ("an uncommonly good man") will "imbibe some of his spirit, and be warmed by a portion of his zeal." Enlarging on this he encapsulates the tension on which we have been focusing.

> I believe, there never yet was a really good man, I mean, a zealous, decided christian, whose lively expression of his own feelings, did not, more or less, reach the hearts of those who heard him.
>
> ... christian preaching can arise, only, from a christian mind and heart. This is the great want in the preaching of to-day: there is no spirit in it. It is the result of a kind of intellectual pumping; there is no gushing from the spring ...
>
> "What do I conceive to be the mean, between cold morality, and wild enthusiasm?" To this, I answer, that the mean between all extremes, is christianity, as given in the New Testament. An attention to the exhibition of Christ's religion, as taught, by himself; as exemplified, in the acts of the apostles; and as expanded and ramified, in the epistles, particularly of saint Paul, ... is the best, and only preservative, against coldness, against fanaticism, and against superstition ...
>
> Coldness is a far more dangerous extreme, than over much heat. The one, may consist with real goodness: nay, may be the consequence of real goodness, commixing with a perturbed imagination, or an ill-formed judgment. But coldness, can be

---

46. Bellett, *Memoir of the Rev. George Bellett*, 29.

resolved, only, into an absolute want of feeling. Enthusiasm is excess, but coldness is want of vitality.[47]

The fellows at Trinity in the early nineteenth century exhibited a wide range of political and religious temperament. Of course there were eccentrics, like the strangely memorable vice provost Jackie Barrett (c.1754–1821), and there were cynics like the embittered diarist, Thomas Prior (c.1769–1843), but there was a solid core of Protestant piety ranging from the exact churchman to the evangelical and from the coldly analytical to the warmly enthusiastic. At a later stage, after 1830, there would be sustained conflict between these very different wings of piety, described by Nigel Yates as "trench warfare,"[48] but in the earlier period they could sometimes cooperate, as when in 1825 the high churchman and former Trinity fellow Archbishop Magee finally licensed the incurably evangelical Bethesda Chapel in Dublin.[49] For a while at least the lines of demarcation were blurred and often shifting.

COMMITMENT

Although the details are far from exact, John Darby's later recollections make clear that he became a Christian a year or two *after* he graduated at Trinity,[50] and in those first years of Christian commitment he was a high churchman, although a few years later (c. 1827) he was increasingly connected with the evangelical wing of the Irish church. There are a few indications, however, that in the later part of his time at Trinity he was engaged in religious enquiry.

He had grown up in what was probably a nominally Anglican family, with all the "rationalist self-confidence and optimistic faith in humanity" that we associate with the eighteenth-century enlightenment.[51] Exposure to the high church piety prevalent in the college was liable to have some

---

47. Foster, *Thirty Years' Correspondence*, i, 17–19.
48. Yates, *The Religious Condition of Ireland*, 266.
49. Carter, *Anglican Evangelicals*, 68.
50. The autobiographical notes are in the margin of Darby's Greek New Testament, which is now at Manchester in the John Rylands University Library, Christian Brethren Archive, Darby Sibthorp Collection, Box 157. The text is carelessly written with hardly any punctuation but includes the extraordinarily imprecise statement, "[I] loved Christ, I have no doubt sincerely and growingly since June or July 1820 or 21, I forget which," quoted in Weremchuk, *John Nelson Darby*, 204.
51. For the learned and philanthropic enlightenment of Darby's family on his mother's side, see Stunt, "Influences in the Early Development," 123–124.

effect on the thinking of a serious young man of this background, and the inclusion of some of the works of Cicero in the later part of the Trinity curriculum may have been the occasion (which he later described more than once) of his questioning whether any rational knowledge of God was possible.[52] We know too that in 1819 he had his own copy of a controversial pamphlet written during the early years of the non-juring controversy, which would suggest that Darby was already interested in questions of episcopal succession, the relationship between church and state, and the authenticity of Anglican orders.[53] But matters were not that simple.

On his arrival at Trinity, Darby's choice of tutor had immediately introduced him to that other more assertive evangelical piety to which we have made reference. Of all the tutors at Trinity, the youthful Joseph Henderson Singer (1786–1866)[54] would soon be recognized as one of the most outspoken and uncompromising evangelicals in the 1820s. It is quite possible that the fourteen-year-old Darby was originally unaware of his tutor's ecclesiastical position, and it may well be that his choice reflected rather his preference for one of the youngest tutors who had been a gold medalist when he graduated.

We have an interesting description of Singer, made by another student who chose him for his tutor a few years later:

> My tutor was Dr. Joseph Henderson Singer, afterwards Bishop of Meath. He had obtained his fellowship at the early age of 23, and was a man of universal and accurate information, possessing very polished manners and a kind and winning address. He was a prodigious reader, not even despising the lighter literature of the day, which he swallowed, but probably did not care to digest; a steady preacher of Evangelical truth and a bold upholder of Scriptural education . . .
>
> His pet name among the college alumni was "Cantor."[55] We liked to see him ascending the chapel pulpit. His sermons were neither original, profound, nor dogmatic, but they were

---

52. For Darby's recollection of this experience when reading Cicero's *De Officiis* before his conversion, "when I was a poor dark creature," see ibid., 122.

53. The writer has recently deposited in the Christian Brethren Archive of the John Rylands University Library of Manchester a copy of *The Character of a Primitive Bishop*, which has the MS endorsement "J. N. Darby 1819." The pamphlet is usually attributed to John Pitts, himself a non-juror.

54. J. H. Singer, admitted as a fellow (1810); BD and DD (1825); Professor of Modern History (1840); Bishop of Meath (1852). "Mr. Singer" is named as Darby's tutor in the TCD Admissions Register for 3 Jul. 1815, 234.

55. The Latin for "Singer."

gentle, sound and moderate, and thoroughly fluent. He had, if anything, too much of the *copia fandi*.⁵⁶

With Singer as his tutor for four years, we may reasonably assume that Darby became familiar with the new evangelicalism. This awareness would have been further augmented by Darby's friendship with the Bellett brothers, who in their later time at Trinity were coming under the influence of Henry Kearney at Kilgobbin. It is fascinating to find that the new incumbent's impact affected the brothers so differently, George developing into an exact churchman with a preference for Arminian theology while John rapidly became a fully committed Calvinist evangelical. Confronted by these two varieties of piety, John Darby could be forgiven for some uncertainty in committing himself.

With his conversion soon after his graduation, Darby made a commitment, submitting to God both intellectually and morally. But during the next five years it is clearly the high church piety that dominates his thinking, and many years later, when answering John Henry Newman's *Apologia pro Vita Sua*, he described how

> years before Dr. Newman . . . I fasted in Lent so as to be weak in body at the end of it; ate no meat on week days—nothing till evening on Wednesdays, Fridays, and Saturdays, then a little bread or nothing; observed strictly the weekly fasts, too. I went to my clergyman always if I wished to take the sacrament that he might judge of the matter. I held apostolic succession fully, and the channels of grace to be there only. I held thus Luther and Calvin and their followers to be outside. I was not their judge, but I left them to the uncovenanted mercies of God. I searched with earnest diligence into the evidences of apostolic succession in England, and just saved their validity for myself and my conscience. The union of Church and State I held to be Babylonish, that the Church ought to govern itself, and that she was in bondage, but was the Church.⁵⁷

---

56. Brooke, *Recollections of the Irish Church*, 8–9. A later anecdote in Brooke's account describes an older fellow addressing Singer as "Dulcissime Doctor" and using the words of the poet Horace to warn him to "take care lest you stumble." The implication is that in his older colleague's estimation, Singer may have been perhaps a little too popular with the students. The phrase *copia fandi* (abundance of talk) suggests that words came to him a little too easily. For the anxieties that Singer's evangelicalism could produce in a high churchman like James Henthorn Todd, some twenty years later, see Stunt, *From Awakening to Secession*, 158n17.

57. Darby, *Analysis of Dr. Newman's Apologia pro Vita Sua*, 19–20; reprinted in Darby, *Collected Writings*, vol. 18, 156. For this stage in Darby's experience see Stunt, "Influences in the Early Development," 129–130.

Later when Darby was associated with evangelicals, the word "rationalist" always had negative connotations for him; and yet throughout his life, Darby retained a decided caution with regard to anything that might be described as enthusiasm, and his thinking remained highly rational and analytical.[58] His systematic rebuttal of Francis Newman's *Phases of Faith* reflects this in its uncompromising title: *The Irrationalism of Infidelity*.[59] Darby's rational appreciation of analysis and analogy is very apparent in the notes (more than a hundred pages) that he jotted down when reading J. S. Mill's *System of Logic*. They were originally published without his permission, and he considered them "quite unfit to be published,"[60] but they are the product of a mind trained in analysis and exercising evaluative skills—a mind similar to those of the disciples and apostles, as confidently described by Dean Graves in his dismissal of Gibbon's claim that they were enthusiasts. In his roots, John Darby was a child of the Age of Reason, sanctified with the piety that he imbibed at Trinity.

On the other hand, there is unquestionably a romantic element in Darby's later career. From the emaciated parish priest laboring among the Irish peasants of Calary, Co. Wicklow, to the isolated Englishman trudging from one remote Swiss village to another, identifying with rustic believers whose language he adopts as his own, there is an almost Rousseauesque simplicity in his lifestyle. Darby's abandonment of the establishment and his fearless readiness to engage in controversy with archbishops and celebrities has an undeniably heroic quality. His intervention in an Oxford controversy has a particular relevance.

In 1831, during a University sermon which the provost of Oriel described as "incurably enthusiastic," Henry Bulteel proclaimed that the establishment was all but apostate and a few days later presented a signed copy of his published sermon to John Darby, who was visiting Oxford. When the Regius Professor of Divinity published a reply insisting, in opposition to Bulteel, that justification should not be confused with

---

58. There is a certain irony that early critics of Darby and the Brethren accused them of playing into the hands of "modern liberalism." On the other hand, there is an intellectual originality about the dispensational hermeneutic, when it categorizes the Gospels as Jewish rather than Christian teaching, that could be regarded as rationalism. When critics like F. C. Baur of the Tübingen School categorized the New Testament books in a different way, they were dismissed as "rationalists." See Stunt, "Trinity College, John Darby and the Powerscourt Milieu," 73n93.

59. Darby, *Irrationalism of Infidelity*.

60. Letter to R. T. Grant from London, 1877, in Darby, *Letters of J. N. D.*, vol. 2, 401. The notes were later published as "Examination of Mill's Logic" in Darby, *Collected Writings*, vol. 32, 54–162. One does not have to agree with the reasoning, but the analytical approach is manifest.

salvation, and that the Thirty-nine Articles were not Calvinist, Darby took up the cudgels and entered the fray, publishing a sixty-four-page reply to the professor and quoting at some length extracts from the works of Martin Bucer, Peter Martyr, and John Jewell. Significantly, when his answer was published, he sent a copy of it (together with Bulteel's sermon) to his former tutor, endorsed "Revd. J. Singer from the Author."[61] He seems to have recognized that this would meet with Singer's approval. Clearly he was now identified with his tutor's variety of evangelical piety.

For many of his admirers, Darby is *par excellence* an expositor of biblical prophecy, and more specifically the pioneer of dispensationalist premillennialism. Following some tentative leads made by Floyd Elmore,[62] more than ten years ago Dr. Gary Nebeker valiantly tried to analyze Darby's later eschatology in terms of the ways in which it contrasted and conflicted with the postmillennial positions of the few Trinity fellows who ventured into the troubled waters of prophecy.[63] Wrongly assuming that Dean Graves had been Darby's tutor, he focused unduly on Graves's postmillennial and Arminian theology, which was completely at variance with Darby's later positions. Such issues have not been the concern of the foregoing analysis. Knowing that his conversion came later, we may assume that at Trinity, Darby was unlikely to have been concerned with eschatology. My purpose has been to find some of the features of intellectual inquiry in which a student of Darby's day (before 1820) would have been engaged and to identify some of the elements characterizing the piety to which he would have been exposed at Trinity. Perhaps these have pointed us to a more useful set of intellectual and spiritual parameters within which Darby operated in subsequent years.

BIBLIOGRAPHY

Acheson, Alan R. *A History of the Church of Ireland, 1691–2001*. 2nd ed. Dublin: Columbia, 2002.

Akenson, Donald Harman. *Discovering the End of Time: Irish Evangelicals in the Age of Daniel O'Connell*. Montreal: McGill-Queen's University Press, 2016.

Barker, G. F. Russell, and Alan Stenning, eds. *The Record of Old Westminsters: A Biographical List of All Those Who are Known to have been Educated at Westminster School from the Earliest Times to 1927*. 2 vols. London: Chiswick, 1928.

---

61. Both pamphlets are preserved in the Library of Trinity College, Gall.0.8.48 No 5 and Gall 0.8.49 No 6.

62. See Elmore, "Critical Examination of the Doctrine."

63. See Nebeker, "John Nelson Darby and Trinity College."

Bellett, Diana. *Memoir of the Rev. George Bellett: Autobiography and Continuation by His Daughter*. London: Masters, 1889.

Bellett, L. M. *Recollections of the Late J. G. Bellett*. London: Rouse, 1895.

Brilioth, Yngve. *The Anglican Revival: Studies in the Oxford Movement*. London: Longmans, 1925.

Brooke, Richard Sinclair. *Recollections of the Irish Church*. London: Macmillan, 1877.

Burlamaqui, Jean-Jacques. *Les principes du droit naturel*. Translated by Thomas Nugent. London: Nourse, 1752.

Burtchaell, George Dames, and Thomas Ulick Sadleir, eds. *Alumni Dublinenses. A Register of the Students, Graduates, Professors and Provosts of Trinity College in the University of Dublin*. London: Norgate, 1924.

Carter, Grayson. *Anglican Evangelicals: Protestant Secessions from the Via Media, c.1800–1850*. Oxford: Oxford University Press, 2001.

The Character of a Primitive Bishop in a Letter to a Non-Juror by a Presbyter of the Church of England. London: Bragg, 1709.

Conybeare, John. *Defence of Revealed Religion*. London: Wilmot, 1732.

Darby, John Nelson. *Analysis of Dr. Newman's Apologia pro Vita Sua: With a Glance at the History of Popes, Councils and the Church*. London: Broom, 1866.

———. *Collected Writings*. 47 vols. Edited by William Kelly. Kingston-on-Thames: Stow Hill Bible and Tract Depot, n.d.

———. "Examination of Mill's Logic." In *Collected Writings*, vol. 32, edited by William Kelly, 54–162. Kingston-on-Thames: Stow Hill Bible and Tract Depot, n.d.

———. *The Irrationalism of Infidelity: Being a Reply to "Phases of Faith."* In *Collected Writings* vol. 6, 1–358. Kingston-on-Thames: Stow Hill Bible and Tract Depot, 1853.

———. *Letters of J. N. D.* 3. vols. Kingston-on-Thames: Stow Hill Bible and Tract Depot, n.d.

Dickson, N. T. W. "Darby." In *Biographical Dictionary of Evangelicals*, edited by Timothy Larsen et al., 178–81. Downers Grove, IL: InterVarsity, 2003.

The Discipline of Dublin University. 2nd ed. Dublin: n.p., 1828.

Dublin University Calendar for the year 1838. Dublin: Curry, 1838.

Elmore, F. S. "A Critical Examination of the Doctrine of the Two Peoples of God in John Nelson Darby." PhD diss., Dallas Theological Seminary, 1990.

Elrington, Thomas, ed. *Euclidis Elementorum, sex libri priores, cum notis*. Dublin: Grierson, 1793.

Farrell, Stephen. "Dublin University." In *The History of Parliament: The House of Commons 1820–1832*, edited by D. R. Fisher. Cambridge: Cambridge University Press, 2009. http://www.historyofparliamentonline.org/volume/1820-1832/constituencies/dublin-university.

Foster, Charles, ed. *Thirty Years' Correspondence Between John Jebb, D.D., Bishop of Limerick, Ardfert and Aghadoe, and Alexander Knox, Esq.* 2 vols. Philadelphia: Carey, 1835.

Graves, Richard. "Essay on the Character of the Apostles and Evangelists." In *The Whole Works of Richard Graves*, vol. I, edited by Richard Graves, 1–223. Dublin: Curry, 1840.

Hempton, David N. "Evangelicalism and Eschatology." *Journal of Ecclesiastical History* 31 (1980) 179–94.

Knox, Alexander. *Remains of Alexander Knox Esq.* London: Duncan, 1834.

Leland, John. *Advantage and Necessity of the Christian Revelation.* London: Clark, 1762.

Lewis, George Cornewall. "Public Schools of England: Westminster and Eton." *The Edinburgh Review* 53 (1831) 64–82.

Liechty, Joseph. "Irish Evangelicalism, Trinity College Dublin, and the Mission of the Church of Ireland at the End of the Eighteenth Century." PhD diss., St. Patrick's College, Maynooth, 1987.

McDowell, Robert B., and D. A. Webb. *Trinity College, Dublin, 1592–1952: An Academic History.* Cambridge: Cambridge University Press, 1982.

———. "Trinity College in 1830." *Hermathena* 75 (1950) 1–23; and 76 (1950) 1–24.

Murray, Richard. *Artis logicae compendium: in usum juventutis Collegii Dubliniensis.* Dublin: Sleater, 1759.

Nebeker, G. L. "John Nelson Darby and Trinity College, Dublin: A Study in Eschatological Contrasts." *Fides et Historia* 34 (2002) 87–108.

Nockles, Peter B. "Church or Protestant Sect? The Church of Ireland, High Churchmanship, and the Oxford Movement, 1822–1869." *Historical Journal* 41 (1998) 457–93.

Porteus, Beilby. *Evidences for the Truth and Divine Origin of the Christian Religion.* London: Cadell, 1800.

Purdon, Richard Francis. *Theory of some of the Elementary Operations in Arithmetic and Algebra.* Dublin: Parry, 1814.

Sandeen, E. R. *The Roots of Fundamentalism: British and American Millenarianism, 1800–1930.* Chicago: University of Chicago Press, 1970.

Stunt, Timothy C. F. "Darby." In *Oxford Dictionary of National Biography* vol.15, edited by H. Colin G. Matthew and Brian Harrison. 61 vols., 117–18. Oxford: Oxford University Press, 2004.

———. "Influences in the Early Development of John Nelson Darby." In *The Elusive Quest of the Spiritual Malcontent: Some Early Nineteenth-Century Ecclesiastical Mavericks*, 119–42. Eugene, OR: Wipf & Stock, 2015.

———. *From Awakening to Secession: Radical Evangelicals in Switzerland and Britain, 1815–35.* Edinburgh: Clark, 2000.

———. "John Nelson Darby: Contexts and Perceptions." In *Protestant Millennialism, Evangelicalism, and Irish Society, 1790–2000*, edited by Crawford Gribben and A. Holmes, 83–98. New York: Palgrave Macmillan, 2006.

———. "John Nelson Darby: The Scholarly Enigma." *Brethren Archivists and Historians' Network Review* 2:2 (2003) 70–74.

———. "Trinity College, John Darby and the Powerscourt Milieu." In *Beyond the End: The Future of Millennial Studies*, edited by Joshua Searle and Kenneth G. Newport, 47–74. Sheffield, UK: Sheffield Phoenix, 2012.

"University of Dublin." *The Quarterly Journal of Education* 6 (April 1833) 5–27; (July 1833), 201–37.

Vuilleumier, Henri. "La société de Bible du canton de Vaud et son fondateur." *Revue de Théologie et de Philosophie* 3 (1915) 177.

Walker, John. *A Familiar Commentary on the Compendium of Logic Used by Under-Graduates in the University of Dublin.* Dublin: printed by Robert Napper and sold by the author, 1805.

Weremchuk, Max S. *John Nelson Darby: A Biography.* Neptune, NJ: Loizeaux, 1992.

Wesley, John. *Journals and Diaries*. Works of John Wesley 21, edited by W. R. Ward and R. P. Heitzenrater. Nashville: Abingdon, 1992.

Yates, Nigel. *The Religious Condition of Ireland, 1770–1850*. Oxford: Oxford University Press, 2006.

4

"An Awful Mystery"
William Magee on the Atonement

EPHRAIM RADNER

WILLIAM MAGEE (1766–1831) HOLDS a prominent place in the history of Trinity College and the Church of Ireland. Having become a fellow at the college in 1788, he went on to become a professor of mathematics there, and finally the Archbishop King lecturer in Divinity in 1808. His later career saw him become Dean of Cork (1814), Bishop of Raphoe (1819), and finally Archbishop of Dublin (1822).[1] Although an important actor in the ecclesiastical politics of his era, he was more widely known for his large work on the atonement, *Discourses on the Scriptural Doctrines of Atonement and Sacrifice*, originally published in 1801 and subsequently greatly expanded into *Discourses and Dissertations* over several more editions.[2] Magee pub-

---

1. Magee, *Works of William Magee*, vol. 1, ix–lxxx (digest in *Christian Observer* 65 [1843] 257–64, and 66 [1843] 321–29); Wills, *Lives of Illustrious and Distinguished Irishmen*, vol. 4, 353–409. For a modern treatment of Magee's role in the ecclesial politics of early nineteenth-century Ireland, see Bowen, *Protestant Crusade in Ireland, 1800–70*, 83–95; see also Bowen, "Magee, William (1766–1831)."

2. Magee worked through a fourth edition in 1816, with the final title as follows: *Discourses and Dissertations on the Scriptural Doctrines of Atonement and Sacrifice*. Most of the original editions were published by Cadell and Davies in London. American editions appeared in 1813. The final edition expanded the original notes and "dissertations" to seventy-four in number, and was divided into three total volumes (volume two being divided into two parts). The last reprint was by Bohn in 1867.

lished nothing besides this huge tome, apart from a few sermons collected in his *Works*. The fact that the *Discourses* were included in the curriculum at Trinity for several decades assured its influence in the Irish Church for some time.³ The work itself became a standard reference work among English-speaking Protestants well into the nineteenth century.

It is difficult to assess the formative influence of Magee's writing either on his students or the wider church, but it is certainly possible to analyze its theological import, which is the purpose of this essay. Magee was seen as the champion of orthodoxy, especially in the context of late eighteenth-century debates over Christology. These, unlike earlier seventeenth-century Unitarian controversies, had shifted away from strict biblical literalism to a critical rationalism, denying the virgin birth and other scriptural claims altogether.⁴ Hence, arguments for traditional christological doctrines in Magee's era were tied to formal claims regarding scriptural authority, and orthodoxy became increasingly identified with biblicism. Magee was orthodox in both respects, and his orthodoxy, for many, was linked to his reputation as a rigid and arrogant man. Certainly he was committed, both personally and as an academic and episcopal leader, to a life of "diligence and zeal" in the service of the divine calling of Christian minister, and he pressed this commitment with student and clergy to a notable degree. To those who knew him personally, or were the objects of his pastoral care, he was "tender" and beloved. But his polemical edge, constantly in view in his dealings with Unitarians and Catholics especially, was notorious. Among Anglicans, he was for Coleridge and Maurice the epitome of what was distasteful, both intellectually and personally, with establishment traditionalism. Magee was just the kind of churchman who, in the eyes of some, rendered orthodoxy synonymous with cold-heartedness.

ORTHODOXY

But how orthodox was Magee in fact? By the second quarter of the nineteenth century, some were already beginning to wonder about his approach. That H. L. Mansel (see below) could still make use of Magee in his famous lectures on *The Limits of Religious Thought* (1858) was an interesting sign: Was there something overly skeptical about Magee, too much like Mansel

---

3. Power, "'Of No Small Importance,'" 170.

4. For a relatively detailed discussion which locates Magee's place in the controversy more generally, see Wilbur, *A History of Unitarianism*, chapters 12–18. For a nontheological overview, see Greenwood and Harris, *An Introduction to the Unitarian and Universalist Traditions*, 32–71.

himself, for both broadchurchmen and more conservative theologians, whether high or low? Some contemporary proponents of the penal substitution view of the atonement see him as actually opposed to their fundamental vision. The American Reformed theologian William G. T. Shedd had early on (but without polemical point) disagreed with Magee on the latter's reticence to use the term "punishment" to refer literally to Christ's sacrifice.[5] Magee continued to be on the School of Divinity reading list in Dublin until 1868[6], but it is clear that his wider influence waned by the late nineteenth century and mostly disappeared altogether.

Whether truly orthodox or not, Magee's book on the atonement is a remarkable volume. It began as two sermons delivered at Trinity College on the Good Fridays in the successive years of 1798 and 1799. These two sermons were then published together in 1801, along with the first set of notes that were to multiply in subsequent editions.[7] Magee takes as their occasion his concern over recent anti-Christian movements in Britain, which he characterizes as the "avowed invader" of the Church, that is, the open deist and the "concealed and treacherous foe" of the "rationalizing Christian philosopher."[8] Although antagonists proliferate in the notes, Magee's main opponents are Unitarians like Joseph Priestley and Thomas Belsham, as well as liberalizing Anglicans like Henry Taylor.[9] Magee's arguments, at least on this topic, were viewed by many as having effectively undercut their anti-sacrificial reasoning, while at the same time eliciting strong reactions from his named opponents.[10] From Magee's perspective, the larger issues were socially and not only ecclesially relevant. There had been much political agitation in the 1790s for the removal of civil penalties against non-Trinitarians, a movement that finally resulted in the 1813 "Doctrine of the Trinity Act," which granted Unitarians relief and was spearheaded, ironically, by William Smith, a friend of one of Magee's most respected writers,

---

5. Magee had argued this on the basis that punishment is subjectively denoted, and Christ, while he truly suffered, did not himself suffer as one "punished" (Note 13). See Shedd, *Dogmatic Theology*, vol. 2, 457–59. The critique pinpointed Magee's fundamental weakness in the eyes of the penal substitution group.

6. *Dublin University Calendar* (1868), 64.

7. Magee, *Works of William Magee*, vol. 1, xxxiv.

8. Unless otherwise noted, I will be citing the third edition of Magee's *Discourses and Dissertations*, due to its accessible one-volume format. The quotations here come from Magee's own "Prefatory Address to the Students," ix.

9. On Taylor, an earlier eighteenth-century Anglican biblicist Arian, see the summary in Price, "Memoir of the Late Rev. Henry Taylor," 65–78; on Priestley, see Bowers, *Joseph Priestley and English Unitarianism in America*.

10. E.g., Belsham, *An Address to the Inquirers*.

the Anglican evangelical William Wilberforce.[11] But while the Unitarian controversy continued for several decades, especially in America, there is something peculiarly eighteenth-century in Magee's concerns, not only in his self-conscious worries over deism and Socinianism, but in the sentiments of his response. It is the latter especially that seems not to have worn well as the nineteenth century progressed.

The two Good Friday discourses, which form the basis for Magee's book, are relatively simple in their focus. The first treats the atonement specifically, basing itself on 1 Corinthians 1:23 and 24 ("We preach Christ crucified . . ."), while the second, on the notion of sacrifice, comes under the heading of Hebrews 9:22 ("And without the shedding of blood is no remission"). Taken together, they are no more than thirty-four pages. Yet these two discourses, independent of the vast array of dissertations that accumulated in their wake, establish Magee's basic theological orientation.

DISCOURSE 1 ON THE ATONEMENT

Magee's argument proceeds against two sets of opponents: deists and "philosophical" theologians, who are effectively or explicitly "Unitarian." Their key claim, Magee states, is that repentance of the sinner is sufficient for God's forgiveness, and therefore there is no need for an atoning sacrifice. This is where Magee aims his self-styled "apologetical" and "polemical" response. In addition, the rationalist argues that, since there is no reasonable connection between forgiveness and the killing of another life, the very idea of atonement undercuts the credibility of scriptural claims more broadly. Magee is certain that this argument is fundamentally destructive of Christian faith, and so the issue of atonement and sacrifice is central to the apologetic task of the age. For his part, he wants to affirm, openly and starkly, the divine truth of the cross as an "expiatory sacrifice," to which properly attach the various terms that have been, in both Old and New Testament discussion, attached to it: propitiation, vicariousness, even (with some qualifications), punishment.

From the start, Magee follows an argumentative strategy associated with the great eighteenth-century Anglican thinker and bishop Joseph Butler (1692–1752). Butler's *Analogy of Religion* (1736) had become the standard orthodox response to deist attacks, particularly on the reasonableness of accepting scriptural revelation, and his *Analogy* became a common fixture in British (and American) divinity curricula well into the nineteenth

---

11. Davis, *Dissent In Politics*. On earlier background, see Ditchfield, "The Parliamentary Struggle," 551–77.

century (Newman being among the most famous direct heirs of Butler's ideas). Trinity College was no exception here, and Butler figures consistently in its reading lists.[12] Butler's approach—and Magee's in his wake—was to look at "nature," including common human experience and history, and determine how the Christian faith correlates or not, especially in areas where uncertainties seem built into the context at issue. On the basic question of forgiveness, Magee tells us that repentance in human relations is almost always seen as insufficient: demonstrations and reparations are usually required. Repentance cannot remove the "effects of past transgressions."[13] If "something else" is required, the divine economy's analogous form vis-à-vis nature should open us to the fact that any number of possible ways this "something else" could be embodied will likely be hard for us to fathom, but no less necessary or divine for all that. Just as the natural world is a highly complex "system," governed by "connections" we are unable to identify yet which are all the same intrinsic to the system's functioning, so God's moral economy is also a vast and infinitely complex system of interrelations, of whose individual "purposes" we are "ignorant." The fact that God reveals to human beings that "sacrifice" is the way that sin is forgiven is not arbitrary; it is deeply connected with the breadth of God's wisdom—only we cannot say exactly how, just as we do not understand gravity in any fundamental way. It is "mysterious," but intrinsically coherent.

Magee's argument here is broad, but also stark. The "awfully mysterious truths of revelation"[14] by which atoning sacrifice is made known to human beings as the means of forgiveness are themselves reasonably expected given the intrinsic ignorance and sinfulness of human beings: how else would they know, except that God would speak to them?[15] Here Magee relies on some of the deeper elements of Butler's orientation: we act in the world, making decisions about what is "reasonable" out of a tremendous abyss of ignorance. Doing so, however, is not foolish, but bound to an inte-

---

12. While Butler's *Analogy of Religion* is rarely mentioned explicitly in Magee's work, his influence hovers over the entire production. He is "the profound Bishop Butler," a "great Divine, and genuine philosopher" (116), whose refusal, within the bounds of human ignorance, to limit God's possible determinations regarding (e.g.) the means of forgiveness, must defer nonetheless to the revealed truths of divine self-offering, something whose "fittingness" amounts in the end to a "moral necessity." Butler was long part of the divinity curriculum in Dublin, at least since the end of the eighteenth century, and continued to be required in 1837. See O'Brien, *An Introductory Lecture*, 62, 77, and 79. Butler remained in the curriculum in 1868; see *Dublin University Calendar*, (1868) 64. Still the best discussion of Butler's philosophical orientation is Penulham's *Butler*.

13. Magee, *Discourses and Dissertations*, 20.

14. Ibid., 27.

15. Ibid., 24–26.

grated sense of likelihoods, probabilities, uncertainties, and pragmatic affirmations. In going after the deists, or the more "philosophical" Christians who would render the sacrificial language of the Bible into figurative modes of moral metaphor, Magee, like Butler before him, points out how utterly arbitrary are the "systems" used by these opponents of orthodoxy, whose criteria of rationality are as deeply mired in ignorance of the systemic whole of reality as any Christian's. Yet without the (rationally) compelling direction of divine revelation, their claims are useless, while the scriptural Christian's, ordered by an acknowledgment of divine omniscience and omnipotence, fall into place, however mysterious it might be in its hidden details.[16] God "chooses" and "determines" expiatory sacrifice,[17] God "reveals" its place in the divine system of the world, and the revelation in which this is located is itself consistent and coherent in a way that the humility drawn from human ignorance properly grasps. What we will emphasize later as Magee's scriptural "nominalism" is really a reflection of his sense of human reason's basic impulse to self-offering in the face of its own ignorance and the majesty of God.

DISCOURSE 2 ON SACRIFICE

The second discourse, specifically on sacrifice, is mostly a long exegesis of Cain and Abel's offerings. This acts as an entrée to a history of sacrifice, figurally ordered to Christ. Magee ends with a final figural hinge between the Law's prescribed Day of Atonement ceremony and the Cross, each joined by their common "vicarious" dynamic. The tone here is quite different from the first sermon; and now, in an almost practical and concrete way, Magee works out his theory of divine mystery and its revelation to human ignorance. He argues against what had become a genre of "history of religion" as applied to the practice of sacrifice—e.g., Sykes and Warburton[18]—as if Israelite sacrifice, even back to its origins with Cain and Abel, was patient of some rational genealogy of human discovery and development. There is no reason for sacrifice other than direct divine revelation, Magee argues,

---

16. Ibid., 30.
17. Ibid., 39, 36.
18. Sykes, *An Essay on the Nature, Design, and Origin of Sacrifices*. Sykes' rationalizing history of sacrifice sought in it a deeper principle—repentance for friendship with God—that could then become the touchstone for understanding development and corruptions within Israel, and, obviously, the revelation of a purer form of moral sacrifice by Christ. Warburton's theories of sacrifice, elaborated across a range of his vast output, provide a kind of historical typology of human religiosity, bound to different forms of sacrificial practice.

stressing the point over and over in a way that is almost perverse in its flouting of social logic. Rather, the very fact that Abel's sacrifice was one of living animals, a sacrifice acceptable to God instead of the more reasonable "gift" offering of Cain's harvest bounty, is itself a sign, Magee insists, of its manifest *irrationality* in human terms, and hence its utterly divine origin.[19] The argument here is an astonishing *tour de force* exposition, in which Cain becomes the proto-deist, "obedient to reason," in a way that rebels against the true nature of human reason's constraints.

At this point, Magee lays out his scriptural hermeneutic in all its breadth, and in a way that, despite the scholarly erudition he will muster in his lengthy notes, marks his basic attitude as essentially anti-Enlightenment in its understanding of history and its relation to God's providential ordering of time and events. *All* sacrifices, Magee argues, both pagan and Israelite, derive from the first revelation of sacrifice to Abel, and they constitute "figures" of the one sacrifice of Christ that alone is ultimately effective for the forgiveness of sins and that alone gives any meaning to any other sacrificial practice in history. All of human and biblical history, taken in terms of its semantic and causal force, exists with this divine system of Christological signification.[20] That is simply part of its divinely systemic, though mysterious, character. To the degree that Magee accepts more modern notions of historical development, he places them in an Irenaean framework: as Israel, through divine pedagogy, adapts the degraded forms of sacrifice that have spread around the world towards more specific religious purposes, bound up with their scriptural accounting, the human mind is made ready for the revelation of the one true sacrifice of Christ.[21] This is not, however, a developmental history, but rather the chronology of divine "institutions," whereby the Bible simply traces the marks of God's determining acts that refer to the Cross. Magee's is more a "sacramental" history (the word is his) than it is an evolutionary one.[22] He ends the sermon, in fact, by exhorting his student listeners to the upcoming Sunday communion service, wherein the "stupendous sacrifice" of Christ is "commemorated." Failure to obey the summons or to do so "irreverently" will bring with it God's further judgment: "Allow me to remind you, that his is an awful call, and upon an awful occasion."[23]

---

19. Magee, *Discourses and Dissertations*, 43–45.
20. Ibid., 42.
21. Ibid., 48–49.
22. Ibid., 47.
23. Ibid., 51.

This sense of "awfulness" or "awe" was actually central to Magee's entire orientation. It shapes his generally skeptical and fideist arguments for the biblical revelation's compelling plausibility, the deontological approach to the substance and forms of sacrifice as divinely given, and the enveloping reality of "mystery"—a word and its cognates that appear repeatedly in the work—that defines the precincts of God's being and will within which the great sacrificial act of Christ emerges. Sacrifice, for Magee, opens a window onto this holy and transfiguring reality. It is a "mysterious transaction," a "mysterious scheme," a "mysterious subject," a "mysterious sublimity," not primarily in its obscurity (although that too), but in its quite tangible and overpowering self-manifestation of God in relation to human beings. Hence, for Magee the reality of sacrifice—which is, at root, nothing less than the very self-giving of God in Christ on the Cross—drives us to humility, and from this posture opens us to its grace.

None of this, with respect to fundamental doctrine, was particularly exceptional. A standard text used for decades within the Episcopal Church in the nineteenth century, Robert Gray's late eighteenth-century *Key to the Old Testament* had used very similar arguments for the sake of similar general doctrinal conclusions, when discussing the character of scriptural sacrifice.[24] Gray even adopted a loose Butlerian framework to make his point, in a way that founded acceptance of this divine system on the basis of human ignorance before the wider ordering of the world. By the end of the eighteenth century, in fact, the Butlerian argument had assumed a certain currency in these kinds of debates, aimed at silencing the rationalist and moralist notions of the divine economy. Having said that, Magee's approach clearly stood in some real tension with those currents which still held on firmly to just these rationalizing and moralizing impulses, and which it seems managed to persevere and outlast Magee's work—which, though it towered above others for a decade or two, would then disappear from the scene. If, in the mid-nineteenth century, Trinity College's curriculum still had a place for Magee, it also still promoted the semi-Arian Samuel Clarke's views on revelation, in all their serene and humanistic logic.[25]

Beyond the overall theological argument of Magee's *Discourses*, his "dissertations" or notes on various points in the sermons proved the most lasting element of Magee's efforts. Finally seventy-four in number, the first and relatively short half of the collection of these explications focused on the anti-Unitarian debate and specific theological arguments involved, mostly

---

24. Gray, *A Key to the Old Testament*, published in 1790 with multiple editions thereafter through the nineteenth century. See especially the treatment of Leviticus.

25. O'Brien, *Introductory Lecture*, 70.

covered in the first sermon. The second set of notes, almost three hundred pages' worth, were related to the second sermon. These became ever more elaborate studies on Israelite and heathen sacrificial practice, history, and religious significance. They proved to be an amazing collation of sources on these topics, delving into a dazzling array of ancient and recent authors, and laying out evidence in encyclopedic breadth. It was this latter set of notes that survived well into the nineteenth century, providing references for countless discussions of sacrifice in its historical development.[26]

The notes also shelter some of Magee's more philosophical presuppositions. So, for instance, we find in Note 53, "On the Divine Origin of Language," a remarkable discussion of human reasoning drawing on Plato and Aristotle, a host of ancient authors and medieval philosophers, Locke, Berkeley, Adam Smith, Dugald Stewart, Condillac, Herder, and many others. Magee argues for a strict nominalism, in which universals and abstract terms act only *as* terms, and do not reference some actual reality.[27] Not only is language directly given by God to Adam, but "terms of worship and adoration were among those which were first communicated."[28] This is the point of his nominalism: revelation alone establishes the reality of biblical practices, like sacrifice, and certifies their divine origin. Such practices cannot be derived from reason at all, as the following Note 54 makes clear ("The Natural Unreasonableness of the Sacrificial Rite").

It is because of this, however, that probing the rationale of scriptural worship and its theological presuppositions can at best be a limited affair, and this includes those classical terms associated—by divine revelation—with the Cross, like "propitiation" or "expiation." In what would become later a matter of concern for stricter Calvinists, Magee demurs from pressing the rational referent of the term "punishment" applied to the sacrifice of Christ.[29] The word strictly speaking cannot describe subjectively (and, from God's side, even objectively) what is happening to the Son, even if the word is "justified" in a vague way. "It were better, perhaps, to adopt the phrase of *suffering for sins*," Magee writes. On the one hand, recognizing that such words are appropriate simply because they are given by God, he affirms their usage in an absolute sense: they are God's individual words given over in Scripture. On the other hand, because they are distinct words, whose

---

26. See *The Bible Cyclopedia*, where Magee is extensively cited in articles on "Abel" and "Sacrifice"; or John McClintock and James Strong's popular *Cyclopedia of Biblical, Theological, and Ecclesiastical Literature*, where he is cited and discussed under "Calvinism" and "Sacrifice," among other articles.

27. Magee, *Discourses and Dissertations*, 294.

28. Ibid., 300.

29. Ibid., 252.

abstracted sense cannot be ascertained if it exists at all in human terms, we can adjust their rationales more loosely. "This view of the subject, completely removes all those objections, derived from a rigorous acceptation of the nature of punishment" that have been raised by rationalist Unitarians against a view of the Cross as a "sacrifice for sin."[30] God determines the use and application of a biblical word, specifically; but that means that we shall never quite understand its full meaning; and consequently, semantic breadth, in human terms, is opened up.

Magee is able to engage this breadth, not so much out of a deferral to human incapacity, but out of an acknowledgement of the divine usage of linguistic terms themselves. This comes up in his repeated attack on the Unitarian description of sacrificial language (among other things) as "figurative" rather than "real." In Note 31, "On the Pretence of Figurative Allusion in the Sacrificial Terms of the New Testament," Magee makes use of the distinction between figuration as imaginative "allusion," and "analogy" as depending on a parallel of "similar relations." The discussion is a bit confusing but hinges very clearly on the notion of divine historical sovereignty. If *God* orders "dispensations" in a relational fashion—e.g., Christ's sacrifice as semantically engaging an earlier era of Israelite sacrifice—this divine act will determine a "real," not a "figurative" sacrificial meaning for the Cross. The latter intrinsically means the former by divine *fiat*, at least minimally. Magee's point is seriously misunderstood if, as some modern scholars have done, his "figural" reading of Cain and Abel in Discourse 2 is viewed as somehow *reducing* the historical reality and integrity of Israelite religion to a referential prop for Christianity. Rather, the past of the Old Testament constitutes the divinely appointed substance of the New's referential character.[31] The substance, which is divinely given, is actually the same.

Taking these elements together, the most significant aspect that was frequently seized upon in later quotes from Magee's work was his idea that the sacrificial reality of Christ is itself a place of mystery into which the human creature enters with awed humility. This text, quoted in dozens of magazines and handbooks, including those lying behind Strong's *Cyclopedia* (where it is given in the article on "Calvinism") represents the center of Magee's theology of revelatory receipt:

> The sacrifice of Christ was never deemed by any, who did not wish to calumniate the doctrine of atonement, to have made God placable, but merely viewed as the means, appointed by divine

---

30. Ibid., 252.

31. Wein, "Fixing Ireland," especially 11–17, where Wein interprets Old Testament figuration as essentially turning Judaism into an ahistorical cipher for Christian truth.

> wisdom, by which to bestow forgiveness. And agreeably to this, do we not find this sacrifice every where spoken of, as ordained by God himself? (John iii.16. 1 John iv.10. 1 Pet. i.18, 19, 20. Rev. xiii.8.) . . . But still it is demanded, "in what way can the death of Christ, considered as a sacrifice of expiation, be conceived to operate to the remission of sins, unless by the appeasing of a being, who otherwise would not have forgiven us?" To this the answer of the Christian is, "I know not, nor does it concern me to know, in what manner the sacrifice of Christ is connected with the forgiveness of sins; it is enough that this is declared by God to be the medium, through which my salvation is effected. I pretend not to dive into the councils of the Almighty. I submit to his wisdom, and I will not reject his grace, because his mode of vouchsafing it, is not within my comprehension."— . . . All that we know, or can know of the one, or of the other, is, that it has been appointed as the means, by which God has determined to act with respect to man. So that to object to the one, because the mode of operation is unknown, is not only giving up the other, but the very notion of a mediator; and if followed on, cannot fail to lead to pure deism, and perhaps may not stop even there.[32]

As others have noted, however, in this posture Magee was simply elaborating on Butler's own views of the matter:

> How, and in what particular way, the sacrifice of Christ had this efficacy, there are not wanting persons, who have endeavoured to explain: but I do not find that the scripture has explained it. We seem to be very much in the dark, concerning the manner, in which the ancients understood atonement to be made, i.e. pardon to be obtained by sacrifices. And if the scripture has, as surely it has, left this matter of the satisfaction of Christ mysterious, left somewhat in it unrevealed, all conjectures about it must be, if not evidently absurd, yet at least uncertain. Nor has any one reason to complain for want of further information, unless he can shew his claim to it. [. . .] It is our wisdom thankfully to accept the benefit—without disputing how it was procured.[33]

It is useful to compare the Butlerian form of Magee's argument for "mystery" here with orthodox contemporaries. In general, Magee was seen as having dealt a hard blow to Unitarian arguments.[34] But at a certain point,

---

32. Ibid., 28–29.

33. Butler, *The Analogy of Religion*, 305–6.

34. "[Magee's work] did more, perhaps, than any other work of its time, to dissolve the charm of those pretensions to philosophic distinction, and those claims to critical

this was no longer the main issue among Protestants. The Dissenter John Pye-Smith, for instance, published a lengthy discourse with notes in 1813 that proved popular in Protestant circles through the 1870s, and that was, like Magee's work, enlarged over time to four discourses with extended notes.[35] Pye-Smith provides a long and laudatory note regarding Magee's work,[36] which he initially read only after his first discourse was delivered. In many ways, the two works converge in their "general" teaching, and it is clear that Pye-Smith is, in his later additions, deliberately covering matters that Magee had already staked out. But, as Pye-Smith notes, there are differences; and they pertain specifically to the degree to which one can properly draw out a logical rationale for the sacrificial meaning of Christ's death. Although Pye-Smith offers a fulsome admission of human ignorance before the great act of the Atonement, in fact he wishes to draw more on Clarke's notion of divine "attributes" to explain matters, and he only rarely touches on the divine determination as the only admissible founding of the sacrificial reality.[37] Instead, moral sentiments emerge as the shaping force and goal, and the tone of the volume turns away from the (seldom mentioned) awful mystery of God to something both more reasonable and "experimentally" uplifting (e.g., "assurance").[38]

It is difficult to gauge the influence Magee's work might have had on the many Trinity students who, over the years, studied his discussion. He guided his readers through a decidedly conservative retention of the traditional forms of Atonement theology, and in this way provided them a basis for more classic sixteenth-century construals of the sacrifice of the Cross. To this extent, his arguments shored up a standard Prayer Book theology that could be taken in more Reformed or High Church directions. His Butlerian skepticism, however, which stressed the mystery of human existence and of that existence's sovereign God, was not only scripturally conservative, but decidedly set against the speculative attractions of modern thinking. At a certain point, Magee's outlook must have seemed not only old-fashioned but obstructionist in the face of the clamoring debates over science, idealism, and historical development that began to swirl about theological discussion by the mid-nineteenth century. Divinity students (and their

pre-eminence, which had obtained for the Unitarians of Great Britain a partial and temporary ascendency" (Anonymous, Review of *Discourses and Dissertations*, 486).

35. Pye-Smith, *Four Discourses*. Originally published in 1813, a fifth edition appeared in 1876.

36. Ibid., note 15, 88–91 in the original edition; cf. Pye-Smith, *On the Sacrifice of Christ*.

37. Pye-Smith, *Four Discourses*, 51–52.

38. Ibid., 60–64.

teachers) more and more, perhaps, demanded means of addressing these debates forthrightly, and Magee was finally dropped from the curriculum. A glance at some of his major critics indicates the drift of intellectual interests in this regard.

CRITICS: COLERIDGE

There was something too austere about Magee's approach, which, in the eyes of those less given to Calvinist commitments, marked the entire path of Reformed reflection on the Atonement, even as Magee's Butlerian skepticism finally proved unacceptable to Reformed rationalism and its drift into evangelical "experimental" religion. Among the first group of critics, Coleridge and (more publicly) F. D. Maurice stand out. Coleridge simply disliked the whole notion of a "forgiveness" that doesn't actually *change* a person in their spiritual being. Magee was taken to be a representative of "imputed" righteousness, which hangs like a sign before God's eyes but without any transformative power:

> I can conceive nothing more hollow or unsatisfactory than the present orthodox notion, as explained by Bull, Horsley, Magee, and other Arminian Church of England divines, that the incarnation and Cross of Christ acts only retrospectively—which they call Justification—by re-instating the sinner in a—real? no! a legal and imputed Innocence. A mere wiping off of old Scores!—O it forcibly reminds me of the Scottish Lady's answer to her Lord who wishing to divorce her on account of barrenness offered to restore her Dowry.—Alas! the *fallen* Spirit—not the fallen *nature* . . . The Spirit has fallen into *a* Nature [. . .] if the Cross be no Antidote to this, no effectual succor at least—if in *this life* only we have hope! [. . .][39]

Coleridge had no real interest in Magee's thinking. For him, he was just another Protestant servant of *sola Scriptura*, groveling at the feet of an arbitrary Deity,[40] following incoherent commands, and unwilling to engage the "Aid of the Spirit" within the Church.[41] And it is true that Magee's vision valorized humble receipt beyond all else.

In this way, however, Magee's Christian was neither an unfeeling automaton nor a repristinated slave. To be sure, Magee rejected Wesley's

---

39. Coleridge, *The Notebooks of Samuel Taylor Coleridge*, vol. 5:1, note 5631.
40. Ibid., vol. 4:1, notes 5215 and 5384.
41. Ibid., vol. 5:1, note 5792.

(let alone the Deistic) search for perfected feeling,[42] and would scoff at sentimentalized Christianity.[43] His remarks concerning sanctification or the "influence of the Holy Spirit" upon the interior will and heart of the Christian are few.[44] In the place of Methodism's "overweening" emotionalism, however, Magee did not leave some "experimentally" neutralized heart, but (quoting Wilberforce at length) the deeply felt reality of a torn spirit, a kind of hope offered through the Cross that could drag corruption into the light of God's redeeming presence.

CRITICS: MAURICE

This kind of sentiment, however, was hardly enticing to many. In 1853 F. D. Maurice had commented on the arguments being held with Unitarians who were concerned that claims regarding a divine propitiatory sacrifice were incoherent with the God of traditional doctrine. Opponents of these claims were frequently "[m]en of the Evangelical school, who did not like Archbishop Magee's book, because they found nothing in it which responded to the witness of their hearts, yet accepted it on the poor calculation that it was a learned book, and might defend what they were pleased to call the outworks of the faith." Maurice then starkly announced that, for his part, "I must give up Archbishop Magee, for I am determined to keep that which makes the Atonement precious to my heart and conscience; to keep the theology of the Creeds and of the Bible."[45] The issue was "the heart," touched by the infinite love of God. For Maurice, this was shown in the sacrifice of Christ—one to which he, furthermore, was willing to apply the term "punishment," based indeed on a divine "wrath."[46] All this was a given, but given only to unveil the divine love itself, which could indeed reach out and reshape the being of a human person. Debate over the doctrine itself that might erect a discussion that obscured this deeper reality was, for Maurice, mistaken and pernicious. He could sympathize with Unitarian worries, even if he could not embrace their extreme conclusions. Yet he somewhat blamed people like Magee for stirring up such worries themselves.

Maurice's fuller theology on the matter is worked out in his series of sermons *The Doctrine of Sacrifice Deduced From the Scripture*.[47] In this

42. Magee, *Discourses and Dissertations*, Note 12.
43. Ibid., 443, Note 72.
44. Ibid., 464.
45. Maurice, "On The Atonement," 114.
46. Ibid., 108.
47. Maurice, *Doctrine of Sacrifice*.

work, he famously lays out his conviction of sacrifice as a central Trinitarian reality, outside of creation itself, the inner character of God itself, as the Son gives himself over to the Father "before the foundation of the world."[48] This establishes a kind of metaphysical "law of sacrifice" that founds the universe itself, and which, historically enacted in the Cross, draws human beings into its transformative reach and reorders their own life according to its shape.[49] In some ways, Maurice almost platonizes Magee's figural approach, and the two are closer together, perhaps, than certainly Maurice believed. Still, it is this inner logic of the world that the Cross expresses, and hence its ontological reordering of lives undergirds Maurice's unrelenting affective approach, so much in contrast with Magee. For Maurice, everything is filled with "sympathy," "anguish," "heart," "spirit," "love," which spread from Christ to human beings. In place of Magee's "awful mystery" of God, Maurice insists that there is an inner divine drive to the self-manifestation of God's "character": it is this that the Atonement displays most fully.

OTHER CRITICS

Other Calvinists shared some of Maurice's emphases, as for example in the influential work of John McLeod Campbell, whose *On the Nature of the Atonement* (1856) has continued to inform thinking well into the twentieth century.[50] For Campbell, the Atonement is properly seen as drawing us into the very sacrificial life of Christ in its "spiritual" realities of submission, confession, obedience, and love, so that the "in Christ" aspect of the Christian's existence, established by the Cross, involves in itself a transformative human dynamic. Later nineteenth-century interest in the "mystical" union wrought by the Atonement is related to this.[51] In contrast to Magee, this developing explication of the Atonement is focused, not on the sovereign determinations of the holy God which themselves constitute divine love, but rather on the relational refashioning of the human heart and its practical expression within the world. Magee was simply too cold and bloodless in this light. Though he was immensely articulate in demonstrating "the sinfulness and spiritual impotence of man" and, in conjunction to this, the "essential" place of the atonement of Christ "in the Christian economy," one

---

48. Maurice, *Doctrine of Sacrifice*, Sermon 7, 100–14.

49. Ibid., 113.

50. Campbell, *Nature of the Atonement*.

51. See Auguste Sabatier's popular work on Paul, *The Apostle Paul*, originally published in French in 1870.

mid-century critic summed up the growing dissatisfaction with Magee's work by noting that

> we could have wished to have seen in the narrative before us a full and clear account of the practical bearings of Scripture doctrine upon the heart, in regard to justification, peace with God, the implantation and growth of holy affections, and the hopes and fears, the trials and consolations, of the renewed mind. We do not imply that the prelate would have denied or doubted that in the regenerate there is "the life of God in the soul of man"; but we regret that what is shewn to be lovely and of good report in his temper and conduct, is not distinctly traced up to the operation of those principles which the world accounts fanatical, but which are the germ of all that is spiritual-minded and holy.[52]

The relational and pneumatic aspects of the Atonement are indeed missing in Magee, and his usefulness to later evangelical religion was thin, just as his strangely skeptical views seemed inadequate for reformed rationalists and fundamentalists. "At times the author speaks like a follower of Bishop Butler . . . At other times his language is such as would be expected from an adherent of the Westminster Assembly, or the Synod of Dort."[53] It was hardly a winning combination as the theological battle lines took shape in the later nineteenth century. Magee's insistence on the mystery of divine determination seemed to end up with a commendation to assert "just the facts" as Scripture described them, even in their confusing variety, and this approach easily ended up with a theology that had neither reason nor feeling heart behind it.[54]

LATER DEVELOPMENTS

Within Britain, Magee's influence faded. In the form of a "concentrated" version of the larger work, the Anglican missionary in India (and briefly the Indian Ocean) Thomas Morton transmitted the kernel of Magee's work

---

52. *Christian Observer* 65 (1843), 258.

53. Porter, *Lectures on the Doctrine of the Atonement*, 165. Porter was an Irish Presbyterian of Unitarian sympathies.

54. See Hicks, "Atonement Theology in the late Nineteenth Century," 116–27, on how the Campbellite stress (for the sake of avoiding speculative dispute) on "just the facts" of biblical atonement claims ended up with a denuded doctrine that no longer had any human purchase. Alexander Campbell himself commended Magee's book as a standard for a Christian's library: see Campbell, "A Good Library," 492.

to the mission field, beginning in the Seychelles.[55] And one sees him still rattling around the edges of theological discussion into the early twentieth century.[56] But the monopoly held by experimentalism and rationalism in Protestant theology during this period and beyond meant there was little place for Magee's submissive brand of revelatory receipt.

Magee's approach was not without creative traces, however, in part because it grew organically out of central aspects of Anglican thinking about the Scriptures themselves. H. L. Mansel's 1858 Bampton Lectures, *The Limits of Religious Thought*, involved him in a notorious debate with Maurice, and Mansel himself became the object of an almost irrational antipathy as a soulless philosopher out of touch with the living spirit of God.[57] Mansel, for his part, found Magee still useful.[58] Indeed, Mansel was perhaps one of the few later writers who understood and appreciated Magee's Butlerian skepticism and humility, tied to the gratuity of scriptural revelation, for it was an argument he was to make famous on his own terms, framed in a post-Kantian set of concepts.[59] Like Magee,

> Mansel was not over-committed on the theological sore spots of his era: penal substitution, predestination or eternal damnation.[60] But nor was he willing to deny that the Scriptures, at times, spoke in these terms. Theological skepticism, properly configured, requires that the Church must make sense of these realities along with the whole range of canonical writings for the simple reason that, somehow, they describe the character and activity of God.[61]

Again, like Magee before him,

> Mansel's theology belongs more securely in the tradition of Anglican theology that combines a skepticism toward speculative theology and an intense devotion to the centrality of Scripture

---

55. See Morton, *The Doctrine of Atonement Vindicated*. A subsequent edition was published in 1829. See also Taylor, *Launching Out Into the Deep*, 42. It was apparently still on the list of books for clergy examination in Jamaica in 1870. See "Religious Denominations."

56. Ralston, *Elements of Divinity*. This was an abridgement of the original Ralston work of 1847, and was republished several times through 1924.

57. For an outline of the theological stakes in this once notorious controversy, see Reardon, *From Coleridge to Gore*, 223–42.

58. Mansel, *Limits of Religious Thought*, 247.

59. Neufeld, "Scripture, Skepticism and the Character of God," 304.

60. Cf. Mansel, *Limits of Religious Thought*, 152.

61. Neufeld, "Scripture, Skepticism and the Character of God," 307.

in the Church's common life. Critics argued that Mansel's skepticism and theory of regulative truth separated the reality of God from the language and narrative of Scripture. However, it can be argued that Mansel's skepticism provides a context in which the entire canon of Scripture can speak truthfully and coherently about the character of God's action in the world.[62]

Though Mansel himself was much misunderstood (and not only by Maurice), the creative and sophisticated way he responded to the confusing tides of idealism for the sake of traditional Christian belief is today being rediscovered; and with this, perhaps Magee's own powerful if unusual approach can be more positively reassessed.[63] Bowen's estimation of Magee as "the epitome of the rational, sober-minded High Church Prelate"[64] is therefore only partly right. To be sure, Magee's commitment to establishment, Prayer Book devotion, and traditional doctrine placed him squarely within this stream of Anglicanism. Yet Magee's theological method was, like Butler's, daring in many ways; and his own religious vision was, like his intellectual mentor's, profound in its apprehension of and submission to God's untamable yet gracious mystery. Theological students of the twenty-first century could stand to be exposed, once again, to this discipline.

BIBLIOGRAPHY

Anonymous. Review of *Discourses and Dissertations on the Scriptural Doctrines of Atonement and Sacrifice* by William Magee. *The American Biblical Repository*, 2nd Series, 4.36 (1839) 486.

Belsham, Thomas. *An Address to the Inquirers after Christian Truth, in Reply to the Extracts from Dr. Magee's Book on Atonement and Sacrifice*. Glasgow: Glasgow Unitarian Fund, 1813.

The Bible Cyclopedia: Or, Illustrations of the Civil and Natural History of the Sacred Writings. 2 vols. London: Parker, 1841–43.

Bowen, Desmond. "Magee, William (1766–1831)." In *DNB* (online edition), edited by David Cannadine. Oxford: Oxford University Press, 2004. http://www.oxforddnb.com.myaccess.library.utoronto.ca/view/article/17778.

---

62. Ibid., ii.

63. To be sure, Magee was not the philosopher Mansel was, and this was noted. See Adam Storey Farrar who, in 1859, gently implied that Magee was not sufficiently clear about the "limits" of ontology, or perhaps just intellectually lazy, in comparison with Mansel. Farrar is reflecting on whether a psychology of guilt can tell us anything regarding metaphysical reality, and hence whether there is anything truly theological at all that one can draw from human sentiments of guilt. Farrar, *Science in Theology*, 197–98; Magee himself had used Adam Smith on this topic, in a "common sense" way that arguably undercut, somewhat, his commitments to revelation vs. mystery.

64. Bowen, *Protestant Crusade in Ireland*, 95.

———. *The Protestant Crusade in Ireland, 1800–70: A Study of Protestant-Catholic Relations between the Act of Union and Disestablishment*. Montreal: McGill-Queen's University Press, 1978.

Bowers, J. D. *Joseph Priestley and English Unitarianism in America*. University Park, PA: Pennsylvania State Press, 2007.

Butler, Joseph. *The Analogy of Religion*. 3rd ed. London: Knapton, 1740.

Campbell, Alexander. "A Good Library." *Millennial Harbinger* 5.10 (Oct. 1834) 490–93.

Campbell, John McLeod. *The Nature of the Atonement, and Its Relation to Remission of Sins and Eternal Life*. Cambridge: Macmillan, 1856.

The Christian Observer (New Series) 65 (May 1843) 257–64.

Coleridge, Samuel Taylor. *The Notebooks of Samuel Taylor Coleridge*. Edited by Kathleen Coburn and Anthony John Harding. 5 vols. Princeton, NJ: Princeton University Press, 2002.

Davis, Richard W. *Dissent in Politics, 1780–1830: The Political Life of William Smith, M.P.* London: Epworth, 1971.

Ditchfield, G. M. "The Parliamentary Struggle over the Repeal of the Test and Corporation Acts, 1787–1790." *The English Historical Review* 89.352 (July 1974) 551–77.

The Dublin University Calendar, for the Year 1868. Dublin: Hodges, 1868.

Farrar, Adam Story. *Science in Theology: Sermons*. London: Murray, 1859.

Gray, Robert. *A Key to the Old Testament and Apocrypha: In Which is Given an Account of Their Several Books, Their Contents, and Authors, and of the Times in Which They Were Respectively Written*. London: Rivington, 1790.

Greenwood, Andrea, and Mark W. Harris. *An Introduction to the Unitarian and Universalist Traditions*. Cambridge: Cambridge University Press, 2011.

Hicks, John Mark. "Atonement Theology in the Late Nineteenth Century: The Pattern of Discussion." *Discipliana* 56.4 (Winter 1996) 116–27.

Magee, William. *Discourses and Dissertations on the Scriptural Doctrines of Atonement and Sacrifice*. 3rd ed. London: Cadell, 1816.

———. "Prefatory Address to the Students in Divinity in the University of Dublin." In *Discourses and Dissertations*, 3rd ed., ix–xi. London: Cadell, 1816.

———. *Works of William Magee, Archbishop of Dublin, with a Memoir of his Life*. 2 vols. Edited by A. H. Kenney. London: Cadell, 1842.

Mansel, Henry Longueville. *The Limits of Religious Thought Examined in Eight Lectures*. 4th ed. London: Murray, 1859.

Maurice, Frederick Denison. *The Doctrine of Sacrifice Deduced from the Scriptures: A Series of Sermons*. Cambridge: Macmillan, 1854.

———. "On the Atonement." In *Theological Essays*, 2nd ed, 98–115. New York: Redfield, 1854.

McClintock, John, and James Strong. *Cyclopedia of Biblical, Theological, and Ecclesiastical Literature*. New York: Harper, 1891.

Morton, Thomas. *The Doctrine of Atonement Vindicated Against the Opponents of that Doctrine as Held by Our Church*. London: Rivington, 1821.

Neufeld, Dane. "Scripture, Skepticism and the Character of God: The Theology of Henry Mansel." ThD diss., University of Toronto, 2015.

O'Brien, James Thomas. *An Introductory Lecture Delivered in the Divinity School in Trinity College, Dublin on the First Lecture Day of Michaelmas Term, 1837*. Dublin: Milliken, 1837.

Penulham, Terence. *Butler.* London: Routledge, 1985.

Porter, John Scott. *Lectures on the Doctrine of the Atonement.* London: Whitfield, 1860.

Power, Thomas P. "'Of No Small Importance': Curricular Change in the School of Divinity, Trinity College Dublin, 1790–1850." In *Change and Transformation: Essays in Anglican History*, edited by Thomas P. Power, 140–183. Eugene, OR: Pickwick, 2013.

Price, D. B. "Memoir of the Late Rev. Henry Taylor." *Christian Reformer, or, Unitarian Magazine and Review*, new series, 5 (Feb 1849) 65–78.

Pye-Smith, John. *Four Discourses on the Sacrifice and Priesthood of Jesus Christ, and the Atonement and Redemption Thence Accruing; with Supplementary Notes and Illustrations.* Edinburgh: Oliphant, 1876.

———. *On the Sacrifice of Christ; Its Nature, Value, and Efficacy: A Discourse Delivered at the Rev. George Burder's Meeting House, March 11, 1813.* London: Stower, 1813.

Ralston, Thomas N. *Elements of Divinity.* Edited by Thomas O. Summers. Nashville: Methodist Episcopal Church South, 1903.

Reardon, Bernard M. G. *From Coleridge to Gore: A Century of Religious Thought in Britain.* London: Longman, 1971.

"Religious Denominations: Ecclesiastical Island Establishment." *1870 Jamaica Almanac.* http://www.jamaicanfamilysearch.com/Members/1870co6.htm.

Sabatier, Auguste. *The Apostle Paul: A Sketch of the Development of His Doctrine.* New York: Pott, 1891.

Shedd, William Greenough Thayer. *Dogmatic Theology.* New York: Scribner, 1888.

Sykes, Arthur Ashley. *An Essay on the Nature, Design, and Origin of Sacrifices.* London: Knapton, 1748.

Taylor, Donald. *Launching Out Into the Deep: The Anglican Church in the History of the Seychelles to 2000 AD.* Victoria, Seychelles: Board of Church Commissioners, Diocese of the Seychelles, 2005.

Wein, Toni. "Fixing Ireland / Fixing the Jew in *Melmoth the Wanderer*." *Patterns of Prejudice* 40.1 (2006) 1–24.

Wilbur, Earl Morse. *A History of Unitarianism.* Boston: Beacon, 1969.

Wills, J. *Lives of Illustrious and Distinguished Irishmen.* Dublin: Fullerton, 1847.

5

A Question of Possession—Who Owned the Church of Ireland's History?

JAMES BLAKE KNOX

IN THE COURSE OF the early nineteenth century, there were a number of developments that challenged the dominant position of the Established Church in Ireland. These included tithe reform, the Church Temporalities Act of 1833, and Catholic Emancipation. Perhaps above all, there were increasing calls for the disestablishment of the Church of Ireland. In response to all of the above, Irish Anglicans attempted to legitimize their church's position in the face of mounting internal and external pressure. To many within the Irish Anglican community, it seemed that one way of ensuring a viable future in Ireland was to present a convincing narrative of their history. In so doing, they hoped to establish the status of their church as an authentically Irish institution. This essay examines two of the most significant works of nineteenth-century Irish Anglican historiography in that context. One is the Bishop of Down and Connor, Richard Mant's (1775–1848) *The History of the Church of Ireland from the Reformation to the Revolution*. The other is Charles Richard Elrington's editions of *The Whole Works of the Most Rev. James Ussher*. Elrington (1787–1850) was the Regius Professor of Divinity at Trinity College, Dublin.

These works were also pivotal in the education of generations of Irish clergymen. When many of those clergy left Ireland to minister abroad, they brought these works and their influence with them. One of the destinations of these clergy was North America and the territory that would become Canada. Anglican immigrants to Canada included the Cork-born John Travers Lewis, the first bishop of Ontario, who acknowledged the pivotal role that Elrington had played in his own education.

The first of these two works to be published was Mant's *History*. At almost seventeen hundred pages, its two volumes are a demanding and at times a tortuous account of the Church of Ireland's development from the Reformation to the Act of Union. The second work that will be examined was conceived on an even larger and more ambitious scale, and runs to multiple volumes. In 1825, the board of Trinity College resolved to publish the collected works of Archbishop James Ussher, and appointed Charles Richard Elrington as overall editor of the project.[1] It took more than twenty-five years to complete the publication of *The Whole Works of James Ussher*. Indeed, by the time the final volume appeared, Elrington was dead, and the publication of Ussher's works had become the most prolonged and expensive project undertaken by either the Dublin University Press or Trinity College in the whole of the nineteenth century.

It is hardly surprising, then, that Irish Anglican historians regarded these two historical projects with the utmost seriousness of purpose. Indeed, they could not have been completed without the intellectual and financial resources of the Church of Ireland and of Trinity College. It is equally significant that the hierarchies of the Church of Ireland and Trinity College who commissioned these landmark projects were dominated by high churchmen. In this context, the two publications not only served as a response to external critiques, but also as a strategic riposte to the low church faction within the Church of Ireland. They were also intended to counter Presbyterian and Roman Catholic interpretations of the Anglican Church's history. The selection of Mant and Elrington for such important undertakings was highly controversial and provoked immediate opposition. It will be argued here that their works are linked at a more fundamental level than has previously been acknowledged.

NEED FOR HISTORY

It is indisputable that the Church of Ireland displayed a greater commitment to Calvinist theology in the beginning of the seventeenth century than did

---

1. Kinane, *History of the Dublin University Press*, 140.

its English "Mother Church." For high church Irish Anglicans such as Mant and Elrington, this represented something of a dilemma. They were, to say the least, not sympathetic to the fundamental tenets of Calvinism. They tended to associate these with the Presbyterians of Ulster, whose robust denial of church hierarchy they found both extremely disagreeable and deeply unsettling. At the same time, the notion of an unbroken spiritual continuity in the Irish church appealed strongly to them. If they wanted to claim any direct connection with the early Irish Church, or with the notion of apostolic succession, then it was clear that they could not simply ignore the history of the Church of Ireland in the early seventeenth century. This led them to attempt to de-Calvinize the history of their church, by understating the influence of Calvinist clergy and the presence of Calvinist theology in that history.

As late as 1843, Robert King (1815–1900), a fellow of St. Columba's College, complained that Irish Anglicans had allowed the "candle of sacred history" to be hidden.[2] The first priority for many Irish Anglicans was to establish a clear and certain sense of their own identity and separate existence from the Church of England. In 1837, James Henthorn Todd had written to a former provost, Samuel Kyle, outlining his fear that

> there is a serious and radical defect in the education of our clergy. They are not taught to be churchmen. The peculiarities of our own church polity are all studiously kept out of sight and that in a country where they have to contend with Presbyterians on the one and the Papists on the other.[3]

He continued: "How can we hope to have our clergy Episcopalian in their feelings, when we sap the very foundations of Episcopal principles by teaching them Presbyterian Church History?"[4]

These concerns were not confined to Todd: they appear frequently in the correspondence of other leading high church figures—such as Charles Richard Elrington, William Reeves, Archbishop John George Beresford, and John Godley—throughout this period.[5] The lack of historical publications

---

2. King, *Primer of the History*, x.

3. TCD Todd papers MS 2214/54. In 1834, a reviewer in Tait's *Edinburgh Magazine*, quoting from the Presbyterian scholar James Seaton Reid (1798–1851), argued that the Church of Ireland was "without a historian" and that this had left "a chasm" in Ireland's ecclesiastical history. Review of *History of the Presbyterian Church*, 210.

4. Ibid, 210.

5. John Godley wrote that "the great fault of the Irish clergyman is ignorance. Most of her ministers are zealous, pious, hardworking men, but with few exceptions, wholly uniformed in the writings of churchmen either from their own or foreign countries." LPL, Selborne papers, MS 1861, fos. 85–86, Godley to R. Palmer, 16 Mar. 1843.

was perceived as a significant handicap for Irish Anglican clergy since it restricted their knowledge of their own church, and made it harder for them to defend it from Presbyterian and Roman Catholic critiques. Reminiscing about the early 1830s, Archdeacon Edward Stopford of Meath later claimed that "there was scarcely a clergyman in Ireland who knew anything of the Church in Ireland. We were required at ordination to know something of the history of the Church in England, but of our own (church)—nothing."[6]

In this context, the imperative articulated in Todd's letter becomes understandable. Todd was also insistent on the specific need for this church history to be written "by an Episcopalian," and he identifies the ideal choice as Charles Richard Elrington.[7] It is also evident that this idea had been one which Todd had toyed with for some time; in fact, it had first arisen in a discussion with Samuel Maitland two years earlier.[8] It soon became clear that Elrington would not be viewed as an acceptable candidate to write a comprehensive history of the Church of Ireland: he was strongly identified with the high church faction, and he had engaged in a number of bruising theological contests with evangelical clergymen. The commissioning of Mant to write the *History* needs to be set against the factionalism that had come to dominate what might be termed the theological politics of the Church of Ireland—and, specifically, those within Trinity College. Austin Cooper has noted that at this time—and "in typically Anglican fashion"—the university "spoke with several voices."[9] Todd's choice of phrase here is revealing. In this context, it is clear that by "Episcopalian" Todd means a high churchman. His emphasis on the need for a specifically "Episcopalian" version of the Church of Ireland's history is reflective of a tendency among certain Irish high churchmen to regard Protestant dissent in terms of heresy and schism, rather than mere denominational difference. In marked contrast, evangelicals within the Church of Ireland were more conscious of the common ground that they shared with Protestant dissenters.

Despite his impeccable social background, Elrington's appointment as the editor of Ussher's works proved to be highly controversial. An anonymous letter—from an "Ex-Scholar T. C. D." and self-proclaimed "admirer of Ussher's character and learning"—to *The Christian Examiner* noted that there were many within Trinity who were of the opinion, from the beginning, that the board of the college was "rather infelicitous in their selection

---

6. Edward Stopford to E. P. Shirley, 9 May 1853: Public Record Office of Northern Ireland, MS D3531/G/11.
7. TCD MS 2214/53 Todd to Samuel Kyle, 1 Jul. 1837.
8. TCD MS 2214/16 Samuel Maitland, 15 Dec. 1835.
9. Cooper, "Ireland and the Oxford Movement," 70.

of an editor, from the almost acknowledged want of sympathy, and this too, on points of importance" between Elrington and Ussher.[10] The chief thorn in Elrington's side was a senior fellow, Joseph Henderson Singer, who had begun to promote evangelical opinions in the college. Indeed, a consistent complaint amongst other evangelicals was that Singer should have been selected for the work instead of Elrington.[11]

REFORMATION CHALLENGE

The Reformation presented particular difficulties for Irish Anglican historians. In England, the Reformation was often understood as a victory for rational religion over primitive Roman Catholic superstition. However, the Reformation in Ireland was a prolonged and tortuous affair in which the Church of Ireland did not manage to finalise its confession of faith, or disciplinary canons, until the third decade of the seventeenth century. Of greater significance, however, was the fundamental and inescapable gulf between some of the formal claims made by the Church of Ireland and the obvious reality. The Church of Ireland was simply not the church of the majority of Irish people. Indeed, it could even be argued that a genuine Irish Reformation had never taken place; and, if it had, it could only be considered to have been a spectacular failure.

The Presbyterian historian James Seaton Reid had, in his depictions of the early Irish Reformation, emphasized Irish Protestant unity and contrasted this unfavorably with what had happened in England. *The Christian Examiner*, founded in 1825 by two leading Church of Ireland evangelicals, Caesar Otway and Joseph Singer, had also pioneered the idea of a broad-based Irish Reformation in one of its early volumes. They appealed for Protestant unity based on the example of the early seventeenth-century Reformation in Ireland: a comprehensive and inclusive Calvinist church founded on Archbishop Ussher's Articles of 1615. *The Christian Examiner* contrasted the good relations between the Established Church and dissenters in Ireland with the deep-seated hostility which persistent persecution had caused in England. It argued that the Irish Articles of 1615 had allowed Ulster-Scots settlers and their clergy to be incorporated into the Church of Ireland in the early seventeenth century. They deeply regretted their subsequent deprivation under Wentworth and Bramhall.[12] Appeals for Protestant solidarity in the face of the apparently overwhelming nature of the

---

10. "Letters to the Editor," 492.
11. Ibid., 492.
12. "Horae Hibernicae," 10; "On the Advantages," 82–84.

threat posed by the Roman Catholic Church not only made pragmatic sense to many, it also carried a powerful emotional appeal that resonated across all of Ireland's Protestant denominations, including the Church of Ireland.

In 1838, Dr. Henry Cooke—a leading northern Presbyterian—wrote to Mant, complaining about his support for an anti-Presbyterian sermon delivered by an unnamed clergyman in Mant's diocese. Cooke warned Mant that "our common enemies the Romanists and Radicals are able to employ it against our common cause."[13] It is evident, however, that Cooke's plea for friendly cooperation made little impression upon Mant. He opposed Cooke's calls for pan-Protestant unity between Anglicans and Presbyterians in defense of the Union, and the Protestant character of the British state. Along with Todd and Elrington, he was increasingly alarmed that evangelicals looked for their roots to the Calvinist Irish Reformation of the early seventeenth century, which the low church faction interpreted as the basis for an inclusive Irish Protestantism, united against the common Catholic threat.[14]

MANT'S HISTORY

At first sight, Mant may seem like an unlikely choice to write a definitive history of the Church of Ireland. It was true that he enjoyed the reputation of a respected author and scholar. However, he was not Irish, had no discernible Irish connections, and had not arrived in Ireland—as a bishop in the Church of Ireland—until he was already in advanced middle age. However, that background was also regarded by some as a positive advantage: since Mant had not lived in Ireland for most of his life, he was not closely associated with either the high church or evangelical factions within the Church of Ireland. In fact, Mant's personal sympathies were high church, but although this was suspected by some of his northern congregation, he was not clearly identified as such.

Given that background, it is not surprising that Mant sought assistance from some of his clerical colleagues. In the preface to the first volume of his *History*, Mant alluded to the difficulties that he had faced in locating and obtaining the source material necessary for his work. However, he acknowledged that "in some cases advantage has now and then been taken of kind assistance." Although Mant claimed that this had been for the "most part acknowledged on the occasion," the extent and nature of this assistance

13. NLI, MS 15, 561 (2).
14. Bowen, *Protestant Crusade in Ireland*, 62; and Ridden, "Forgotten History of the Protestant Crusade," 79.

remained obscure.[15] He did reserve his "special thanks" for the "friendly zeal and intelligence" of James Henthorn Todd, then a junior fellow and librarian in Trinity College.[16]

This is one of only two references to Todd in the first volume; he does not appear at all in the second, which might suggest that his contribution to the final text was fairly modest. However, there is ample evidence to indicate that the role that Todd played in the overall work was an important and even a formative one. Todd was not only engaged in the collating of research material for Mant, he was also involved in editing and shaping the final drafts. This role is explicitly acknowledged in a letter that Mant sent to Todd on 11 November 1840, regarding the second edition of the work: "I thank you for your letter (undated) received this morning," he wrote, "and for your corrections whenever they come. On their arrival, my proof corrected by yours will be returned to the press."[17]

The notes and preliminary drafts for the two volumes of Mant's *History*, along with Mant's correspondence, allow for new and revealing insights into how his work was conceived and written. The role of Mant's various assistants in this his major work has never been examined until now. Aside from Todd and Elrington, there are also contributions from some of the most promising members of a new generation of Irish Anglican antiquaries and historians, including William Hardinge ("WmH"), William Gowan Todd ("WGT"), Henry Cotton ("HC"), James Graves ("JG"), William Reeves ("WmR"), and Robert King ("RK"). It is clear that their task was to provide Mant with memoranda summarising the relevant documentary evidence that he sought. Indeed, Mant often incorporated these memoranda in their entirety within his own text. These research and briefing documents are filled with extracts and selections from a wide variety of libraries and archives throughout Great Britain and Ireland, and almost each note is credited to the source that brought it to Mant's attention. All of these scholars were active in or had recently graduated from Trinity College, Dublin, and they constitute the channels through which Mant's work was directly connected with contemporary Anglican scholarship at that university.[18]

Significantly, some of these authors also played important roles in the drafting and editing of Elrington's *The Whole Works of the Most Rev. James Ussher*. Indeed, both Todd and Reeves would oversee the completion of the project upon Elrington's death. Apart from editing many volumes of

15. Mant, *History of the Church of Ireland*, v.
16. Ibid., vi.
17. TCD Todd papers MS 2214/112.
18. NLI MS 15, 361 (1) (2) (3).

Ussher's *Works*, Elrington also wrote a *Life* of Ussher. This had not been part of his original intention, but he responded to the demand from the Church of Ireland community and from the board of Trinity College. This in itself gives some idea of the unique and commanding position that James Ussher occupied in the history of the Church of Ireland.[19] He had played a pivotal role in the history of that church, and one that was acknowledged even by those who were opposed to him for theological or political reasons. This is not only because he served as the Archbishop of Armagh and the Anglican Primate of All Ireland for more than thirty critical years. It is also because of his remarkable personal qualities and intellectual distinction. He was a prolific scholar who had entered Trinity College just a few years after Dublin University was founded. Later he became Professor of Theological Controversies at the university, and vice provost of Trinity. He was born into a family that was closely connected with the Church of Ireland: indeed, his uncle had served before him as Archbishop of Armagh and Primate of All Ireland. Ussher was also closely involved in drawing up the first confession of faith for the Church of Ireland. In other words, he played a central role in the formative years of the Irish Anglican Church. However, despite his voluminous letters and publications, Ussher's forms of expression could, at times, seem indirect or allusive, which allowed a certain ambiguity to develop about his precise views.[20] Defining Ussher's theological views presented both an intellectual and an ideological challenge for Irish Anglicans, and—given the primate's important historical role—it was one which was, as Alan Ford has argued, of "considerable importance in identifying the character and thrust of the Irish Reformation."[21]

---

19. Ford, "Ussher, James"; McCafferty, "Ussher, James."

20. This apparent lack of clarity had been exploited by biographers and scholars who were anxious to secure his posthumous endorsement: a process that began, arguably, with the eulogy at Ussher's funeral—which was published by his Calvinist chaplain, Nicholas Bernard, in 1656. Ford has noted that Bernard's claims "faithfully to interpret his master's voice were far from uncontested." Ford, "Making Dead Men Speak," 49; Bernard, *Life and Death*. Peter Heylin even accused Bernard of being a kind of necroventriloquist, robbing graves and making dead men speak, offering a false portrait of Ussher as a saintly bishop: Heylin, *Respondet Petrus*, 3. Bernard, in turn, was outraged by Heylin's characterization of Ussher as a "Calvinist" and "Puritan"—an indication of the dangers associated with labelling anyone at this time. Bernard, *Judgement of the Late Archbishop of Armagh*.

21. Ford, "'High or Low'?," 10.

MANT AND REID

In his *History* of the Presbyterian Church, James Seaton Reid had discussed in detail how Robert Blair, the leader of the Scottish clergy in Ulster, came to serve within the Church of Ireland. Blair was unhappy at the imposition of episcopacy in Scotland, and had sought greater freedom in the Ulster Plantation. Reid was particularly interested in Blair's interactions with Bishop Robert Echlin of Down and Connor. He claimed to be drawing from Blair's own testimony that, when faced with the conflict between Blair's desire to serve in the Established Church and his reluctance to be ordained by a bishop, Echlin had sidestepped the issue by agreeing to join with other Presbyterian clergy in laying their hands on Blair in 1623. Reid believed that this accommodation suited both parties. It meant that Echlin could claim that, as an Anglican bishop, he had ordained Blair. At the same time, Blair could claim that he had been ordained by Echlin acting simply as one of a number of presbyters.[22]

Reid provided another similar example of interdenominational accommodation, one which he again claimed was derived from Blair's own account. According to Reid, Blair had met with the Archbishop James Ussher on two occasions, first with a group of nobles and clergy from Ulster. At this meeting, it seems that Blair had become uneasy by the use of the Anglican Prayer Book. Ussher, sensing his unease, had suggested that he come to his residence in Drogheda for a private conversation. According to Blair, they conversed amicably, concurring in fundamental doctrinal matters, while agreeing to differ on ceremonies. For Reid, it seemed prophetic that Ussher had warned Blair that, although he did not wish to move against the Presbyterian clergy in the Church of Ireland, there were others in his communion who would. For Presbyterians like Reid, Ussher's sense of tact had been exemplary: he praised him as a model of episcopalian gentleness and discretion.[23]

Mant was unequivocal in his rejection of Reid's narrative. He described Blair as a "delinquent," and characterised Reid's account as a "perfect delusion."[24] In conferring holy orders, Mant argued that a bishop is

> personally nothing: he has nothing whatever to say or to do about conditions on his own account. He is the trustee, the representative, the minister, the organ of the Church: in her name

---

22. Reid, *History of the Presbyterian Church in Ireland* 1, 102.
23. Ibid., 136.
24. Elrington, *Life of James Ussher*, 146; Mant, *History of the Church of Ireland*, 514.

he acts; his course of proceeding is prescribed by her, and he has promised and is pledged to faithfulness in following it.[25]

He quoted directly from Reid to dismiss in its entirety Blair's claim that he had asked Echlin to submit to ordination from the adjacent brethren, and "to let him come in among them in no other relation than a presbyter." Mant also dismissed any notion that Archbishop Ussher would ever have countenanced the accommodation that Reid had described. For Mant, this was "too flagrant a breach of discipline," and was "not within the limits of credibility."[26]

There are many points in which Mant took issue with Reid. It is not surprising that one of these was his view of the Ulster-Scots clergy, and their relationship to the Church of Ireland. One aspect of the Ulster Plantation which Mant felt was "deeply to be lamented" was the influx of ministers from Scotland who, following Calvin and Knox, preferred a "studied affectation of a bare . . . abstract and frigid simplicity in the service of God" to "the apostolical form of church government by bishops and the liturgical mode of worship both of which had been transmitted from earliest Christianity."[27]

ORDER OF WORKS

In the advertisement for the sixteenth volume of Ussher's *Works*, Todd included a timetable detailing the date of publication of each of the preceding volumes. This schedule revealed that the timespan—from the publication of the first volume to the project's completion—was a quarter of a century. Given this extraordinarily extended period of publication, Todd lamented that it is "attended with this inconvenience, that there will no doubt ultimately be left unsold a large number of old volumes."[28] He reassured readers that all those who were in possession of the incomplete works could, however, have their sets made whole on application to the university printers, Hodges, Smith, and Co. of Dublin. The cost of complete collections would have been well beyond the means of most individuals at that time, since

---

25. Mant, *History of the Church of Ireland*, 455.
26. Ibid., 455.
27. Ibid., 365.
28. Todd and Elrington, advertisement in *Whole Works of James Ussher*, vol. 16, xiii.

each volume cost 12s.[29] It is not surprising, therefore, that only a few people seem to have taken up this offer.[30]

Todd had drawn attention to what he termed the "chronological arrangement of the works" that Elrington had adopted.[31] When read sequentially—with a few minor omissions—the volumes do indeed run in chronological order, as Todd claimed. However, the sequence in which they were actually published was very different—and highly significant. The timetable of the publication included by Todd revealed what might seem like a random or haphazard order. Volume II, for example, was published eighteen years before volume I, and volume XV appeared twenty-eight years before volume XIV.

According to Todd, the decision to adopt this uncommon non-sequential approach was not Elrington's but one that he had been advised to follow by the board of Trinity. In fact, Todd claimed that this stricture had "greatly displeased Dr. Elrington who submitted with reluctance to the arrangement."[32] Todd gave a number of explanations for the peculiar order: he described in detail the numerous difficulties that Elrington had faced, and the acute "embarrassment" he had felt at his own limitations in transcribing, sourcing, and editing some of Ussher's writings as a further contributing factor to the unorthodox order of publication.[33] However, it is tempting to believe that he protested rather too much about these difficulties.

There may be certain underlying reasons which Todd did not choose to acknowledge—or, perhaps, even to recognise—and these relate to the way in which Elrington seems to have wished for Ussher's work to be interpreted and understood by contemporary readers. It would appear that these volumes were not initially intended to be published in what might seem like a random sequence. Indeed, it is only in volume I of *The Whole Works of James Ussher*, to which Elrington prefixed a comprehensive biography of

---

29. "Advertisement for Vol I," *The Publishers' Circular* 6 (1848) 91; "Advertisement for Vol I," *Foreign Literature* (1848). See the advertisement for vol. 6 from *The Edinburgh Review or Critical Journal* 76 (1843) and the advertisement for vol. 13 contained within *The Churchman's Monthly Review* (1844) 628, *The Athenæum* (1843) 22, and *Bent's Literary Advertiser* 9 (1848) 16.

30. Kinane, *History of the Dublin University Press*, 142. Indeed, just before the current millennium commenced, hundreds of unsold volumes of *The Whole Works of Ussher* were found in the basement and cellars of House 6 of Trinity College. Sadly, the large majority of these had succumbed to mold, mildew, and fungus, produced by the damp conditions in which they had been stored for many decades, and it took several days to remove their damaged remains.

31. Todd, *Whole Works of James Ussher*, vol. 16, xiii.

32. Ibid., xiii.

33. Ibid., iv–x.

Ussher, that the perspective from which he wanted Ussher's writings to be viewed becomes apparent.

Far from being completely random or haphazard, it seems evident that their order was systematically chosen by Elrington. One instance of the underlying considerations that helped to determine the sequence of publication may be found in a letter to Elrington that he received from his father. Bishop Thomas Elrington was also a distinguished scholar, and he wrote to his son advising him how best to deal with Ussher's problematic legacy. He asserted his own view that "the chronological order of Ussher's works *can not* be followed" (his emphasis). Instead, he recommended that his son take a different approach: "in short I would bring all his work on similar subjects together."[34] Although this letter is simply dated June 29, it clearly predates 1835—the year in which Bishop Elrington died. The purpose of this intervention is evident in one of the questions that Bishop Elrington asks his son: "Have you ever read a letter of his (Ussher) on Predestination—I think it worth while to make special reference to it in a note."[35] The issue of predestination was one of particular sensitivity for high church Anglicans like the Elringtons—*pere et fils*—since it could be regarded as one of the defining features of Calvinist theology. It seems clear it was for that very reason that Bishop Elrington advised his son that it needed "special" attention.

Following this letter, Charles Richard Elrington began to compile a series of categories or, as he preferred to describe it, to prepare himself for the "division of Ussher's work."[36] He wrote frequently to Francis Lynch Blosse, and to Bulkeley Bandinel, the head librarian of the Bodleian. In one response to Elrington, Blosse discusses the process by which they had begun to group Ussher's works into various categories. Blosse divided them into seven basic themes: six works relating to ecclesiastical history and antiquities; six chronological and geographical works; fourteen polemical works; four critical disputations; four practical works; four political works; and the letters, which are not sub-divided into specific categories.

However it might have been rationalized, the system of classification devised by Elrington and Blosse reveals many of the inherent ideological contradictions in trying to group Ussher's works along strictly thematic lines. It was, for example, impossible to deny that Calvinist influences were present in Ussher's writings throughout his life. Despite his pronounced dislike of the works, Elrington still published *Gotteshalci et Praedestinatianae Controversiae ab eo motae Historia* and the *Veterum Epistolarum*

---

34. TCD Elrington papers MS 2489/15.
35. Ibid., 2489/15.
36. TCD MS 2489/12, MS 2489/15.

Hibernicarum Sylloge in Volume IV. They were released on 9 June 1830, and followed by the *Brittanicarum Ecclesiarum Antiquitates*, which was released on 16 October of the same year. The grouping of these works corresponds directly with those described by Blosse: they are numbered 3, 4, and 2 on his list of Ussher's works on ecclesiastical history and antiquities. In other words, there was a degree of deliberate continuity in the ways in which Ussher's various works were grouped together for publication, and they did not appear in a more or less random sequence.

Similarly, those works which held a direct and obvious polemic appeal to Irish Anglicans, such as Ussher's *A Discourse of the Religion Anciently Professed by the Irish and British* and *An Answer to a Challenge Made by a Jesuit in Ireland*, which had been placed together by Blosse and Elrington, were released in close proximity. Evidence of the contemporary currency that these works still held can be found in Blosse's bold assertion that the *Veterum Epistolarum Hibernicarum Sylloge* successfully refuted Charles O'Conor's *Rerum Hibernicum Scriptores*, a work which he noted had recently been reissued by the Irish Historical Library.[37]

ELRINGTON'S LIFE

Like Mant, Elrington sought to deny and excise the Church of Ireland's Calvinist heritage by identifying it as the alien import of disaffected English and, in particular, Scottish Puritan nonconformists. As part of this process, the complete works of James Ussher were edited and, to a considerable extent, remoulded by him. This process involved the construction of an elaborate narrative, one which depicted Ussher's involvement in the drafting of the Irish Articles as the product of mere youthful folly, while at the same time asserting his impeccable high church credentials.

It could be argued that significant parts of Elrington's *Life* are polemic thinly disguised as history. Certainly, Elrington signalled from the start of his book and in unambiguous terms that he intended to claim Ussher for high church Anglicanism as opposed to Calvinism. This is expressed in his vehement rejection of Nicolas Bernard's account of Ussher's "born-again" conversion at the age of ten. For Elrington this claim was "a mere attempt to support the doctrines of Calvin by a remarkable example."[38] He made his own doctrinal preferences clear, by insisting that Ussher was "one of those happy individuals" who had daily grown in the grace conferred on him by the rite of baptism, making later conversion unnecessary and even

---

37. TCD MS 2489/12.
38. Elrington, *Life of James Ussher* 1, 2.

irrelevant.[39] If Ussher had indeed experienced any adolescent religious experience, Elrington maintained that it had been safely sacramental, and occasioned by him receiving holy communion in the Anglican rite for the first time.[40]

Elrington lamented the prevalence of Puritanism in the early years of Trinity, which he attributed to the unsavory habit of the Church of England disposing of its Puritan waste in Ireland. As a consequence, he argued, the Trinity College of Ussher's youth was a "refuge for puritans, who would not have been tolerated in any similar position in England."[41] Elrington accepted that this "must have materially contributed to influence the early theological opinions of Ussher," and marvelled that "any germ of affection for the doctrine of the Church of England could have survived in so corrupted an atmosphere."[42] In this profound antipathy to Trinity's Calvinist history, Elrington was by no means exceptional.

Members of Trinity had often expressed a deep ambivalence towards the college's founding fathers. James Henthorn Todd's *University Calendar* contained the first officially authorized history of the university. It had a somewhat unusual structure in that it did not begin—as one might expect—with the period directly prior to the college's foundation. Instead, Todd chose to begin by discussing the early Irish Church, and tried to place Trinity within an earlier indigenous Irish tradition—such as the University of Armagh, which he noted was "said to have been founded by St. Patrick." It is striking that it is not until the twenty-sixth page of Todd's work that the foundation of Trinity itself is mentioned. Todd also rigorously ignored anything in the college's history that could be construed as Calvinist. Although he made reference to Adam Loftus, James Ussher, William Bedell, Henry Alvery, and Walter Travers, he made no mention that they had all been influenced by Calvinist doctrine. Instead, he placed great emphasis on the development of the statutes and regulations of the college—lavishing praise on the manner in which these were amended and finalized by Bramhall and Laud.[43]

Elrington was prepared to concede that the young Ussher had been susceptible to some malign influences, and "had held rigidly the opinions of Calvin."[44] The detrimental hold of Calvinism on the early progress of

39. Ibid., 1, 2.
40. Ibid., 7.
41. Ibid., 15.
42. Ibid., 17.
43. Todd, *Dublin University Calendar 1833*, 3.
44. Ibid., 270.

the Irish Reformation was confirmed for Elrington by the decision of the Church of Ireland to draw up its own confession, rather than use the Thirty-nine Articles of the Church of England.[45] Elrington further conceded that "there is not any thing contained in the Articles, which is not in strict conformity with the opinions [Ussher] entertained at that period of his life."[46] Elrington accepted that the Irish Articles had been "framed with a strong desire to conciliate the non-conformists" and reflected Ussher's opinions "at that period of his life." However, he sought to play down their longer-term importance, and to limit Ussher's responsibility by advancing a number of mitigating arguments.[47]

Elrington argued that the Irish Articles were never, in any case, properly sanctioned by parliament.[48] Some of the articles such as the tenth and twelfth, dealing with the service of God and of each individual's duty towards their neighbor, were dismissed by Elrington simply as being "of a character unsuited to articles of faith, and approach that of a homily." Others—with "rigid precision"—determined questions which Elrington maintained "had hitherto never been introduced into articles of faith."[49] He rejected Heylin's objection that the Articles supported the Sabbatarian doctrine of a judicial rest on the Lord's Day. He suggested that "it may be doubted whether this passage ought to form part of an article of faith," but for Elrington, the doctrine put forward was in any case "unexceptionable."[50]

ELRINGTON, REID, AND THE IRISH ARTICLES

Elrington combined this down-playing of Ussher's Calvinist history with a sustained attack on James Seaton Reid's *History of the Presbyterian Church in Ireland*, which he felt had reasserted Heylin's views too strongly and had "carried his proofs far beyond what he is justified in doing."[51] The Irish confession had omitted the English article 36 *Of consecration of bishops and ministers*. Alan Ford has maintained that Reid saw this as meaning that "the validity of ordination by presbyters was implied"; that the doctrine of absolution was condemned; and that the forgiveness of sins was understood

---

45. Ibid., 43.
46. Ibid., 44.
47. Ibid., 44.
48. Ibid., 49.
49. Elrington, *Life of James Ussher*, 44.
50. Ibid., 44.
51. Ibid., 46.

to be only declaratory.[52] Elrington, on the other hand, denied that such an inference could be drawn: pointing out that Reid had misquoted the English article in order to strengthen his case. He had attributed his claim to Heylin, but could not "find authority for it."[53] Instead, Elrington maintained that the condemnation seemed to be confined to the "Popish doctrine of absolution," and that the words of the prayer in the morning and evening service were copied exactly.[54]

The most important ground of objection that Elrington held in relation to the Irish Articles was the introduction of the Lambeth Articles, which had been recently rejected by the Church of England. By this unfortunate inclusion, Elrington argued, a "serious impediment was interposed to prevent any agreement between the Churches of England and Ireland."[55] He lamented that Ussher and those who acted with him "must have been aware of this evil." He speculated that their belief in the necessity of introducing the Lambeth Articles was because they must have "considered that the English Articles expressed imperfectly, if at all, their views of Christian doctrine." Elrington then rounded on the "advocates of Calvinistic opinions in the English Church," arguing that the Thirty-nine Articles were exclusively Calvinistic, and that "they cannot admit an interpretation at variance with those particular views."[56]

Elrington complemented his hostility to Puritanism by a trenchant defense of the actions of Charles I, William Laud, John Bramhall, and Thomas Wentworth. For Elrington, these individuals were responsible for saving the errant Irish church and bringing it back into conformity with the Church of England. He felt that "every friend to the Irish church must feel grateful to those distinguished individuals for the zeal and energy with which they endeavoured to rescue the property of the Church from the hands of

52. Ford, "High or Low'?," 13.

53. Elrington, *Life of James Ussher*, 46.

54. Reid's assertion that Lent was disclaimed as a religious fast was similarly dismissed as not in the Articles. Elrington took exception to Reid's argument that no authority was claimed for enforcing ecclesiastical canons or decreeing rites and ceremonies. Elrington noted that "this is certainly a very bold assertion," drawing Reid's attention to the seventy-seventh article, which gave "the power as fully as it is claimed by the English Church." He acknowledged that Reid was correct in stating that no allusion is made to the mode of consecrating the higher orders of the ministry, but insisted that he should have added that "the ordination of presbyters and deacons was equally omitted, and while the Liturgy remained in force neither was necessary." Ibid., 47.

55. Ibid., 45.

56. Ibid., 45. In refuting the conduct of the "predestinarian party," Elrington drew heavily upon Laurence, *An Attempt to Illustrate*, initially released as a Brampton Lecture in 1805 and then again in 1820.

its unprincipled plunderers."[57] This was, by Elrington's own admission, the only part of the second edition of his *Life* that was "entirely new."[58] It included an account of the disputes which arose in relation to the second charter granted to Trinity College, respecting the appointment of William Chappell to the provostship and, subsequently, to the bishopric of Cork. Elrington asserted that it was this appointment that had, in the end, engaged the notice of parliament, and swelled the list of charges brought against Wentworth.

Ussher had played a central role in this, and Elrington was forced to acknowledge that he had "at one time" supported Laud and Wentworth, and "at another" had been involved "in opposing them."[59] Sensitive to the suspicion of Tractarianism and other high church tendencies that many Irish Anglicans exhibited, Elrington went out of his way to defend Laud, Bramhall, and Wentworth from charges that they favored popery, and stressed their close theological links to Ussher.[60] He noted that there was "no part of the Life of Archbishop Ussher about which I was so anxious to obtain accurate information, as that which related to the transactions connected with the death of Lord Strafford."[61]

In this context, it is revealing that Elrington explicitly stated his wish to vindicate the character of Wentworth from the "foul calumnies which have been thrown upon it by those who ought to have acted differently." While Wentworth's character was not faultless, Elrington believed that "its failings arose from the most amiable weaknesses of our nature."[62] Elrington's description of the 1634 convocation and the imposition of the Thirty-nine Articles and the new canons sought to minimize the disagreements between Wentworth and Ussher, and to downplay the differences between the Irish canons and the English canons of 1604.[63]

At the same time, Elrington took great pains to detail the friendship and regular correspondence of Ussher and Laud: a pattern which, he claimed, was established about 1629, and continued without a break through the 1630s.[64] He was not the first of Ussher's biographers to develop this theme: it had also been endorsed by Richard Parr, the first post-Restoration

---

57. Elrington, *Life of James Ussher*, popular edition, vii.
58. Ibid., vi.
59. Ibid., vii.
60. Ibid., 92, 108, 113, 153.
61. Ibid., vii.
62. Ibid., viii.
63. Ibid., 165–87.
64. Ibid., 129–30, 198–200, and in Knox, *James Ussher, Archbishop of Armaugh*, 45–46.

biographer of Ussher, who had made a convincing case for Ussher's friendship with Laud. Parr had acknowledged that most of those letters written between the two in the early 1630s had perished. Elrington also lamented that not many letters exchanged between Laud and Ussher are extant. In fact, the number of letters used by Elrington is precisely the same as Parr, who admitted that he had "selected" them "out of a far greater number."[65]

For Elrington, the real significance of Ussher's "friendship" with Laud was very clear. He asserted that "the point at issue is whether the Archbishop (Ussher) found reason, at a subsequent period, to change these opinions."[66] He maintained that a "rigid Calvinist could not honestly have spoken in such terms of Laud's promotion—to the Archbishopric of Canterbury—as are to be found in Archbishop Ussher's letters."[67] In later years, however, he argued that "the effects of this prava disciplina were almost obliterated" within Ussher's work.[68]

Elrington explicitly rejected James Seaton Reid's interpretation of Wentworth and Laud's reform of Trinity College as being inspired by a wish to remove Puritanism and install Arminian leaders. According to Elrington,

---

65. Parr, *Life of the Most Reverend*, 40–41. Recently, Ford has published an additional twenty-two letters between Ussher and Laud which he found transcribed at the Bodleian: Ford, "Correspondence between Archbishops Ussher and Laud," 5–21. Amanda L. Capern has argued that Ussher's past biographers have presented "a picture of friendship through misrepresentation," and that Ussher "did not like or approve of Laud to the extent suggested by them." Capern, "The Caroline Church," 57–85. As evidence for this, she has focused on the qualitative difference found between Ussher's correspondence with Laud and his exchange of letters with those he numbered amongst his friends in the English clergy. Hugh Trevor-Roper also pointed out that one would expect letters between Ussher and Laud to be formulated by the rules of professional courtesy, and that letters between the two and their respective friends must be more enlightening. Trevor-Roper, "James Ussher, Archbishop of Armagh," 140. Such letters do, indeed, provide just that degree of insight. Laud's letters to Thomas Wentworth, for example, show that he felt an intense irritation towards Ussher—for reasons that were sometimes of an ideological nature. It must also be noted that on two occasions after Wentworth went to Ireland, Laud complained about Ussher's apparent reluctance to write to him at all. See *Earl of Strafford's Letters*, William Laud to Thomas Wentworth, 1 Nov. 1633, 1, 156, and 29 Dec. 1638, 11. Capern believes that ideological reservations were passed on to Peter Heylin in his *Aerius redivivus* and *Cyprianus Anglicus*, which posthumously accused Ussher of "Calvinism" and "Puritanism" because of the Irish Articles. Heylin, *Aerius redivivus*, 394; *Cyprianus Anglicus*, 24, 192–95. This indicates the degree to which both Laud and Heylin accepted Richard Montagu's proposition that the Irish Articles were as "foreign" as the doctrinal decisions of the synod of Dort; equally it indicates their acceptance of Montagu's pejorative meanings for the term "Calvinism."

66. Elrington, *Life of James Ussher*, 290.

67. Ibid., 290.

68. Ibid., 17.

Ussher had approved Laud's attempts to replace a discredited provost to restore the sense of order to the university, and to introduce new statutes that would help to maintain conformity and discipline.[69] It was true that Ussher had supported the appointment of Archbishop Laud as chancellor of Dublin University in 1633. However, the following year, Laud had imposed on the college an Arminian provost, William Chappell, whose autocratic style and theological views were clearly at odds with those of Ussher.

Reid had focused on the policy that Wentworth and Laud had followed in relation to Trinity College. Reid interpreted all of these actions as symptomatic of Laud's interference in the affairs of the Irish church. He believed Laud's underlying purpose was to rid Trinity College of Calvinist influence and to introduce an Arminian ethos to the university. For Elrington, Wentworth and Laud had acted out of honorable motives which were simply to ensure that university affairs were conducted with some sense of order and decorum: he believed whatever changes had been made by Laud and Wentworth had been directed for this admirable purpose. Reid did not dispute that the university needed reform, but he attributed to Laud a desire to change the ethos of the university to coincide with his own theological views.[70] Elrington challenged Reid "to produce one single change from the statutes of Bishop Bedell, which could be construed by the most decided Calvinist into a measure for the establishment of Arminianism."[71]

In short, it seems evident that Elrington used his *Life* to deal with—even neutralize—some of the more questionable elements, from a high church perspective, of Ussher's written legacy. Elrington's narrative of events has proved to be remarkably enduring in terms of Irish Anglican scholarship. John Walton Murray described how Ussher as the draftsman of the "entirely Calvinistical" Irish Articles "modified his views" late in his life.[72] James Carr related Ussher's metamorphosis from "an extreme Calvinist"

---

69. Ibid., 155, 191–98.

70. Ibid., 155; Reid, *Seven Letters to Dr. Elrington*, 21–28.

71. Elrington, *Answer to Dr. Reid's Animadversions*, 16. On this matter, Elrington can claim some support from recent historiography: his interpretation of Laud's policy with regard to Trinity anticipates that advanced by Kevin Sharpe in relation to Laud's dealings as Chancellor with Oxford. Sharpe, "Archbishop Laud and the University of Oxford," 156–62. However, a close examination of the Trinity statutes suggests that— *pace* Elrington—there were a large number of significant changes which reflected the concerns of what most historians would label the English Arminians. Alan Ford has argued convincingly that it is "incontrovertible that Chappell—the Provost appointed by Laud—was, theologically, an Arminian." Ford, "'That Bugbear Arminianism,'" 147–60.

72. Murray, *Sketches of the Life*, 43, 50.

into "a man of reasonable views" on the extent of atonement, election, and reprobation.[73]

CONCLUSION

It may be deduced from all of the above that Mant and Elrington shared certain similar goals. In particular, they both wanted to present the high church faction within the Church of Ireland as the rightful heirs to the founding fathers of their church. Their different backgrounds are reflected in the different degrees of emphasis that they brought to their respective projects. However, it seems clear that they shared certain impulses such as a fear and detestation of Presbyterians, evangelicals, and low church practices in particular. Doubtless, both men acted in good faith and genuinely believed that the histories they wrote expressed some essential truths. However, it is hard to resist the conclusion that they both chose to conceal or misrepresent their sources, and it is equally difficult not to conclude that this was done to advance their arguments. What is also hard to challenge is the influence and impact of their work. Their two texts became imposing features of the historiography of the Church of Ireland. They were written at a time of growing crisis for their Church in Ireland, and, for all their faults, these works met an immediate and pressing need: the desire for both Irish Anglican clergy and laity for authoritative accounts of their church's history. The texts produced by Mant and Elrington did not exert influence only upon those Anglican clergy who were born, or educated, or ministered in Ireland. The texts were also carried by clergy and members of the Church of Ireland who left their native country and emigrated to North America, Africa, and Australia. As those individuals entered and became assimilated into the Anglican (and other) churches of the countries in which they had settled, the influence of Mant and Elrington's work was also dispersed. For many years their texts were regarded as close to definitive both inside and beyond Ireland, and it is only in relatively recent times that some of their underlying assumptions have been subjected to rigorous scrutiny, and critically re-assessed.

BIBLIOGRAPHY

Anonymous. Review of *History of the Presbyterian Church in Ireland*, by James Seaton Reid. *Edinburgh Magazine* (April 1834) 210.

Bernard, Nicholas. *The Judgement of the Late Archbishop of Armagh*. London: Printed for John Crook, at the ship in St. Paul's Churchyard, 1657.

---

73. Carr, *Life and Times of James Ussher*, 203.

———. *The Life and Death of the Most Revered and Learned Father of our Church Dr. James Ussher*. Dublin: Printed by William Bladen, 1656.

Bowen, Demond. *The Protestant Crusade in Ireland, 1800–70: A Study of Protestant-Catholic Relations between the Act of Union and Disestablishment*. Montreal: McGill-Queen's University Press, 1978.

Capern, Amanda L. "The Caroline Church: James Ussher and the Irish Dimension." *The Historical Journal* 39.1 (1996) 57–85.

Carr, James. *The Life and Times of James Ussher*. London: Wells, Gardner, Darton, 1895.

Cooper, Austin. "Ireland and the Oxford Movement." *Journal of Religious History* 19.1 (June 1995) 62–74.

The Earl of Strafforde's Letters and Dispatches with an Essay towards His Life by Sir George Radcliffe. From the Originals in the Possession of His Great Grandson the Right Honourable Thomas Earl of Malton, Knight of the Bath. By William Knowler, LLD. Rector of Irthlingborough. London: Printed for the editor, by William Bowyer, 1739.

Elrington, Charles Richard. *An Answer to Dr. Reid's Animadversions upon the Life of Archbishop Ussher*. Dublin: Hodges, 1849.

———. *The Life of James Ussher, Lord Archbishop of Armagh*. Dublin: Hodges, 1848.

———. *Life of James Ussher*. Popular edition. Dublin: Hodges and Smith, 1849.

Ford, Alan. "Correspondence between Archbishops Ussher and Laud." *Archivum Hibernicum* 46 (1991–92) 5–21.

———. "'High or Low'? Writing the Irish Reformation in the Early Nineteenth Century." *Bulletin of the John Rylands Library* 90.1 (Spring 2014) 10.

———. "'Making Dead Men Speak': Manipulating the Memory of James Ussher." In *Constructing the Past: Writing Irish History, 1600–1800*, edited by Mark Williams and Stephen Forrest, 49. Woodbridge, UK: Boydell, 2010.

———. "'That Bugbear Arminianism': Archbishop Laud and Trinity College, Dublin." In *British Interventions in Early Modern Ireland*, edited by C. F. Brady and Jane Ohlmeyer, 147–60. Cambridge: Cambridge University Press, 2005.

———. "Ussher, James (1581–1656)." In *DNB*, 1–20. Oxford: Oxford University Press, 2004.

Heylin, Peter. *Aerius redivivus: or, The Prehistory of the Presbyterians*. Oxford: Printed for John Crosley, 1670.

———. *Cyprianus Anglicus: or, The History of the Life and Death of William Laud lord Archbishop of Canterbury, containing also the ecclesiastical history of the three kingdoms*. London: Printed for A. Seile, 1668.

———. *Respondet Petrus*. London: Printed for R. Royston at the Angel in Ivy Lane, and R. Marriot in S. Dunstan's Churchyard, Fleet Street, 1658.

"Horae Hibernicae." *The Christian Examiner and Church of Ireland Magazine* 2.1 (Jan 1826) 8–11.

Kinane, Vincent. *A History of the Dublin University Press 1734–1976*. Dublin: Gill & Macmillan, 1994.

King, Robert. *A Primer of the History of the Holy Catholic Church in Ireland, from the Introduction of Christianity to the Formation of the Modern Irish Branch of the Church of Rome*. 2nd ed. Dublin: Grant, Bolton, and J. Robertson, 1843.

Knox, Robert B. *James Ussher, Archbishop of Armaugh*. Cardiff, UK: University of Wales Press, 1967.

Laurence, Richard. *An Attempt to Illustrate Those Articles of the Church of England Which the Calvinists Improperly Consider Calvinistical*. Oxford: Hanwell & Parker, 1805.

"Letters to the Editor." *The Christian Examiner* 23 (August 1848) 492.

Mant, Richard. *History of the Church of Ireland from the Reformation to the Revolution*. London: Parker, 1840.

McCafferty, John. "Ussher, James." In *Dictionary of Irish Biography*, vol. 9, edited by James McGuire and James Quinn, 621–29. Cambridge: Cambridge University Press, 2009.

Murray, John Walton. *Sketches of the Life and Times of Imminent Irish Churchmen, from the Reformation Downwards*. Dublin: George Herbert, 1847.

"On the Advantages of an Union amongst Irish Protestants." *The Christian Examiner and Church of Ireland Magazine* 2.8 (Feb 1826) 82–84.

Parr, Richard. *The Life of the Most Reverend Father in God, James Usher, Late Lord Archbishop of Armaugh*. London: Printed for Nathanael Ranew, 1686.

Reid, James Seaton. *History of the Presbyterian Church in Ireland*. Dublin: Curry, 1837.

―――. *Seven Letters to Dr. Elrington, Professor of Divinity in Trinity College, Dublin, occasioned by his Animadversions in his "Life of Ussher" on certain Passages in the History of the Presbyterian Church in Ireland*. Glasgow: Ogle & Son, 1849.

Ridden, Jennifer. "The Forgotten History of the Protestant Crusade: Religious Liberalism in Ireland." *Journal of Religious History* 31 (2007) 78–102.

Sharpe, Kevin. "Archbishop Laud and the University of Oxford." In *History and Imagination: Essays in Honour of H. R. Trevor-Roper*, edited by Hugh Lloyd-Jones et al, 156–62. London: Duckworth, 1981.

Todd, James Henthorn, and Charles Richard Elrington, eds. *The Whole Works of James Ussher*. 17 vols. Dublin: Hodges & Smith, 1847–64.

―――. *Dublin University Calendar 1833*. Dublin: Dublin University Press, 1834.

Trevor-Roper, Hugh. "James Ussher, Archbishop of Armagh." In *Catholics, Anglicans and Puritans: Seventeenth Century Essays*, 120–65. London: Secker, 1987.

6

James Henthorn Todd, an Irish High Churchman and Early Tractarian at Trinity College, Dublin

PATRICIA MCKEE

JAMES HENTHORN TODD SUFFERED, when accounted for by others in his own church and beyond, from strong condemnation of the reasons he gave for hope for the long-term survival of the minority Church of Ireland. The spiritual affinities and devotional model of church which he put forward to the public during the 1830s and 1840s in Ireland were shaped by his debate with the early Tractarian and Oxford Movements. However, the church which he so passionately outlined and presented for acceptance was not immediately popular. It was rejected by the Puritan majority within his own church, Irish Presbyterians, Methodists, and Roman Catholic ultramontanists like Paul Cullen, later Cardinal Cullen of Dublin.

It is, therefore, essential to establish the underlying reasons he gave for governing the kind of church which he sought to revive and why he believed that it would be possible. In the reordering of things, this Irish Anglican Church would be clearly apostolical, refer frequently to pre-Reformation church history, be strongly sacramental, definitively episcopal, revive a high liturgical tradition, and be catholic. It would affirm the early universal catholic church saints, revive the Irish saints' days in the liturgical calendar, foster the tradition of translation of the Scriptures and the Prayer Books in

Irish and the holding of services in Irish, and be the reformed, Protestant Church of Ireland. He saw no contradiction in such a model of revived parish networks across the country, the key being to produce, from Trinity College Dublin Divinity School, many young, well-trained local parish clergy who would support what he termed strong church principles. He therefore began to campaign, from early on in his career, for a better system of educating the clergy at Trinity, in order that they would be highly educated in the current need for strong church principles among a disaffected laity.

Todd hoped that the provision of parish clergy for the parish system of the Church of Ireland would reduce the damage done in the 1820s by the Second Reformation movement, which he thought encouraged the more Presbyterian element within the Church of Ireland to flourish, and he hoped it would be replaced by a clergy from the divinity school in Trinity who would foster faith and practice in a much higher Anglican tradition, where both the majority of Roman Catholics and the minority Church of Ireland would feel at home. To him, the leaders in the Church of England who formed the nucleus of the early Tractarian and Oxford Movements were very attractive. They were essentially revivalists like himself, and so he began to correspond with them and met in Oxford with them, in order to learn more of how to revive his own church, which he thought had sunk into a low reformation position which left the laity exposed to other denominational cross-tastings. He probably never suspected at this point that his own brother William Gowan Todd, fed up with the controversies of the Church of Ireland over catholic historical truths and influenced by the spellbinding attractions of Newman, would jettison his own wife and career in the Church of Ireland in order to become a Roman Catholic priest in England. The fluctuations and fascinating twists and turns of this historical period are such that fact becomes as unexpected as any historical fiction.

Todd, the elder brother in Trinity, suffered no such qualms; and even though he liked Newman, he still argued with him as to where his ultimate aims were taking him and the Church of England during the 1830s and 40s. In addition, given his own strong revivalist aims for the Church of Ireland, he was in a strange way no different from the Second Reformation evangelical movement of the 1820s in Ireland he sought to overcome. He had a very different revivalist hope for the church, yet it was a revivalist hope for an all-Ireland Protestant majority church, nonetheless. In other respects, the Irish Anglican church which he envisaged was different. Although he looked to

England for inspiration, the Tractarianism represented by the early Oxford Movement in England was different from the one he hoped would succeed in Ireland.

This essay examines the underlying similarities and differences between the two and explores his life as representative of a brief, flamelike backlash into high Catholicism within the Protestant church in Ireland, from 1830 to 1860. The legacy of this Tractarianism in Ireland is ambivalent, firstly because it was time-based in that it followed the failure of the Second Reformation movement in Ireland and sought to replace it; secondly because it was deliberately suppressed by later Church of Ireland historiography; and thirdly, because the conclusions of Stewart Brown regarding the influence of the Oxford Movement in Scotland, where some of the reforms became mainstream after a very long period of time, could legitimately be applied to Ireland.[1]

BIOGRAPHICAL OVERVIEW

Todd came to his task of revival of the Church of Ireland amidst a background of academic, ecclesial and literary reform movements in Ireland, occurring between 1830 and 1850 and was appointed Regius Professor of Hebrew at Trinity College, Dublin, in 1849. During the 1830s and 40s he came to be regarded as a considerable promoter of university and church reform, the critical study of Irish literature, and a biblical scholar of some importance and controversy in Ireland.[2] A valued member of the chapter of St. Patrick's Cathedral in Dublin, his clerical life began shortly after when he went to study at Trinity College, Dublin, as an undergraduate. He took deacon's orders in 1831 and priest's orders in 1832. Appointed to the city cathedral chapter soon after his ordination, he was finally recognized by the crown as chancellor of the cathedral chapter in 1864. In the meantime, he took a great interest in the history, buildings, sermons, and choral music of the historic city cathedral of St. Patrick's in Dublin, together with the ordering of the furniture and fabric of all the church buildings of the Church of Ireland. The highlight on every occasion of worship within the church building was a proper high church liturgy. In addition, he was greatly interested in documenting and preserving ancient Irish religious monuments and artifacts of the Church of Ireland, the early Irish church religious relics of which were scattered across the country. He was, at the end of his

---

1. Brown, "Scotland and the Oxford Movement," 56–77.

2. Welch, *Oxford Companion to Irish Literature*, 561–62, erroneously refers to him as the Regius Professor of Greek.

life, buried in 1869 where he most desired to be remembered, in the little graveyard adjacent to St. Patrick's Cathedral in Dublin, his grave marked by a simple Irish cross. Described by Alfred Webb in his *Compendium of Irish Biography* as being in Archdeacon Cotton's words in 1850 "the *sine qua non* of every literary enterprise in Dublin" yet leading "a quiet life," he was nonetheless considered "an eminent scholar" who "contributed largely to the literature of his country and who took part in various movements for its advancement in arts and literature."[3]

Todd was born in Dublin on 23 April, 1805, entered Trinity College, Dublin, on 6 November 1820, graduated with honors in 1824, and took his BA in 1825. He tutored pupils and gave grinds as a Trinity College grinder and may have been associated with the *Christian Examiner*.[4] He began writing articles for the *British Critic* when introduced in 1833 to the editor, Samuel Roffey Maitland, who shortly afterwards became the librarian at Lambeth Palace, London. Todd was elected a fellow in Trinity in 1831 and became a senior fellow in 1850. He was considered a "popular tutor," "conservative," "high church," "in doctrine rather than in ritual," someone who "disliked but accepted reform," and he wrote a brief history of the University of Dublin which was published in 1833 in the first college calendar. He graduated from TCD with a BD in 1837 and a DD in 1840.[5]

The 1833 history showed the importance of the founding of Trinity as a religious educational establishment for the clergy of the Church of Ireland and was based on his early research work among the manuscripts in Trinity, among them handwritten legal documents and letters by the early Puritan provosts and famous graduates whom he admired, like Jonathan Swift.[6] Todd then traced both the origins of the university and the Church of Ireland to the early Irish church, the Irish saints, and the English Bede, whom he admired for his appreciation of the Irish church. He treated the foundation of Trinity College, Dublin, by Queen Elizabeth I in 1592 as a continuation in detail of an earlier church life, and continued his history up to the late seventeenth century. Thus, he tied together, in several controversial ways, the history of Ireland as a country, the lineages of the Church of Ireland, and the *raison d'etre* of Trinity College, Dublin. He made his final

---

3. Webb, *Compendium of Irish Biography*, 525–26.

4. *Oxford Dictionary of National Biography*, http://www.oxforddnb.com. The *Christian Examiner* was founded by Caesar Otway and Joseph Henderson Singer, both "Second Reformation" Church of Ireland clergymen. Singer was a fellow in Trinity at the same time as Todd. Though there is no proof, it is possible that Todd could have been an editor/contributor to the anonymously authored magazine.

5. Ibid.

6. Todd, *Catalogue of Graduates*.

contribution to the yearly calendar of 1868/9 shortly before his death in 1869, at a time when his eyesight had seriously begun to fail. In this way, early in his academic and clerical life, he revived an interrelated, threefold foundation which bound together in Irish ecclesiastical historiography the early Irish church, the University of Dublin at Trinity College, and the establishment of the Church of Ireland.

REPRESENTATIONS OF TRACTARIANISM

The term "Tractarian" was first mentioned at the end of the 1830s by the Master of the Temple in London, Christopher Benson, in a sermon preached in 1839. He used the term to describe writers such as Newman and Pusey in relation to their *Tracts* and their followers who supported them.[7] There were other, more disparaging names applied: that they were suffering from "Newmania," a term used by Richard Whately, who also described Newman and his followers as "Neomanics."[8] Todd was sometimes called a "Puseyite" by disparagers in Ireland, after his Tractarian colleague and friend at Oxford.

The majority of evangelical and low church Irish bishops and clergy and also some later academic historians of the Whig variety regard all aspects of the catholic nature of Tractarianism as a form of narrow bias to be avoided. Take, for example, the distaste with regard to Todd's modest Tractarian explorations as expressed in a private letter written to Archbishop Whately by William Fitzgerald, bishop of Killaloe, in 1851, about the candidates who were being considered for the then vacant post of provost. "Anyone I do believe, would be better than Todd ... I have a great regard for him but I am convinced he would throw the whole weight of his position into the Tractarian scale."[9] The rather harsh assessment by Fitzgerald was repeated and even caricatured by the historians who contributed to the three-volume history of the Church of Ireland edited by Walter Phillips, published in 1933, which took an extreme dislike to the Tractarians.[10] McDowell and Webb in their 1982 academic history of Trinity took a similar stance with regard to Tractarianism.[11] Such criticism makes no case for respecting Todd's inner convictions as an Irish Victorian high churchman. In addition, his minority outlook illustrates the tensions between the acceptance of diversity along an

7. Nockles, *Oxford Movement in Context*, 36n155.
8. Ibid., 36n155.
9. Ibid., 207.
10. Phillips, *History of the Church of Ireland*.
11. McDowell and Webb, *Trinity College Dublin*, 207.

Anglican theological and historical spectrum in the 1830s and 40s, and a Protestant Irish uniformity, the shorthand version for which is the descriptive epithet "the low Church of Ireland."

UNIVERSITY CAREER

Todd progressed steadily at Trinity despite being barred from becoming provost. He loved books and was early in his career appointed as an assistant librarian in 1831, a post that did not become formally ratified until 1852. There was much to do in the library to preserve the Ussher manuscripts which, according to Todd and also Franc Sadleir, another of the junior librarians, were "in a state of decay by worms"; a Dublin bookbinder had recommended that they be unbound and washed, in 1831.[12] Librarian duties for Todd included care of the *Book of Kells*, which to his horror had some of the page numbers cut off by an earlier bookbinder, upgrading the college book copyright law and therefore greatly helping to increase the holdings of the university library, and adding to the manuscript archives for research. Todd devised a new system of cataloging for the whole library, based on his observations and improvements of the system in the Bodleian Library at Oxford. He built up the Muniments Room as a storehouse for college records, acted as bursar for the library and college for a time, and gathered together much that had been difficult to locate regarding the manuscript history of the university. He also dedicated himself to publicizing the rare Irish manuscript collections held in the library and showed the *Book of Kells* and other manuscripts to Queen Victoria and Prince Albert on their first visit to Ireland in 1849. He expanded the library collection of print books by buying those with color illustrations rather than the black and white editions and built up the German and European language book collection. In his private library, in addition to his Irish manuscript collection, he was attracted to purchasing polyglot language variant translations of the Bible and other rare translation editions. He gathered works of Hebrew exegesis by the rabbinic schools and sought out works by famous rabbis.[13] He was familiar with the mystics of the Kabbalah—all of which enhanced his teaching abilities in the divinity school at Trinity and his reputation as a biblical

---

12. Ibid., 525n11.

13. See the subtitle in Jones, *Catalogue of the Valuable Library of the Late Rev. James H. Todd*: " . . . Comprising Select Biblical Literature, the History, Antiquities and Language of Ireland, Miscellanea, Embracing many works of Rarity, with Copious Manuscript Annotations . . . Patristic, Irish and Other Manuscripts on Vellum and Paper, to be Sold at Auction."

and manuscript scholar who had a fine degree of versatility in matters of translation.

Cutting a donnish figure as an energetic, lively, learned college man, a lecturer who specialized in all things related to biblical and Irish exegesis, on the downside perhaps for him, in becoming an ordained teaching fellow, he was not allowed by the college statutes on celibacy to marry. It was, however, an ambivalent area of college life and there were certainly fellows' wives.[14] The celibacy statute was repealed in 1840, but for Todd this began a sustained change to the founding statutes and intention of Elizabeth I, and he opposed the change on these grounds as he saw this as opening the way for Roman Catholic teaching fellows. He also objected as he thought the college board would stagnate, as there would be no incentive for married tutor priests and fellows to leave and find a parish. It would mean less turnover and less space for the junior fellows to take their place amidst the senior men of the college governing authority. It is here that we must wonder at his ability to both support change and resist it, in relation to the survival of the Church of Ireland, compared with the needs of the long-term growth of the university; and yet he was weighing up various options which are now obsolete. He seems to have never softened his stance regarding the admission, not of Roman Catholic students, of which there were a minority, but of Roman Catholic teaching fellows, an instance of an understandable but faulty survival mechanism at work which sought to preserve the church ethos of the university, but worked against long-term growth. In mitigation, Oxford and Cambridge faced similar problems and tackled them in much the same way.

Meanwhile, he proved to be a committed lecturer, continually revising and expanding the tutoring, teaching, curriculum, and press output of the divinity school. He was critical of existing divinity texts by Mede and Mosheim in particular, which supported what he considered to be an erroneous, ultra-Protestant line of interpretation found in nearly all Anglican Church history books, which argued that the pope and the papacy were the Antichrist of the book of Revelation. An area of consistent successful reform carried through was his challenge to the older system of tutor staff relationships, which he thought encouraged excessive self-promotion by individual tutors and individual coteries of students. He was awarded an honorary *ad eundem* degree by the University of Oxford in 1860. In sum, his career was one of trying to better the existing college system by extensive

---

14. McDowell and Webb, *Trinity College, Dublin*, 107. Women kept their maiden names and were addressed as "Mrs."

and consistent reform based on his high church principles, rather than by encouraging radical or revolutionary change.

BOARDROOM TENSIONS

The dedication of over thirty years of his life to fostering the collegiate life of Trinity proved Todd's point that college life required commitment. But because the board of the college held to differences of conviction within a religious and political range of opinion and belief, the more low church view was usually the stronger party, and his genial nature was gradually subsumed under the reputation given to Tractarian and Oxford Movement sympathizers by men like his contemporary, James Thomas O'Brien. A dominant college man, O'Brien was elected a junior fellow in 1830 and appointed to an Irish bishopric twelve years later; from then until his retirement, he lost no opportunity to preach openly against the Tractarians. O'Brien also managed to retain his Archbishop King's Lectureship at Trinity on becoming incumbent of Clondahorky and then Dean of Cork, finally relinquishing his university post when appointed bishop of Ossory, Ferns, and Leighlin in 1842. He published a series of controversial pamphlets, one of which Todd passed on to Newman as it was against *Tract 90*, and held the line against what was considered to exemplify the "verbal subtleties of Tractarian metaphysics," which in general the college rejected.[15]

The boardroom meetings of the college were frequent, and it was the duty of the provost to resolve conflict and tensions among the fellows, and to distinguish between harmful and beneficial outside influences, especially those coming from the parliament at Westminster. At a time of great political upheaval in Ireland—centered on the granting of Catholic Emancipation—the passing of the Irish Church Temporalities Act, the great Reform Act of 1832, and limited college graduate franchise meant that shifting Tory and Whig politics at Westminster and the rise and fall of government majorities played a significant role in determining the running of college life. Those who supported either a strong Whig or a strong Tory government program, when it was in power, were handsomely rewarded by promotion within the university, as ultimately government ministers made the final decisions. Although the provost and board appeared to hold sway with regard to higher appointments such as the provostship, the role of the lord lieutenant was influential. In Todd's case, his rejection as a nominee for the post of provost was based on his being perceived by the lord lieutenant, then Lord Hettysbury, as being disloyal to the educational reforms put forward

---

15. Ibid., 164.

by the government to accommodate Catholic aspirations in the sphere of higher education.

In the early 1830s the upper echelons of the board consisted of the Chancellor, who was the Tory Hanoverian Duke of Cumberland and who seldom attended any meetings, the Vice-Chancellor Lord John George de la Poer Beresford as the Primate of all Ireland and Archbishop of Armagh—a moderate and kindly prince bishop and a generous benefactor to Todd—and the provost Samuel Kyle, a high churchman with evangelical and high church views, soon to be made a bishop, who was influenced by Bishop John Jebb and Alexander Knox. He was a close confidant of Todd who looked to him for guidance. When he was elected bishop of Cork in 1831, his place was taken by Bartholomew Lloyd, a distinguished mathematician whom Todd liked and worked well with in terms of various innovative projects of reform. He was soon requesting help from him and the board for a new print type for the University Printing Press to aid in the production of the first college history he had begun to research. The visitors were the Vice-Chancellor Beresford and the Archbishop of Dublin, Richard Whately, a Whig supporter, who became a firm enemy of Todd at the very beginning of his appointment to Dublin, due to the controversy surrounding his proposed new college for graduate ordinands of Trinity. Todd accused him of calling the whole system of training for the Church of Ireland clergy in Trinity into question, a view which the provost modestly rejected, but the point rankled for a long time among the fellows, who were almost united in rejecting Whately's first initiative as archbishop, though they declined to say so too openly. Todd's letters to Kyle are very humorous on this point and recount the whole saga in detail.[16]

Whately's appointment to Dublin was considered by many to be unusual. He was appointed by the Whig prime minister, Charles Grey, to succeed William Magee. Whately himself may have been surprised at this turn of events, and he arrived in Dublin having skipped the rank of bishop, for at Oxford he had become the second ever Professor of Political Economy. Whately was also a member of an Oxford group at Oriel College called the *Noetics*, led by Edward Copleston, a group which Newman came to dislike when it supported Robert Peel in an Oxford election campaign. Peel was firmly against the Tractarians and Todd. Newman briefly wondered if he should go to Dublin with the archbishop in 1831, but Charles Dickinson was appointed as the archbishop's curate instead. The tensions between Whately and the fellows were gradually dissolved over time, though they

---

16. See TCD MSS 2214 for various references in his correspondences of the early 1830s.

were never fully eradicated. Whately has been described as "an unharmonious blacksmith," a phrase that evokes the actions of one who inadvertently offends all around him.[17]

The senior fellows on the board at the time of Whately's appointment were the vice-provost Francis Hodgkinson, who died in 1840, the Regius Professor of Civil Law and Erasmus Smith Professor of Modern History; Robert Phipps the registrar; Thomas Prior, the Regius Professor of Greek and Archbishop King's Lecturer in Divinity; Bartholomew Lloyd (soon to be provost), a senior lecturer and Erasmus Smith's Professor of Natural and Experimental Philosophy; Henry Wray, senior proctor; and Franc Sadleir, bursar, librarian, Erasmus Smith Professor of Mathematics, Donnellan Lecturer, and an Irish Whig. He was, in a way, Todd's greatest political and personal rival for promotion. Charles William Wall, the Senior Dean, was Professor of Hebrew, and Todd's early tutor. The senior men were considered by Todd to be somewhat slow on the uptake, their average age being sixty in 1830. Henry Wray, the senior proctor, was neither a Second Reformation man nor a strong churchman. There were twenty-five fellows who had lecturing posts in 1830 and thirteen professors who did not hold a fellowship. The fellows were higher in rank than the professors, and fellows had to resign on taking up a chair, as happened to Whitley Stokes, William Rowan Hamilton, and the high churchman and friend of Todd, Charles Elrington, who became a young Regius Professor of Divinity.[18] It was important to canvas the board in order to get what was sought by an individual fellow past the vote. Todd had to consider his allies, but in the end could lose out to a majority, as support from Beresford, the provost, and men like Elrington was sometimes not enough. However, his general reforms were supported by all in quite a number of cases, as they made sense to all shades of opinion.

TODD'S CONTRIBUTIONS OUTSIDE COLLEGE

In what proved to be an enhancement of his academic career and an extension of his scholarly influence, Todd took up a role in the development of the intellectual, literary and scientific society known as the Royal Irish Academy. First elected as a member in 1833, he became secretary from 1847 to 1855, and was elected president from 1856 to 1861. The list of his papers and contributions in the Academy *Proceedings* is long and wide-ranging, especially with regard to the development of the study of the manuscript sources of Irish history, the study of Irish artifacts, and the development of

---

17. Clarke, *Richard Whately*.
18. McDowell and Webb, *Trinity College, Dublin*, 96–98, 108, 110.

the study of the Irish past. A Todd lectureship was devised in his honor and greatly enhances, to this day, the broad discipline of Irish studies.

Todd, John O'Donovan, and Eugene O'Curry, both native Irish scholars, were involved with Edwin Wyndham-Quin, the third Lord Adare, and many other ascendency Irish families in the founding of a strong and eventually ecumenical society for the study of the Irish past, in 1840, which expanded on a joint footing to become the Irish Archaeological and Celtic Society. Todd became secretary and editor of some of the society's publications and formed a lifelong working partnership with O'Donovan and O'Curry. The work of the Irish Archaeological Society was accompanied by his contributions as editor to the English Camden Society and the Scottish Bannatyne Book Club in Edinburgh. All of these extracurricular activities meant that Todd was known far beyond the university campus and had an enhanced and wide circle of readers for his academic publications, extending to the Victorian reading public of the United Kingdom and beyond to the Continent.

Todd also, with Wyndham-Quin, William Monsell (Lord Emly), and others, founded in 1843 St. Columba's College, Rathfarnham, county Dublin, with Beresford as chief patron and the English Tractarian William Sewell as one of the early wardens. It became an attractive Irish alternative and a first role model for an Irish public school network, fostering a specifically Irish, Protestant spiritual life. Initially, the school recruited native Irish speakers from Kerry in an attempt to teach Irish to the new students alongside the classics, the arts, and sport, with extra-curricular subjects catered for like fencing and drawing.

Todd found he had a part to play in Dublin, Ireland and beyond, and the Irish intellectual revival of the time provided a very important stimulus to this process of the expansion of the common grounds for scholarship, debate, and the formation of public opinion and comment. The main voice of the Dublin intellectual revival was the *Dublin University Magazine*, a journal which provided the city with a forum for writers, historians, storytellers, poets, philosophers, scientific, and mathematical men and clergymen alike. It was founded in 1833 and ran until 1877, when it became the *University Magazine* (1878–1880). It was the first successful monthly magazine begun by a literary coterie "excited by reform" and was for a time edited by Isaac Butt, then a trainee barrister and later MP, judge and "father of home rule," following some early issues by Charles Stanford. Clearly Todd was encouraged by the print media of his day and the way in which topical magazines could contribute to shaping public opinion, as he founded his own high church journal in Dublin for a growing readership interested in comment on public and church matters.[19]

Todd began to specialize in editing a definitive book for the Irish reading public which would explain the variant manuscript editions of the lives of the early Irish saints, including their hymns, focusing on the lives of St. Patrick and St. Brigid in particular.[20] He saw this research as re-establishing a part of the heritage of the pre-Reformation catholic church that had been lost at the time of the Reformation, yet valuable and essential for understanding the full history and devotion of the Church of Ireland. He thought it would be of interest to the wider reading public, as the academic study of Irish church history began to be supported by archival research. However, in his long Introduction, which gave a high church and Victorian history of the Church of Ireland, he somewhat spoiled his own considerable scholarly research on the extant manuscript sources for Patrick, as Roman Catholic converts such as Margaret Cusack began to complain. He was accused by her of turning St. Patrick into an Irish Protestant, and the most vocal Roman Catholic commentators were, like her, converts to Catholicism from the Church of Ireland. In all, the responses to his work, typified by Margaret Cusack, indicate the resource for Irish history, debate, claim, and counterclaim, which his work often provided.[21]

APOCALYPTIC TIMES

While research has been done on the importance of the apocalyptic interpretations generated in the 1830s and 40s in Ireland and their relationship to Irish history writing of the period and beyond, more needs to be done on Todd's own contributions, which were dismissed by the more conservative fellows and clergy graduates as betraying their Puritan, Reformation heritage.[22] Similarly, more needs to be said on the ultra-Protestant reaction to his biblical exegesis after his Donnellan lectures on the interpretation of prophecy, presented to the university and public in the college chapel in 1838 and 1841.[23] He published his first book in 1840 and a second book continuing the history of the Continental, English, and Irish interpretations

---

19. Nineteenth Century Index at http://c19index.chadwyck.co.uk/contributors/intDUM.jsp.

20. Todd, *Leabhar Imuinn* and *St. Patrick, Apostle of Ireland*.

21. Cusack, *Life of St. Patrick*.

22. Bebbington, *Evangelicalism in Modern Britain*; Gribben and Stunt, *Prisoners of Hope?*.

23. Todd, *Discourses on the Prophecies (Daniel and Paul)*.

of the Antichrist in 1846 to somewhat less acrimony, after he had taken a long vacation and got on with other projects and books, especially on Wycliffe and his men or followers.[24]

In addition to work on the apocalyptic texts in their contexts and in current biblical exegesis and interpretation, he began to edit for publication the manuscript history of Wycliffe, the Waldensians, and the Albigensians, sifting out why the latter were wrongly blamed for being the origin of the papal Antichrist and Protestant theology in Europe, and wrongly persecuted because of it. He began his research using the Ussher manuscript collection on Wycliffe, held in the library at Trinity.[25] He later went on to find a missing Waldensian manuscript when he travelled to the public library in Nantes, France, which substantiated his earlier manuscript research evidence and argument, begun during his earlier Oxford years in conjunction with Maitland. The lifelong fidelity he displayed to integrating a nonsectarian interpretation of the Antichrist into the teaching of the divinity school and in his wider publications on ecclesiastical history did so much to discredit earlier ultra-Protestant Anglican teaching and doctrine that it was not long before the papal Antichrist argument had been replaced by a more biblical re-formation.

NEWMAN AND TODD

By 1842 Todd had begun to distance himself from Newman, although the differences between them had emerged earlier. Christopher Dawson has called attention to the essence of the Oxford Movement as being a spiritual and devotional movement and has pointed out that from it sprang a more irenic and ecumenical theology.[26] Todd too based his commitment to scholarly work on a monk-like deepening of the spiritual life and in finding common ground for scholarship based on intellectual religious toleration with Roman Catholics in Ireland. He was of the generation of Irish Protestant clergymen who, in rejecting the excesses of the French Revolution and the subsequent Deist debates, still held to a strongly religious and spiritual outlook combined with scholarly research. He, like Newman and Pusey, valued the importance of the liturgy to impart religious experience, and sought

---

24. Todd, *Six Discourses on the Prophecies (John)*.
25. Todd, *Three Treatises by John Wycliffe, D.D.* and *Book of the Vaudois*.
26. I am thinking here of the corrective which came about from a tendency to see the Tractarians and Oxford Movement leaders as merely a collection of evolving dogma, party spirit, or promoters of liturgical change for its own sake. See Dawson in *The Spirit of the Oxford Movement*.

to combine it with an intellectual grasp of the faith via the study of the full library of Catholic and Reformed writings of the Anglican Church.

Most importantly, and unlike Newman, Todd did not see the European Enlightenment legacy as necessarily omitting or undermining religious experience, revelation, devotional life, or scholarly forms of religious toleration with Roman Catholics.[27] He studied pre-Reformation Mass texts like the Sarum Use and owned a copy of a thirteenth-century parchment called "The Dublin Troper of the Sarum Use," later acquired by the University of Cambridge.[28] In this his was a paradoxical and Irish religious toleration, as it was also combined with devotion to the denominational preservation of the university of his choice, with regard to teaching fellows, and he was distinctly wary of Dissenters. He did, however, wholeheartedly support the expansion and development of teaching and research at the Roman Catholic seminary at Maynooth, combined with his shared love of research into Irish manuscript sources.

In the beginning, the relationship between Newman and Todd was about the Irish reaction to the continual pace of parliamentary reform at Westminster. Newman wrote to Todd in Dublin to find out more about the views of Irish churchmen, both from the point of view of finding out their traditional context and to see out how they viewed the current changes to the status of the Established Church. Newman by this time had begun to hive off his own select following from among the older high churchmen, whom he came to regard as too Anglican and staid. These included the Irishman at Oxford, William Palmer of Worcester College, and also Maitland and Hugh James Rose. In the mind of Newman, these men lacked the passionate conviction of his close university companion Richard Hurrell Froude and were ambivalent about the publication of Froude's *Remains*. It is interesting that Todd did not side with Newman over Froude but kept faith with Maitland, Palmer, and Rose.[29]

Newman in 1836 was anxious to establish that Todd was not the son of a Cromwellian planter, tinged with the Orange of the followers of William of Orange, or a sympathizer with his long Williamite wars in Ireland and the legacy of the battle of the Boyne. Todd had little Orange sympathies. Newman did know Robert Bentley Todd, his medical brother, who had completed his Trinity medical studies at Oxford and had been invited, with Todd, for breakfasts at Oriel with Newman and his inner circle. He wrote to check that Todd, in the "department of Romanism," would fit with his

27. I hope to pursue this important point in a forthcoming publication.
28. University of Cambridge, GB-CU Add. 710 (Digital Image Archive).
29. Froude, *Remains of the Late Reverend Richard Hurrell Froude*.

new plans for the journal he had in mind to take over the editing of from Maitland and Rose. Simon Skinner has described the distinctions emerging between the old high churchmen and Newman at this point as a defining moment in Tractarian history and "the parting of the ways between Hackney and Oxford."[30] Skinner goes further and suggests that

> Newman's conviction that the movement required a periodical voice in order to complement the tracts and permit commentary on contemporary public affairs, his protracted machinations to secure one and his leverage over the *Critic* even after relinquishing formal control, graphically demonstrate the extent to which the austerely cerebral figure of historical convention was in fact constantly immersed in the maneuvres necessitated by church partisanship ... and disclose a capacity for intrigue and even duplicity which, unsurprisingly, has not been acknowledged within an overwhelmingly hagiographical literature.[31]

It is surprising, at one level, concerning the historiography of the Oxford Movement, that Todd's own sounding out of Newman's arguments and sympathies are not more well known.[32] Todd was drawn right into the heart of this defining battle for the emerging identity of the Tractarian and Oxford Movements. Newman, in a letter to him dated 19 March 1838, sets out his own tactics for advancement:

> I will try to say what I mean as simply as I can. We wish of course that the Review should speak with one voice, and not write against itself in its separate articles. Now as far as I know, I really do not think you would disapprove of anything we were likely to say. The point on which, judging at a distance, disapproval on your part was most likely, was the Revolution question; but from what I have read or heard you say, I think you are not bigoted to King William. We are as strongly opposed to the Romanists as an existing system in these countries as you can be, though we do not like abusing them.[33]

30. Skinner, "Newman, the Tractarians and the British Critic," 716–59, 716; Skinner, *Tractarians and the "Condition of England."*

31. Skinner, "Newman, the Tractarians and the British Critic," 716.

32. This may be because some of his letters in reply to Newman are either tied up in unpublished correspondence at Trinity College, Dublin, were once misfiled at Pusey House in Oxford among the Newman and the *British Critic* papers, or those in the *Letters and Diaries of John Henry Newman* by Gerard Tracey in volume five are not in proper sequence.

33. Newman to Todd, 19 Mar. 1838 (TCD MS 2214/65); Newman, *Via Media and Froude's Remains*, 201.

Todd received the subtle sword point held in the last sentence and was somewhat unclear as to what Newman was referring to regarding the review. He had previously sent Maitland and Rose some material he hoped would be published in England, but wondered what had become of it, not realizing perhaps that Newman had taken over the editorial voice. Newman may have read his copy, for he continues:

> I am not aware that you are especially attached to Luther either—as we are not. We do not praise Cranmer or Jewel, but keep silent; and I think ever should. We have perhaps very high views of the abstract process and position of the Church as a ruling body—but then—considering it to be in captivity, we hold it a Christian duty to obey our Masters, as the Jew obeyed Nebuchadnezzar. Is there any point on which there is likely to be any serious difference between us? And now pray pardon me if I have gone beyond the remit of candour.[34]

Todd replied to Newman on 26 March 1838, addressing him as "My dear friend,"

> I should feel no difficulty whatsoever in writing for the British Critic, so far as principles are concerned. I am not, as you rightly conclude, at all bigoted to William III—the Revolution which he headed seems to me to have been affected altogether on grounds of worldly expediency, and I know not how it can be defended on higher principles—it broke down the outward defence of our Church, as an establishment church, and placed us in our present anomalous situation, in which we are regarded as a mere creation of an act of Parliament, like a corporation of alderman whose corporate existence may be at any time dissolved.[35]

So far this is the same reaction in both countries to parliamentary interference in the running of the Established Church, then theoretically joined by the Act of Union of 1801. Todd went on to mention his favorite complaint that "in the eyes of the people" the Irish Established Church was "mixed up with various sects and persuasions," and worse still, "regarded as one of them," and that the fault lay with "the policy introduced at the Revolution . . . in reference to the Church and Dissenters."[36] Then again, it was remarkable that "most of the changes . . . in the doctrine and liturgy of the Church have had a tendency rather to return to antient practice and be-

34. Newman to Todd, 19 Mar. 1838, Dublin, (TCD MS 2214/65).

35. Todd, 26 Mar. 1838, Oxford (Pusey House, envelope marked "Newman and the British Critic," found in 2005).

36. Todd to Newman, 26 Mar. 1838, Dublin (TCD MS 2214/65).

lief, than to amalgamate our communion with that of the foreign Reformed Churches."[37] Here too he shares with Newman the advantages of going behind the Reformation to the ancient past, and adds that he thought those who spoke most loudly about the venerable Reformers were not prepared to put their teaching or principles into effect:

> With our respect to our Established Church, I am fully persuaded that the present theory of our endowments being the property in fact of the State, held by us in trust for the performance of certain political functions expedited or beneficial to society, does place us in a sort of captivity and tie up our hands—it gives our political rulers an influence in sacred things especially in appointments to bishoprics and other spiritual promotions, which is highly injurious and corrupting to the Church.[38]

Todd was in sympathy with Newman and Keble regarding Keble's sermon on national apostasy of July 1833. Yet, in what followed of their correspondence, there was a voice of dissent from Todd, and it began to emerge around his "scientific method" for the exegesis of Scripture.

Todd wrote again to Newman on 28 May 1838, saying that he had "lost a great deal of time in waiting for an answer from the *British Magazine* as to the fate of my paper" and "it would have saved me a great deal of time in writing the article for you."[39] Here he seems to recognize that Newman is the new editor in chief. News follows from him about the *Churchman*, the *Church of England Gazette*, and the *Dublin Review*. In a coy excuse, he tells Newman that he is forced to hold off sending material to him because he has to reply to the *Dublin Review*, and the Camden Society of London wants him to edit a fifteenth-century mystery play he had discovered in the TCD library archives. He is

> truly glad to find how little we really differ on the subject of literal interpretation of Scripture, I would probably go farther than you in rejecting what are called spiritual interpretations, but I quite agree with what you say of the many meanings of the words of Scripture and even spiritual interpretations I have no objection to provided they do not imply the rejection of the literal meaning...[40]

37. Ibid.

38. Todd to Newman, 26 Mar. 1838, Oxford (Pusey House, found in an unfiled envelope marked "Newman and the British Critic," June 2005).

39. Todd to Newman, 28 Mar. 1838, Oxford (Pusey House found in an unfiled envelope marked "Newman and the British Critic," June 2005).

40. Ibid.

Here Todd means by the "literal meaning" the biblical texts as read in a more "scientific" way.

There is a gap in their correspondence and then Newman reviews Todd's first publication of his Donnellan lectures, entitled *Prophecy and the Antichrist*, for the *British Critic*. The gulf between them is now based on Newman's arguments for the unbridgeable gap between reason and revelation. Todd, on other hand, is in Enlightenment mode, elevating enlightened reason with hermeneutical exegesis of the major prophetic and apocalyptic passages of the Old Testament and the New Testament into an interpretative form of early scientific positivism. Newman more or less refutes this approach in his review, which appeared in October 1840. He writes using the plural pronoun "we," perhaps to emphasize that the journal is speaking with one voice:

> Dr. Todd's Discourses are, perhaps, the first attempt for a long course of years in this part of Christendom to fix a dispassionate attention and a scientific interpretation on the momentous prophecies which he specifies in his title-page.[41]

In doctrine "we entirely agree with Todd," as "the Discourses are methodical, careful, accurate," also "clear and unaffected" in manner of presentation:

> If they have a fault it is that far from imposing a meaning upon Scripture, in order to make it tally with events in the history of the day, if he has a fault, it rather lies in his proving too little from it; that is, in his being rather bent on disproving what others advance than in establishing, according to the sense of the Catholic church, anything positive and substantial instead.[42]

This is a good point, as Todd did have a tendency to show up the errors of Mede, Miller, Faber, and the rest and assume that this rectified what was amiss. Yet Newman added that Todd earned the gratitude of all churchmen for seeing that the Antichrist will be coming to judge the earth in the future tense and has not done so in the past. Despite his lapse into scientific mode, Newman is prepared to say that the Irish publication is "seasonable" and "important," as "if any branch of the Church be Antichristian, it will be found that all the Church is so, our own branch inclusive."

In the end the impression remains that English churchmen like Newman and indeed his sparring partner at Oriel, Whately, greatly suspected that none of the Irish clergymen could be even-tempered about religion,

41. Newman, "Protestant Idea of Antichrist," 391.
42. Ibid., 391.

unlike Englishmen; so finding common cause in the long term was bound to be a difficult task. In 1831 Whately wrote regarding the true nature of Irish Protestants to his old friend Edward Copleston from Oriel, now the bishop of Llandaff, including a possibly facetious solution:

> The English apply all they hear of the Irish national character to the Roman Catholics and imagine that Protestants—men of their own church—are much such men as themselves: whereas a Roman Catholic and an Orangeman (with of course individual exceptions) are much more like each other than either of them to an Englishman; the chief difference, in respect of the present point, is implacability.[43]

The solution in his view was:

> ... the *entire* extermination of at least all the adult males of the Roman Catholics. If any are left, mark my words, there will be, on the one side, oppression and vexatious insult; on the other assassination, burning, houghing of cattle in outbreak after outbreak until the end of time.[44]

He finished his remarks by advising the bishop not to keep his letters lying about the house, for fear both their houses would be burned down.

Todd was very much in the midst of the maelstrom created by the high achieving and emboldened churchman that Newman was in this period, while at the same time seeking to further his Irish academic career and life as an Irish clergyman and feeling undermined by Whately's attitude to the Tractarians. He tried hard to make sure that he did not become, for the sake of his career prospects in Ireland, a minority within a minority with regard to his involvement in all things Oxford. Yet that was what in part happened because of the usual divisions within the college and the Church of Ireland. He found that at crucial times he had little support from within the rank and file of some of his academic colleagues, especially those who held Second Reformation views among the Irish clergy who had graduated from the college. At times he had to fight for his academic life and freedom.[45]

---

43. Whately, *Life and Correspondence*, vol. 1, 33.

44. Ibid., 33.

45. This aspect will be referred to in greater detail in a forthcoming longer work on Todd.

IRELAND, ENGLAND, AND THE TERM "HIGH CHURCHMAN"

One of the contemporary problems in interpreting Todd with regard to the Tractarian and Oxford Movements and of assessing his overall contribution from Ireland is the differing context of his Irish background and how the overall term "an Irish high churchman" is to be interpreted, as used for example by Peter Nockles.[46]

Today, in Oxford Movement historiography, the Church of Ireland high churchmen usually somehow blur into the workings of the Church of England, as seen in the ground-breaking but also problematic essay by Nockles. We can see that, in some ways, in order to interpret Todd, he has to remain within the more volatile political context of his day in Ireland, and that means being sadly mistaken, depending on your point of view, for being an Orangeman by Englishmen, which is what Newman and Whately thought all Irish Protestant males were, to a greater or lesser irrational degree.

In addition, even in Todd's day the differences between the Irish high churchmen and the English high churchmen were obvious. Desmond Bowen, writing of the nineteenth-century Church of Ireland, uses the phrase "the High Church Evangelical mentality that characterized the leadership of the Established Church," referring to men who were considered mainstream material for promotion, like James T. O'Brien, bishop of Ossory, Ferns, and Leighlin from 1842 until 1874.[47] Generally, the Irish high churchmen like Todd were perhaps lower in their liturgical practices than England, but still very high for Ireland. Others have noted that in the earlier pre-Tractarian high church tradition, Alexander Knox and John Jebb were thought of as catholic Evangelicals, again with this mix of evangelical and high church. Jebb has been viewed as embracing the Romantic age and empathizing with the Evangelical revival as a pre-Tractarian high churchman.[48] George Otto Simms, in a brief biography of Todd, would only speak of him as a strong churchman and someone who argued in favor of strong church principles, thus eschewing all reference to nineteenth-century church party politics in his descriptions of his church loyalties. He preferred to see him instead as irenic in intention with regard to his churchmanship and scholarship.[49]

---

46. Nockles, "Church or Protestant Sect?," 457–93.
47. Bowen, *Protestant Crusade in Ireland*, 77.
48. Barrett, "Alexander Knox, Lay Theologian," 40; Acheson, *Bishop John Jebb*, xiv.
49. Simms, "James Henthorn Todd," 5–23.

The Church of England diverged into a three-way church party split as described in the usual accounts of the development of the nineteenth century.[50] It is not necessarily true that this unfolded in the same way in Ireland, as even Nockles in his work makes little reference in detail to an emerging clear influence from the Broad Church movement, as led by Cambridge. It seems also that the old high church and the new high church or Tractarian and Oxford Movement sympathizers were pushed into a very narrow corner by the later historiography of the Church of Ireland, more so than in the Church of England, where in academic history they are more linked to ritualism. Links with the old Irish Caroline high churchmanship are not common. The founding figure in the Puritan tradition in Ireland was James Ussher, Archbishop of Armagh (1625–1656), who set out the initial parameters of a very polemic relationship between Roman Catholics and the Church of Ireland, in the wake of a weak Irish reformation, followed by the Ulster and Cromwellian plantations.[51] High Church in England simply did not transfer to the Irish situation in this regard, unless the transition is made by an Englishman in Ireland, innocent of being anyway out of place, as in the 1840 publication of a history of the Church of Ireland by Richard Mant.[52]

The phrase "high as a steeple and no better for it" or "high, dry, and two bottles orthodox," as Newman liked to refer to the older high churchmen, was also understood to apply to the select few like Todd, in Ireland, with no distinction between the older high churchmen and those like Todd and Elrington, who came under the influence of Newman. Irish ecclesiastical memory sees them as one, as far on as 1916–17 when the *Church of Ireland Gazette* referred to a church service where an "Old Prebendary" "high, dry, and gouty" limped into his stall, late for a Dublin cathedral liturgy. Unfortunately, as the *Gazette* explained, his lateness meant that the whole service had to begin again in order to accommodate him, much to the ire of the celebrant.[53] It is this sort of anecdote which remains in the collective memory, influenced no doubt by a low church reaction of fear to Tractarianism and ritualism. Yet here there was and is greater diversity and important rapports

---

50. Frances Knight, who lectures at Lampeter, Wales, on the nineteenth-century Church of England, kindly introduced me to the topic long ago, together with Nigel Yates and Thomas O'Loughlin, all of whom remain part of the reason I continued with this particular topic.

51. Ussher, *A Discourse of the Religion*; Ussher, *Prophecies Concerning the Return of Popery*.

52. Mant, *History of the Church of Ireland*.

53. "Dublin Cathedrals and Chapters," 492.

than the received historiography permits us at present to remember about the positive value of diversity.

Take for example the description of the divinity school reading list in 1838 by McDowell and Webb:

> From the list of books prescribed for the examinations, as well as from the writings of the Professors and lecturers, we can infer the prevailing tone of the Divinity course: a conservative, robust, but reasonably balanced Protestantism. There was needless to say no flavour of Tractarianism, but neither was there a marked reaction against it: the doings of the Ritualists in England provoked disgust but little alarm.[54]

Todd, in fact, mixed in the circles of Tractarians and Oxford interests, and discriminated in things theological and historical more than this summary of teaching and learning permits.

CANADIAN INTERPRETATIONS OF THE CHURCH OF IRELAND

In Canada, the meaning and use of high church and low church shifts again in the use of three models of church exported from different countries to Canada or British North America.[55] It is commonly agreed that they form the basis of the identity of the blended Anglican Church of Canada today. The three comprise the English Church, the American Church, and the Irish Church, with the latter coming in as representative of a main low church model, and one containing greater sectarian tensions. The shorthand is that the term "high church" is based on traditional English Tory parliamentary divisions. The term "Tory" has a religious meaning in this sense, standing for the importance of the divine right of kings and the subordination and cooperation of parliament, especially concerning the restriction of dissenters. The term "low church," again using the English model, Hayes suggests, stands for Whig politics.[56] This is amusing to consider for the Church of Ireland. To be low church is to be Whig! However, we may take the theological and political sense as meaning less emphasis on the divine right of kings and more on a democratic diversity of representation in parliament, which then accords with the American model.

---

54. McDowell and Webb, *Trinity College, Dublin*, 163.
55. Hayes, *Anglicans in Canada*.
56. Ibid.

To further complicate matters, this might just refer, in the early and mid-nineteenth century, to moderate Irish Tories who could also be Irish liberals who, in practice, favored modest and pragmatic reform. There may yet be a word or phrase that incorporates this shifting set of boundaries, shaded in the middle perhaps, or even forming a *via media*. Perhaps Simms is right. It is better to look for the irenic than to rule it out as impossible, for the Church of Ireland. Bowen too seeks the *eirenicon,* or the moment when things turn out in favor of ecumenical endeavor within the Irish Church. Nockles and others explore another territory—i.e., the difference between a sect and church—and hopes that the Church of Ireland is more than a Protestant sect. The differences between Nockles, Simms and Bowen are therefore clear: the latter two cautiously optimistic for the survival and flourishing of the Church of Ireland, the former inclined to think more in terms of a legacy of Irish sectarianism.[57]

CONCLUSION

Austin Cooper sees the loss of ten Irish sees and two archbishops as having prompted Keble to preach the 1833 assizes sermon at Oxford and Newman to turn to Ireland, though he later denied it.[58] A common distrust of Westminster rule at the beginning of the Tractarian and Oxford Movements did form significant common ground between Ireland and England. If we examine Keble's words, they could have been written by Todd to Newman:

> Can we conceal from ourselves that every year the practice is becoming more common, of trusting men unreservedly in the most delicate and important matter, without one serious inquiry, whether they do not hold principles which make it impossible for them to be loyal to their Creator, Redeemer, and Sanctifier?[59]

Keble could also have been speaking for the Irish churchmen at the time of the dissolution of the Irish parliament and the bringing in of the Act of Union of 1801 when he went on to add: "Are not offices conferred, partnerships formed, intimacies courted . . . and if it be true . . . that such

---

57. One of Todd's first innovative suggestions to the board, even before he was made Junior Fellow, was to request a new print type for the College Print Room which would enable him to reproduce accurately documents from the history of the College: Bartholomew Lloyd to James Henthorn Todd, 18 Aug. 1827 (TCD Todd Correspondence, MS 2214/2).

58. Cooper, "Ireland and the Oxford Movement," 62–74.

59. Keble, "National Apostasy," 136–40, and quoted by Chapman, *Firmly I Believe,* 15.

enactments are forced on the Legislature by public opinion, is apostasy too hard a word to describe the temper of that nation?"[60] By 1833, the issues were of allowing Roman Catholic, Dissenter, and Jew to take their democratic place in parliament. If a measure of disillusionment between church and state was common and ever present even before 1833, then early Tractarians in England and Ireland were merely hitting a nerve together, though it soon became clear that they were united and divided in different ways. It is mere speculation that Todd may have attended Newman's lectures on *The Idea of a University* in the Rotunda rooms during 1851, although a lot of Trinity men did turn up. Newman and Todd certainly both had the ideal of a modern university in common and Newman was said to have based his ideas for the new Catholic University of Ireland on his time as an Anglican at Oxford.

The Irish forms of "high" churchmanship and their development into Tractarian and Oxford Movement sympathies in a predominantly "low" church were beset by subsequent problems of memory and recall, and received little sympathetic treatment from histories of the Church of Ireland, even in memorial passing. Yet for all the gaps and undercurrents, the loss of the ten Irish sees and two archbishoprics was a catalyst for quite radical change. It is very interesting to attempt to put the pieces together and see how they fit in new ways. Todd was correct in both agreeing with and parrying Newman at various times and brave in taking on a project which Newman never attempted, that of bringing into the public domain the major flaws of a sectarian apocalyptic theology carried uncritically into the teachings of the Church of England. So Whately and Newman, in their assessment of the Orange nature of the Irish church and its deeply sectarian nature, were wrong. On this point at any rate, Todd brought the Church of Ireland into line with European Enlightenment thinking by outlining a more "scientific" approach to the Bible.

Perhaps, in retrospect, it was not all that scientific in the long run, being more of an attempt to be fair and not to create or inflame sectarian tensions in Ireland or England, from the point of view of the teachings of the divinity school in Dublin. It was a project that was, as he said himself, a bit too Roman for the Puritan Church of Ireland. In addition, the period from 1830 to 1850 has been characterized as one of intellectual stimulus and new intellectual exploration with regard to the destiny of Ireland. The resulting complex reactions of Irish Protestants to a series of rapid political changes with far-reaching consequences is a most interesting topic which

---

60. Ibid.

confronts church narratives with forms of agreement, subversion, and dissent.[61] If the Irish were forced by circumstance to find a new destiny for Protestantism at large, then Todd in his own way added significantly to this most compelling debate. Stewart Brown has pointed out that the sense of apostolical and catholic continuity and many of the devotional, liturgical, and church practices that the Tractarians and Oxford Movements sought to recover, and for which they suffered ignominy, were incorporated over time into the mainstream Scottish Episcopal and Presbyterian Churches.[62] It is what occurred also, by degrees, in the "low" Church of Ireland.

BIBLIOGRAPHY

Acheson, Alan R. *Bishop John Jebb and the Nineteenth-Century Anglican Renaissance.* Toronto: Clements, 2013.

Barrett, Peter F. "Alexander Knox, Lay Theologian of the Church of Ireland." *Search* 18 (2000) 40.

Bebbington, David W. *Evangelicalism in Modern Britain: A History from the 1730s to the 1980s.* London: Routledge, 2002.

Bowen, Desmond. "Magee, William (1766–1831)." In *DNB*, edited by David Cannadine. Oxford: Oxford University Press, 2004. http://www.oxforddnb.com.myaccess.library.utoronto.ca/view/article/17778.

———. *The Protestant Crusade in Ireland, 1800–70: A Study of Protestant-Catholic Relations between the Act of Union and Disestablishment.* Montreal: McGill-Queen's University Press, 1978.

Brown, Stewart J. *Providence and Empire, Religion and Society in Britain, 1815–1914.* Harlow, UK: Pearson Education, 2008.

———. "Scotland and the Oxford Movement." In *The Oxford Movement: Europe and the Wider World, 1830–1930*, edited by Stewart J. Brown and Peter B. Nockles, 56–77. Cambridge: Cambridge University Press, 2012.

Chapman, Raymond, ed. *Firmly I Believe: An Oxford Movement Reader.* Canterbury, UK: 2006.

Clarke, Richard. *Richard Whately: The Unharmonious Blacksmith.* Armagh, UK: The Church of Ireland Historical Society, 2002.

Cooper, Austin. "Ireland and the Oxford Movement." *Journal of Religious History* 19.1 (June 1995) 62–74.

Cusack, Margaret F. *The Life of St. Patrick.* London: Burns and Oates, 1871.

Dawson, Christopher. *The Spirit of the Oxford Movement.* London: Saint Austin, 2001.

Dickson, David. "Trinity College and the Intellectual Revival, 1830–1850." In *Treasures of the Mind: Trinity College Dublin Quatercentenary Exhibition*, edited by David Scott, 45–54. London: Sotheby's, 1992.

"Dublin Cathedrals and Chapters." *Church of Ireland Gazette*, Compendium (7 Jul 1917) 492.

---

61. Dickson, "Trinity College and the Intellectual Revival," 45–54.
62. Brown, "Scotland and the Oxford Movement," 56–77.

Froude, Richard Hurrell. *Remains of the Late Reverend Richard Hurrell Froude, M.A.* 2 vols. London: J. G. and F. Rivington, 1838.

Gribben, Crawford, and Timothy S. Stunt, eds. *Prisoners of Hope? Aspects of Evangelical Millennialism in Britain and Ireland, 1800–1880.* Carlisle, UK: Paternoster, 2004.

Hayes, Alan L. *Anglicans in Canada: Controversies and Identity in Historical Perspective.* Chicago: University of Illinois Press, 2004.

Jones, John Fleming. *Catalogue of the Valuable Library of the Late Rev. James H. Todd.* Dublin: M. H. Gill, 1869.

Keble, John. "National Apostasy." *Sermons Academical and Occasional.* London: John Henry Parker/Rivington, 1848.

Mant, Richard. *History of the Church of Ireland from the Reformation to the Revolution.* London: Parker, 1840.

McDowell, Robert B., and D. A. Webb. *Trinity College, Dublin, 1592–1952: An Academic History.* Cambridge: Cambridge University Press, 1982.

Newman, John Henry. "The Protestant Idea of Antichrist." *British Critic* (Oct 1840) 391–440.

———. *The Via Media and Froude's Remains, January 1837 to December 1838.* In *The Letters and Diaries of John Henry Newman*, vol. 6, edited by Gerard Tracey. Oxford: Oxford University Press, 1989.

Nockles, Peter B. "Church or Protestant Sect? The Church of Ireland, High Churchmanship, and the Oxford Movement, 1822–1869." *Historical Journal* 41 (1998) 457–93.

———. *The Oxford Movement in Context: Anglican High Churchmanship, 1760–1857.* Cambridge: Cambridge University Press, 1997.

Oxford Dictionary of National Biography. Oxford: Oxford University Press, 2004.

Phillips, Walter, ed. *History of the Church of Ireland from the Earliest Times to the Present Day.* 3 vols. Oxford: Oxford University Press, 1933.

Simms, George O. "James Henthorn Todd." *Hermathena: A Dublin University Review* 109 (Autumn 1969) 5–23.

Skinner, Simon A. "Newman, the Tractarians and the British Critic." *Journal of Ecclesiastical History* 50.4 (Oct 1999) 716–59.

———. *Tractarians and the "Condition of England": The Social and Political Thought of the Oxford Movement.* Oxford: Oxford University Press, 2004.

Todd, James Henthorn. *The Book of the Vaudois, the Waldensian Manuscripts Preserved in the Library of Trinity College Dublin.* Dublin: Hodges & Smith, 1865.

———. *A Catalogue of Graduates Who have Proceeded to Degrees in the University of Dublin from the Earliest Recorded Commencements.* Dublin: Dublin University Press, 1833.

———. *Discourses on the Prophecies Relating to Antichrist in the Writings of Daniel and St. Paul, Preached before the University of Dublin, at the Donnellan Lecture, 1838.* Dublin: Dublin University Press, 1840.

———. *Leabhar Imuinn.* 2 vols. Dublin: Dublin University Press, 1869.

———. *Six Discourses on the Prophecies Relating to Antichrist in the Apocalypse of St. John. Preached before the University of Dublin at the Donnellan Lecture by James Henthorn Todd.* Dublin: Dublin University Press, 1846.

———. *St. Patrick, Apostle of Ireland.* Dublin: Hodges & Smith, 1864.

———. *Three Treatises by John Wycliffe D.D.* Dublin: Hodges & Smith, 1851.

Ussher, James. *A Discourse of the Religion Anciently Professed by the Irish and British*. London: printed for Benjamin Tooke, 1623.

———. *Prophecies Concerning the Return of Popery in England, Scotland and Ireland*. London: printed for A. Bancks, 1682.

Webb, Alfred. *Compendium of Irish Biography Comprising Sketches of Distinguished Irishmen, and Eminent Persons Connected with Ireland by Office or by Their Writings*. Dublin: M. H. Gill & Son, 1878.

Welch, Robert, ed. *The Oxford Companion to Irish Literature*. Oxford: Oxford University Press, 1996.

Whately, Elizabeth. *Life and Correspondence of Richard Whately, D.D., Late Archbishop of Dublin*. 2 vols. London: Longman, Green, 1866.

7

The Role of Bible Societies in Identity Formation, 1800–1850

Miriam Moffitt

ASSOCIATIONAL CULTURE PLAYED AN important role in inculcating a sense of identity and in promoting societal cohesion within the Church of Ireland in the early nineteenth century, particularly through the agency of Bible societies, which served to promote dissemination of the Scriptures and/ or the provision of education and charity. These objectives were regularly conjoined, as the provision of education or relief was often contingent on engagement with the Scriptures, although this connection was often unacknowledged. Parish-based societies also played a role in fostering the conception that the Church of Ireland, although numerically small, was a component of a larger entity and connected to a wider Protestant community, both inside and outside the Anglican diaspora. This paper will review the activities of parish organizations in Ireland in the early decades of the nineteenth century, and will explore the manner in which participation in Bible agencies facilitated a sense of shared community, both inside and outside home localities. It will pay particular attention to the manner in which Protestant missionary work was promoted in the western county of Sligo in the period.

FORMATION

A large number of Irish Protestants, horrified at the level of violence that accompanied the rebellion of 1798, came to believe that further insurrections might be averted if Ireland's Catholic population had access to a scriptural education. This resulted in the establishment of numerous church-based organizations whose objective was the dissemination of the Scriptures: the Hibernian Bible Society (1806), London Hibernian Society for Establishing Schools and Circulating the Holy Scriptures in Ireland (1806), Hibernian Sunday School Society (1809, renamed the Sunday School Society for Ireland in 1818), the Irish Society for Promoting the Education of the Native Irish through the Medium of Their Own Language (hereafter the Irish Society) (1818), and the Scripture Readers Society (1822).[1] Some Bible societies were specifically associated with the Church of Ireland, while others were pan-Protestant in nature. Irish organizations promoting access to the Scriptures often operated in tandem with a British counterpart; for instance, the London Irish Society and the Irish Society were segments of the same organization. As home missionary activities ran parallel to mission work in foreign lands, participation in missionary and scriptural societies enabled members of the Church of Ireland to play a role in promoting the expansion of Protestantism in general, and the Anglican Church in particular, both inside and outside the island of Ireland. On foreign soil, supporters hoped to gather in the heathen population to scriptural Protestantism, while the intended home beneficiaries were persons within and without the established church.

The Act of Union of 1800 which followed the rebellion of 1798 provided a context whereby like-minded lay and clerical persons of an evangelical disposition came together to organize a campaign for the mass conversion of Irish Catholics, hoping that a religious approach would remedy Ireland's political problems.[2] John Wolffe's observation of popular religious organizations in England is applicable to Ireland: that participation in societies of this nature enabled the grafting of a spiritual dimension onto what had previously been racial, nationalist, or anti-Catholic prejudices, and that this validated ethnic or political motivations by transforming them into religious crusades.[3] The blurring of boundaries between religious, educational, and sociocultural expectations is evident in the annual reports of these societies. For example, the Hibernian Sunday School Society asserted in 1818

---

1. Whelan, *Bible War in Ireland*, 53–85.

2. Maguire, "Church of Ireland Parochial Associations," 97–109; Whelan, "Bible Gentry," 52.

3. Wolffe, "Evangelicalism in Mid-nineteenth-century England," 194–95.

that "the moral or immoral habits" of the Irish impacted on "the welfare of the United Empire," and hoped that exposure to "the principles of decency, order, social harmony and true religion" would counter some of the "worst evils" prevalent in Ireland.[4]

The conflation of religion and politics in Ireland, combined with the denominational composition of the country, meant that Protestant efforts to disseminate the Scriptures, to provide education, and to alleviate poverty became completely fused as low levels of literacy made the provision of classes in reading and writing an integral part of home missionary work. The consequent intermingling of religion and education led to the allegation that Bible societies were attempting to subvert the confessional allegiance of Irish Catholics with offers of schooling. While this accusation is perfectly valid, it should be remembered that Bible societies merely applied to Ireland the *modus operandi* employed by similar associations in Britain, where the expected recipients were Protestant, or at least nominally Protestant. In Ireland, however, most of the poor were Catholic, and Protestant intervention, whether missionary, charitable, or educational in nature, was condemned as proselytism by the Catholic clergy and middle classes, who mounted a strenuous campaign to counter "the extent, the power, the funds, the patronage, the systematic organization . . . the fanatic energy of that anti-Catholic alliance."[5]

Many Bible societies established to promote free access to the Scriptures had, at their core, a desire to eradicate or at least contain Roman Catholicism in Ireland. It was no coincidence that these societies flourished in the 1820s when large segments of Irish Protestantism felt threatened by the campaign for Catholic emancipation,[6] expressed in warnings that "As long as Popery exists, a cloud of darkness will overspread the world."[7] Protestant missions to Irish Catholics were also inspired by an evangelical obligation to actively promote a knowledge of the Scriptures, and were motivated by the need to reassert the Church of Ireland as the legitimate descendant of the early Irish Church, to position her as the church of the majority, and to atone for England's introduction of Roman influences in the twelfth century.[8] Protestant fears should be considered against the backdrop of Pastorini's prophecies, which promised Catholic retribution against Protestants at an

---

4. Hibernian Sunday School Society, *Annual Report* (1818), 9, 18.
5. *Freeman's Journal* (7 Sept. 1824), 3.
6. Blackstock, *Loyalism in Ireland*, especially chapter 6.
7. Spoken by Col. Irwin at a meeting in Sligo, *Ballina Impartial* (11 Aug. 1828), 4.
8. Bebbington, *Evangelicalism in Modern Britain*, 5–17; Hill, "Church of Ireland and Irish Church History," 9–31.

unspecified date between 1821 and 1825.[9] The activities of Irish biblical societies in the early decades of the nineteenth century (termed the Second Reformation) were strongly supported by persons with an evangelical or low-church leaning and were inspired by the growth of a conservative premillennialism which considered that the world was deteriorating rapidly and which sought to gather "lost" souls for the Lord.[10] Such opinions found urgent voice in British publications such as the *Record*, and in Ireland in the *Dublin Record* and the *Christian Examiner and Church of Ireland Magazine*.

ORGANIZATION

Parish-based Bible societies adopted a uniform organizational structure whereby a national parent body was supplemented by local auxiliaries, which were comprised of both male and female volunteers. In connecting parish associations with a national or transnational infrastructure, participation at local levels strengthened parochial and societal cohesion by building on the shared objective of a collective crusade. The promotion and maintenance of ongoing horizontal (parish-to-parish) and vertical (parish-to-central) connections created a community of dedicated supporters, united in a common pursuit, whose belief in the validity of their cause was reinforced by a sense of solidarity and by the extent and perceived status of the wider organization.

Participation in religious charities took various forms, depending on one's social status. Aristocratic persons, both male and female, could assume a public role as patron; the middle classes might be actively involved in collecting weekly, monthly, or quarterly subscriptions within their social circles, or in ensuring the smooth operation of the charity. As Bible societies provided education and/or the care of children, they afforded opportunities for female participation at a time when there were few ways in which women could play an active role outside the home. In a complex way, the gathering of subscriptions, the organizing of fundraising, and the execution of the mission work answered the religious and social needs, not only of the intended recipients of mission, but also of donors and activists, and provided a method whereby supporters were enabled to carve out a significant and public role by engaging in worthwhile activities. The compilation and publication of subscription lists which detailed monies donated by, and

---

9. Using the pen name Pastorini, Charles Walmesley, a Roman Catholic bishop, prophesised that punishment for heretics would be delivered fifty years after 1771. Whelan, *Bible War*, 143–46.

10. Brown, *Providence and Empire*, 70–74.

collected by, named individuals enabled persons of moderate means to define their status within the parish. This has provided a permanent record of their activities and social interactions so that, over time, the records of parish auxiliaries captured the lives and social status of the ordinary parishioners who comprised their membership, to parallel the wall memorials of the wealthier classes.

The Hibernian Church Missionary Society (HCMS), founded in 1814 to advance mission work overseas, was an associate of the London-based Church Missionary Society (founded 1799). The HCMS applied the methodologies of the British and Foreign Bible Society (founded 1804) by agreeing to "extend itself through Ireland by Associations." Members were urged:

> Let each of us, when we go to our respective destinations, carry in our bosoms a live coal which we have taken off this altar, and endeavour to kindle a hallowed fire in our towns, our cities and our countries. Let us solicit the splendid offerings of the affluent, and the more limited contributions of the poor—not disdaining even the widow's mite, when cast into the treasury of the Lord![11]

The annual reports of the HCMS informed supporters of work undertaken by its CMS parent in India, Africa, Ceylon, and on the North American continent. CMS operations were clearly targeted not only at the Indigenous people but also at North America's European immigrants, who were in danger of falling prey to Catholic missionaries from Quebec:

> Not only may we hope that this place will extend the blessings of religion and education over the trackless wastes of North America—reclaim the wandering hunter to a settled and pastoral life, and render those inhospitable deserts accessible;—but it will restore to religion many hundred Europeans, who have either become heathens in fact, living without God in their world, or have been seduced from the religion of their fathers.[12]

The detailed year-by-year information contained in HCMS annual reports reveals that financial support was strongest in town parishes with larger numbers of middle-class parishioners, and it also shows that its principal collectors and donors were female.[13] It was noted that, in Sligo, "the Ladies have borne the burden and heat of the day" and that these women raised £24 18s. 3d. in 1821, supplemented by an additional £9 10s. collected by Mrs. Trafford and Miss Faussett for educating a missionary in Africa,

---

11. HCMS, *Annual Report* (1814), 31.
12. HCMS, *Annual Report* (1823), 35–36.
13. See, for example, HCMS, *Annual Report* (1823), 149–50.

who was to be known as Williams Chambers Armstrong.[14] This practice of raising subscriptions for the support of individual children in Africa was commonplace, their names chosen by the benefactor. In 1823, forty-three children were maintained in this manner at an annual cost of £5 8s. 4d. per child, raised by various individuals from all over the island of Ireland: Miss L. Blacker collected this sum from twenty-one named persons, while twenty-two contributors are listed on Miss Elizabeth Scriven's list, the monies in each case to be spent on two African children called Lucinda Blacker and Samuel Scriven, respectively.[15]

The HCMS focussed its activities on "heathens" overseas, supporters believing that its parish-based activities would add weight to the contemporaneous home missionary impetus: "Meeting will strengthen meeting, and hand will strengthen hand . . ."[16] Although the objectives of the Hibernian Bible Society (HBS) resembled those of the HCMS, the HBS engaged in active mission work in Ireland in addition to supporting overseas mission. In contrast to the HCMS (a Church of Ireland society), the HBS was pan-Protestant in nature, being affiliated to the (also pan-Protestant) British and Foreign Bible Society (BFBS), which had led the way in translating the Scriptures into local languages. Its first translation was in 1804 when St. John's gospel was translated into Mohawk-English by Captain John Norton, a chief of the Six Nations Indians in Upper Canada; and in 1825, the BFBS reprinted the Irish-language translation of the Bible prepared by Bishop Bedell two centuries earlier.[17] The dual objectives of the HBS (home and overseas mission) are confirmed in a letter from an unidentified Irishman (1816), then resident in St. John's, Newfoundland, who congratulated the society for its home evangelization activities and who thanked the Wexford auxiliary of the HBS for sending bibles, which he had distributed to Irish fishermen working at the outlying ports "where ignorance and sensuality begin to prevail over early religious prepossessions."[18]

SLIGO ORGANIZATION

The papers of the Sligo HBS enable an analysis of the function and objectives of the organization, the levels and locations of support, and the role played by women. The Sligo HBS was structured in the usual manner; at

14. HCMS, *Annual Report* (1819), part 2, 60; ibid. (1821), 45.
15. HCMS, *Annual Report* (1823), 100.
16. HCMS, *Annual Report* (1814), 40.
17. Canton, *History of the British and Foreign Bible Society* 1, 25, 370–71.
18. HBS, *Reports of the Hibernian Bible Society*, 163–64.

its inception in 1814, its president was George Beresford, Church of Ireland bishop of Elphin, and its vice presidents included the two MPs for the county, Charles O'Hara and Edward Synge Cooper, along with several other persons of note.[19] It adopted the general *modus operandi* of church-based societies, enlisting supporters, organizing sermons and lectures, taking up collections, identifying likely recipients of Scriptures, and establishing a female branch—the "Fair Auxiliaries"—whose special affinity with scriptural dissemination was noted.[20] Within a year, 212 bibles and 465 copies of the New Testament had been distributed, some sold at full cost, some subsidized, and others given gratuitously.[21] It is clear that participation entailed a substantial commitment: the male section of the Sligo HBS met on nine occasions during 1824, and the Sligo Ladies' Auxiliary collected quarterly subscriptions from 151 named individuals in 1822 (sums ranging from 5s. 6d. to 1s. 3d.), in addition to undertaking domestic visits to advance missionary work.[22]

Mirroring the situation in England,[23] women's auxiliaries in Ireland were expected to remit monies raised to their male counterpart, and funds raised by the Sligo Ladies' Auxiliary were managed by the male branch as outlined in the 1830 report:

> It has been found the best—for the Ladies Association to hand over the Adm. of their collection annually to the Trr. of the Gentlemen's Society, and to receive supplies of copies of the Scriptures from their Depository.[24]

Support for the HBS in County Sligo was strongest among those living in or associated with the town of Sligo, and an effective auxiliary (parish) network was only established in the 1830s. From this time, specific clergymen were designated as HBS deputation secretaries and tasked with visiting parishes to speak on behalf of the society, after which collections were taken up. The success of deputation lectures varied according to location; the report of the 1835 deputation tour confirms low levels of support in the less prosperous rural parts of County Sligo—as at Coolaney, where the speaker attributed the disappointing attendance to a fear among poorer Protestants

---

19. Ibid., 122.
20. HBS, *Report of the Managing Committee*, 17.
21. Sligo HBS papers, Minute book of Sligo HBS (henceforth "Sligo Minute Book"), 17, 10 Jan. 1815, MS 212/1 (RCBL).
22. Sligo Minute Book, 23 Oct. 1823, 1824 MS 212/1 (RCBL).
23. Davidoff and Hall, *Family Fortunes*, 107–18.
24. Sligo HBS papers, Annual Report, 1830, MS 212/2/2 (RCBL).

that a donation might be expected.[25] No collection was taken at the Lissadell meeting because "nearly all the persons present are in a very humble line of life," and Rev. John Garrett of Ballymote did not promote the society in his parish because "we are so badly provided in the way of common necessities of life and the education of the poor that if you were to ask for any subscriptions it would be for these purposes."[26]

ACTIVITIES

While the stated objective of the HBS was the dissemination of the Scriptures to the entire population, correspondents were particularly delighted when they managed to engage with Roman Catholics. Rev. George Mostyn of Tubbercurry reported in 1835 that he had distributed two bibles gratuitously, "one to a firm Protestant, the other to a Roman Catholic," had given three testaments to Catholic children who attended Sunday School, and another three to teachers at a night school under the management of the Baptist Society, for distribution "to the most worthy and faithful."[27] Rev. John Dawson of Easkey was confident that, by 1835, every Protestant family in his parish already owned a copy of the Scriptures, and he hoped to persuade the Roman Catholic population to accept and study them, which would "with God's grace tend to Emancipate them from the degrading Superstition and thraldom in which they are held by a despotic Priesthood."[28] Rev. Dawson's strong desire to diminish the influence of the Catholic clergy, and the reluctance of the Ballymote and Lissadell rectors to embark on public fundraising activities in the mid-1830s, might be attributed to the heightened interdenominational tensions arising from the contemporaneous anti-tithe agitation. The appeal of scriptural education had diminished among the Catholic population following the provision of government-funded primary education from 1831.[29] However, as some Roman Catholic bishops did not permit the introduction of national schools into their dioceses, fertile areas remained especially among the adult population.

Protestant societies which promoted the dissemination of the Scriptures among Irish Catholics, whether pan-Protestant (e.g., HBS) or exclusively Anglican (e.g., Irish Society), were ostensibly religious in character

25. Sligo HBS papers, notes of a deputation tour, MS 212/3/12 (RCBL).
26. Sligo HBS papers, reports from Lisadell and Ballymote branches, 1835–6, MSS 212/3/5, 212/3/7 (RCBL).
27. Sligo HBS papers, report from Tubbercurry branch, 1835, MS 212/3/1 (RCBL).
28. Sligo HBS papers, report from Easky branch, 1835, MS 212/3/2 (RCBL).
29. *Belfast News-Letter* (7 Jun. 1839).

but encompassed strong unvoiced political and sociocultural agendas. The establishment of two Bible societies in Sligo in 1814 (HBS, and the Sligo and Western Evangelical Society) is partly attributable to the ongoing war with France,[30] as is the commencement of mission work in the town of Sligo in the same year, undertaken by Albert Blest, an agent of the London Hibernian Society.[31] The rapid development of Protestant mission in Ireland at this juncture should be seen in the context of a worldwide expansion, the missionary impetus being given an additional fillip with the passage of the Charter Act in 1813, which facilitated the advancement of Protestant mission in India.[32]

The Sligo HBS acknowledged a political agenda from the outset; it hoped its work would inspire in its recipients "love to their neighbour, loyalty to their King, and reverence to their God."[33] An account of the Irish Society emits a strong whiff of superiority regarding the morals and character of Irish Catholics and their propensity to be led astray by a scheming political priesthood, but claims that many years of mission work had diminished the influence of the Roman clergy.[34] By 1846, Rev. Lewis Potter of Dromard in County Sligo could report that people were no longer "terrified by the wrath of the priest"; he continued in a hopeful vein: "it is not easy to say where the spirit of liberty, thus begun in small things, may stop; it is quite clear they are judging for themselves."[35]

Advancement in civility was an expected and intended by-product of a scriptural education; and Bible societies, whether operating in home or foreign fields, believed that their remit extended beyond the sphere of religion. Their unvoiced intention was a desire to reshape missionary regions as mirror-images of English society, as explained by the Sligo and Western Evangelical Society, which observed that, by disseminating the Scriptures, Ireland had "trodden in the steps of her illustrious Sister" and had "imbibed her spirit."[36] The Sligo HBS hoped to replace all the "weeds of Ignorance and vice" with the "happy fruits of Righteousness, Industry, Loyalty and Peace"[37] and acknowledged that an intrinsic part of its work was the promotion of

---

30. HBS, *Report of the Managing Committee*, 10–18.
31. Motherwell, *A Memoir of the Late Albert Blest*, 98; Whelan, *Bible War*, 10, 94–98.
32. Copland, "Christianity as an Arm of Empire," 1025–54.
33. HBS, *Report of the Managing Committee*, 2.
34. Mason, *History of the Origin*, 99.
35. Ibid., 101–2.
36. Sligo and Western Evangelical Alliance notice, MS 36,649/7 (NLI).
37. Sligo Minute Book, p. 25, MS 212/1 (RCBL).

"civilization."[38] By 1830, it was able to report that its work among the inmates of Sligo gaol had effected "moral regeneration" in these "most abandoned and worthless creatures," and that

> in those districts where the Scriptures have been circulated, a moral reformation has been observed among the lower orders of Society, drunkenness is by no means as prevalent as formerly, and a greater respect is paid to the Sabbath than before the introduction of the Scriptures.[39]

It is clear that missionaries in foreign lands hoped for a similar sociocultural impact. Writing in 1821 from a fledgling mission zone in the Red River area of Hudson's Bay, the CMS missionary Rev. John West likened the Indigenous people to "the wretched gypsies in England" and believed it necessary to remove children "from an idle and wandering mode of life" in which they were "prejudiced in their ignorance and barbarous habits."[40] Twenty years later, Rev. J. Smithurst, CMS missionary in this region, delighted in the "adoption of the habits of civilized life" evident at a convert wedding, where everyone was

> dressed in the costume of dear Old England . . . Had Mr. West been at the Indian Church this morning, and seen a fine-looking young man of twenty-seven, dressed in an English blue frockcoat, dark cloth trowsers [sic], handsome waistcoat, and a silk handkerchief neatly tied about his neck, he would hardly have recognised the naked, oily little urchin put into his canoe, at York by Withaweecapo [child's father] more than twenty years ago.[41]

Supporters of parish-based societies in Ireland, although belonging to local auxiliaries organized on a county or diocesan basis, were ultimately part of national or transnational organizations which came together once a year, at well-attended Easter meetings. The first annual meeting of the HBS in Dublin's Rotundo attracted an audience of over 3,000 ladies and gentlemen in April 1815.[42] In subsequent years, the HBS arranged its annual meetings for the second last Thursday in April, with HCMS annual

---

38. Sligo HBS, Report for 1829 (handwritten), in Sligo Minute Book, MS 212/1 (RCBL).
39. HBS, *Annual Report* (1819), 13; ibid. (1820), 27.
40. HCMS, *Annual Report* (1823), 64.
41. *Church Missionary Gleaner* (1842), 10.
42. *Freeman's Journal* (21 Apr. 1815), 3.

meetings scheduled for the following day.[43] The clustering of annual meetings facilitated social interaction between persons espousing similar objectives. For instance, the meetings of the Irish Society, London Missionary Society, Society for Promoting Christianity among the Jews, Sunday School Society, Hibernian Bible Society, Church Missionary Society, and Church Education Society were scheduled to be held in Dublin in April 1846.[44]

HOME AND ABROAD

Promotional material published by Bible societies forged connections between mission work at home and abroad. The 1815 report of the HBS first outlined Protestant missionary work in Iceland, Jamaica, Cepholonia, Lithuania, Podolsk, St. Petersburg, Massachusetts, Buenos Aires, Louisiana, Calcutta, and Persia, and then informed readers of the expansion of the HBS in Ireland, including the establishment of the County Sligo branch the previous year. The monthly *Christian Examiner* provided information on foreign and domestic missionary advances. Its issue of July 1825 reported on meetings of Bible societies in Wexford, Enniscorthy, New Ross, Waterford, Athy, and Maryborough, told that HBS had been represented by two persons at the annual meeting of the BFBS in London, and described the conversion of the formerly Catholic village of Gallneukirchen in Austria to Protestantism. Success in this location validated the methodologies employed by Bible societies in Ireland, as Gallneukirchen's inhabitants "were convinced, by reading the Scriptures, of the errors of their church, and a very visible change was wrought in their habits."[45] The next issue of the *Christian Examiner* outlined Protestant advances in Italy, told that monasteries and convents had been suppressed by government order in Paraguay and, on the home front, provided details of a controversial episode involving the Carlow Auxiliary Bible Society, gave an update on the activities of the Sunday School Society, and related that a Rev. Hannan, formerly a Roman Catholic priest, had conformed to the established church in St. Stephen's Church Dublin the previous month.[46]

Just as Irish publications told of advances against Romanism in Ireland and abroad, together with reports of mission work in foreign lands, overseas periodicals juxtaposed the Bible campaign in Ireland with accounts of

---

43. HCMS, *Annual Report* (1819), front page and included on subsequent HCMS annual reports.
44. *Belfast News-Letter* (24 Mar. 1848).
45. *Christian Examiner* (Jul. 1825), 33, 70–71.
46. *Christian Examiner* (Aug. 1825), 239–44.

missionary advances in un-Christianized and Roman Catholic countries. The *American Monthly Magazine* of September 1817 reported on the tenth anniversary meeting of the BFBS held in London, at which Dr. Thorpe, secretary to the HBS, told of progress in Ireland. Dr. Thorpe's presentation was supplemented by accounts of Protestant advances in Scotland, in New York, and in Savannah. Alongside this report were accounts of missionary successes in Ceylon, Bombay, West Indies, Russia, and throughout the North American continent.[47] *The Spirit of Missions,* published under the auspices of the Episcopal Church of America, provided regular updates on the operations of the CMS; and, as part of a lengthy overview of the operations of BFBS throughout the globe, it informed readers that 33,500 bibles and 47,000 testaments had been distributed among the Irish in North America.[48]

Irish persons engaged in mission work, whether to foreign "heathens" or to Roman Catholics at home were thereby encouraged to see themselves as part of a worldwide crusade; this created an "imagined community" of activists by connecting fundraisers and mission agents across miles of terrain, and even across miles of ocean. The formation of this global network bolstered the conviction and determination of Protestant-born supporters of Irish Bible societies, and also Ireland's convert communities who identified with fellow converts in other jurisdictions, as when the Irish Society's convert-teachers identified with the *Deutschkatholisch* reform movement in Germany,[49] rejoicing that over 100,000 persons had deserted the Church of Rome and hoping that "What a living 'Rongé' has effected in Germany, the immortal 'Bedell' may yet effect in Ireland."[50]

CONCLUSION

Locally based parish auxiliaries were designed to function as part of a church-based associational culture, creating and maintaining relationships between parishioners, and between parishioners and diocesan/national/transnational parent bodies. By internalizing attitudes contained in the speeches and printed output of biblical societies, supporters were secured in their convictions and were made part of a global network, thereby ensuring

47. *American Monthly and Critical Review* (Sept. 1817), 384–85.

48. *The Spirit of Missions* (Jan. 1840), 26–28; ibid. (Mar. 1840), 93.

49. In 1845, Johannes Ronge, an excommunicated Roman Catholic priest who founded the *Deutschkatholisch* (General Christian) Church, was hailed in the Protestant press as the "Reformer of the nineteenth century." Weir, *Secularism and Religion,* 39–54.

50. Mason, *History of the Origin,* 110. Bishop Bedell of Kilmore produced the first Irish-language Bible in the seventeenth century.

that however far they might travel, they were likely to find a ready-made group of like-minded persons. By setting theological and ideological criteria for entry to these church-based groupings, missionary societies were positioned to provide and control social interactions which helped to keep members secure in the rightfulness of their objectives and to ensure such attitudes were transmitted from generation to generation.

By depicting mission work at home and abroad as two sides of the same coin, Irish Bible societies were able to build upon the vast extent of the nineteenth-century Protestant missionary endeavor. They fostered in their supporters a sense of belonging to a worldwide movement which was actively playing its part in combatting the dual forces of Romish error and heathen ignorance; and, by regularly outlining the urgent necessity for mission, these organisations nurtured the conviction that Protestantism and even Anglicanism were under threat. This sense of foreboding was particularly strong among Irish Protestants in the early nineteenth century, and the movement of numerous Irish evangelicals to the North American continent brought a particularly virulent form of anti-Catholic Protestantism to the New World as these migrants, preconditioned by their religious, political, and cultural home environment, sought to promote strong resistance to the development of any Roman-style influences within their own denomination, associated with the growing numbers of Catholics who crossed the Atlantic.[51] In some host communities such as Canada, this contributed to the development and persistence of a strong anti-Catholic socio-political culture which was firmly established prior to the arrival of the large numbers of Catholic Famine emigrants at the midpoint of the century.[52]

BIBLIOGRAPHY

American Monthly and Critical Review. New York: Kirk and Mercein, 1817.
Ballina Impartial. Ballina, Ireland: Gillmore, 1823–35.
Bebbington, David W. *Evangelicalism in Modern Britain: A History from the 1730s to the 1980s.* London: Routledge, 2002.
Blackstock, Allan. *Loyalism in Ireland, 1789–1829.* Woodbridge, UK: Boydell, 2007.
Brown, Stewart J. *Providence and Empire, Religion and Society in Britain, 1815–1914.* Harlow, UK: Pearson Longman, 2008.
Canton, William. *A History of the British and Foreign Bible Society.* 2 vols. London: 1904.
Christian Examiner and Church of Ireland Magazine. Dublin: Curry, 1825.
Church Missionary Gleaner. London: Watts, 1842.

---

51. Katerberg, *Modernity and the Dilemma*, 25.
52. Smyth, *Toronto, the Belfast of Canada*, 5.

Copland, Ian. "Christianity as an Arm of Empire: The Ambiguous Case of India under the Company, c.1813–1858." *Historical Journal* 49.4 (Dec 2006) 1025–54.

Davidoff, Leonore, and Catherine Hall. *Family Fortunes: Men and Women of the English Middle Class, 1780–1850*. London: Hutchinson, 1987.

Freeman's Journal. Dublin: Freeman's, 1806–1900.

HBS. *The Fourteenth Report of the Hibernian Bible Society, 1820*. Dublin: Goodwin, 1820.

———. *Reports of the Hibernian Bible Society from its Commencement in the Year 1806 to 1817, Inclusive*. Dublin: Goodwin, 1818.

———. *Report of the Managing Committee of the Sligo Branch of the Hibernian Bible Society for the Year Ended 5th January 1816*. Sligo, Ireland: Alex Bolton, 1816.

———. *The Thirteenth Report of the Hibernian Bible Society, 1819*. Dublin: Goodwin, 1819.

HCMS, *Annual Report, 1814*. Dublin: Jones, 1814.

———. *Annual Report, 1819*. Dublin: Goodwin, 1819

———. *Annual Report, 1821*. Dublin: Graisberry, 1821.

———. *Annual Report, 1823*. Dublin: Goodwin, 1823.

———. *The Fifth Report of the Committee of the Hibernian Church Missionary Society*. Dublin: Goodwin, 1819.

———. *The Ninth Report of the Committee of the Hibernian Church Missionary Society*. Dublin: Goodwin, 1823.

Hibernian Sunday School Society. *Annual Report*. [S.l.]: HSSS, 1818.

Hill, Jacqueline R. "The Church of Ireland and Irish Church History c.1790–1869." In *Ireland's Polemical Past. Views of Irish History in Honour of R. V. Comerford*, edited by T. Dooley, 9–31. Dublin: University College Dublin Press, 2010.

Katerberg, William H. *Modernity and the Dilemma of North American Anglican Identities, 1880–1950*. Montreal: McGill-Queen's University Press, 2001.

Maguire, Martin. "The Church of Ireland Parochial Associations: A Social and Cultural Analysis." In *Confraternities and Sodalities in Ireland: Charity, Devotion and Sociability*, edited by Colm Lennon, 97–109. Dublin: Columba, 2012.

Mason, Henry Monck. *History of the Origin and Progress of the Irish Society*. Dublin: Goodwin, 1844.

Motherwell, Maiben Cunningham. *A Memoir of the Late Albert Blest*. Dublin: William Curry, 1843.

Smyth, William J. *Toronto, the Belfast of Canada: The Orange Order and the Shaping of Municipal Culture*. Toronto: University of Toronto Press, 2015.

The Spirit of Missions. New York: Dana, 1840.

Weir, Todd H., *Secularism and Religion in Nineteenth-Century Germany*. New York: Cambridge University Press, 2014.

Whelan, Irene. "The Bible Gentry: Evangelical Religion, Aristocracy and the New Moral Order in the Early Nineteenth Century." In *Protestant Millennialism, Evangelicalism and Irish Society, 1790–2005*, edited by Crawford Gribben and Andrew E. Holmes, 52–82. Basingstoke, UK: Palgrave MacMillan, 2006.

———. *The Bible War in Ireland: The "Second Reformation" and the Polarization of Protestant-Catholic Relations, 1800–1840*. Dublin: Lilliput, 2005.

Wolffe, John. "Evangelicalism in Mid-Nineteenth-Century England." In *Patriotism, the Making and Unmaking of British National Identity*, edited by R. Samuel, 194–95. New York: Routledge, 1989.

8

"That Ultra-Protestant Nursery"[1]
Trinity College, Dublin, and the Supply of Anglican Clergy to England, 1830s–1880s

ANN MCCORMACK

IN ENGLISH PARISHES THROUGHOUT the nineteenth century, there was a significant presence of Anglican clergymen who had been educated at Trinity College, Dublin (TCD). As the empire expanded, Trinity fulfilled the demand for educated men who could take up management positions in military or civilian life, on the railways, or in the civil service. Closer to home, a significant number of Trinity men gained distinction—or notoriety—as Church of England ministers, though of course many will have blended in seamlessly, attracting little attention. Unprecedented urban growth prompted demand for the subdivision of parishes, additional churches, and therefore more clergy. This need was served by a steady stream of Irish-trained clergy. Alan Haig noted that one in five of the clergy in the Northern Province of York came from universities other than Oxford and Cambridge and, of that one in five, the majority were from TCD.[2]

---

1. *Rochdale Observer* (20 Dec. 1916), obituary Rev. R. S. Rowan; see note 55 below. I am grateful to Rev. William Jacob for helpfulness on aspects of London parishes, on clarifying theological nuances, and for comments on earlier drafts.

2. Haig, *The Victorian Clergy*, 119.

FORMATIVE INFLUENCES

Generations of Church of England clergy, therefore, had come under a unique combination of Irish influences. These included the rather particular social, political, and religious circumstances in Ireland. The security and confidence of the minority Church of Ireland was threatened by a series of legislative reforms. The Act of Union (1801) marginalized Ireland politically, Catholic Emancipation (1829) permitted Catholics to enter public life, and the Church Temporalities Act (1833) reduced the number and power of Irish bishops. Economic decline, local famines, and tithe wars (1831–1836) contributed to social destabilization. Parliament and other institutions were no longer the bastion of Anglicanism, as Catholics and Nonconformists now sat in the House of Commons. At home, the Church of Ireland was regarded with contempt by the majority Catholic population. As Donald Akenson has defined it, not only was it a tool of the state, it was a tool of the English state; it had in previous centuries engaged in attempts to limit the religious freedom and economic prosperity of Catholics; and it was identified with the despised Irish landlord class.[3] Domestically, Irish Anglicans felt besieged and betrayed politically by the Tories, and experienced further alienation by the election of a Whig government in 1832.

Within Trinity, some tutors had high church or moderate evangelical leanings. There was, however, a strong legacy of the Evangelical Revival. This passion was augmented by the hoped-for "Second Reformation in Ireland" and by a level of Orange activism.[4] Various reforming measures gradually improved academic standards. The key individuals involved were Charles R. Elrington (1787–1850)[5] as professor of Divinity (1829–1850) and Bartholomew Lloyd (1772–1837),[6] provost (1831–1839). Trinity was one of the first institutions to introduce a divinity testimonium. The admission of non-resident students also attracted clerical candidates from across Britain and Ireland. Another figure who had a strong influence on students was Joseph Singer (1786–1866). A fellow since 1811 and a leading evangelical, he succeeded the more moderate Elrington as Regius Professor of Divinity (1850–1862).[7] This atmosphere created an earnest sense of personal respon-

3. Akenson, *Church of Ireland*, 5.

4. Luce, *Trinity College, Dublin*, 65.

5. Blacker, "Charles Richard Elrington (1787–1850)." For claims that he was isolated in the evangelical environment, and derided as "high and dry," see McDowell and Webb, *Trinity College, Dublin*, 192.

6. Hamilton, "Lloyd, Bartholomew (1772–1837)."

7. Carlyle, "Joseph Henderson Singer (1786–1866)"; McDowell and Webb, *Trinity College, Dublin*, 192.

sibility for the salvation of lost souls, bringing them into the fold of true religion, an ambition that was considered both urgent and achievable. David Hempton has remarked that "it is striking to note the number of prophetical writers who were educated at TCD or who had strong Irish links."[8] McDowell and Webb also note the strong evangelical ethos at Trinity: "[Along] with deep and wide-ranging scholarship there existed an extraordinarily intense conviction that the narrowly defined path of the evangelical to salvation was the only one."[9] They also note that, on average, 115 Trinity men each year—approximately one-third of all BAs—were intended for ordination, a number which could not be absorbed into the minority Irish church.[10]

A major concern at Trinity was the constant prospect of English interference—a fear realized in 1831 when the Whig Prime Minister, Earl Grey, nominated the English-born, Oriel-educated Richard Whately (1787–1863) as archbishop of Dublin. He was the arch-representative of the planted English bishop in the Irish church. He quickly became unpopular in the Church of Ireland, showing "genuine amazement that the Irish do not at once imitate whatever is the latest reform to have been adopted in England."[11] Whately commented on a fellowship examination at Trinity: "It is very strange to us Oxford men, and, we should think very absurd, being in Latin, all oral, and all the candidates together, jostling each other."[12] Trinity was sensitive to outside criticism, believing itself to be equal, if not superior, to other institutions. They regarded Oxford and Cambridge as academically lax and incapable of providing good clerical training. The Church of Ireland evangelical tradition was distinct within Anglican evangelicalism in that it emphasized the importance of apostolic succession. The catholic and apostolic identity of Irish Anglicanism, they believed, made the Church of Ireland the true catholic church in Ireland, and rightful successor of St. Patrick.

In this period of political and religious turbulence, many English parishes were served by men who were Irish-born, Irish-educated, or who may have married into Irish Anglican—often ecclesiastical—families. Their theological and political outlook was, inevitably, shaped by Irish opinions and Irish events. Although Trinity men were represented amongst deans, college principals, canons, and chaplains to the aristocracy, they were not

8. Hempton, "Evangelicalism and Eschatology," 179–94; Hempton and Hill, *Evangelical Protestantism in Ulster Society*, 15; Whelan, *The Bible War in Ireland*, 19, 57.

9. McDowell and Webb, *Trinity College, Dublin*, 150–51.

10. Ibid., 138, 149–50.

11. Ibid., 127–28.

12. Quoted in McDowell and Webb, *Trinity College, Dublin*, 127–28; Maxwell, *History of Trinity College, Dublin*, 194. Until 1853 fellowship exams were in Latin and viva voce.

particularly prominent in the upper tiers of the Church of England. There was one bishop, William Connor Magee (1821–1891),[13] Bishop of Peterborough (1868–1891) and, briefly, archbishop of York (1891). Of the deans, Hugh McNeile (1795–1879, BA 1842), dean of Ripon (1868–1875),[14] was the best known. Both were appointed as Disraeli tried to shore up evangelical support. Other Trinity deans included two Irish-born evangelicals, Archibald Boyd (1803–1883, BA 1823), dean of Exeter (1867–1883),[15] and William Lefroy (1836–1909), dean of Norwich (1889–1909).[16] Irish-trained clergy were, however, an identifiable force in English public life.

LANCASHIRE, LIVERPOOL, AND HUGH MCNEILE

The Church of England was perceived to be under threat from Nonconformists, delinquent Anglicans, Tractarians, and particularly Roman Catholics. Protestantism, they claimed, was the reason that England was blessed. Catholicism was regarded as a threat to family values, political stability, and religious orthodoxy. Anglican clergy could present a formidable political power. It has been long recognised that the Anglican Church had an extreme wing in Liverpool, dominated by a prominent cohort of Irish, TCD evangelical clergy, and allied with the Tories. Radical and energetic on the pastoral front, they also demonstrated political strength. Between 1840 and 1880, over a hundred Dublin-educated clergymen were listed as active in Liverpool and Birkenhead.[17] At least forty-five parishes in the wider Liverpool district had Irish or Irish-trained incumbents. Some parishes had two or more Irish clergymen serving simultaneously, or had a succession of Irish clergy. Occasionally, the sons of Irish incumbents succeeded their fathers, establishing small pockets of Irish ecclesiastical dynasties. Owen Chadwick remarked that Trinity College, Dublin, gave more of its graduates to Lancashire than to other areas of England.[18] Theological affinity with John Bird Sumner (1780–1862), the evangelical Bishop of Chester (1828–1848),[19] was an important influence, and the fact that Irish clergy "provided the only means of filling the complement of unbeneficed staff in

---

13. Macdonnell, "William Connor Magee (1821–1891)."
14. Wolffe, "McNeile, Hugh Boyd (1795–1879)."
15. Boase, "Boyd, Archibald (1803–1883)."
16. Wellings, "Lefroy, William (1836–1909)."
17. Based on the author's analysis of entries in *Crockford's Clerical Directories 1878*.
18. Chadwick, *Victorian Church, Part II*, 250.
19. Sumner was considered to be a strong but moderate evangelical, not Recordite or premillennial in view. Scotland, "Sumner, John Bird (1780–1862)."

unpleasant industrial parishes."[20] Sumner's mindset was made clear when, as archbishop of Canterbury (1848–1862), he commented on "the constant immigration from Ireland of men who have imbibed superstition from the cradle." He pleaded for a special mission to "the godless English poor of the towns exposed to Celtic proletarian Jesuits."[21] Trinity clergy undertook a varied workload. They were notably active in several evangelical missionary societies, with either local or international focus, including the CMS and the CPAS,[22] supporting their causes through preaching, fundraising, and administrative services. A myriad of parish schools, Sunday schools, and adult education classes were initiated by Irish incumbents. Irishmen were tutors at the teacher-training facility, Liverpool College, and at St. Aidan's Theological College, Birkenhead, one of the first Anglican theological colleges.[23]

Philip Waller has noted the involvement of Irish Anglican clergy in political activities in Liverpool and the importance of the Tory-Anglican connection in local government.[24] An anti-Catholic card was often played, with the collusion of some Irish clerics, to defeat Liberal reforms. A major force in this movement was Hugh McNeile, dubbed the "real creator" of Liverpool Conservatism.[25] Between 1826 and 1830, McNeile was the moderator of the Albury conferences, hosted by Henry Drummond, M.P. (1786–1860).[26] Greatly influenced by premillennialist Edward Irving (1792–1834),[27] they were much concerned with the conversion of Catholics and Jews. He became well known nationally for his oratorical powers, his evangelical stance, and his willingness to challenge opponents in public debate and to meddle

---

20. Ward, *Religion and Society in England*, 221.

21. Sumner, *Charge to the Archdeacons and Clergy of the Diocese of Canterbury*, (1849), quoted in Sheridan Gilley, 'Protestant London: No Popery and the Irish Poor 2 (1850–60), *Recusant History*, 11, 1971–2, 23.

22. The Church Missionary Society (1799) was founded by leaders of the Clapham Sect. The Church Pastoral Aid Society (1836) raised funds to provide stipends for clergy in areas of great need, such as new parishes which had not yet been endowed by the Ecclesiastical Commission, or to provide extra curates to assist in populous districts: CPAS, "History," n.p.

23. See Heiser, *The Story of St. Aidan's College*. Heiser was principal from 1929 until at least 1947: Dowland, *Nineteenth-Century Anglican Theological Training*, 103.

24. Waller, *Democracy and Sectarianism*, 11. For broader discussion of the Tory-Anglican relationship, see McLeod, *Religion and Society in England*, 86–87, 93–94, 96–99..

25. Waller, *Democracy and Sectarianism*, 11.

26. Flegg, "Drummond, Henry (1786–1860)."

27. Brown, "Irving, Edward (1792–1834)."

in local politics.[28] He published numerous sermons, lectures, and theological papers. In 1835, only a year after his arrival in Liverpool, McNeile led a successful campaign to defeat the attempt of Liverpool Corporation to set up a non-sectarian system of education, dubbed "the Irish system," designed to benefit poor children, both Catholic and Protestant.[29] Through organizations such as the Protestant Operatives Association[30] and the Orange lodges, anti-Catholic, anti-Liberal, and anti-reform sentiments were aggravated amongst the Protestant working classes, further galvanizing sectarian attitudes. Frank Neal noted that,

> Central to the success of this campaign were the efforts of McNeile and a group of fellow Irish clergy who put their time, church pulpits and school halls at the disposal of the Tories, which, combined with their fanaticism, overwhelmed the Liberals.[31]

The parishes of St. Bride's and St. John's Liverpool and St. Mary's and Holy Trinity Birkenhead were run by a succession of Irish evangelicals who gained notoriety for their staunch anti-Catholic rhetoric, but also respect for their energetic devotion to pastoral duties. Prominent figures include William Marcus Falloon (1814–1891, BA 1837), a native of Co. Antrim. His preaching talent brought him to the attention of McNeile, who invited him to become his curate at St. Jude's, Liverpool. It was said of him that "nature had bestowed upon him many excellent gifts," and he was not "destined to hide his light in this obscure corner [of Antrim]."[32] Falloon demonstrated the distinctive nature of Irish evangelical belief when he reiterated that the Established Church was "catholic as regards truth, evangelical as regards doctrine, apostolic as regards order and protestant as regards error."[33] Richard Paul Blakeney (1820–1884, BA 1842), together with Falloon, co-founded the Church Association, to combat ritualism. Blakeney was an evangelical polemicist who had wide influence in bringing legal challenges against Anglo-Catholic clergy. He had a deep hatred of Roman Catholicism, claiming that his wife was "torn from me by the demonical machinations of Popery."[34]

28. Bullock, *Hugh McNeile and the Reformation Truth*, 21.
29. Murphy, *Religious Problem in English Education*, 50–56.
30. Protestant Operative Association (1838), formed by McNeile.
31. Neal, *Sectarian Violence*, 48. There were numerous Irish or TCD graduates in McNeile's circle.
32. Falloon, *Memoir of William Marcus Falloon*, 8.
33. Ibid., 55.
34. Wolffe, "Blakeney, Richard Paul (1820–1884)."

JOSEPH BAYLEE AND OTHERS

Some veterans of the proselytizing campaigns to Irish Catholics progressed to ordination and on to careers in the Church of England. Joseph Baylee (1808–1883, BA 1834), is one such example, though not a typical one.[35] Born to a Quaker family in Co. Limerick and taught by Elrington, he underwent conversion at Trinity and felt a personal calling "to preach the Gospel to every creature."[36] Under the influence of Edward Nangle (1800–1883), he embarked on a combative career as a Bible Reader at the Achill mission.[37] His controversial reputation preceded him to Birkenhead, thanks to the efforts of his Irish Catholic adversaries.[38] He was alleged to have used such confrontational tactics as stopping priests on the road, or forcing entry to a priest's house, to engage in theological argument.[39]

In Birkenhead, he conceived the idea of founding a theological college in response to the shortage of trained clergy. He gathered the support of powerful evangelicals, English and Irish, lay and clerical, and began theological classes at his home in 1846. Baylee's erratic style of management, fiscal ineptitude, and nepotism led to his forced resignation as principal in 1859. He was distracted by every possible public controversy, travelling to speaking engagements and challenging opponents to public debate. He is notoriously regarded as the catalyst for the Garibaldi riots (1862).[40] He had advertised a meeting in support of Garibaldi, reportedly by displaying orange placards inscribed "Sympathy with Garibaldi" outside his church and school. In a city with a tradition of violent clashes between Catholics and Orangemen, the outcome was hardly surprising.[41] Irishmen stoned the church and school. The proceedings were cancelled but subsequently went ahead with the protection of special volunteer Orange constables and a thousand police.[42] In Sheridan Gilley's words, the principal was "a Reformation Bulwark at the heart of a tangle of narrow streets [now] occupied by

---

35. Cooper, "Baylee, Joseph Tyrrell (1808–83)."

36. Friends Historical Library, Dublin, portfolio 36a, 7. Letter to Society of Friends, 18 May 1830.

37. Branach, "Edward Nangle, and the Achill Island Mission" 35–38; McDonald, *Achill Island, Archaeology, History, Folklore.*

38. These included John McHale (1791–1881), Roman Catholic Archbishop of Tuam: *Freeman's Journal* (22 May 1841), 2.

39. *Freeman's Journal* (9 Aug. 1838), 3.

40. Gilley, "Garibaldi Riots of 1862," 697–732.

41. Dowland, *Nineteenth-Century Anglican Theological Training,* 64.

42. Roman Catholic priests, magistrates, and Baylee's son, John Tyrrell, had tried to prevent violence. Fourteen policemen were sent to the hospital and, of the estimated 300 rioters, eleven were arrested, including two women.

some five thousand Irish dock labourers and their families."[43] McNeile, Falloon, and Baylee were supportive of the Orange Order, but one TCD cleric who opposed it was Philip Hains,[44] who found himself its victim. "An ardent supporter of Liberal reforms," and accused of desiring "the destruction of the Established Church in Ireland," he was severely beaten by an Orange mob, while he accused the police of being members of the Orange Order.[45]

Another less conventional clergyman was Richard Hobson (1831–1914), who served in various parishes in Liverpool and Birkenhead. Although he attended classes at TCD, he did not graduate. He deserves inclusion here, however, because he represents so much of the TCD, Irish, and evangelical legacy in Liverpool. From a poor Protestant background, his family were adversely affected by the Irish famine of the 1840s. Self-educated—he paid for tutors when he could—he led the Louth Mission, attended St. Aidan's College, and was taught by Baylee. A strong proponent of lay involvement, he declared that "to prevent there being drones in the church hive, the pastor shall not do work which might be done by others,"[46] and lamenting:

> Often, I have wished that our bishops would follow the example of their Canadian brethren, by licensing suitably qualified laymen to read ... the service ... I do not see how all the work of the church is to be done. On my resignation, I left over 50 men fit and ready to lead in prayer ... some far more competent than many young curates ... the training of candidates for ordination in our church is lamentably deficient.[47]

Also concerned with education provision and the extreme levels of poverty in Liverpool, Abraham Hume (1814–1884, BA 1843), assisted by St. Aidan's students, undertook pioneering statistical surveys to ascertain the living conditions of Liverpool poor.[48] He proposed a revised administrative

---

43. Gilley, "Garibaldi Riots of 1862," 720–22.

44. Philip Frost John Bird Hains b. 1828 Jersey; *Crockford's Clerical Directory 1897*, 894, states he attended Birkenhead (St. Aidan's) and TCD, but gives no information on degree. He does not appear in *Alumni Dublinenses*, www.http://digitalcollections.tcd.ie.

45. *Pall Mall Gazette* (28 Nov. 1868) and *Liverpool Mercury* (5 Dec. 1868, 2 Aug. 1969). For McNeile and the Orange Order, see Murphy, *Religious Problem in English Education*, 50.

46. Hobson, *What Hath God Wrought*, 56, 70.

47. Ibid., 70.

48. Sutton, "Hume, Abraham (1814–1884)"; Hume, *Condition of Liverpool, Religious and Social*. A friend and correspondent of Gladstone, they were both members of the Historic Society of Lancashire and Cheshire. See also Murphy, *Religious Problem in English Education*, 266–67.

system for distribution of charitable donations, claiming "the bounty rarely reaches the class of persons for whose benefit it was especially given."⁴⁹

RITUALIST CONTROVERSIES

Despite its evangelical reputation, there was a high church faction at Trinity—J. H. Todd (1805-1869), elected fellow in 1831, being a popular advocate.⁵⁰ While the Oxford Movement did not receive support in Ireland, Trinity-educated clergy were to be found at the heart of the ritualist controversies in England. Of George Herring's list of 686 Tractarian clergy between 1840 and 1879, forty-seven were educated at TCD, five of whom converted to Roman Catholicism.⁵¹ Improbably, even in Protestant Lancashire, twelve TCD graduates listed by Herring as Tractarians served at some point in Cheshire or Lancashire under evangelical bishops of Chester and Manchester. The founder and first chairman of the English Church Union branch in Rochdale, Robert S. Rowan (1828-1916, BA 1846), was for forty years the vicar of St. James's, Wardleworth. On his death, the *Rochdale Observer* remarked, "he was a graduate of Trinity College, Dublin, and it is the more surprising, therefore, that in theological matters, Mr. Rowan, in mature life, displayed High Church sympathies."⁵² An advanced Trinity ritualist was Richard William Enraght (1837-1898, BA 1859), vicar of Holy Trinity, Bordesley, Birmingham, and member of the extreme ritualist Society of the Holy Cross. An aggressive case was brought against him by the Church Association, and he was imprisoned in Warwick in 1879. While Bishop Philpott of Worcester permitted the prosecution, Nigel Yates suggests that Philpott tried to be as supportive as possible to the unapologetic Enraght.⁵³

Two clerical friends of Enraght in nearby Bordesley were brothers James and Thomas Pollock. J. S. Pollock was appointed curate of St. Alban the Martyr in 1865 and elected to the Society of the Holy Cross.⁵⁴ Despite

49. Hume, *Condition of Liverpool, Religious and Social*, 23.

50. Todd, "Todd, James Henthorn (1805-1869)."

51. Herring, *Oxford Movement in Practice*, 251-352.

52. *The Rochdale Observer* (23 Dec. 1916). R. S. Rowan, born Co. Down, was the son of Hill Wilson Rowan, Hillsborough.

53. Yates, *Anglican Ritualism in Victorian Britain*, 259-62. Richard William Enraght, the son of Matthew Enraght, was curate of Moneymore, Ireland (TCD, BA 1859; MA 1861); curate Corsham, Wilts., 1861-1864; Sheffield 1864-68; St. Paul, Brighton, 1869-72; curate in charge Portslade-by-Sea 1872-74; vicar Holy Trinity, Bordesley 1874.

54. The Pollocks do not appear in *Alumni Dublinenses*, although it is widely written

their dedicated pastoral work, their church services courted controversy. The evangelical Simeon Trustees, patrons of the parish, objected to their "false teaching." The mission was publicly denounced and months of rioting ensued. Public controversy loomed again for the Pollocks in 1867 in an alleged case of excommunication of Letitia Jane Taylor. This brought forth claims of "unmitigated Romanism" and appeals to Bishop Philpott to reverse the sentence and sanction James Pollock. Although Philpott said that Pollock was "worthy of some reproof" and reprimanded him, critics were not satisfied, one declaring that Pollock "did not seem to be swallowed up with overmuch sorrow."[55] At a hostile public meeting, in a speech littered with anti-Irish remarks, the Protestant laity were urged to take the matter up. The speaker threatened, "If I were a man of Irish temperament, I should have knocked his altar about for him." While ostensibly not advocating violence, the speaker declared it his Christian duty to defend the Protestant cause to the death, "with rifle or a six-barreled revolver." The Pollocks were not Irish but Manx.[56] J. S. Pollock subsequently published a lecture defending his Anglo-Catholic position, claiming that the Tractarians who converted to Rome were people like Newman who had originally been evangelicals.[57] He was instrumental in providing a new church in 1871, and a report in *Church Bells* noted that after twenty-five years, the Pollocks had achieved four churches with space for 2,200 worshipers, free pews, and the largest day schools in Birmingham not under the control of school boards.[58]

LONDON TRACTARIANS

Eleven TCD graduates noted as "Tractarians" served at some time in the London area. One of the most prominent was Richard Carr Kirkpatrick (1823–1916; BA 1846),[59] who resigned as curate of St. Mary's, Kilburn, in 1867 when the new vicar was unsympathetic to his extreme liturgical practices. He secured permission from the Bishop of London to start a mission in the parish, which was an area of significant Irish settlement. He commissioned J. L. Pearson (1817–1897)[60] to design a church, St. Augustine's, Kil-

---

that they were Trinity graduates. James Samuel Pollock (1858) and Thomas Benson Pollock (1859) are the TCD dates given in *Crockford's 1878*.

55. *Oxford Chronicle and Reading Gazette* (21 Dec. 1867), 8.
56. *Birmingham Daily Gazetteer* (15 Oct. 1867), 3. The speaker was Mr. T. H. Aston.
57. Pollock, *Romanizing*, 18–19. See Reed, *Glorious Battle*, 305.
58. *Dublin Daily Express* (4 Jul. 1891), 2.
59. He was the son of a County Kildare landowner, William Kirkpatrick of Donaghcumper, Celbridge.
60. Waterhouse, "Pearson, John Loughborough (1817–97)."

burn, which remains one of the finest examples of Victorian gothic revival, with soaring vaults and elaborate decoration.[61] Kirkpatrick had six curates and, controversially, two women's religious communities in the parish.[62] He was an active member of the English Church Union and the Society of the Holy Cross, and a leading opponent of the Deceased Wife's Sister Bill, claiming it would "go far towards disestablishment, and that would lead to much graver results; it would lose the bands of society and the throne would not stand much longer."[63] At a meeting of the Kilburn branch of the Church of England Working Men's Society, he threatened to "turn out" any member of his Bible class who voted for any politician who supported the bill.[64]

Following the Public Worship Act (1874), he took up the cause of Anglican clergy prosecuted for ritualist practices, especially the Rev. James Bell-Cox of Liverpool, who was prosecuted for eleven charges of ritualism but refused to cease his activities and to recognize the right of a secular court to pronounce on religious matters.[65] Kirkpatrick called for "a renewal of more vigorous efforts on the part of . . . the Church for the free exercise of her right to decide . . . for herself in spiritual causes," demanding "an increase in the Episcopate and the restoration of true Diocesan Synods."[66]

Soho, Seven Dials, and St. Giles-in-the-Fields were major areas of Irish settlement. As well as evangelical missions to convert Irish Catholics, there were also Tractarian missions to the Irish, notably at St. Anne's, Soho, where the rector was Nugent Wade (BA 1829), one of Gladstone's "oldest friends."[67] It was said that Wade's highly trained choir and orchestra at St. Anne's influenced St. Paul's Cathedral and Westminster Abbey to introduce music during Passiontide. Charles Ingham Black was a curate there in 1849 (BA 1835).

There was also a mission church, St. Mary's, adjoining Seven Dials, where Walter Atkins (BA 1841) was curate 1854–1856 and Richard Littledale was curate 1857–1861 (1833–1890, BA 1855).[68] Littledale was the chief scholarly exponent of ritualism in the Church of England in the 1860s and 1870s. A critic of the Reformation, he was also a leading defender of An-

61. St. Augustine, Kilburn: http://www.saugustinekilburn.org.uk.
62. The Community of the Sisters of the Church and the Community of St. Peter.
63. *Kilburn Times* (16 Mar. 1883), 5. The meeting was in Hampstead.
64. Ibid. (4 May 1888), 5.
65. Ibid. (12 Feb. 1886), 5.
66. Ibid. (10 Jun. 1887), 6.
67. *The Sketch* (16 Aug. 1893), 53. Wade was incumbent at St. Paul's, Finsbury, 1839–46: Foot and Matthew, *The Gladstone Diaries*, vol. 3, dated 26 May 1847, where Gladstone records attending Nugent's 7:30 a.m. service at St. Anne's, Soho.
68. Herring, "Littledale, Richard Frederick (1833–1890)."

glicanism against Vatican I and the claims of papal infallibility. A prolific writer of pamphlets, he argued in defense of ritualism and further expansion of the ceremonial aspect of Anglican worship. This, he claimed, made conversion to Roman Catholicism both unnecessary and morally dubious.[69]

LONDON EVANGELICALS

Several TCD evangelicals operated in the crowded areas of London, where poor Irish Catholics had settled. John Armstrong (BA 1831), priest-in-charge of St. Paul's, Bermondsey, an Irish speaker, received Bishop C. R. Sumner's permission to officiate in Irish. Together with two agents from the Irish Church Mission they concentrated on recent Irish arrivals, not yet attached to a Catholic chapel. Converts were badly treated by their fellow Irish. Armstrong collaborated with Samuel Garratt (1817–1906),[70] millenarian minister of Holy Trinity, St. Giles-in-the-Fields (1851–1867), to establish the English Church Mission, with the support of *The Record* and Lord Shaftesbury, and the Duke of Manchester and the Earl of Roden, two evangelicals with large Irish estates. In 1855, Armstrong was succeeded in Bermondsey by William Long (BA 1837) who continued open air preaching and employed an Irish convert priest to work among the Irish. He was less able and less enthusiastic, and the work came to an end.[71]

Robert Maguire (1826–1890, BA 1847) had been secretary for ICM in Cork before becoming head of Islington Protestant Institute in 1852, where there were free schools for Irish children; he was described as bigoted and conceited, a gifted orator, who successfully organized two lay missionaries and an operative auxiliary with 300 members. In 1853 Bishop Blomfield granted him a special license to evangelize the Irish. He came into violent conflict with a Catholic parish priest, former Anglican Frederick Oakley (1802–1880), who threatened to excommunicate the Catholics who sent their children to his schools. Joseph Kingsmill (1805/6–1865, BA 1831), chaplain at the newly built Pentonville Prison, was a prominent advocate of the "separate system" for prisons and of pressing for the evangelical conversion of prisoners. He feared the expansion of the Roman Catholic Church and resisted attempts to establish Catholic ministry to prisons, although he

---

69. *Liverpool Daily Post* (22 Aug. 1868), 4.

70. Lewis, *DEB*, sub Garratt, Samuel. Samuel Garratt was English and Cambridge-educated. Shaftesbury was also a supporter of Baylee and St. Aidan's College.

71. Gilley, "Protestant London," 24–27.

permitted access to a Roman Catholic priest if a Catholic prisoner specifically pressed for this.[72]

In 1850, Robert Bickersteth (1816–1884) became honorary secretary of the Irish Church Missions, succeeding his uncle, the founder, Edward Bickersteth (1786–1850). In 1851, he became rector of St. Giles-in-the-Fields and saw the inconsistency of working for the conversion of the Irish in Ireland, while ignoring the Irish in his parish.[73] Both Englishmen, they illustrate the great interest amongst English evangelicals for the conversion of Irish Catholics.

Catholic bishops responded by providing schools, welfare, and self-help societies. The Bishop of Southwark appointed an Irish-speaking priest, Daniel Donovan, to persuade converts to return to Catholicism.[74] Cardinal Wiseman reacted by providing rival services, and Catholic priests publicly denounced Irish families whose children attended Protestant schools. Gilley suggests Protestant conversion tactics were largely unsuccessful, as they divided family and community links.[75] Not all TCD evangelicals were quite so controversial. William Pennefather (1816–1873, BA 1840), who worked in various London parishes, was a committed evangelical who also believed in ecumenism. He was founder of the Mildmay Conference Centre and organizer of the deaconess movement.[76] In many populated areas, however, TCD clerics found themselves continually engaged in campaigns for the conversion of Catholics. For Irish Catholics in England, there was seemingly no escape from the painstaking efforts of people like Richard Hobson:

> I would say here that neither I nor our visitors ever neglected to call at the houses of Romanists . . . It requires great tact, if not even special training, to deal successfully with Romanists. They must not be allowed to feel that we are in any way afraid of them. We ought not to begin by offering tracts, particularly to Irish Romanists, as they have a strong prejudice against them . . . We should make common ground with them, on say, the immortality of the soul, heaven, hell, the Trinity, etc.[77]

---

72. Ibid., 30; Forsythe, "Kingsmill, Joseph (1805/6–65)." See Kingsmill's *On the Idolatry of the Church of Rome*.

73. Gilley, "Protestant London," 22.

74. Ibid., 25. Donovan was convicted of attacking a convert with his umbrella.

75. Ibid., 34.

76. Bebbington, "Pennefather, William (1816–73)."

77. Hobson, *What Hath God Wrought*, 137.

CRITICISM OF THE CHURCH OF ENGLAND

Some TCD clerics were outspoken in their criticism of the Church of England. The austere Hobson complained about the failure of financial provision for the clergy: "There are people who seem to think a clergyman ought to live on air, yet those same individuals look very carefully after their own bread and butter, though they are highly spiritual persons."[78] New parishes were not always immediately financed by the Ecclesiastic Commissioners, and clergy had to be resourceful in cultivating funds. When Falloon moved to the affluent St. Bride's (1851–1871), he utilized resources to help his former parishioners at St. John's parish (1843–1851), sending lay workers there "to sustain and to develop the various parochial agencies formed to win the masses."[79]

Evangelicals blamed poor church attendance on poor preaching. Hobson recorded, "I have always found the masses ready to hear plain speaking . . . they like a minister to hit out straight from the shoulder."[80] He disapproved of the circuit of celebrity preachers, which included McNeile and Baylee, who were invited to grace pulpits and public platforms. Hobson boasted that in his parish "there was no need to bring 'great guns' from afar . . . I am satisfied that . . . if the vicar be not as able to in his own pulpit as a stranger, there is something wrong."[81]

Hume was angered by evidence of class division in the Church of England congregations, which he felt was a factor in keeping the working classes out. The Established Church, he claimed, was built for the rich, not the poor.[82] In a scathing criticism, Hobson wrote, "the ignorance of some of the rich country clergy as to the actual condition of a slum parish is surprising and lamentable."[83] Both evangelicals and Tractarians despised the pew rent system, as it fostered class distinction.

REPUTATION

The distinct Irishness of a clergyman could be either an advantage or hindrance. One admirer of McNeile noted he had the gift of eloquence, such

---

78. Ibid., 62.
79. Falloon, *Memoir of William Marcus Falloon*, 37.
80. Hobson, *What Hath God Wrought*, 74.
81. Ibid., 81.
82. Hume, *Condition of Liverpool, Religious and Social*, 7.
83. Hobson, *What Hath God Wrought*, 106.

that "thousands hung breathlessly to his accents."[84] On the other hand, Hugh Falloon identified what he regarded as a less attractive and anecdotal "Celtic" style, and contrasted this with his father's preaching:

> Never an impassioned style, formed upon the models of Celtic oratory but was more akin to the calm, dignified, convincing eloquence of the Teutonic nations, he was very sparing in the use of anecdote and illustration and was almost deficient in action, seldom doing more that raising his hand now and then.[85]

The impact of English politics on Irish affairs was a concern for the vicar of St. Michael's, Woolwich, Hugh Ryves Baker (1833–1898, BA 1854), "a diligent writer in the correspondence column."[86] Angered that, in his former parish in Devon, where he was still an elector, the "Whigs" had put J. B. Phear as a candidate, Baker demanded that Devonshire men choose a local candidate rather than a "Home Ruler" and "Radical." "As an Irishman and an Ulsterman [I don't wish to see] the loyal Protestant minority in Ireland under the domination of a priesthood which has ever been hostile to the best interests of the Empire."[87]

Both nationality and class were conscious elements in TCD identity. Haig notes that "despite its many distinguished scholars and its solid Divinity teaching, TCD was regarded as providing graduates of lower social standing and lesser cultural attainments than the English universities."[88] TCD's reputation was harmed by allegations that its non-resident degree facilities provided a "back-door" to graduate status for impecunious Englishmen, especially during the first quarter of the century, when student numbers rose exponentially.[89] Until about 1870 TCD provided more graduate clergy than anywhere outside Oxford and Cambridge. St. Aidan's was founded and, during its first twenty-five years, managed by Irish and TCD graduates. Specifically aimed at non-graduate students of limited means, such as Richard Hobson, it was affected by class bias, Baylee constantly having to state that all his students were "gentlemen."

Countless schools and churches were built and led by Trinity clergy, many of whom were active in difficult and unpopular locations. They were adept at harnessing wealthy sponsors and lay helpers. Diligent and caring

---

84. Bullock, *Hugh McNeile and the Reformation Truth*, 15.
85. Falloon, *Memoir of William Marcus Falloon*, 15.
86. *Illustrated London News* (24 Dec. 1898), 11.
87. *Exeter and Plymouth Gazette* (11 Jul. 1892), 3.
88. Haig, *Victorian Clergy*, 123.
89. McDowell and Webb, *Trinity College, Dublin*, 87.

pastoral work could ward off the sanctions of a disapproving bishop and earn maverick clerics loyal grassroots support. When J. E. Sedgwick (BA 1852), curate of St. Alban's, Manchester (1856–1874), was sanctioned by his bishop for ritualist practices, his congregation published a defense, asserting that, "a crowded congregation has been gathered together; a large and beautiful church erected . . . Singlehandedly, he has conducted sixteen services a week in a district which was aforetime almost destitute of the means of grace."[90] Similar tributes were paid to the evangelical clerics in Liverpool.

CONCLUSION

The fact that, in the public mind, several TCD clerics were associated with high-profile polemical controversies can best be understood in the context of turbulent Irish affairs. These clergy were important figures in keeping Irish issues to the fore in English politics, often leading opposition to disestablishment Board schools and any increase in Roman Catholic power. A few were instrumental in stoking sectarianism, especially in districts with poor Irish of either persuasion. Trinity-trained clerics had a demonstrable impact on both religious and social affairs in Victorian England, St. Aidan's Theological College and the Church Association being two defining Irish-led projects. Vacancies in the English church provided opportunities for educated Irishmen with drive and ambition to carve out their own niche. They could embrace professional opportunities not available in Ireland, while helping shore up allegiance to the Established Church. They were a significant and effective workforce, at a time when church infrastructure was overwhelmed by the sheer scale of population increase and there was an acute shortage of trained clergy.

BIBLIOGRAPHY

Akenson, Donald Harman. *The Church of Ireland: Ecclesiastical Reform and Revolution, 1800–1885*. New Haven, CT: Yale University Press, 1971.

Bebbington, David W. "Pennefather, William (1816–1873)." In *DNB* (online edition). Oxford: Oxford University Press, 2009. http://www.oxforddnb.com/view/article/21868.

Blacker, B. H. "Charles Richard Elrington (1787–1850)." In *DNB* (online edition). Oxford: Oxford University Press, 2009. http://www.oxforddnb.com/view/article/8756.

90. *Liverpool Daily Post* (3 Dec. 1868), 9. John Edmund Sedgwick (1829, Preston, Lancs); BA 1852; DD 1874; Priest 1835 Bishop Manchester; curate St. Simon, Salford, 1853–56; St. Alban, Manchester, 1856; Rector Stanford le Hope, Rochdale, 1874.

Boase, G. C. "Boyd, Archibald (1803–1883)." In *DNB* (online edition). Oxford: Oxford University Press, 2009. http://www.oxforddnb.com/view/article/3102.

Branach, Niall R. "Edward Nangle and the Achill Island Mission." *History Ireland* 8.3 (2000) 35–38.

Brown, Stewart J. "Irving, Edward (1792–1834)." In *DNB* (online edition). Oxford: Oxford University Press, 2009. http://www.oxforddnb.com/view/article/14473?docPos=1.

Bullock, Rev. C. *Hugh McNeile and the Reformation Truth: The Characteristics of Romanism and Protestantism.* London: Home Word, 1882.

Burtchaell, George Dames, and Thomas Ulick Sadleir, eds. *Alumni Dublinenses. A Register of the Students, Graduates, Professors and Provosts of Trinity College in the University of Dublin.* London: Norgate, 1924.

Carlyle, E. I. "Joseph Henderson Singer (1786–1866)." In *DNB* (online edition). Oxford: Oxford University Press, 2009. http://www.oxforddnb.com/index/25/101025640/.

Chadwick, Owen. *The Victorian Church, Part II.* London: Black, 1970.

Cooper, Thompson. "Baylee, Joseph Tyrrell (1808–1883)." In *DNB* (online edition). Oxford: Oxford University Press, 2009. http://www.oxforddnb.com/view/article/1747.

CPAS. "History." https://www.cpas.org.uk/about-CPAS/history.

Crockford's Clerical Directory 1878. London: Crockford, 1878.

Crockford's Clerical Directory 1897. London: Crockford, 1897.

Dowland, D. A. *Nineteenth-Century Anglican Theological Training: The Redbrick Challenge.* Oxford: Oxford University Press, 1997.

Falloon, Hugh. *Memoir of William Marcus Falloon, MA, Rector of Ackworth and Honorary Canon of Chester; with Selections of Letters, Sermons and Papers.* Liverpool: J. A. Thompson, 1892.

Flegg, Columba Graham. "Drummond, Henry (1786–1860)." In *DNB* (online edition). Oxford: Oxford University Press, 2009. http://www.oxforddnb.com/view/article/8067.

Foot, M. R. D., and H. C. G. Matthew, eds. *The Gladstone Diaries, vol. 3: 1840–1847.* Oxford: Oxford University Press, 1974.

Forsythe, Bill. "Kingsmill, Joseph (1805/6–1865)." In *DNB* (online edition). Oxford: Oxford University Press, 2009. http://www.oxforddnb.com/view/article/56015?docPos=7.

Gilley, Sheridan. "The Garibaldi Riots of 1862." *The Historical Journal* 16.4 (Dec 1973) 697–732.

———. "Protestant London: No Popery and the Irish Poor 2 (1850–60)." *Recusant History* 11 (1971) 21–46.

Haig, Alan. *The Victorian Clergy.* London: Croom Helm, 1984.

Hamilton, Thomas. "Lloyd, Bartholomew (1772–1837)." In *DNB* (online edition). Oxford: Oxford University Press, 2009. http://www.oxforddnb.com/view/article/16817.

Heiser, F. B. *The Story of St. Aidan's College, Birkenhead, 1847–1947.* Chester, UK: Philipson & Golder, 1947.

Hempton, David. "Evangelicalism and Eschatology." *The Journal of Ecclesiastical History* 31.2 (1980) 179–94.

Hempton, David, and Myrtle Hill. *Evangelical Protestantism in Ulster Society, 1740–1890.* London: Routledge, 1992.

Herring, George. "Littledale, Richard Frederick (1833–1890)." In *DNB* (online edition). Oxford: Oxford University Press, 2009. http://www.oxforddnb.com/view/article/16778?docPos=2.

———. *The Oxford Movement in Practice, the Tractarian Parochial World from 1830s to the 1870s*. Oxford: Oxford University Press, 2016.

Hobson, Richard. *What Hath God Wrought: An Autobiography*. London: Eliot Stock, 1903.

Hume, Abraham. *Condition of Liverpool, Religious and Social*. Liverpool, UK: Brakell 1858.

Kingsmill, Joseph. "On the Idolatry of the Church of Rome." In *Sermons on some of the Leading Points of Difference between Protestantism and the Church of Rome, Delivered in the Parish Church of Newcastle-under-Lyme*. Newcastle, UK: Hyde, 1836.

Lewis, Donald M. *The Dictionary of Evangelical Biography, 1730–1860*. 2 vols. Oxford: Oxford University Press, 1995.

Luce, J. V. *Trinity College, Dublin: The First Four Hundred Years*. Dublin: Trinity College Dublin Press, 1992.

Macdonnell, J. C. "William Connor Magee (1821–91)." In *DNB* (online edition). Oxford: Oxford University Press, 2009. http://www.oxforddnb.com/view/article/17779.

Maxwell, C. *A History of Trinity College, Dublin, 1591–1892*. Dublin: Dublin University Press, 1946.

McDonald, T. *Achill Island, Archaeology, History, Folklore*. 2nd ed. Offaly, UK: IAS Publications, 2006.

McDowell, Robert B., and D. A. Webb. *Trinity College, Dublin, 1592–1952: An Academic History*. Dublin: Trinity College Dublin Press, 2004.

McLeod, Hugh. *Religion and Society in England, 1850–1914*. Houndmills, UK: Macmillan, 1996.

Murphy, James. *The Religious Problem in English Education: The Crucial Experiment*. Liverpool, UK: Liverpool University Press, 1959.

Neal, Frank. *Sectarian Violence: The Liverpool Experience, 1819–1914*. Manchester, UK: Manchester University Press.

Pollock, J. S. *Romanizing: The Substance of a Lecture Delivered in the Town Hall, Birmingham, 23 Jan. 1867*. London: Masters, 1867.

Reed, John Shelton. *Glorious Battle: The Cultural Politics of Victorian Anglo-Catholicism*. Nashville: Vanderbilt University Press, 1996.

Scotland, Nigel. "Sumner, John Bird (1780–1862)." In *DNB* (online edition). Oxford: Oxford University Press, 2009. http://www.oxforddnb.com/view/article/26785.

Sumner, John Bird. *The Charge of the John Bird, Lord Archbishop of Canterbury to the Clergy of the Diocese at his Primary Visitation, 1849*. London: J. Hatchard and Son, 1849.

Sutton, C. W. "Hume, Abraham (1814–84)." In *DNB* (online edition). Oxford: Oxford University Press, 2009. http://www.oxforddnb.com/view/article/14132.

Todd, E. M. "Todd, James Henthorn (1805–1869)." In *DNB* (online edition). Oxford: Oxford University Press, 2009. http://www.oxforddnb.com/view/article/27491.

Waller, P. J. *Democracy and Sectarianism: A Political and Social History of Liverpool 1868–1939*. Liverpool, UK: Liverpool University Press, 1981.

Ward, W. R. *Religion and Society in England, 1790–1850*. London: Batsford, 1972.

Waterhouse, Paul. "Pearson, John Loughborough (1817–1897)." In *DNB* (online edition). Oxford: Oxford University Press, 2009. http://www.oxforddnb.com/view/printable/21720.

Wellings, Martin. "Lefroy, William (1836–1909)." In *DNB* (online edition). Oxford: Oxford University Press, 2009. http://www.oxforddnb.com/view/article/34476.

Whelan, Irene. *Bible War in Ireland: The "Second Reformation" and the Polarization of Protestant-Catholic Relations, 1800–1840.* Dublin: Lilliput, 2005.

Wolffe, John. "Blakeney, Richard Paul (1820–84)." In *DNB* (online edition). Oxford: Oxford University Press, 2009. http://www.oxforddnb.com/view/article/2590?docPos=2.

———. "McNeile, Hugh Boyd (1795–1879)." In *DNB* (online edition). Oxford: Oxford University Press, 2009. http://www.oxforddnb.com/view/article/17711.

Yates, Nigel. *Anglican Ritualism in Victorian Britain, 1830–1910.* Oxford: Oxford University Press, 1999.

9

"A Zealous, Well-educated, and Well-informed Body of Clergy"

Trinity College, Dublin, and the Church in Upper Canada in the 1830s*

THOMAS P. POWER

IN THE ORIGINS OF Canadian Anglicanism three foundational strands were contributory. First there were the American loyalists who came north in the 1780s following the American Revolution. With no experience of episcopal structures, they brought with them both a sense of independence from the mother church and a commitment to local control and lay leadership. Secondly, there was the English model of church with its emphasis on episcopal authority and the church's links to the state. A third model emerged with the arrival in the early 1800s of large numbers of Irish Anglicans who emphasized scriptural truth and doctrinal purity. The Irish brought a strong evangelicalism that came to be demonstrated in missionary work, anti-Catholicism, lay leadership, and scholarly endeavors.[1]

*Earlier versions of this essay were given at the Canadian Church Historical Society Conference, Trinity College, Toronto, Nov. 2014, and as the Founders' Day Memorial Lecture, Wycliffe College, Toronto, Oct. 2016.

1. Hayes, *Anglicans in Canada*, 3–7, 117–8.

Writing of the distinctive Irish contribution, James Talman in 1938 claimed: "The Church of England in Upper Canada owed its greatest debt to Trinity College, Dublin."[2] In a similar vein, the author of *Leaders of the Canadian Church* (1918) asserted: "Ontario owes a great deal to the Irish Church. There is no doubt that in the middle of the nineteenth century the great central part of Ontario was indelibly stamped with the die [sic] of Trinity College Dublin."[3]

What that stamp was and the nature of its indelibility could not have been foreseen in 1834 when John Strachan, archdeacon of York, famously wrote to Richard Whately, archbishop of Dublin, offering his critique of the many Irish clergy who were then arriving in Upper Canada:

> The clergymen who come to this country from Ireland are strongly Calvinistic in their sermons and go much further than those who are called Evangelical in England. Some of them have also a foolish fancy of preaching without notes. From conversing with them it seems to me that they adopt this plan from laziness[,] for the stuff they utter requires no thoughtful preparation—and one might preach it by the day if conscience would let. They brandish a little Bible in their hand fastened with brass clasps and open it from time to time to read their quotations, but they . . . repeat them long before they find the place where they are recorded. These persons are so wild in their doctrines and unguarded in their statements that I really am afraid to allow them to preach, for they seem never to have known the distinctive principles of the Church of England or to have thrown them away on the voyage.[4]

It is clear from Strachan's remarks that Irish clergy came with a distinctive theological formation that was unsettling to him. His reaction is not surprising, for in the 1820s Strachan had transitioned in his churchmanship from a liberal Anglicanism which he had hitherto embraced, to one distinguished by high church doctrines.[5] This shift accounts for his disavowal of the Irish clergy.[6] It is significant that Strachan was struck by their facility

---

2. Talman, "Some Notes on the Clergy," 62.

3. Heeney, *Leaders of the Canadian Church*, 204.

4. Strachan to the archbishop of Dublin, 28 Apr. 1834 (AO Strachan Letter Book, 1827–1839 [MS 35 reel 10]); also printed in *John Strachan's Papers and Letterbooks* 2, 243. They had corresponded from at least 1826: AO F 983-1 Strachan Papers Whately to Strachan, 27 Jun. 1826 (MS 35 reel 2).

5. Fahey, *In His Name*, 99–100.

6. In Australia some recruiters for the SPG were also wary of taking on Irish clergy for much the same reasons as articulated by Strachan and tended to prefer English clergy if they could be had: Gladwin, *Anglican Clergy in Australia*, 50.

and readiness with preaching, their easy familiarity with the Bible to the extent of being able to quote from it with ease, and how in all this their zeal exceeded expectations of what "evangelical" had come to represent in England. Indeed, one contemporary noted that in contrast to the clergyman in England who confined his preaching to the Sunday pulpit, "An Irish clergyman does not shake hands with you without leaving a text or two in your palm."[7] Despite his reservations about the Irish clergy, Strachan—given the shortage of clergy in Upper Canada—was prepared to tolerate them for the benefit of the spiritual needs of the settlements being formed there. What were the formative influences that gave Irish Anglican clergy in particular, and its laity more generally, such distinctiveness?

OLD WORLD FORMATION: EDUCATION

Trinity College, Dublin (TCD) was the gathering point for Anglicans of different backgrounds, and as such acted as a great leveler and formative center where laity and aspirant clergy were educated together under a common curriculum. At the outset of the nineteenth century, Trinity—like the colleges of Oxford and Cambridge—had no further professional education beyond the BA degree for those wishing to enter ordained ministry. Basic education at the undergraduate level was deemed sufficient. Significantly, those studying for the BA degree were obliged to take lectures in divinity, irrespective of whether they were intended for the holy orders or not.

More specifically, four aspects of the curriculum are noteworthy. Firstly, the arts undergraduate curriculum was formative for divinity studies. The study of mathematics, moral and natural philosophy, and the ancient languages were foundational for divinity studies in terms of content, reasoning skills, and mental discipline. At Dublin study of logic, mathematics, and physics led to the acquisition of inductive habits, classes in moral philosophy and metaphysics allowed connections to be made to important issues in theology, and an exposure to ancient languages and classics was clearly advantageous for biblical studies. Undergraduates were exposed to the New Testament in the original Greek language as well as Latin and Hebrew, all of which was an excellent preparation for the study of Scripture.

Secondly, Strachan's reference to the Irish clergy's easy recall and facility with the Bible comes as no surprise when we discover its place in the curriculum. Competence in the Bible was a prerequisite for college entrance for there was an examination in the Greek testament, the four gospels and Acts. After entrance all students studied the Bible. Examinations for the degree of

---

7. Trollope, *Clergymen of the Church of England*, 106.

BA, which were oral, required that students be able to translate the Greek New Testament into Latin, have knowledge of Hebrew grammar, and be capable of translating the first two Psalms from Hebrew into Latin. Exposure to the Bible was central to the curriculum. Thirdly, students were exposed to regular catechetical instruction. The college catechist instructed in the Bible, held examinations, and granted prizes for effective answering. The practice prevailed of having the two junior classes instructed catechetically in scriptural knowledge and history, as well as Christian doctrine. Students were tested on Genesis and Exodus, the historical books of the Old Testament, the gospel of Luke, the Acts of the Apostles, and the Creed. Fourthly, there was chapel attendance. Trinity was, like the colleges of Oxford and Cambridge, a religious foundation, thoroughly Anglican in its ethos. Attendance at chapel services where they were exposed to preaching was expected of students on a regular basis.

Whether intended for the church or not, from early on in their college careers students at Trinity were infused with a strong catechetical formation through which they acquired an oral facility for expounding scriptural knowledge and the essentials of the faith.[8] The Trinity undergraduate curriculum had clear strengths in terms of formation, and those who graduated from the school—even if they did not enter the ministry of the church—had a strong foundation in terms of knowledge of the Bible and an oral articulation of the faith. This ready facility made its clerical graduates, in particular, adept at preaching without notes, an attribute noted with some distain by Strachan, and its laity knowledgeable in the faith.

By the time many of the Irish clergy arrived in Upper Canada in the 1830s, improvements to an already robust curriculum had occurred. These were of such an order that in 1833 a formal school of divinity emerged at Trinity, in advance of such a development at Oxford or Cambridge. In the process there was a transition from an undergraduate curriculum where the emphasis was on the classical languages, mathematics, and the liberal arts, to a two-year graduate degree specifically in divinity studies. For the first divinity year (which, significantly, could be taken concurrently in the final undergraduate year), they were lectured on the evidences of natural and revealed religion including prophecy, apologetics, the gospel of Luke in Greek, Acts of the Apostles, Galatians, and Philippians, and the Creed. In their second year, they studied the epistle to the Hebrews in Greek; church history covering the first three centuries and the sixteenth; liturgy and church polity; and Roman Catholic controversies, the latter of which equipped them with the intellectual arguments in theological debates with

8. The following section draws on Power, "'Of No Small Importance,'" 140–83.

their denominational rivals. Professorial classes were supplemented by catechetical ones. The combination of professorial and tutorial instruction benefited students, distinguished the Trinity approach, and made it highly regarded. A mandatory examination was required at the end of each year which all divinity students had to pass. Candidates for ordination had to possess a certificate of attendance and demonstrate an ability to write in Latin and read New Testament Greek. The new arrangement was solidified because Irish and English bishops now came to regard the certificate as the preferred qualification for ordinands and in time came to require it.[9]

The result of these reforms was that the academic standard was raised, and the program of study proved to be more rigorous than what preceded it. Those who succeeded were well prepared, with one observer offering the following assessment of the caliber of the clergyman ministering in the Church of Ireland and the quality of education they had received:

> The superior professional qualifications of the Irish clergy, their personal character, their parochial activity and usefulness [are notable] ... Their increased attainments in professional learning has been equally observable, and is to be traced to the efficiency of the divinity school of our university, and the care and labour there bestowed on the candidates for the ministry ... [10]

What all this amounts to is that from an early stage (and accentuated as a result of the reforms of 1833) clergy graduates of TCD came out imbued with a classically based education supplemented with a strong biblical literacy and catechetical facility along with a grounding in apologetics (honed for debate with Roman Catholics) and a vibrant missionary spirit. So despite Strachan's disavowal of Irish clergy in certain respects, in another respect they fulfilled his preference for candidates who had a classical education and who had the ability to read the Greek New Testament.[11]

It is one thing to determine that the Irish clergy and their lay siblings were well educated and theologically and biblically literate. It is another to situate this fact within the broader social, economic, political, and mental world of the period within which Irish Anglicans subsisted, and thereby discern the factors that brought them to Canada in the 1820s and 1830s. This dimension can be considered in terms of push and pull factors.

9. For an example of a certificate produced by James Smith for Strachan from TCD, Jul. 1839, see AO F 983-1 Strachan Papers MS 35, reel 3, and certificate of his MA, 4 Mar. 1840 (ibid.).
10. *Dublin University Magazine* 27 (1846), 374.
11. Westfall, "'Some Practical Acquaintance with Parochial Duties,'" 44.

OLD WORD FORMATION: PUSH FACTORS

In this period the position of the Church of Ireland and its adherents was undermined due to external and internal forces and circumstances. Despite the established nature of its position, historically Church of Ireland adherents had always been vulnerable because of their minority status in Ireland. Their position as a minority served, on the one hand, to sharpen their sense of self-identity, and on the other, gave them a missionary purpose. The circumstances of the 1820s and 1830s sharpened the sense of vulnerability and minority status. Increased mobilization by Catholics resulted in the emancipation act of 1829. Added to this was a rising sense among Protestants as a whole of an apocalyptic end times in the 1820s and early 1830s. Adding to the unease among Anglicans was the presence in their own ranks of a growing number of secessionist laity and clergy. The church's legal privileges came to be undermined. Despite a series of church reforms since 1800 the institution was still in a precarious position, for the government was intent on dismantling its privileged position.

Agrarian violence was to coalesce around the unresolved issue of tithe, the main source of clerical income. Initial legislation allowed for the payment of tithes in kind in lieu of cash, but continued resistance resulted in the accumulation of large arrears of tithe payments, a situation ultimately emanating in the eventual virtual abolition of the tax by the late 1830s. The decimation of tithe as a prime source of income was the prime cause of so many Irish clergy emigrating to Canada. Referring specifically to this, in 1833 Bishop Charles Stewart of Quebec commented, more charitably on this occasion than Strachan: "This [i.e., tithe] is one instance, amongst others in which Providence has turned the distress of the Church and people in Ireland to the advantage of Canada. Many good Protestants and their ministers have . . . been constrained to leave their native country and have found refuge in this and are now benefiting themselves and others . . . This will especially apply to several of our new missionaries."[12] Already in 1832 Archbishop Whately of Dublin had written to Archdeacon John Strachan in York (Toronto) inquiring about openings in Canada for Protestant clergymen who were "thinking of emigration from finding themselves destitute thro' the existing troubles of the Church."[13]

In the 1820s and 1830s, therefore, the prospects for the Church of Ireland, its adherents, its existing and aspirant clergy were not propitious. Political upheaval in the form of Catholic emancipation, tithe arrears, the

---

12. Hawkins, *Annals of the Diocese of Toronto*, 87–88. Until 1839, Upper Canada was part of the diocese of Quebec.

13. Quoted in Talman, "Cronyn, Benjamin," para. 3.

breaking of a monopoly on education, the reduction in the number of bishoprics, a detrimental economic environment coupled with secessionism and a rising apocalyptic fervor, informed the mental world of Irish Anglicans. These factors coalesced to push large numbers from Ireland to Canada.

NEW WORLD: NEED FOR CLERGY

What made the decision to emigrate relatively easy was the fact that Canada was opening up, with the prospect of good, relatively cheap land, the concomitant demand for labor to work it, and the cost of living much less.[14] Canada, Upper and Lower, had a growing need for resources, human and financial. For Irish immigrants Canada was an appealing destination, for they came with clear advantages, notably a facility with the English language and with British legal and political institutions prevailing there. For Anglicans, their religion made them more acceptable to the host society and so they were able to adjust and move more freely. Substantive growth in Irish arrivals occurred in the 1820s and continued into the 1830s.

Clergy were needed to minister to the growing immigrant population. Strachan's delineation of the situation was grim. In 1827 he calculated that twenty-four Anglican clergy were serving a population extending over 28,000 miles, that 112 additional clergy were needed immediately, and that by 1846 a total of 272 would be needed to service a growing population estimated to then reach 400,000.[15] Yet, during the 1830s, only eighty-one new clergy in total are recorded as officiating and this to a population estimated in 1838 at 150,000 Anglicans.[16] In 1841 in a circuit of 300 miles that brought him through Thornhill, Newmarket, Barrie, Penetanguishine, Gwillimburg, and Tecumpseth, Strachan estimated that because of the increase in settlers, instead of seven or eight clergy there would be need for one hundred.[17] In the same year, Strachan estimated that there were forty-five stations covering a population of 100,000 for which missionary clergy were needed.[18] In addition, the need for clergy was heightened because of the fear of inroads being made among the new arrivals by the Methodists.[19]

14. Hawkins, *Annals of the Diocese of Toronto*, ix–x.

15. Fahey, *In His Name*, 72. On the continuing need for clergy, see AO Strachan Letterbooks, Strachan to Thomas Dunscombe, Cork, 28 Oct. 1840 (F-983-2 Ms 35 reel 11); same to Rev. W. J. D. Waddilove, 9 Jun. 1841 (ibid.).

16. Fahey, *In His Name*, 60–61; Hawkins, *Annals of the Diocese of Toronto*, 95.

17. Hawkins, *Annals of the Diocese of Toronto*, 128.

18. Ibid., 155.

19. Flint, *John Strachan*, 24; Talman, *Authentic Letters from Upper Canada*, 112, 114, 115; AO Strachan Papers F 983-1 Flood to Bp. of Montreal, 1 Oct. 1838 (MS 35 reel 3).

Prior to 1830 there was a scarcity of candidates for the church. In general, clergy from the old world were unwilling to serve in Upper Canada because it was viewed not as an opportunity for advancement but as demotion to a backward region. Hence educated clergy from elsewhere had been difficult to secure, expensive, and not always suited to the country. This deficiency brought into focus the urgent need for Canadian-educated clergy, something Strachan had a preference for, but this goal was not to materialize until the 1840s.[20] Only after he became bishop of the newly created diocese of Toronto in 1839 was there an opportunity to implement his desire to have locally trained clergy with the establishment of his own training school in Cobourg in 1842, from which forty-five graduated prior to its absorption into the newly established Trinity College in 1851.[21] For his Cobourg initiative Strachan hoped to attract candidate officers from the army and navy, professionals, and from among the more respectable classes.[22] Prior to that there was no university or college where future clergy could be trained, with Strachan opting to train candidates at his own expense.[23] Whatever training Strachan could provide locally before 1842, it was in the context of declining recruitment from Oxford and Cambridge and was clearly insufficient to meet demand given the new settlements being established in the 1820s and 1830s and their immediate need for clergy.[24] Fortunately for Strachan, despite his initial reservations, it was this need that was filled in significant numbers by Irish university-educated clergy. So whereas the prospects for graduating clergy in Ireland, however well formed, were increasingly inauspicious, demand in Upper Canada was increasing. How was their arrival mediated or facilitated?

MEDIATING/FACILITATING FACTORS: SOCIETIES

Because few clergy from the old world were willing to voluntarily go to remote Upper Canada, from the 1780s to the 1830s financial incentives were provided by the Society for the Propagation of the Gospel (SPG). From 1814 to 1833 parliamentary grants for religious purposes were administered in

---

20. Flint, *John Strachan*, 62; AO Strachan Letterbook 1812–1834 F 983-2: letter from John Strachan reporting on the condition of the church (MS 35 reel 10); Strachan to Bp. of Quebec, 7 Apr. 1829 (Letterbook 1827–1839, Ms 35, reel 10).
21. Hawkins, *Annals of the Diocese of Toronto*, 199; Glazebrook, *Church of England in Upper Canada*, 20.
22. Hawkins, *Annals of the Diocese of Toronto*, 123.
23. Thompson, *Into All the Lands*, 151.
24. Hardwick, *An Anglican British World*, 46.

British North America by the SPG.[25] In that period SPG applicants showed a preference for coming to Canada rather than Australia.[26] Many of the Irish who came prior to 1833, including Rev. Benjamin Cronyn in 1832, did so through sponsorship by the SPG.[27] In the 1830s, however, the SPG had to retrench when its funds were cut by parliament. In 1832 the new Whig government reduced the grant to the SPG from £12,000 in 1832 to £4,000 in 1834, with all funding to cease thereafter, with the hope that the deficiency would be made up from other sources.[28] This expectation failed to materialize, leaving the government to continue to provide the reduced annual grant of £4,000 after 1834.[29] This decision left the emergent church in Canada with a serious shortage of funds as it tried to organize clerical human resources at a time when immigrants from Britain and Ireland were flooding in.

A key organizational expression of evangelical commitment in the old world was through new societies that advanced a variety of causes.[30] Such societies allowed a newly affluent and literate middle class a means of tangible identification with the aims of the evangelical revival.[31] Their existence meant a challenge to the more traditional and establishment basis of the SPG.[32] The first departure from the SPG monopoly came with the founding of the Society for Converting and Civilizing the Indians and Propagating the Gospel Among Destitute Settlers in Upper Canada in 1830, which the SPG refused to cooperate with.[33] The new society had as its objective the soliciting of lay support for itinerant missionaries.[34] The Society's dual pur-

25. Hayes, *By Grace Co-Workers*, 28. It first gave support in 1812 with £200 for four students: Thompson, *Into All the Lands*, 146.

26. Gladwin, *Anglican Clergy in Australia*, 37.

27. Thompson, *Into All the Lands*, 250.

28. Kenyon, "Influence of the Oxford Movement," 83.

29. Ibid., 83.

30. Bradley, *Call to Seriousness*, 135–44.

31. Twells, *Civilising Mission*.

32. There was competition between the evangelical Church Missionary Society (CMS) and the more high church SPG which influenced missionary policy, popular engagement, and financial support. This reflected a fundamental difference in origin and approach: the SPG was the older of the two, emphasized the unity of church and state, was committed to service to colonies composed of settlers from the old world, and identified with the colonial regimes and the imperial principle. The CMS, on the other hand, was more committed to missionary work to Indigenous peoples. Though the CMS had better financial assets reflecting its broad, lay evangelical base, the SPG had more political influence. On these points see Maughan, *Mighty England Do Good*.

33. Ruggle, "Itinerant Clergy in Upper Canada," 65.

34. Fahey, *In His Name*, 222.

pose of sending travelling missionaries to evangelize the Indigenous people and to service the pastoral needs of immigrant groups through an itinerant ministry was seen in its early choice of clergy, who included William McMurray (1810–1894) who served at the remote Sault Ste. Marie from 1832 to 1840. The Portadown-born McMurray came with his parents to York in 1811, attended Strachan's school, and acted as a catechist before his appointment as a travelling missionary in 1832.[35] Even before he had taken orders, he was the first to establish a mission among the Ojibwa in 1832; following his ordination and return, he was the first to conduct Anglican services; and in his six-year stay he baptized 160 Indigenous people (forty of whom became communicants) in what was to become the diocese of Algoma.[36]

The withdrawal of funding to the SPG after 1834 opened the way for laity to become more involved in support of the church in Canada. The bishop of Quebec, Charles Stewart (1775–1837), produced an address in which he appealed to the British public for funds and support.[37] In response, Rev. W. J. D. Waddilove, who was one of Bishop Stewart's English relatives, established the Upper Canadian Travelling Missionary Fund, to support missionaries. There followed the Upper Canada Clergy Society (UCCS), a largely lay-driven organization, which filled the gap left by the demise of SPG support. Founded in 1835, it became operational in 1837, and existed until 1840 when it merged with the SPG.[38] Its stated purpose was to "send out clergymen and catechists to labor among the destitute settlers and others in that province [Upper Canada], and to assist in the building of churches."[39] Cronyn supported the foundation of the Upper Canada Clergy Society on the model of what his former rector, Rev. Peter Roe, had initiated in Kilkenny.[40] Thus the purpose was to provide human and physical resources supportive of the church's ministry.

The initiative represented a trans-Atlantic partnership between interested evangelical clergy and laity intent on bringing a clerical presence to isolated Anglican communities in Upper Canada. In the 1830s the Fund supported the activities of missionaries many of whom were of Irish origin including Richard Flood, Thomas Greene, Frederick Mack, and James Usher.[41] In this capacity, it served to bring many clergy (including Irish) to Can-

35. Ibid., 44; Millman, *Life of the Right Reverend*, 209–10; Ruggle, "McMurray, William," paras. 1–3.
36. *Algoma 100*, 9–10.
37. Waddilove, *Stewart Missions*, 137–40.
38. Hawkins, *Annals of the Diocese of Toronto*, 192.
39. UCCS, *First Report* (1838), iv; Hardwick, *Anglican British World*, 35–37.
40. Vaudry, *Anglicans and the Atlantic World*, 143, 258 n56.
41. Millman, *Life of the Right Reverend*, 199–200, 201, 208, 221; AO Strachan F 983-1 Papers, letters missive 18 Jan. 1836 (Ms 35, reel 3).

ada in the 1830s. In January 1836 alone Strachan made five appointments of Irish clergy: Rev. Francis Evans to Woodhouse (near London), Rev. Frederick Mack to Wellington Square (now Burlington), Rev. Arthur Palmer to Guelph, and Rev. Dominick Blake to Adelaide.[42]

As well as its lay basis, a notable aspect of the UCCS was that it attracted support from Irish donors including Irish peers who were patrons or vice presidents, the earls of Roden and Mountcashel, and Viscount Bernard, Rev. Richard Murray, the dean of Ardagh (the only clergyman among the society's vice presidents), and Arthur Guinness; while the committee of fifteen included members of parliament (e.g., John Ponsonby), officers in the navy (e.g., Hon. F. Maude), and other gentlemen. Its evangelical credentials were indicated by the society's address at Exeter Hall, the hub of British evangelicalism by the early 1830s. The selection of missionaries was in the sole hands of the society, subject to the approval of the bishops of London or Quebec, in respect of persons to be ordained as missionaries. From an early stage the society was obliged to clarify its role vis-à-vis the SPG in order to counter an impression that its activities would impinge on the role of the latter. The Society was keen to make clear that it wished to cooperate with the work of the SPG.[43]

Five of the first seven and two of the first three missionaries appointed by the Society were Irish: Henry H. O'Neill and Frederick A. O'Meara. O'Neill (BA TCD 1831) came to Toronto in 1835 and was appointed by Stewart as a travelling missionary. O'Meara and Dominick Blake (BA TCD 1829, emigrated 1832) were other Irishmen who came to Canada under the auspices of the Society at this time.[44] Born in 1814, O'Meara entered Trinity in 1832 aged 18 years.[45] Ordained deacon in 1837, the year of his graduation, he arrived in Toronto in March 1838 under the auspices of the UCCS. Another missionary who came out under UCCS auspices was Rev. Bold Cudmore Hill (1799-1870) (BA TCD 1831) of Bandon, where he ministered. Significantly Castle Bernard was located west of Bandon and was the seat of Viscount Barnard, one of the patrons of the Society.[46] Hill arrived in Toronto in September 1838 and was dispatched by the bishop

---

42. AO Strachan F 983-1 Papers, letters missive 16, 18, 21 Jan. 1836 (Ms 35, reel 3); Millman, *Life of the Right Reverend*, 191, 199, 208, 214.

43. UCCS, *The First Report*, 10-11.

44. Millman, *Life of the Right Reverend*, 134, 191; Hardwick, *Anglican British World*, 36.

45. Burtchaell and Sadleir, *Alumni Dublinenses*, 639.

46. Hardwick, *Anglican British World*, 159-60.

as a missionary to the Grand River tract of the Niagara district, where his ministrations were to cover a vast area.[47]

Thus many agencies from the traditional SPG to the more lay-driven ones like the UCCS acted to facilitate the coming of Irish clergy to Upper Canada to minister to the needs of the vast numbers of newly arrived immigrants. The fact was that in practice these agencies facilitated the arrival of evangelical clergy from Ireland with the recruitment of clergy from England being less successful.[48] While the Society for Converting and Civilizing the Indians and Propagating the Gospel Among Destitute Settlers in Upper Canada and the Upper Canada Clergy Society did not raise significant funds for the support of travelling missionaries, they did fill a gap until the founding by Strachan in 1842 of the more successful Church Society and the re-emergence of the SPG in 1840.[49] During a critical time in the 1830s both societies, given the financial challenges faced by the SPG, served a function in promoting clergy, including Irish, to key areas.

MEDIATING/FACILITATING FACTORS: FAMILY AND BISHOPS

In addition to these agencies, the arrival of clergy was made possible by emigrant literature and personal family communication. Information trickled back to advertise opportunities for emigrants to Canada. For the 1830s alone it has been estimated that over one hundred accounts were published descriptive of Upper Canada.[50] Notable in this respect is Thomas William Magrath's *Authentic Letters from Upper Canada; with an account of Canadian field sports* published in Dublin in 1833. Magrath was the son of James Magrath (1766–1851), who was born in Ireland, graduated from TCD in 1790, was ordained, served in various clerical positions, came to Canada in 1827, and became a missionary in Toronto township.[51] He became the

47. UCCS, *The Second Report* (1839), 11, 23–24.
48. Hardwick, *Anglican British World*, 37, 40, 158.
49. Fahey, *In His Name*, 223–29. The Church Society absorbed the SCCIPGDS: ibid, 223.
50. Talman, *Authentic Letters from Upper Canada*, v. In the 1830s Canada as a specific destination for Irish Protestants was treated in the columns of the newly founded *Dublin University Magazine* (hereafter *DUM*)—see, e.g., i (1833) 600–11; xi (1838) 326–53—while emigration in general was also covered, e.g., i (1833) 471–83; iv (1834) 1–12.
51. Burtchaell and Sadleir, *Alumni Dublinenses*, 546; Millman, *Life of the Right Reverend*, 209; Grant, *A Profusion of Spires*, 71. He was rector of Shankill, diocese of Ferns (Talman, *Authentic Letters from Upper Canada*, 2n). Another source says he came out

first rector of St. Peter's, Erindale. When he died in 1851 he was the senior missionary and oldest clergyman in the diocese of Toronto.[52] Works such as Magrath's and others like G. A. Hill's *A Guide for Emigrants from the British Shores to the Woods of Canada* (Dublin, 1834) disseminated knowledge of the country among prospective emigrants in Ireland, highlighting settlement potential, economic opportunities, and the needs of the church for clergy.[53]

Personal family communication through letters achieved a similar purpose. Writing from Adelaide Township near London in December 1832, William Radcliff informed his brother Arthur in Dublin:

> Let my brother John know that clergymen are in great demand. Had he been here he would probably have been appointed to the rectory of this township. I am informed that the governor has thirty clerical situations to fill up. If my brother comes soon, he may get one near us. They are very desirable preferments and afford a fine field for active zeal.[54]

In 1833 Thomas Radcliff wrote from Adelaide to his father in Dublin, lamenting the lack of clergy in the new settlements and indicating that there was a demand for thirty or forty of them. In their selection he offered the following advice:

> If care be taken to select able, zealous and active men, the happiest results will follow; but if a swarm of drones be sent among us, attracted merely by the temporal advantages of a settlement, without higher motives and anxieties, the degradation of our religion and general contempt of inefficient ministers, must be contemplated...
>
> How delightful would it be, in this great and improving country, rising so rapidly into a state of civilization, which is extending every hour, through the medium of British emigration, to have this numerous body fully supplied with pastors of their own church? and how cheering would it be to have their respective settlements anxiously superintended by a zealous, well-educated, and well-informed body of clergy?[55]

---

in 1819 sponsored by the SPCK (Houston and Smyth, *Irish Emigration and Canadian Settlement*, 168), but gives no source other than a commemorative plaque: ibid., 357.

52. On Magrath see AO Strachan Papers F 983-2 Letterbook, 1827–1839 (Ms 35 reel 10), 2.

53. Hill, *A Guide for Emigrants*.

54. Talman, *Authentic Letters from Upper Canada*, 110–11. The number of thirty or forty clergy is confirmed: 114.

55. Ibid., 114–15.

The missionary potential of the new country and the attractiveness of openings for clergy as pioneers were emphasized in the public presses in Ireland. Rev. Thomas Green, a Trinity graduate of 1834, following his settlement as an itinerant missionary in the London district, in his correspondence and publications was keen to underscore the potential of missionary and pioneer openings as mutual. Writing in 1838 he appealed:

> I am astonished that so little should be known of this country and its wants, presenting, as it does, so ample a field for missionary labour, and with a prospect (humanly speaking) of such abundant success . . . There are openings for ministers at Port Burwell and Vienna, with the neighbouring parts [of] Burford, Dereham [Durham], Norwich, Walpole, and Huron Tract. Ministers in these townships could act as pioneers, and I trust very quickly mission stations could be opened.[56]

Coming at a time when prospects for clergy in Ireland were grim, such appeals and family correspondence encouraged the exodus of significant numbers of Trinity-educated clergy to Upper Canada.

In the realm of personal contact, bishops acted as facilitators in easing the transfer of clergy from Ireland to Canada. Contacts between Archbishop Richard Whately in Dublin, and Archdeacon John Strachan in York, as well as Bishop Charles Stewart of Quebec, opened channels of communication where the plight of the Irish clergy domestically and the needs of the nascent Canadian church coalesced. Given Strachan's preference for university educated clergy, testimonials from bishops in Ireland were critical to have for a clergyman wishing to establish himself in the new world. One correspondent writing from Adelaide near London in 1832 advised his Dublin counterpart about clerical opportunities, "Make him bring out proper testimonials from his Bishop."[57] Rev. Thomas Green, mentioned above, was brought to the attention of Charles Stewart, bishop of Quebec, by his nephew, Rev. W. Waddilove, and brought to Canada, ordained by Stewart in January 1836, and sent as an itinerant missionary to the London district, where many Irish were already settled.[58] Similar cases of episcopal recommendation are documented for others.[59]

---

56. *DUM* 11 (1838), 346n.

57. Talman, *Authentic Letters from Upper Canada*, 111.

58. Millman, *Life of the Right Reverend*, 201.

59. Arch. of Dublin to Bp. of Toronto, 29 Apr. 1844 (AO Strachan Papers F 983-1 [Mic 35, reel5]); same to same, 12 Jan. 1848 (ibid.); Strachan to Thomas S. Dunscombe, Cork (ibid., F-983-3 Letterbooks, 1839-43, MS 35, reel11).

The family dynamic continued to be a feature of life in the new world with a distinct pattern of intermarriage, which built on connections existing prior to the parties emigrating. The majority of the emigrants prior to the 1840s travelled in some form of kinship group. Thus, led by the Trinity-educated Thomas Radcliff (b.1794), thirteen members of the Radcliff family came in 1832 and settled in Adelaide township in Middlesex County, where they were ministered to by Rev. Dominick E. Blake, as part of a plan to have a clergyman in every township.[60] Blake and Benjamin Cronyn were fellow students at Trinity College and both proceeded to ordination in the Church of Ireland. Samuel and Edward Blake, sons of Dominick Blake who had come over in 1832 on the *Anne of Halifax* with Cronyn and others, married two of his daughters: Margaret Cronyn married Edward Blake, Rebecca Cronyn married Samuel Hume Blake; while Cronyn's son Verschoyle married Sophia Blake, a sister to Edward and Samuel Hume, all children of William Hume Blake.[61] Similarly, two of the sisters of Dominick Edward Blake (1806–1859) married pioneer clergymen in Upper Canada, Richard Flood and Charles Brough.[62]

This element of family cohesiveness was reinforced in many cases where Irish clergy were appointed to Irish settlements, something Strachan encouraged where he could. This would be true of the London area and also around Peterborough where many Irish settled in the 1820s; in one such settlement, Cavan township in 1841, there were many Irish Protestants under Rev. Samuel Armour.[63] Thus family communication not only acted as a mediating and facilitating factor in bringing Irish clergy to Upper Canada, but it was perpetuated in their appointment to Irish settlements and in select but influential alliances.

CONSEQUENCES: CONTINUITIES AND ADAPTATIONS

There were important changes that occurred as a result of the arrival of Irish Protestants in Upper Canada.

---

60. Talman, *Authentic Letters from Upper Canada*, ix, xvi, 83. The party included his brother, William Radcliff (1806–1883), who terminated his Trinity studies to emigrate: ibid., x.
61. Talman, "Cronyn, Benjamin."
62. Millman, *Life of the Right Reverend*, 191.
63. Hawkins, *Annals of the Diocese of Toronto*, 131.

Minority Status Reversed

The first is that their minority status was reversed by virtue of their large numbers. The numbers of Irish coming to British North America (BNA) grew from 53,463 in 1825–1829 to 185,952 in 1835–1839.[64] In each of the individual years between 1829 and 1837 (except 1836), the number of Irish emigrating to BNA exceeded that for England, Scotland, and Wales combined.[65] Though many of them proceeded to the United States, significant numbers stayed in Canada. Secondly, the proportion of Irish relative to other ethnic emigrant groups is notable. The Irish were the single largest ethnic group in English Canada from the 1830s to the 1880s. Already by the mid-1840s the Irish outnumbered the total of English, Welsh, and Scots as migrants.[66] By 1871 they composed 24.3 percent of all Canadians, ahead of the English (20.3 percent) and the Scots (15.8 percent).[67]

Thirdly, Protestants made up a majority of the Irish arrivals in this period. In 1841 the Church of England was the single largest denomination in Upper Canada.[68] Of those of Irish ethnicity, the largest single denomination was Roman Catholic at 38 percent with over 60 percent Protestant, of whom 23 percent were Anglicans.[69] Significantly, in Upper Canada (what became the province of Ontario) where from the early 1830s the majority of Irish settled, the ratio of Protestants to Catholics was 2:1.[70] The 1842 census of Upper Canada showed that the Church of England had 107,291 members, followed by the Church of Scotland (77,929), Roman Catholic (65,203), and Methodist (55,667).[71] Thus the large influx of Anglicans from Britain and Ireland in the 1820s and 1830s propelled the Anglican Church membership into a majority status, in large part due to the Irish influx.

In Ireland, Protestants comprised about 25 percent of the population, whereas in British North America they made up more than 50 percent, primarily because Ontario held two-thirds of the Irish in Canada and

---

64. Wilson, *Irish in Canada*, 5; Graham and Proudfoot, *An Historical Geography of Ireland*, 344.

65. Murray, *An Historical and Descriptive Account*, vol. 3, 172–73.

66. Wilson, *Irish in Canada*, 9.

67. Ibid., 11.

68. Fahey, *In His Name*, 218. On the denomination composition in general of Irish emigrants, see Houston and Smyth, *Irish Emigration and Canadian Settlement*, 67–78, 226–37.

69. Houston and Smyth, *Irish Emigration and Canadian Settlement*, 226.

70. Wilson, *Irish in Canada*, 8; Graham and Proudfoot, *An Historical Geography of Ireland*, 347.

71. Fahey, *In His Name*, 38–39.

three-quarters of Irish Protestants were located there.[72] This new world reversal of the minority status that had prevailed in the old gives credence to the comment made by one Irish Anglican settler at Adelaide in 1833 that "Of Roman Catholics there are comparatively very few in our province."[73] Thus on the basis of numbers, ethnicity, and denomination, Irish Anglicans came to constitute an important and influential group.

Clergy Impact: Short Term

The result of the combined impact of the mediating role of missionary societies, family contacts, and episcopal initiative was an increase in the number of clergy ministering in Upper Canada in the 1830s. The number of clergy increased from two in 1790 to twenty-two in 1820, to forty-four in 1830, to ninety-one in 1840, with a total of 150 different clergy serving in the period up to 1840.[74] Between 1826 and 1836 the number of clergy grew from twenty-six to fifty-six, a significant number of whom were supported in whole or in part by the SPG.[75] The 1830s emerge, therefore, as a critical decade when clerical numbers more than doubled. Yet these numbers were insufficient to keep pace with the growing population, highlighting the need for more clergy, including travelling missionaries.[76]

The largest single source for trained clergy in Upper Canada in the formative phase was Trinity College Dublin. It has been estimated that of the 150 clergy who had served in Upper Canada by 1840, about seventy derived from colleges and universities. Of these, ten or twelve were graduates of Oxford University, thirteen or nineteen from Cambridge, but the bulk (up to twenty-seven) came from Trinity College Dublin, with the balance comprised of those locally trained or those whose background is undetermined.[77] Of the ninety-one clergy ministering in the newly-created diocese of Toronto in 1841—where the country of origin of those clergy can be de-

---

72. Houston and Smyth, *Irish Emigration and Canadian Settlement*, 226.

73. Talman, *Authentic Letters from Upper Canada*, 114.

74. Talman, "Some Notes on the Clergy," 57. Another source gives the figures as 1819 (10), 1825 (22), 1827 (30), and 1833 (46): *Church of England Magazine* 12 (1842), 21–22. In 1832, there were fifty-six Anglican clergy serving in Upper Canada: Thompson, *Into All the Lands*, 147.

75. Hawkins, *Annals of the Diocese of Toronto*, 86, 94.

76. Millman, *Life of the Right Reverend*, 145; Hawkins, *Annals of the Diocese of Toronto*, 72; AO Strachan Papers F 983–1 A. Palmer to Bp. of Toronto, 30 Nov. 1841 (MS 35 reel 3), Francis Evans to the archdeacon of York, 29 Feb. 1848 (ibid.).

77. Talman, "Some Notes on the Clergy," 61–63.

Power—"A Zealous, Well-educated, and Well-informed Body of Clergy"   179

termined—the largest were from England (thirty-two) followed by Ireland (thirty-one), Scotland (three), with the remainder from a scattering of other locations.[78] In terms of education of this ninety-one, at least nineteen and possibly twenty-four were TCD graduates or had attended there, most of whom had come since 1830.[79] Overall in 1840 one-third of all clergy serving in Upper Canada were of Irish birth or education.[80] There were an estimated thirty-three clergy in the province c.1840 who could be described as evangelical.[81] Of this number, twelve were Irish-born, of whom eleven had been educated at Trinity College Dublin.[82] The Irish clergy derived from the higher class of student compared, for instance, with Cambridge clergy.[83]

Fulfilling Strachan's preference for an educated clergy, the Irish who came were a distinguished group not merely because of the rigor of the program to which they were exposed at Dublin, but also because of their individual attainments academically. For instance, Benjamin Cronyn, following his BA (1822), became a divinity prizeman (1824), and then achieved MA (1825), and he was later in 1855 to be made DD.[84] Frederick O'Meara returned to Ireland in 1839, receiving his MA from TCD in the same year.[85]

The influx of educated clergy in the 1830s established a foundation that was built on subsequently. Clergy continued to come directly from Ireland even after mid-century. Writing from Goderich in 1859, Jane White reported that "We have got six clergymen out from Dublin lately, some of them very talented men."[86] After becoming a bishop, Cronyn continued to recruit aspirant clergy on his visits to Ireland. In 1857 when he journeyed to Lambeth to be consecrated by the archbishop of Canterbury, he availed himself of the opportunity to visit Ireland where in Dublin he spoke to a Bible class impacting three of his listeners (Edward Sullivan, John Philip

78. Ibid., 63; Hawkins, *Annals of the Diocese of Toronto*, 152.

79. Talman, "Some Notes on the Clergy," 63. This compares with the situation in Australia in the same period, where 81 percent of the clergy who came were educated at TCD, compared to Oxford (6 percent) and Cambridge (2 percent): Gladwin, *Anglican Clergy in Australia*, 48. This was at a time when in 1836 there were thirty-two clergy (excluding bishops) in the Australian colonies, a number that was to increase to 161 in 1850: ibid., 48.

80. Talman, "Some Notes on the Clergy," 63. This compares with thirty-two born in England. See also Westfall, "'Some Practical Acquaintance with Parochial Duties,'" 45.

81. Fahey, *In His Name*, 255.

82. Ibid., 255.

83. Hardwick, *Anglican British World*, 44.

84. *Dublin University Calendar* (1835), 32; Talman, "Cronyn, Benjamin."

85. Millman, *Life of the Right Reverend*, 134, 213.

86. Houston and Smyth, *Irish Emigration and Canadian Settlement*, 299.

DuMoulin, James Carmichael) to commit to Canada for ministry.[87] They made an impression from the time of their first arrival, all three settling in the London area. It was reported of Rev. James Carmichael, who had been placed at Clinton,

> He is very young and very enthusiastic. He seems completely devoted, a little too theatrical but a most attentive preacher. He carries the mind away until you would think you actually saw what he describes. His Good Friday's sermon on the crucifixion was startlingly vivid. He drew crowds from other churches . . . [88]

The same commentator, Jane White, reported that though people were impressed with Carmichael, "they were more taken with a Mr. [Edward] Sullivan who has been once or twice here [Goderich]."[89] The three were to make a significant contribution to the Canadian Church, being recruited to be part of the staff of Huron College (founded by Cronyn) and later becoming bishops: Sullivan in Algoma, DuMoulin in Niagara, and Carmichael in Montreal.[90]

Clergy: Posting

Of those clergy in general who arrived, some found employment as chaplains to regiments, while others gravitated towards teaching positions in Upper Canada College, the latter being mostly English and graduates of Cambridge who took Sunday services in churches close to Toronto in addition to their posts.[91] Despite Strachan's initial reservations about the Irish clergy, as it turned out he was happy to have such a zealous group on hand to serve the needs of the church. Upon arrival Irish clergy became engaged either in ministering to their fellow Irish emigrants, or in missionary work. It was Strachan's policy to try, wherever possible, to place Irish clergy with Irish congregations.[92] It was the Trinity-educated clergy who went to the

---

87. Heeney, *Leaders of the Canadian Church*, 201–31, 265–73, 277–319.
88. Houston and Smyth, *Irish Emigration and Canadian Settlement*, 299.
89. Ibid., 299. Though she had not heard Sullivan preach she was somewhat suspicious of his name, commenting, "The name has a Popish sound with [sic] it." (Ibid., 299.)
90. Crowfoot, *Benjamin Cronyn*, 74; Cooper, "Irish Immigration and the Canadian Church," 16.
91. Talman, "Some Notes, on the Clergy" 61–62.
92. Hardwick, *Anglican British World*, 40.

outlying areas, a pattern exemplified by the placement of Irish clergy associated with the UCCS.

The UCCS initially chose three missionaries, one of whom, Rev. F. Osler, was sedentary; and the other two, Rev. H. O'Neill and Rev. F. A. O'Meara, both Irish and recent graduates of Trinity College Dublin, were itinerant or travelling missionaries.[93] This ratio of a sedentary pastor to double the number of itinerant pastors showed the missionary emphasis of the society. The work of a travelling missionary involved services and preaching in houses, barns, and fields. Secondly, it illustrates how the Irish were given the itinerant role, thereby demonstrating how the new world demanded a different model than the fixed nature of parochial ministry in the old world. This adaptation to itinerant ministry was more akin to the Methodist circuit as the prime unit of ministry and was one precipitated by the large distances to be travelled, scattered settlements, paucity of clergy, and increasing numbers.[94] In fact, itinerancy became normal, the bishop reporting in 1838 that "The clergy . . . except in the few comparatively large towns, are almost all more or less itinerants."[95]

O'Neill was appointed to the Home District, Gore and Niagara. Gore, which in 1837 had a population of almost 44,000 and consisted of 24 townships, was served by four resident clergy in addition to O'Neill, who was a travelling missionary among the European settlers.[96] Niagara consisted of twenty-two townships, a population of over 32,000, with its northern and eastern section ministered to by five clergy (its other parts being unprovided for), with O'Neill the only travelling missionary.[97] In the Home District, O'Neill found no clergyman in the fifty miles between Toronto and Darlington to the east.[98] It was to this neglected area (covering the present counties of York, Ontario, Durham, Peel, Simcoe, Wentworth, Halton and Brant—an area 130 miles by sixty miles from Lake Ontario to Lake Huron) that Rev. Frederick O'Meara was appointed as a travelling missionary.[99]

The frontier and settlement conditions often necessitated cooperation between the bishop and the UCCS. The purpose of the UCCS was to provide clergy to the European immigrant communities in cooperation

---

93. UCCS, *The First Report*, 11; Burtchaell and Sadleir, *Alumni Dublinenses*, 639.
94. Ruggle, "Itinerant Clergy in Upper Canada," 63–69.
95. Hawkins, *Annals of the Diocese of Toronto*, 98.
96. UCCS, *The First Report*, 16.
97. Ibid., 16–17.
98. Ibid., 17. The locations of these clergy were Grimsby, St. Catherine's, Niagara, Chippewa, and Fort Erie: ibid., 17.
99. Ibid., 17.

with the bishop, not to the Indigenous peoples. When the bishop of Montreal wanted to transfer Rev. Frederick O'Meara from the Home District to minister to the native populations at Sault Ste. Marie, the UCCS concurred even though such ministration was not in its mandate.[100] Following his ordination, O'Meara relinquished his position as itinerant missionary and was appointed in 1838 to the Indigenous mission at Sault Ste. Marie.[101] He was to remain there for two years. Then, after Strachan became first bishop of the newly constituted diocese of Toronto in 1839, in 1841 he appointed O'Meara as chaplain to a government-sponsored mission at Manitoulin Island where he ministered among the Ojibwa, succeeding another Irishman, Rev. Charles Brough.[102] It was here O'Meara was to minister for almost twenty years.

From 1830 onwards, despite financial constraints and uncertainty, the church extended itself with missions in Upper Canada to Port Hope, Thornhill, with Irish being appointed to Guelph (Arthur Palmer, 1832), London (Benjamin Cronyn, 1832), and Adelaide (Dominick Blake, 1833), all being ordained clergy of the Church of Ireland, sponsored by the SPG. In 1834 Richard Flood, a friend of Cronyn's while in Ireland and who followed him to Canada in 1833, was made a missionary to Indigenous communities at Caradoc and Delaware, near London.[103] By the time the new diocese of Huron was formed in 1857 there were sixteen Irish rectors or missionaries in it, including in the main centers of London, Woodstock, Goderich, St. Thomas, Owen Sound, Chatham and Amherstburg.[104]

100. UCCS, *The Second Report*.

101. Hawkins, *Annals of the Diocese of Toronto*, 127–28. This appointment was made by the bishop and the lieutenant governor, Sir George Arthur, so that O'Meara and O'Neill (who had returned from Ireland), could be present at Manitoulin in August 1839 when the government made its annual presentation of gifts to the tribes. Before a massive gathering, O'Meara preached to them through an interpreter: UCCS, *The Second Report*, 10, 21; Bleasdale, "Manitowaning," 147–57; E. J. Pratt Library, Victoria College, Toronto, J. W. Grant Papers, "Rendezvous at Manitowaning" (Box 7, file 25), describes the distribution of gifts for military service rendered.

102. Millman, *Life of the Right Reverend*, 127–28; UCCS, *The Second Report*, 10. The Ojibwa lived in a vast stretch from the Ottawa Valley to the Prairies on both sides of the Great Lakes. At the time, the British government was trying to concentrate a large number of the Ojibwa tribes on Manitoulin Island around a mission which had been built at Manitowaning.

103. Millman, *Life of the Right Reverend*, 143.

104. Cooper, "Irish Immigration and the Canadian Church," 15.

ACHIEVEMENT

The contribution of the Irish clergy in the first generation was significant on a number of counts.

Church Planting

Irish clergy proved adept and effective as agents of evangelism and church planting. In this respect as well as others, the most dominant and indefatigable figure was Benjamin Cronyn (1802–1871). After his arrival in York (Toronto) in 1832, Cronyn was appointed to Adelaide near London where already there were friends settled.[105] He found himself in a missionary context serving three congregations. In due course he became the rector of London, had impressive numbers for baptisms and marriages, supported the foundation of the UCCS, and led fundraising and recruitment trips to Britain and Ireland.[106] Under his aegis, the new St. Paul's Church in London was opened in 1846, funds for which came from Ireland.[107] Additionally, a London branch of the Church Society was established to raise funds which were used to place missionary clergy in new districts.[108]

Cronyn soon convened a synod and founded a church society for the diocese, the purpose of the latter being the support of missionaries and clergy, a fund to supplement their income, promotion of education, assistance for those preparing for holy orders, the circulation of religious texts, and the maintenance of churches and buildings.[109] After becoming bishop, Cronyn cooperated with the SPG whereby the Society granted £400 per year (in tandem with a similar sum raised locally) for the support over three years of five travelling missionaries; the arrangement was renewed in 1860 when eight missionaries were at work, and in 1861, eight more were added giving a total of twenty.[110]

In those areas where there was a critical mass of settlers (e.g., Adelaide and London), provision for clergy was more traditional. Reports sent back to Ireland in 1832 suggested that the government would provide new clergy

---

105. Talman, *Authentic Letters from Upper Canada*, 118. He was anticipated to be "a correct, talented, and zealous clergyman" (ibid., 118).

106. Crowfoot, *Benjamin Cronyn*, 37–39, 40–41, 45; Hardwick, *Anglican British World*, 50.

107. Crowfoot, *Benjamin Cronyn*, 52.

108. Ibid., 50.

109. Ibid., 75, 78.

110. Thompson, *Into All the Lands*, 250.

with £150 a year, a house and 400 acres, or £100 annually and 200 acres.[111] However, more typical at least in emergent settlements was the likelihood of an unpredictable income. Rev. Thomas Green, who became rector of Wellington Square (now Burlington) in 1838, following a time as travelling missionary around London, commented in that year (when he was still around London) in his appeal for more clergy that he could not speculate on what income they could expect, for "money is very scare among them."[112] Nevertheless, the amount of £200 made available by the SPG to missionaries in the newly created diocese of Toronto (1839) was a comparable and more stable source of income compared to what obtained in Ireland.[113]

Following Cronyn's elevation to the episcopate as first bishop of Huron in 1857, during the course of the subsequent fourteen years, 101 churches were opened in his diocese, the number of parishes increased from thirty-nine to 160, and the number of clergy doubled.[114] In 1858 Cronyn had forty-four clergy serving the spiritual needs of the older and newly arrived immigrant population, the Indigenous peoples of the area, and escaped slaves from the United States.[115] In ten years as bishop, Cronyn increased the number of clergy to eighty-eight serving 145 churches.[116] Graduates of Trinity were predominant among the clergy of the area.[117] Illustrative of Cronyn's ministry was that in one year he visited eighty-four congregations, confirmed over 1400 persons, consecrated five churches, and ordained fifteen deacons and three priests.[118] With such an expanse of people (the population of the diocese increased by 205,000 between 1852 and 1861) and churches, the need was apparent for the provision of clerical theological training, a need met in 1863 when Cronyn founded Huron College.[119]

Despite differing theologically from Cronyn, fellow Irishman and TCD graduate (1848) John Travers Lewis had a similar missionary purpose of spreading churches staffed with competent clergy throughout his diocese.[120]

111. Talman, *Authentic Letters from Upper Canada*, 111, 119.

112. *DUM* 11 (1838), 346n.

113. Hawkins, *Annals of the Diocese of Toronto*, 122; *DUM* 10 (1837), 735, where the average amount is put at £250; and Townsend, *Facts and Circumstances*, 87–89, where the average is computed as £381.10s.1d. before deductions (e.g., cost of collecting and other expenses), which would put it to £324.9s.

114. Talman, "Cronyn, Benjamin."

115. Crowfoot, *Benjamin Cronyn*, 80.

116. Thompson, *Into All the Lands*, 250.

117. Crowfoot, *Benjamin Cronyn*, 48.

118. Ibid., 80.

119. Ibid., 81.

120. Schurman, "John Travers Lewis," 305.

Following his election as the first bishop of Ontario in 1861, Lewis initially oversaw an area of 152 townships with fifty-five clergy, a number that increased to eighty-six in twelve years, and within twenty years he oversaw the building of 140 new churches.[121] By 1877 alone he had added one hundred new churches, and by the end of the century the number had increased to 283.[122] Thus east and west of Toronto, two Irishmen were to oversee impressive growth in church building, clergy numbers, and pastoral provision.

Efforts by individual clergy were notable. When O'Meara was first posted to the Sault Ste. Marie, aged only twenty-five, his journals and reports show him to have been keenly interested in evangelization and education.[123] On one visit in 1842 Bishop Strachan commended O'Meara for being a "zealous and successful missionary" noting that 400 attended his service.[124] He returned to Ireland late in 1846 seeking money for church building, the funds raised going towards the building of St. Paul's Church, Manitouwaning, a task completed in 1849. When Bishop Strachan visited he commented that: "The new church, a very neat wooden building stands high, and is the most inspiring object in the village. Though not quite finished it was made fit for Divine service."[125] O'Meara remained until 1863. He made another overseas journey in 1854–1855 to gain further support for his mission, and a boys' school was begun. In these ways he demonstrated a commitment to education, fundraising, and church building.

There was a similar achievement by others. Following his posting to London in 1836, Dominick Blake visited outlying settlements in Biddulph, McGillivray, and Osborn in the Huron Tract which, with his station in London, came to constitute nine regular stations which he visited fortnightly.[126] Within a year of being appointed a missionary to Guelph in 1832 and being the only one with a thirty-square-mile radius, Arthur Palmer (TCD 1828) had built a church with a capacity of 400.[127] Rev. Francis Evans (1801–1858) was a TCD graduate who came to Canada in 1824 and by the time he died had formed fourteen congregations in the Woodhouse and Simcoe dis-

121. Thompson, *Into All the Lands*, 251.
122. Schurman, "John Tavers Lewis," 309.
123. USPG Archives, Rhodes House Library, Oxford, C/CAN/503. Two of his reports, both under the title *A Mission to the Ottawhahs and Ojibwas, on Lake Huron*, were published in 1846 at the request of the SPG, and his second report of 1847 reappeared in a third edition in 1849.
124. Hawkins, *Annals of the Diocese of Toronto*, 160.
125. Quoted in *Algoma Anglican* 9.5 (May 1965), 4a.
126. *DUM* 11 (1838), 346n.
127. Hawkins, *Annals of the Diocese of Toronto*, 89; AO Strachan F 983–1 Papers, letters missive, 21 Jan. 1836 (Ms 35, reel 3).

trict.[128] Thus at episcopal and local levels the evidence shows that the Irish pursued a rigorous program of church planting in new frontier areas.

Indigenous Ministry

Strachan was initially more concerned to provide pastors for the settlers than for them to engage in missionary work among the Indigenous peoples. When pressed to address the latter need, he tended to respond with Irish clergy. Such was Rev. William McMurray, the first clergyman at Sault Ste. Marie, who was succeeded by Rev. Frederick O'Meara in 1838. Rev. Richard Flood (1795–1865), a TCD graduate (BA 1820, MA 1832), came to Canada in 1833 and, supported by the Stewart Travelling Mission Fund, became a missionary among the Chippewa along the Thames River from 1834 to 1846.[129] He focused his efforts on the Munsee native settlements on the Thames River, where he had success.[130] Initially for the five townships he was responsible for, there was no church so worship was conducted in barns, attracting fifty to 200 people.[131] Flood's first convert was the chief of the tribe, Capt. James Snake, and within a decade his congregation consisted of one hundred persons, of whom about forty-five were regular communicants.[132] In his 1844 visitation John Strachan remarked that "Large portions of the country remain entirely without Gospel privileges, and have never seen the face of a single Clergyman," yet he could also report that "Missions to the native Indians are, upon the whole, in a prosperous state."[133] In no small way was the success of ministry among the Indigenous peoples due to the efforts of Irish clergy.

---

128. Millman, *Life of the Right Reverend*, 199; AO Strachan F 98301 Papers, letters missive, 16 Jan. 1836 (Ms 35, reel 3).

129. *Upper Canadian Stewart Travelling Mission Fund*, 2–8; Millman, *Life of the Right Reverend*, 199–200.

130. *Upper Canadian Stewart Travelling Mission Fund*, 5–7; Acheson, "Pioneer Clergy in Upper Canada," 133–46. He preached a message from John 14:15 to the Munsee and conducted a Sunday school using signs and his broken Chippewa. He agreed to a specific request that he record their names with a written promise to relinquish the consumption of alcohol among them (a destructive habit they had acquired from the white settlers) for a month. To reinforce this commitment he preached on Galatians 5:14–15, which urged them to live in the fruits of the Spirit (Hawkins, *Annals of the Diocese of Toronto*, 90–91).

131. Hawkins, *Annals of the Diocese of Toronto*, 90–91.

132. Beaven, *Recreations of a Long Vacation*, 81. See also Acheson, "Pioneer Clergy in Upper Canada."

133. Hawkins, *Annals of the Diocese of Toronto*, 195–96.

New Models of Ministry: Dissent Threat

The proliferation of dissenting sects posed a threat to vulnerable immigrants. There was a danger that the thousands of Anglican immigrants arriving in the 1820s and 1830s would choose not to become part of a beleaguered and underdeveloped church, but would rather turn to the Methodists and other dissenting sects.[134] As well as Methodists, there were Mormons, Mennonites, and those holding Unitarian opinions in areas ministered to by Henry O'Neill in the Home, Gore, and Niagara districts.[135] The frontier nature of the scattered settlements meant that the old world model of the sedentary minister in a traditional parochial structure could not function as the sole method of pastoral provision. In the new pioneering conditions the Methodist circuit riders were more effective. In response to both challenges, a model of itinerant missionaries emerged.

The many Irish clergy who came in the 1830s through their service to scattered communities as itinerant clergy, in fact, rescued the church from losing members to the dissenting sects.[136] Their appearance struck a recently arrived immigrant at Adelaide: "The humbler clergyman of our church, when riding through their parishes in travelling dress, resemble the Irish Methodist Preacher."[137] In a fluid and volatile frontier situation, often innovation was necessary. O'Neill, for instance—without a church building of his own—developed such a good relationship with the dissenters that they allowed him the use of their chapels, and it was said "occasionally their ministers have accompanied their congregations to hear him."[138] Indeed, some Irish clergy were responsible for converting some high-profile Methodists to the Anglican fold. Thus Rev. Edward Denroche, a TCD graduate (1828) from Kilkenny and a missionary at Brockville (1833–1854), converted John Flanagan, a fellow Irishman, in 1839.[139] In the contest with Unitarianism, no doubt William Magee's text on the atonement (which was a counter to Unitarian doctrine) would have been foundational as a response by missionar-

---

134. Fahey, *In His Name*, 180; Hawkins, *Annals of the Diocese of Toronto*, 89–90.

135. UCCS, *The First Report*, 18–19; *The Second Report*, 17. Caution about the movement of Methodists over to the Anglican Church, including aspirants to the ministry, was articulated by Strachan to Rev. Edward Denroche in 1840: AO Strachan Letterbooks F 983–2 Strachan to Denroche, 5 Mar. 1840, 23 Mar. 1840 (Ms 35 reel 11).

136. The need for itinerant missionaries was not recognized until 1819: Talman, "Some Notes on the Clergy," 65.

137. Talman, *Authentic Letters from Upper Canada*, 120.

138. UCCS, *The First Report*, 19.

139. Talman, "Some Notes on the Clergy," 64; Millman, *Life of the Right Reverend*, 197.

ies trained in Trinity where it was on the curriculum.[140] Thus in the 1830s in the frontier areas of new settlement, in an exercise of adaptation, the church was able to shed the rigidity of the parish system, something that was the norm in the old world, and adopt a practice of travelling missionaries which in turn served to counter Methodist advances. Nevertheless, it was the hope that at some point the travelling missionaries would be dispensed with and individual communities would come to support a resident clergyman in a stable parish structure.[141]

New Models of Ministry: Pastoral Provision

The urban setting allowed for a more traditional parish structure and the format of religious services. However, in the frontier situation adaptation of the latter was apparent, for instance with Sunday observance and catechetical methods. The expectation that a clergyman's ministrations should be confined only to Sunday was dispensed with because of the pastoral needs of the settlers. As one Irish clergyman, Thomas Green, commented in 1838, "every day must be Sunday," and as a result he had a numerous congregation on weekdays which supplemented his daily house visits.[142] Similarly there was an adaptation of catechetical methods in part to attract dissenters to the church and in part to prevent adherents seceding to the sects. On this matter, Green advocated that "The minds also of those who, from destitution or other causes, have fallen into dissent, ought to be prepared by short lectures on the services of the church, that the charge so frequently made that our prayers etc. are cold and formal, may be practically answered."[143] The frontier context thus solicited flexibility in pastoral provision to which the Irish responded.

Literary Activity

A TCD education came to benefit local communities in ways other than the pastoral. O'Meara's training in classical languages at Trinity no doubt facilitated his becoming fluent in Ojibwa, and producing a number of

---

140. See above Radner's contribution to this volume: "'An awful mystery': William Magee on the Atonement."

141. Noted by Fahey, *In His Name*, 48–51.

142. *DUM* 11 (1838), 346n.

143. Ibid., 346n.

translations into that language.[144] These included a devotional book of select Bible verses, the *Book of Common Prayer*, the four gospels, the psalms of David, a selection of hymns (co-authored with Peter Jacobs, a local Ojibwa man whom O'Meara helped prepare for holy orders, and who, following his ordination by Bishop Strachan in 1856, was his assistant until his death in 1864), and (also with Jacobs) the Pentateuch with Proverbs and Isaiah (Appendix). Strachan's opinion was that O'Meara's works of translation "are still more valuable than his personal exertions as a missionary."[145]

Rev. Richard Flood, whom Strachan assessed as an "excellent missionary," was also involved in translations into the native language for the Munsee and other Indigenous tribes around Lake Huron.[146] In 1847 the SPCK published Flood's translation into Munsee of selections from the *Book of Common Prayer*.[147] Some of this translation work was of wider import; that of O'Meara, for instance, was reprinted and used by missionaries in Rupert's Land and in the Yukon.

Administrative: Diocesan Creation

Prominent Irish clergy were part of the creation of the church's administrative structure. In 1839 the new diocese of Toronto was created out of the larger diocese of Quebec. But it too was to shortly become so populated that its administration became unwieldy, making further subdivision necessary. The plan was to separate the eastern and western parts (centered on Kingston and London respectively) as soon as either could raise the necessary $10,000 for the endowment of its see.[148] Significantly, the first to reach this

---

144. UCCS, *The Third Report*, 13; O'Meara to Bp. of Toronto, 6 Mar. 1840 (AO Strachan Papers F 983-3, Ms 35 Reel 3). Something of his approach to translation is illustrated in the case of his sermons. Initially attempts to deliver the sermons through an interpreter proved inconvenient and cumbersome, so he then wrote out his sermons in English, had the interpreter translate it into Ojibwa, then copied it himself into Ojibwa, and then preached it in that language.

145. John [Strachan], Toronto, 17 Mar. 1857 (GSA, Anglican Church of Canada, M 80-23). O'Meara's work parallels that of another Trinity graduate (of 1833 in classics with prize in Hebrew), the Limerick-born Robert Maunsell (1810-1894) who, following his emigration to New Zealand, made many translations into the Maori language, including the Hebrew text of the Old Testament: Nathan, "Maunsell, Robert."

146. Hawkins, *Annals of the Diocese of Toronto*, 163.

147. Flood, *Morning and Evening Prayers*. It consisted of alternate pages of English and Munsee.

148. Both Cronyn and Rev. Arthur Palmer were to the fore in making suggestions as to how the two new dioceses should be erected: AO Strachan Papers: Report of B. Cronyn and A. Palmer to the Bishop of Toronto, 19 Dec. 1855, F 983-1 (Ms 35 reel 7).

goal was the Irish-dominated area centered on London in 1857 with the election of Cronyn.[149] The decision to create the diocese of Huron (made up of thirteen counties in the western part of Upper Canada) was to lead to a contentious episcopal election between evangelical supporters of Benjamin Cronyn and the high church supporters of Archdeacon A. N. Bethune, who was favored by Strachan.[150] After twenty-five years in the area, Cronyn's election was a crowning achievement. Further, he was the first such bishop in the Canadian church to be elected by a diocesan synod, those up to that point being crown appointments.[151] Significantly, the second area to raise the necessary funds for diocesan creation was the area to the east where in 1861 Travers Lewis was elected the first bishop of the new diocese of Ontario—where, among Anglicans, its rural parts were dominated by Irish.[152]

The creation of Huron and Ontario dioceses—containing significant Irish populations and under the leadership of two Irish bishops—were major markers in the creation of the administrative fabric of the Canadian church. In later years this was added to by the election of Sullivan in Algoma, DuMoulin in Niagara, and Carmichael in Montreal.[153] Collectively all this contributed materially to the institutional and administrative apparatus of the emergent Canadian church. When the first provincial synod of the ecclesiastical province of Canada met in 1861, of the five bishops present, two—Cronyn and Lewis—were TCD graduates.[154] On a wider stage Lewis was a promoter of the first Lambeth Conference in 1867 and of Canadian Anglican church union which materialized in 1893. Thus as the administrative structure of the church in the old world was being dismantled or reconfigured, the new world offered the opportunity for its reconstruction as evident in Huron and Ontario.

---

149. Thompson, *Into All the Lands*, 151.

150. Details of the election are in Horall, "The Clergy and the Election," 205–20; Crowfoot, *Benjamin Cronyn*, 63–74; Kenyon, "The Influence of the Oxford Movement," 89–91.

151. Cronyn's election was novel in that though he was duly elected by the new diocese of Huron, there was no Province of Canada where a group of episcopal peers would consecrate him, hence Cronyn had to go to England for consecration by the archbishop of Canterbury: Crowfoot, *Benjamin Cronyn*, 62–63.

152. Thompson, *Into All the Lands*, 151; Schurman, *A Bishop and His People*, 52, 53–55.

153. Heeney, *Leaders of the Canadian Church*, 218, 267–73, 304.

154. Carrington, *The Anglican Church in Canada*, 129–30. In a photograph of the historic occasion (reproduced in Carrington, 240) only Cronyn and Lewis are standing. Lewis was appointed secretary for the occasion.

Emergence of Distinct Theological Orientations

These developments in the administrative fabric of the church determined the future theological orientation of the dioceses of Ontario and Huron, with Toronto in between becoming the main area of contention. While Strachan lived, opposition was kept in check. His successor A. N. Bethune (the defeated candidate in Huron in 1857 and Ontario in 1861) was less conciliatory and his encouragement of ritualistic innovations spurred the foundation of the Evangelical Association in 1869, aimed at getting more congregational participation in clerical appointments. There followed the foundation of the Church Association (1873), whose goals were to set up institutions parallel to synod. These included the founding of a newspaper, the *Evangelical Churchman*, and the establishment of the Protestant Episcopal Divinity School (later Wycliffe College) in 1877, whose founders (who included O'Meara and Samuel Blake) drew on a strong tradition of low church evangelicalism to which Irish Anglicans contributed significantly. In contrast, Bishop Lewis of Ontario, influenced by the high church ethos of some TCD faculty, notably C. R. Elrington and J. H. Todd, was a supporter of Trinity College, Toronto, and would not ordain graduates of Wycliffe College, where he discerned the teaching to be Calvinistic.[155] Thus theological divisions from the old world (reflective of a fracture in the divinity school of TCD itself) were transported to the new world and institutionalized in dioceses (Huron, Ontario) and in colleges (Trinity, Huron, and Wycliffe).

Lay Leadership

The influx of settlers from Britain and Ireland not only forced the rapid development of church organization and structures, but the arrival of so many Irish, in particular, brought with it an assertion of strong lay leadership in the emergent church. Already in the old world, lay people were well attuned to involvement in church matters at a variety of levels. Laity and clerical aspirants shared a common curriculum at Trinity and hence because of its strong scriptural and catechetical content, there was the experience of a common formation. This latter fact makes explicable how leading Irish settler families were forthright in the qualities they sought in clergymen for the new settlements. Writing in 1822, Thomas Radcliff declared his preference for clergy who were

---

155. Schurman, *A Bishop and His People*, 104, 163, 165, 202.

men of character and high religious attainments, deeply convinced of the responsibility attached to their calling, and determined that every other pursuit and care, shall be secondary to the great purpose for which they are designed and to which they should be principally devoted.[156]

Lay Anglicans came with a heightened sense of the role of the laity in the church and this was extended in a Canadian context.[157]

Such an expansionary dimension to lay involvement in church affairs was in part precipitated by circumstances. With the demise of parliamentary funding for the SPG after 1832, existing resources were insufficient to meet the demand which inaugurated a greater lay involvement in church matters.[158] This is evidenced in the role of lay evangelical societies in promoting clerical recruitment, mission, and church building in lieu of the government-sponsored bodies of long standing.

Irish Anglicans became deeply engaged and lobbied for greater influence over church affairs. In both Huron and Ontario it was the financial support of the laity that produced much of the funding necessary for the founding of new churches and support of clergy.[159] But lay influence did not cease with financial provision. The most notable demonstration of this was in the 1857 episcopal election in Huron where the clerical vote was evenly divided, with Cronyn obtaining twenty-three of the forty votes, but it was the lay vote (twenty-three to ten for Cronyn) that ensured his victory.[160]

Lay and clerical bonds were sealed through marriage alliances. Two of Rev. Dominick Blake's sisters married clergymen, Richard Flood and Charles Brough, both Irish. The TCD cohort produced a new generation of clergy who continued service in the Canadian church. Thus member of the families of Frederick O'Meara, Francis Evans, Rev. Andrew Balfour, Henry Burgess, Edward Denroche, and William Johnson produced clergy in the next generation.[161] Others were influential in other areas of church and public life.[162] Later in the century Samuel Blake, son of Dominick Blake, emerged to be the leading lay Anglican in nineteenth-century Canada.

156. Talman, *Authentic Letters from Upper Canada*, 115.

157. Hayes, "The Struggle for the Rights," 5–17; Hardwick, *Anglican British World*, 79–82.

158. Hayes, *By Grace Co-Workers*, 22.

159. Thompson, *Into All the Lands*, 250–51.

160. Cooper, "Irish Immigration and the Canadian Church," 15.

161. Millman, *Life of the Right Reverend*, 189–90, 192–93, 197, 199, 205.

162. Hannah, daughter of John Grier, was the founder of the Sisterhood of St. John the Divine, while another was a principal of Bishop Strachan School. The son of Samuel Armour (d. 1853), John Douglas Armour, became chief justice of Ontario (Millman, *Life of the Right Reverend*, 188). See also Hayes, "Struggle for the Rights," 5–17.

Ethnic Rivalries

Despite their obvious contribution to the development of the church, there remained a residual resentment against the Irish that was based on theological orientation, personality, style, and ethnic origin. Strachan wrote of Cronyn: "He is a low churchman and better fitted for a political agitator than for a bishop."[163] Cronyn, in large part, enjoyed his success because of the strong lay and clerical support from among the Irish immigrants in the London area, to the extent that one commentator wrote of "[that] combination of clergymen from the Emerald Isle, which exists in this section of the Province, for the purpose of elevating to the dignified post, one of themselves."[164] The extent of such influence is encapsulated in contemporary references to the "Irish compact" and "Trinity College Dublin . . . cliqueism" as characterizing Huron diocese.[165] But such antipathies to the Irish were not focused only on areas where they were concentrated. Rev. John Driscoll reported of Bishop Charles Stewart of Quebec, "The Bishop dislikes Irishmen . . . In speaking of me lately he said: 'He is a good man, but an Irishman.'"[166] These comments bespeak the confrontational style that Irish evangelicals, clerical and lay, brought to public debate on church matters ranging from governance to liturgical style to theological emphasis.

In many ways such attitudes were reflective of those prevailing in the old world, where they had extended to the realm of divinity training. Thus William Connor Magee, a TCD graduate who became archbishop of York, commenting on the Church of England clerical establishment, remarked: "I am only a poor wild Irishman, and they [are] learned and wise and thoughtful Englishmen, who look down with all the fine contempt of an English University upon the man whose degree is not of Oxford or Cambridge."[167]

Complementing this is evidence of an anti-English antipathy informing Irish emigrant attitudes. In 1838, reporting on the ministrations of the English clergyman Rev. F. L. Osler in the townships of Tecumseth and Essa, Rev. Frederick O'Meara observed that

---

163. Quoted in Carrington, *Anglican Church in Canada*, 110. He was writing in 1851, six years before Cronyn became a bishop.

164. Quoted from an unreferenced source in Cooper, "Irish Immigration and the Canadian Church," 15.

165. Ibid., 15.

166. Quoted in Millman, *Life of the Right Reverend*, 165.

167. MacDonnell, *Life and Correspondence*, vol. 2, 283 (quoted in Haig, *Victorian Clergy*, 119).

the inhabitants of those townships which are under his charge, are chiefly Irish of the lower order, and were at first rather prejudiced against Mr. Osler, merely because he did not happen to be a countrymen (sic) of their own (a clannish spirit, which I am sorry to say pervades most of my countrymen who have emigrated to this province).[168]

This sentiment likely reflected a feeling among the Irish that they had been forced from their country because of the push factors described above, among which were the reformist policies of the government at Westminster. It is clear that the new world brought together clergy and people from different parts of Ireland, as well as primarily Irish congregations and English clergy, and that although there were ethnic tensions, these were likely reflective of deeper theological differences.[169] An anti-Catholic bias was likely derivative of this also. Certainly, an anti-Catholic animus was present among some of the early Irish missionaries such as Charles Brough, which, in his case, derived from competition with Catholic priests to gain converts among the Ojibwa.[170]

Maintenance of Contacts with Old World

The maintenance of links and contacts with Ireland were important on a number of fronts. First, Ireland was a source of funds for church and school building projects in Canada. This was the case with O'Meara in Sault Ste. Marie, Cronyn in St. Paul's Church London, and in Lewis's Ontario diocese.[171] Indicative of the vibrancy, wealth, and enduring Irish communal connections between old world and new, was the fact that the fundraising effort was a two-way process. Thus in 1855 a visitor from Ireland successfully raised £120 in the London area for the purposes of supporting the

---

168. UCCS, *The Second Report*, 20.

169. Hardwick, *Anglican British World*, 86–87.

170. Bleasdale, "Manitowaning," 153; AO Strachan Papers F 983-1 Brough to Rev. H. Grasett, 1 Aug. 1839, Ms 35 reel 3 (printed in "The Manitoulin Letters," 71–72).

171. Henderson, "Bettridge, William Craddock." In 1837, William Bettridge and Cronyn formed a deputation that journeyed to England, where Bettridge spent almost a year and a half preaching and touring in an attempt to raise public support for the needs of the church in Canada (ibid.). Together their appeals to the British public for funds and their encouragement of the foundation of local associations resulted in the raising of £128.12s.6d. in subscriptions and donations: UCCS, *First Report*, 10–11. For O'Meara, see Millman, "O'Meara, Frederick Augustus." For Lewis, see Schurman, "John Travers Lewis," 308; Schurman, "Lewis, John Travers."

reformation in Ireland.[172] Secondly, Ireland continued to be a source of recruitment. Keeping the old world community informed of progress and the needs of the mission in Canada was a priority of some of the Irish clergy such as Thomas Green, whose letters as a travelling missionary appeared in the *Church of England Magazine, Dublin University Magazine,* and in the reports edited by W. Waddilove.[173] Benjamin Cronyn recruited three candidates directly, as we have seen. Rev Robert McGee (1789–1872), a TCD graduate (BA 1811, MA 1813), the evangelical incumbent of a Dublin parish, was considered as a possible candidate in the 1857 election for bishop of Huron.[174] Thirdly, there was academic recognition by TCD of the achievements of its graduates. In 1855 the college granted Cronyn the degree of Doctor of Divinity, as it did for O'Meara, Lewis, and Thomas Green, who received an LLD.[175] Lastly, there is evidence of returnees, that is, instances of those who returned to Ireland, but these were rare, a witness to how firmly established the church in Canada was becoming.[176] The old world continued to be a source of resources, human and financial, indicating that in the first generation of emigration, departure to the new world did not bring with it finality and severance.

CONCLUSION

This essay has considered the factors that brought Irish Anglicans to Upper Canada in the 1820s and 1830s, and the immediate and long-term impact they had for the development of the church there. It has focused on clerical and lay formation broadly defined in Ireland, the circumstances and modes of its transfer to the new world, and its application there in a critical decade in the evolution of the colonial church in Canada.

The prospects for the Church of Ireland were not auspicious in this period. Its privileged position began to be dismantled. Multiple threats—external and internal—in the form of Catholic emancipation and government-initiated church reform precipitated a large-scale exodus of its adherents to Upper Canada. They included a significant number of university-educated

---

172. Houston and Smyth, *Irish Emigration and Canadian Settlement*, 168–69.

173. Millman, *Life of the Right Reverend*, 201; *DUM* 11 (1838), 346n; Waddilove, *Stewart Missions*.

174. Kenyon, "Influence of the Oxford Movement," 89.

175. Millmann, *Life of the Right Reverend*, 201, 210; Schurman, *A Bishop and His People*, 65.

176. Hardwick, *Anglican British World*, 191.

and experienced clergy, who came honed through robust study, catechetical instruction, and debate at Trinity College.

In Upper Canada the political environment was accommodating, the ecclesiastical needs dire, and land and economic opportunity plentiful, all in a context where their old world minority status was reversed. Upper Canada was not without its challenges, however, for this was a time of transition.[177] The 1830s was the decade when government support of the SPG was withdrawn and when attacks on the privileged status of the church in the colony began. In this situation of flux, there was a danger that the thousands of Anglican immigrants arriving would turn from an underdeveloped church to the Methodists. There was a critical need for well-educated clergy to keep the thousands of immigrants in the Anglican fold. Strachan's shortage of clergy could have led to him accepting non-qualified, non-educated candidates for the ministry. In the absence of local facilities for theological training (that at Cobourg only materializing in the early 1840s and its successor, Trinity College, Toronto coming in 1851), he was fortunate that so many Irish university-educated clergy with parish experience came to Upper Canada in the 1820s and 1830s, given the demise in Oxford and Cambridge graduates arriving. Strachan, finding the Irish clergy unacceptable in theological terms but, on the other, valuing their university training, arrived at the pragmatic accommodation forced by circumstances to accept them.

Brought to Canadian shores through the agency of lay-driven societies, family contacts, and episcopal intervention, Trinity-educated clergy served not only to bring religious services to existing settlements and new, but also demonstrated flexibility in pastoral provision, stemmed the threat from the dissenters and Methodists, and helped the church become established in frontier conditions, including among Indigenous peoples. The foundational base established in the 1830s was to emanate in the rise of a leadership structure and in the formation of key administrative units in the church with the diocese of Huron (1857) and Ontario (1861), their first bishops being Irish. In these ways the Irish contributed to the expansion of the colonial church.

---

177. Fahey, *In His Name*, 19.

APPENDIX

List of Works by Rev. F. A. O'Meara in Ojibwa
with Transliteration of Titles

Kaezhetabwayandungebun kuhya kaezhewaberepun Owh Anuhmeaud Keahneshnahbabeëgahdag. [Selection of verses from the Bible translated into Ojibwa]. Cobourg: Printed at the Diocesan Press for the Church Society of the Diocese of Toronto, 1844. 36 pages.

Shahguhnahshe Ahnuhmeahwene Muzzeneegun Ojebwag Anwawaud Azheuhneke-Nootahbeegahdag. [English prayer book the Chippewa as their language is so translated and put in writing.] Toronto: Printed at the Diocesan Press for the SPG, 1846.

Ewh oomenwahjemoowin owh tabanemenung Jesus Christ kahenahjemoowaud egewh newin manwahjemoojig owh St. Matthew owh St. Mark owh St. Luke kuhya owh St. John: keahnekuhnootuhbeegahdag anwamand egewh Ahneshenahbag Ojibway anindjig: keenahkoonegeawaud kuhya ketebahahmahgawaud egewh mahyahmahwejegajig Society for Promoting Christian Knowledge, ewede London anduhzhetahwaud. [That his good tidings that one our lord ("that one who owns us") Jesus Christ as they have told the story those four who relate good tidings that one St. Matthew that one St. Mark that one St. Luke and that one St. John. Translated and written into as the manner of their language is those Indians Chippewas who are called. As they have determined that it should be done and have paid for it those who are associated together in doing society for promoting Christian knowledge there London where they work.] Toronto: SPCK, 1850. 766 pages.

Oodahnuhmeähwine nuhguhmoowinun owh David Ojibwag anwawaud azheühnekenootahbeëgahdagin. [His religion songs that David the Chippewas as their language is so translated and put in writing.] Toronto: Printed by H. Rowsell for the Upper Canada Bible Society, 1856. 204 pages.

Nuhguhmoowinun: kanuhguhmoowahjin egewh ahnishenahbag ojibwag anindjig.kahanekuhnootuhbeumoowahjin egewh makuhdawekoonuhyag Rev. Dr. O'Meara kuhya Rev. Peter Jacobs. [Songs (or hymns) which they will sing those Indian Chippewas who are called. Which they have translated and written those clergymen, Rev. Dr. O'Meara and Rev. Peter Jacobs.] Toronto: 1861. 93 pages.

Ewh kechetwah-muzzeneëgun. Nahnun muzzeneëgunun Moses kahoozhebeiihmoowahjin keähnekuhnootuhbeëgahdag anwawaud egewh Ahnishnahbag Ojibwag anindjig. Keënahkoonegawaud kuhya ketebahahmahgawaud egewh mahyahmah-wejegejig. Society for Promoting Christian Knowledge, ewede London anduzhetahwaud. [That sacred-book. Five books Moses which-he-wrote as it has been translated into and written as their language is those Indians Chippewas who are called. They having determined that it should be done and have paid for it those who are associated together in work Society for Promoting Christian Knowledge, there London where-they-work.] Toronto: Printed by Lovell and Gibson, Yonge Street, 1861.

BIBLIOGRAPHY

Acheson, Alan R. "Pioneer Clergy in Upper Canada." In *Reformation Worlds: Antecedents and Legacies in the Anglican Tradition*, edited by Sean Otto and Thomas P. Power, 133–46. New York: Peter Lang, 2016.

Algoma 100: 1873–1973. A Documentary Commentary Commemorating the Centennial of the Diocese of Algoma. Sault Ste. Marie, Canada: Diocese of Algoma, 1973.

Beaven, James. *Recreations of a Long Vacation; or A Visit to Indian Missions in Upper Canada.* Toronto: H & W Roswell. 1846.

Bleasdale, Ruth. "Manitowaning: An Experiment in Indian Settlement." *Ontario History* 66 (1974) 147–57.

Bradley, Ian. *The Call to Seriousness: The Evangelical Impact on the Victorians*. London: Cape, 1976.

Burtchaell, George Dames, and Thomas Ulick Sadleir, eds. *Alumni Dublinenses. A Register of the Students, Graduates, Professors and Provosts of Trinity College in the University of Dublin.* London: Norgate, 1924.

Carrington, Philip. *The Anglican Church in Canada: A History.* Toronto: Collins, 1963.

Church of England Magazine. London: Burns, 1836–75.

Cooper, John Irwin. "Irish Immigration and the Canadian Church before the Middle of the Nineteenth Century." *JCCHS* 2.3 (1955) 1–20.

Crowfoot, Alfred H. *Benjamin Cronyn: First Bishop of Huron.* London: Synod of the Diocese of Huron, 1957.

The Dublin University Calendar, for the Year 1835. Dublin: Curry, 1835.

Dublin University Magazine. Dublin: Curry, 1833–77.

Fahey, Curtis. *In His Name: The Anglican Experience in Upper Canada, 1791–1854.* Ottawa: Carleton University Press, 1991.

Flint, David. *John Strachan: Pastor and Politician.* Toronto: Oxford University Press, 1971.

Flood, Richard, trans. *Morning and Evening Prayers, the Administration of the Sacraments, and Other Rites and Ceremonies of the Church. According to the Use of The United Church of England and Ireland.* London: SPCK, 1847.

Gladwin, Michael. *Anglican Clergy in Australia, 1788–1850: Building a British World.* Woodbridge, UK: Boydell Press for the Royal Historical Society, 2015.

Glazebrook, George Parkin de Twenebroker. *The Church of England in Upper Canada, 1785–1867.* n.p. 1982.

Graham, B. J., and L. J. Proudfoot, eds. *An Historical Geography of Ireland.* Toronto: Academic, 1993.

Grant, John Webster. *A Profusion of Spires: Religion in Nineteenth-Century Ontario.* Toronto: University of Toronto Press, 1988.

Haig, A. G. L. *Victorian Clergy: Ancient Profession Under Strain.* London: Croom Helm, 1984.

Hardwick, Joseph. *An Anglican British World: The Church of England and the Expansion of the Settler Empire, c.1790–1860.* Manchester, UK: Manchester University Press, 2014.

Hawkins, Ernest. *Annals of the Diocese of Toronto.* London: SPCK, 1848.

Hayes, Alan L. *Anglicans in Canada: Controversies and Identity in Historical Perspective.* Chicago: University of Illinois Press, 2004.

———. "The Struggle for the Rights of the Laity in the Diocese of Toronto, 1850–1879." *Journal of the Canadian Church Historical Society* 26 (1984) 5–17.

Hayes, Alan L., ed. *By Grace Co-Workers: Building the Anglican Diocese of Toronto, 1780–1989.* Toronto: Anglican Book Centre, 1989.

Heeney, W. B. *Leaders of the Canadian Church.* Toronto: Musson, 1918.

Henderson, J. L. H. "Bettridge, William Craddock." In *DCB* 10. Toronto: University of Toronto Press, 2003–. http://www.biographi.ca/en/bio/bettridge_william_craddock_10E.html.

Hibernian Church Missionary Society. *The Ninth Report of the Committee of the Hibernian Church Missionary Society.* Dublin: [s.n.], 1823.

———. *The Third Report of the Committee of the Hibernian Church Missionary Society.* Dublin: [s.n.], 1817.

Hill, G. A. *A Guide for Emigrants from the British Shores to the Woods of Canada.* Dublin: R. Moore, 1834.

Horall, S. W. "The Clergy and the Election of Bishop Cronyn." *Ontario History* 58 (1966) 205–20.

Houston, C. J., and W. J. Smyth. *Irish Emigration and Canadian Settlement: Patterns, Links, and Letters.* Toronto: University of Toronto Press, 1990.

John Strachan's Papers and Letterbooks. 4 vols. Toronto: Archives of Ontario, 197–?.

Kenyon, John. "The Influence of the Oxford Movement upon the Church of England in Upper Canada." *Ontario History* 51.2 (1959) 79–94.

MacDonnell, John Cotter. *Life and Correspondence of William Connor Magee.* 2 vols. London: Isbister, 1896.

"The Manitoulin Letters of the Reverend Charles Crosbie Brough." Transcribed by Rundall M. Lewis. *Ontario History* 48.2 (1956) 63–80.

Maughan, Steve S. *Mighty England Do Good: Culture, Faith, Empire, and World in the Foreign Missions of the Church of England, 1850–1915.* Grand Rapids, MI: Eerdmans, 2014.

Millman, Thomas R. *The Life of the Right Reverend, the Honourable Charles James Stewart, DD Oxon. Second Anglican Bishop of Quebec.* London, ON: Huron College, 1953.

———. "O'Meara, Frederick Augustus," In *DCB* 11. Toronto: University of Toronto Press, 2003–. http://www.biographi.ca/en/bio/o_meara_frederick_augustus_11E.html.

Murray, Hugh. *An Historical and Descriptive Account of British America.* 3 vols. Edinburgh: Oliver & Boyd, 1839.

Nathan, Judith Morrell. "Maunsell, Robert." *Dictionary of New Zealand Biography. Te Ara—the Encyclopedia of New Zealand.* http://www.TeAra.govt.nz/en/biographies/1m28/maunsell-robert.

Power, Thomas P. "'Of No Small Importance': Curricular Change in the School of Divinity, Trinity College Dublin, 1790–1850." In *Change and Transformation: Essays in Anglican History*, edited by Thomas P. Power, 140–83. Eugene, OR: Pickwick, 2013.

Ruggle, Richard E. "Itinerant Clergy in Upper Canada." *JCCHS* 27.2 (1985) 63–69.

———. "McMurray, William." In *DCB* 12. Toronto: University of Toronto Press, 2003–. http://www.biographi.ca/en/bio/mcmurray_william_12E.html.

Schurman, Donald M. *A Bishop and His People: John Travers Lewis and the Anglican Diocese of Ontario, 1862–1902*. Kingston, ON: Diocese of Ontario, 1991.

———. "John Travers Lewis and the Establishment of the Anglican Diocese." In *To Preserve and Defend: Essays on Kingston in the Nineteenth Century*, edited by G. Tulchinsky, 299–310, 383–4. Montreal: McGill-Queen's University Press, 1976.

———. "Lewis, John Travers." In *DCB* 13. Toronto: University of Toronto Press, 2003–. http://www.biographi.ca/en/bio/lewis_john_travers_13E.html.

Talman, James J. "Cronyn, Benjamin." In *DCB* 10. Toronto: University of Toronto Press, 2003–. http://www.biographi.ca/en/bio/cronyn_benjamin_10E.html.

———. "Some Notes on the Clergy of the Church of England in Upper Canada Prior to 1840." *Transactions of the Royal Society of Canada*, 3 ser., sec. 2, 32 (1938) 62–66.

Talman, James J., ed. *Authentic Letters from Upper Canada Including an Account of Canadian Field Sports by Thomas William Magrath, the Whole Edited by the Rev. Thomas Radcliff*. Toronto: Macmillan, 1953.

Thompson, H. P. *Into All the Lands: The History of the Society for the Propagation of the Gospel in Foreign Parts, 1701–1950*. London: SPCK, 1951.

Townsend, T. S. *Facts and Circumstances Relating to the Condition of the Irish Clergy of the Established Church*. Dublin: William Curry, 1832.

Trollope, Anthony. *Clergymen of the Church of England*. Leicester, UK: Leicester University Press, 1974.

Twells, Alison. *The Civilising Mission and the English Middle Class, 1792–1850: The 'Heathen' at Home and Overseas*. New York: Palgrave Macmillan, 2009.

UCCS. *The First Report of the Upper Canada Clergy Society*. London: [s.n.], 1838.

———. *The Second Report of the Upper Canada Clergy Society*. London: [s.n.], 1839.

———. *The Third Report of the Upper Canada Clergy Society*. London: [s.n.], 1840.

Upper Canadian Stewart Travelling Mission Fund. Hexham, UK: n.d. [c.1836].

Vaudry, Richard W. *Anglicans and the Atlantic World: High Churchmen, Evangelicals and the Quebec Connection*. Montreal: McGill-Queen's University Press, 2003.

Waddilove, W. J. D., ed. *The Stewart Missions: A Series of Letters and Journals, Calculated to Exhibit to British Christians, the Spiritual Destitution of the Emigrants Settled in the Remote Parts of Upper Canada . . . Printed at the Expense of the Venerable Bishop's Upper Canadian Travelling Mission Fund*. London: Printed for J. Hatchard & Son, 1838.

Westfall, William. "'Some Practical Acquaintance with Parochial Duties': Learning and Practice in the Diocese of Toronto in the Nineteenth Century." In *Learning to Practice: Professional Education in Historical and Contemporary Perspective*, edited by Ruby Heap et al, 43–67. Ottawa: University of Ottawa Press, 2005.

Wilson, David A. *The Irish in Canada*. Ottawa: Canadian Historical Association, 1989.

10

Samuel Blake's Projects and Ministries
A Canadian's Church of Ireland Vision

ALAN L. HAYES

DURING HIS ACTIVE YEARS, no Anglican layperson in Canada outshone Samuel Hume Blake (1835–1914) in prominence as a religious leader and controversialist. He made his living, and quite a good one at that, as a skilled lawyer with important clients, and for several years as a judge, but he seemed to have all the time in the world for church affairs. He was uncompromisingly passionate and boundlessly energetic in his conservative evangelical faith. He took on several lay ministries, most notably training Sunday school teachers in many denominations. He exercised a wide-ranging philanthropy, directing his professional wisdom and substantial wealth to a variety of Christian educational, social service, and missionary institutions and associations. He gave inspirational addresses and helped organize religious conferences and preaching missions. He published dozens of conservative tracts on theological controversies and aggressively advocated his causes in church judicatories and other contexts. Whether he was acting in cooperation with the Church's established episcopal and synodical authorities or in defiance of them, his figure loomed large.

Considered a century after his death, Blake's lasting achievements are modest. In his most fervent religious goals—maintaining the pure Protestant identity of Canadian Anglicanism, routing ritualism, restraining Roman

Catholicism, resisting liberalism, protecting the Bible from higher criticism—he failed, and was bound to fail. Several institutions that he helped found, such as Wycliffe College, Havergal College, and Ridley College, do continue to prosper, but they are no longer the instruments of his values and bigotries. But his historical role in his contemporary Canadian Christianity is extremely significant. He wielded clout and shaped discussions, and his ministries, projects, addresses, and writings affected a wide range of people.

Blake's prominence in the church owed partly to his worldly resources: wealth, professional skills, social standing, and friendships. But the character and the effectiveness of his church work depended to a very large extent on his theologically developed, biblically defended, integrated vision for Christian faith and discipleship. That vision was rooted and steeped in the Church of Ireland style of Anglicanism in which he was raised and to which he remained attached throughout his life. Blake can be seen as the last gasp of a traditional Church of Ireland Anglicanism before it was swept away by new intellectual tides, and World War I.

CHURCH OF IRELAND BACKGROUND

The name of the church into which Sam Blake was born was the United Church of England and Ireland. This church had been created in 1801, when the United Kingdom of Great Britain and Ireland was established, and it would disappear when the Church of Ireland was disestablished in 1869. The word "united" was perhaps more aspirational than descriptive. The Church of England and the Church of Ireland, although united in general administrative ways, were distinct in their theological tendencies, their sense of history, their pastoral character, and their social context. Looming over the Church of England was the figure of Archbishop William Laud, martyred by Puritans in 1645.[1] The prototype of high-church Toryism, Laud represented royal rule, episcopal authority, hierarchical governance, liturgical scrupulosity, Arminianism, and uniformity of religion. Looming over the Church of Ireland, by contrast, was the figure of Laud's contemporary and in some ways rival, Archbishop James Ussher, biblical scholar, Irish church historian, ardent Calvinist, and anti-Catholic apologist.[2] Ussher's historical research had led him to the view that the Church of Ireland derived from a primitive Celtic Christianity which to a remarkable degree resembled Calvinistic Protestantism, and he successfully defended the identity and independence of the Irish Church against Laud's attempted encroachments.

1. Milton, "Laud, William (1573–1645)."
2. Ford, "Ussher, James (1581–1656)."

Neither tradition, of course, was monolithic. There were indeed high-church Anglicans in the Church of Ireland, though Peter Nockles describes them as "an embattled minority,"[3] just as there were many Calvinist evangelicals in the Church of England. A TCD background was no guarantee of evangelicalism, as is amply demonstrated by the case of John Travers Lewis, a Tractarian who was elected bishop of Ontario in 1861.[4] Nevertheless, it remains true that the two churches had distinct centers of gravity.

Sam Blake's family of origin was strongly Church of Ireland. His paternal grandfather was a Church of Ireland minister, as was his uncle, Dominick Edward Blake. His father, William Hume Blake (he was called Hume), had begun studying for the ministry too, although he soon lost either interest or patience. Sam's mother, Catherine Hume, the first cousin of his father, was herself a devout Christian with Church of Ireland convictions, strict ethical standards, and a domineering personality. She was also an educated woman, fluent in French and Italian, skilled in harp and piano, and given to reading the classics in Latin.

Sam's father and brother were TCD graduates. Theological education there was arguably the best available in the English-speaking world.[5] The academic curriculum in divinity was demanding, and was enhanced by studies of pastoral application. One sign of the quality of TCD was that its faculty were active in publishing research; typically at Oxford and Cambridge teachers did little publishing, and indeed holders of chairs were generally pluralists and absentees. "The superior professional qualifications of the Irish clergy," wrote an observer in 1846, were to be traced to "the efficiency of the divinity school of our university, and the care and labour there bestowed on the candidates for the ministry." In what's now Ontario, about a third of the active Anglican clergy in the mid-nineteenth century were TCD graduates. The Church of Ireland model of a reasoned Protestant faith, sympathetic to Calvinism and strongly biblical, united to a vigorous intellectual culture in the service of the Church and community, would shape Sam Blake profoundly. Such a model stands behind the prospectuses for Wycliffe, Ridley, and Havergal Colleges.

Two other dimensions of Church of Ireland Anglicanism deserve mention.[6] First, it had to defend itself against a majority Roman Catholic

---

3. Nockles, "Church or Protestant Sect?," 460.

4. "His connections with Ireland and Trinity College, Dublin, probably helped get him elected bishop in 1863 [sic]." Rawlyk, *Aspects of the Canadian Evangelical Experience*, 164. He was elected in June 1861, but not consecrated until March 1862.

5. Power, "'Of No Small Importance,'" 182.

6. The information in this paragraph is drawn from Akenson, *Church of Ireland*, 65–69.

population and a Presbyterianism that were both deeply hostile towards it. Church of Ireland members made up hardly more than a tenth of the population of the country, but they owned most of the property and wielded most of the political influence, and over the years they had grown accustomed to defending themselves against the resentments of the majority. Sam's pugnacity came naturally. And while anti–Roman Catholic sentiments were rampant in the Church of England, they were far more bitter in the vastly outnumbered Church of Ireland. Sam could never bear "papism." Second, generally speaking and compared to other denominations, the Church of Ireland laity were financially comfortable, literate, well educated, and professionally skilled. Under the system of church patronage, they had the authority to appoint many of the parish clergy. Sam was never in the least tempted to acquiesce to clericalism or to be overawed by bishops.

Now, in the Old World, Ireland was in one place and England in another. But in colonial Canada, the Irish and the English were in constant relation. Tensions could result. For one thing, although in Upper Canada people of Irish extraction outnumbered those of English extraction by perhaps two to one,[7] and although a significant portion of the lower clergy were Irish, the bishops, archdeacons, and the officials they appointed were usually English, or Scots Episcopalians whose church style was more English than Irish. Under English oversight, those of a Church of Ireland background could feel like colonized, if not despised, outsiders. The disdain of Anglican leaders for the Irish is easy to spot in the correspondence of John Strachan, the archdeacon of York and later the first bishop of Toronto. "The clergymen who came to this country from Ireland are strangely Calvinistic in their sermons—and go much further than those who are called Evangelical in England," he observed with alarm in 1834.[8] In 1842, when the governor-general Sir Charles Bagot appointed a Church of Ireland minister, John McCaul, to be vice president of Strachan's beloved King's College, an Anglican establishment, Strachan was horrified. "If we are to commence King's College in an imposing, popular, and effective manner," he fired off to Bagot, "the President and leading professors must without exception be from England."[9] When Strachan sought a provost for his Trinity College in

---

7. Akenson, *Irish in Ontario*, 18–19, who notes the imprecision of demographic data.

8. Archives of Ontario, Strachan Papers, John Strachan to the Archbishop of Dublin, 28 Apr. 1834 (F 983–2 Letterbook of John Strachan, 1827–1839, f. 243). Quoted in Magocsi, *Encyclopedia of Canada's Peoples*, 777, where it is mistakenly dated 1836.

9. Friedland, *University of Toronto*, 20.

1850, he made sure to choose from among "true sons of the Church of England" who were not evangelical,[10] and his search was confined to England.

Thus even before the 1860s, two parties were beginning to crystallize in the United Church of England and Ireland in Canada, one with its base in the Church of England, and one with its base in the Church of Ireland.

FAMILY BACKGROUND

Samuel Hume Blake[11] was born in Toronto in 1835, but his spiritual roots, like his ethnic heritage, were Irish. His parents, Hume and Catherine,[12] as well as his uncle Dominick and his wife, had come to Canada in 1832, not as refugees from an Irish potato famine, but as members of comfortable families with social standing. For Dominick, the incentive was to find church employment, since opportunities for parish appointment in the Church of Ireland were drying up as a result of contemporary Irish church reform. For Hume and Catherine, the thought was initially to try farming. Why they chose Canada isn't clear, although Dominick's father-in-law had fought in Canada in the War of 1812 and spoke well of the country. The Blakes and some university friends, including Benjamin Cronyn, the future first bishop of Huron, chartered a sailing ship for their crossing. Hume and Catherine settled on a farm in Strathroy, near London, where their first son Edward was born in 1833. Pretty soon Hume discovered, or, according to family stories, Catherine persuaded him, that he didn't have much talent for farming, so they moved to Toronto, and he began studying the law. Catherine ran a private girls' school.

Sam and Edward and their two sisters had their early education and the heart of their religious formation at home, mainly from their mother, and also from tutors. What he learned at home about Christianity became bedrock. Towards the end of his life, Sam wrote, "I have never been in the

---

10. Headon, "Whitaker, George," para. 3.

11. A general biographical reference on Blake is Blackwell, "Blake, Samuel Hume." For his early family life and other references, see Schull, *Edward Blake*. Obituaries include Cody, "Samuel Hume Blake"; *Canadian Churchman* (25 Jun. 1914); *Globe* (26 Jun. 1914). Contemporary biographical entries include Rose, *Cyclopaedia of Canadian Biography*, 72–73; Dent, *Canadian Portrait Gallery*, 177–180. He published dozens of tracts, most available online through the Canadian Institute for Historical Microreproductions (CIHM record identifiers are given in the bibliography where available). Most of Blake's papers were disposed of by his daughter. A few are at University of Toronto Archives, Blake-Wrong fonds, B2009-0019/001P; several miscellaneous files are at Archives of Ontario; correspondence with Henry Cody is in the archives of St. Paul's, Bloor Street.

12. Swainson, "Blake, William Hume"; Livermore, "Hume, Catherine Honoria."

least shaken in the simple creed as to the Bible given to me as a child over sixty-five years ago"—the creed that God's revelation is given in the Holy Scriptures as the infallible Word of God.[13]

Sam's father moved into a brilliant career as a lawyer, first as a crown attorney (one of his cases was the inspiration for a work of historical fiction by Margaret Atwood called *Alias Grace*), and then in the equity courts, which at the time had a separate existence from courts of common law. (Equity courts had general jurisdiction in a number of areas where the common law didn't work well, such as foreclosures, alimonies, trusts, and guardianships.[14]) He advanced to be the senior judge of the principal equity court, Chancery, which gave him the title Chancellor. His sons Edward and Samuel, too, would become lawyers.

Soon Hume was distracted from the law into a political career, where he followed the family tradition of Whiggish and Reform sympathies. He supported the reformer Robert Baldwin, another evangelical Anglican of Irish extraction, who in the 1840s did as much as anyone to bring down the Tory "family compact" of Upper Canada, of which John Strachan was a prominent member. Their sons Edward and Sam followed in the same political tradition into what in 1861 became the Liberal Party. In a speech late in his life, Sam Blake recalled that, as a child, he sometimes saw Robert Baldwin walk past his window, with a bearing of integrity and uprightness, and he would say to himself, "I would like to live a life as true and as upright as the life of that man!"[15]

Sam Blake, after his early home tutoring, attended Upper Canada College, where he was an unusually able student, with a particular reputation for oratory. After a stint with a mercantile firm, he completed a BA at the University of Toronto and studied law. In 1854 he was admitted to the bar, and partnered with his brother in the law firm that was now called Blake and Blake, or just Blakes. As Edward moved firmly into politics (he would become premier of Ontario, later the leader of the federal Liberal Party), Sam kept the firm going, and indeed led it to become one of the largest, most active, and most prestigious law firms in Canada. Like his father, he specialized in equity, and he too would one day become a judge in the Court of Chancery—one of the assistant judges, with the title Vice Chancellor. In that capacity he won a reputation for efficient administration of cases and able judgments, although some may have worried that his outspoken commitments to evangelical Christianity and the Liberal Party raised conflicts.

13. Blake, *Teaching of Religious Knowledge* (CIHM 74241), 8.
14. Brown, "Equitable Jurisdiction and the Court of Chancery," 274–314.
15. Blake, *Standards* (CIHM 86215), 4.

In 1859 Blake married Rebecca Cronyn, one of the daughters of Benjamin Cronyn, whose family had been fast friends of the Blakes since even before immigrating together to Canada. (Sam's brother Edward married another Cronyn daughter, Margaret; and Sam's sister Sophy married one of Cronyn's sons, Verschoyle.) Cronyn, who had been elected bishop of Huron in 1857, despite (or because of) what his critics called his "Calvinistic cliqueism"[16] (i.e., Church of Ireland roots), was now the single most prominent advocate of Church of Ireland Protestantism in the province, and Blake's family association with him was now as fully cemented as his theological connections. Sam and Rebecca lived in a comfortable house on Jarvis Street, then a very fashionable area. They attended St. James Cathedral for many years, then switched to St. Peter's, Carlton Street, and finally to St. Paul's, when Henry Cody came there as rector.

CONTROVERSIES

In his late teen years, Blake had a ringside seat as controversies developed around Trinity College, which was established by Bishop Strachan in 1851, and which immediately divided Anglicans along what were developing as party lines.[17] Strachan and his supporters wanted a distinctly church university, with religious tests on students for admission and on teachers for appointments; Trinity was intended to form students' moral and spiritual character according to the best kind of Christianity, which was high-church Anglican Christianity. Evangelical Anglicans disliked the monastic character of Trinity and its exclusion of good Christian young people whose churches lacked bishops. Instead, they supported the public university, the University of Toronto, which initially was led by three Irish-born Anglicans who had broken with their bishop: John McCaul, its first president, and Peter de Blaquière and William Hume Blake, its first two chancellors. (Sam Blake would later teach law there, and his brother Edward would become chancellor.) High-church Anglicans were appalled at the adhesion of Anglican evangelicals to a university that one archdeacon publicly termed "a gorgeous temple of infidelity."[18]

A year after Sam Blake's marriage, his father-in-law launched an attack on the theological teaching of the provost of Trinity, George Whitaker. In particular Cronyn alleged that the provost's teaching on the Blessed Virgin Mary, the prayers of the departed, priestly absolution, and sacramental

16. Talman, "Cronyn, Benjamin."
17. A brilliant short study is Westfall, *Founding Moment*.
18. Melville, *Rise and Progress of Trinity College*, 116.

theology was distinctly un-Protestant.[19] These were areas of theology where the Church of England had grown more indulgent of Catholic opinion than the Church of Ireland. Cronyn's dissatisfactions ultimately led him to begin his own theological school, Huron College.

In the 1860s further controversies sharpened the divide between the two Anglican groups.[20] Evangelicals wanted lay oversight of diocesan finances; Strachan's supporters resisted. Evangelicals wanted to discipline clergy who used too much ceremony in their liturgy; Strachan's supporters resisted. Evangelicals wanted the laity to control the appointments of clergy to parish churches; Strachan's supporters resisted. In the mind of the evangelicals, what was at stake in these issues was the rights of the laity. The theological foundation of the rights of the laity was the Reformation principle of the priesthood of all the people, of whom the ordained clergy were representative. But there was another foundation: Church of Ireland laypeople of a certain class were accustomed to be taken seriously in church affairs. Their wealth gave them clout. In reading Blake's many broadsides, one is struck by how often he makes a claim to be heard, and a claim for the laity to be heard, on the basis of the money that they bring to the table.[21] If the clergy wanted a cathedral, or wanted to renovate their buildings, or wanted to run residential schools, he reminded them that they needed to bring the laity on side. To clericalists, this approach was offensive. It sounded to them as if he was saying: "Don't preach the gospel unless what you say suits the fancy of your wealthy laypeople." But to Blake, the faulty assumption in that reaction was that the clergy knew the gospel and the laity didn't. Philanthropic laypeople like Blake wanted to steward their wealth for the businesslike support of gospel goals, and their stewardship required them to discern which of the clergy's aims were both businesslike and evangelical.

For many reasons, notably their personal affection for the aging and venerable John Strachan, evangelical Anglicans in Toronto made an effort to restrain their criticisms of the diocesan establishment until a new bishop, A. N. Bethune, succeeded in 1867. The unfortunate Bethune, a weak, narrow, and indirect man, reaped the whirlwind. At first evangelicals tried to work within the synodical system, but in 1873 that became impossible. An organized majority in the Toronto synod voted all evangelicals out of office.

19. Cronyn, *Bishop of Huron's Objections*.

20. Hayes, "Struggle for the Rights of the Laity," 5–17; Hayes, "Repairing the Walls," 43–96.

21. Just to give one example: in resisting a plan for church extension by Rural Dean Cayley, discussed below, Blake wrote, "I did not think we were justified in appealing to our men of wealth to assist in such an unbusiness-like undertaking." Blake, *Synod of the Diocese of Toronto* (CIHM 86238), 3.

The most scandalous expulsion was that of the loyal and hard-working J. G. Hodgins, the Dublin-born honorary lay secretary of synod, whose day job was the eminent one of deputy superintendent of education in Ontario. This appears to be the provocation that brought Sam Blake fully into the fray of church politics. On the day that the evangelicals were voted out of their synod appointments, he advertised an organizational meeting of a protest group, which led to the formation of what they called the Church Association. Sam Blake became a vice president in title, but he was most of the energy and much of the money behind the organization. For the next six years the group took on projects, wrote tracts, and raised money for a private mission fund, each activity provoking further anger from his critics.[22] The newspaper of the church party, the *Dominion Churchman*, asked in evident exasperation: "Who is to have control of the Diocese? The bishop and the synod, or the Vice-Chancellor Blake and those who are accustomed to do his bidding?"[23]

By a process which the anthropologist Marshall Sahlins calls "deviation amplification,"[24] two mutually hostile church parties took shape, each driven to emphasize the importance of points in dispute and their contrasting justifications, creating contrapositional identity markers that formed them into structural antitypes. In time each had its own weekly newspaper, hymn book preferences, Sunday school curricula, missionary organizations, theological college, and supporters in synod. Probably most church members scorned both extremes, but their perception of the church landscape was inevitably shaped by these two sets of powerful voices, as, inevitably, the perceptions of historians have been as well. Blake became one of the acknowledged leaders of the evangelical party.

Blake's strategies might be political, but his vision was theological: he wanted to strengthen the Church of Ireland character of the Church of England in Canada. He gave leadership in organizing a hugely successful parish revival mission in 1877 at St. James Cathedral led by William Rainsford, an Irish-born Anglican evangelist.[25] It attracted crowds so large that people had to stand in the chancel, thus scandalizing the high-church press which called it a desecration of holy space.[26] In each of the next two years Blake chaired the executive committee for an event called the Christian Confer-

---

22. Hayes, "Struggle for the Rights of the Laity," 11–15.
23. *Dominion Churchman* 3 (1877), 303.
24. Sahlins, *Culture in Practice*, 340. I am grateful to Professor Joseph Bryant of the University of Toronto for a discussion leading to this reference.
25. Rainsford, *Story of a Varied Life*.
26. Bonham, *Church Revived*, 248.

ence, a new idea in Canada which had precedents in Britain and the United States.[27] It centered on Bible readings, a Darbyite idea focusing on strings of short Bible passages with brief commentary, along with inspirational speakers, not quite exclusively of conservative theological outlook, leading up to a mass evangelistic meeting. Another of his projects was to create a non-ritualist parish church to serve the needs of the inner-city poor, just up the road from the ceremonially inclined Holy Trinity Church (at what is now called Eaton Square).[28]

During the Church Association period of the 1870s, Blake's most long-lasting achievement, and the one of which he was always the proudest, was the creation of a new theological school. What became Wycliffe College[29] opened in 1877, promising to train students in a Protestant understanding of justification, Church, ministry, and sacraments, in direct opposition to Trinity College, the diocesan school. The bishop of Huron immediately announced that he would be delighted to ordain its graduates.

But the bishop of Toronto cold-shouldered it. The supporters of Wycliffe wondered whether the college would prove a wasted effort, since students wouldn't come if they couldn't be ordained after graduation. What happened next was recalled many years later by Blake at a Wycliffe College anniversary event. According to a reporter who covered the event for the *Toronto Mail and Empire* named Hector Charlesworth, writing years later in a book of memoirs,[30] Blake "lost control of his emotions—as he was apt to do in moments of excitement." After recounting several obstacles to the founding of the college that God had removed in answer to the prayers of its supporters, he came to what he called "the final obstacle," Bishop Bethune's threat not to ordain the graduates of the college. "We . . . prayed fervently, and again it pleased God to answer our prayers—for shortly afterward *Bishop Bethune died*." Charlesworth recalled, "Mere type cannot do justice to the mordant fire of Mr. Blake's tones. His voice was naturally biting and vibrant, and it was clear that in the rapture of triumphant recollection he had become oblivious to the diabolical implication of his words," which might be "twisted into a charge that the evangelicals had prayed for the death of their bishop." The principal of the college persuaded the reporters

---

27. Sawatsky, "'Looking for that Blessed Hope,'" 134–78.

28. Grace Church, as it was called, where the bus station is now, always struggled for a congregation, and lost several of its leaders through a dispute when a ritualist priest was appointed. In 1911, it was moved to the northern suburbs, where it became Grace Church-on-the-Hill.

29. Blake, *Wycliffe College* (CIHM 86745); Hague, *Jubilee Volume of Wycliffe College*; Edinborough, *Enduring Word*.

30. Charlesworth, *Candid Chronicles*, 49–51.

not to print this part of Blake's speech. The anecdote says a great deal about Blake: his patriarchal role at Wycliffe and in the Anglican evangelical party; his pietistic sense of God's favour for his cause; his voice so naturally fitted to courtroom oratory and so easily adapted to church controversy; his imperviousness to different points of view; and what D. C. Masters called his "complete bluntness and absence of tact."[31]

With Bethune's death, representatives of the two church parties, meeting privately, agreed on a compromise: the Church Association would be terminated, and a bishop who was open to evangelicalism would be elected. The new bishop, Arthur Sweatman,[32] an English priest who had been little known in the diocese of Toronto, proved more evangelical than expected, and at his first synod gave an address which left Blake ecstatic. Blake was still recalling it many years later as the Magna Carta of Anglican evangelicalism in Toronto.[33] However, Sweatman's patience with the provocative Blake, and with Wycliffe College, did sometimes wear thin.

With the dissolution of the Ontario Court of Chancery in 1880, Blake returned to his private law practice. One achievement of his leadership deserves note because of its resonances with church affairs: he supported admitting women to the professions. Perhaps the model of his well-educated mother, who had managed a school, influenced him. In 1892, as one of the Benchers (the governance of the Law Society), Blake seconded the motion that, by a vote of twelve to eleven, allowed Clara Brett Martin to become the first woman lawyer in the British Empire. Later, when Martin's articling placement at a Toronto law firm was being sabotaged by sexist lawyers and clerks, Blake brought her to his own firm and took over her supervision.[34] Around the same time, as will be noted below, Blake was giving strong support to the new Anglican order of deaconesses.

But Blake was giving less and less time to his practice, and spending more and more time on his philanthropy and church activities, until in his last years he was giving virtually all his time to church matters and philanthropy.[35] Blake's projects in these years can be divided (not quite neatly) into two categories, Anglican educational institutions and ecumenical social service and evangelistic associations.

---

31. Masters, "Anglican Evangelicals in Toronto," 55.
32. Hayes, "Sweatman, Arthur."
33. Blake, *Anglo-Roman Priesthood* (CIHM 86222), 21.
34. Backhouse, "To Open the Way," 1–41.
35. "Hon. Samuel Hume Blake, K.C.," 452.

ANGLICAN EDUCATIONAL INSTITUTIONS

With his fellow lay supporters of Wycliffe College and others, Blake was a leader, sometimes *the* leader, among a group of Toronto Anglican evangelicals seeking opportunities to found other schools in the TCD tradition of evangelical faith and intellectual culture.[36] The first was a boys' school, Bishop Ridley College.[37] Their opportunity emerged in 1888 when a suitable property came available in St. Catharines; it was the old Springbanks Sanitarium at College and Yates Streets. The founding group came together first in Principal J. P. Sheraton's office at Wycliffe College. Blake became a member of the board of directors of the school, and a strong financial supporter. (One of its first teachers included Henry Cody, who became a fast friend of Blake's.) Conflict between the two church parties was triggered by the letter of incorporation, which described the school as offering "a religious training of a distinctive evangelical type in accordance with the Protestant principles of the Reformation." The bishop of Niagara, Charles Hamilton, huffed that these were not terms "used in the formularies of the Church of England" and were "in my judgment objectionable." Blake remained connected with the school until the principal accepted an honourary doctorate from Trinity College. Blake immediately withdrew his financial support, and never attended a board meeting again.

The next educational project was Havergal College, an Anglican girls' school, as an alternative to Bishop Strachan School, which Blake regarded as thoroughly papist.[38] In 1894 Blake saw an opportunity when one of his law clients, the proprietor of a girls' school, wanted to dispose of the property. Blake called his friends together. The old school, called Morvyn House, was a rather shabby building, but it was in a fashionable area on Jarvis Street at number 354, near Sam's own home. The group bought the house, guaranteed a year's funding, and recruited a principal, Ellen Knox, the sister of the evangelical Church of England bishop of Manchester, Edmund Knox (1847–1937). They named the school after the English evangelical poet and hymn writer, Frances Ridley Havergal. The prospectus identified its mission as "uniting Evangelical influences with a thorough intellectual culture," in the line of Wycliffe College and Ridley College, which it specifically identified. Again, we see the TCD model in the background. Blake, as chair of the board, and Knox, as principal of the school, were both as stubborn as they were evangelical, and sometimes came to loggerheads, but they respected

---

36. Masters, "Anglican Evangelicals in Toronto," 54.
37. Bradley and Lewis, *Ridley*; Beattie, *Ridley*.
38. Byers, *Havergal*, 8–10.

each other and worked successfully together to build the school up. Blake was a frequent visitor at the school, remembered by the girls as "austere, dominating, yet humorous and kindly." It was a school tradition that he read Dickens' "A Christmas Carol" at the school's annual Christmas party.

A fourth educational institution that Blake supported was the Deaconess School,[39] which the Alumni Society of Wycliffe College took on in 1891, with several laypeople including Blake on the organizing committee. Blake was keen to promote the Christian ministry of women, and was mortified that the high church had already found a way to do so through women's religious orders, a calling which he considered papist. An order of deaconesses was more acceptable to Anglican evangelicals, and this was being gradually instituted in various parts of the Anglican Communion in the nineteenth century, with the rationale that it was a revival of an order in the early church. Blake served on the board that developed the Deaconess School, and gave $10,000 to give it a home at 179 Gerrard Street East, in a seamy neighborhood where deaconess students could test their mettle. A few years later, when the building needed to be expanded, he helped fund a new wing. (Decades later the Deaconess School became the Anglican Women's Training College, and then merged with a United Church school to become what is now called the Centre for Christian Studies, located in Winnipeg.)

Blake played a less prominent part in establishing a non-Anglican school. The Toronto Bible Training School started at Walmer Road Baptist Church in 1894 as an ecumenical institution to train Sunday school teachers, missionaries, and pastors' assistants.[40] Elmore Harris, of the farm machinery company, was the president, and Blake's support was behind the scenes. The school moved four years later to a building on College Street east of Bay, now a parkette next to a subway entrance. This school later became the Toronto Bible College, then Ontario Bible College, then through a merger the Ontario Theological Seminary, and finally Tyndale College and Seminary.

ECUMENICAL SOCIAL SERVICE AND EVANGELISTIC PROJECTS

Blake's major educational projects have survived to this day as established institutions, but he was also deeply involved in ecumenical "social service" projects—although the term hadn't yet been invented—which haven't left

---

39. Griffith, *Weaving a Changing Tapestry*; Haldenby, *Anglican Women's Training College*.

40. Sawatsky, "'Looking for that Blessed Hope,'" 263–78.

permanent identifiable traces. Some of the more important ones can be briefly noted. One was the temperance movement (Blake was a lifelong abstainer). Another was the Prisoners Aid Society, which he founded with W. H. Howland,[41] a successful businessman, a fellow founder of Wycliffe College, and the mayor of Toronto during whose term the city began to be called Toronto the Good. Blake served as its president for many years. Blake, Howland, and a handful of other Wycliffe supporters also began the non-denominational Toronto Mission Union to coordinate a number of associated charities involved with social and medical assistance to the poor, evangelism, and foreign missions. Under the auspices of the Toronto Mission Union, he carried on the Sackville Street mission, which soon had its own building and a large influence over many years. Blake also served on the board of the Toronto Willard Tract Depository, for the publication and distribution of ecumenical evangelical literature.[42] For fourteen years he was the president of the Toronto YMCA,[43] and he served for a while on the International Committee. He also served as president of the Toronto branch of the Evangelical Alliance and the Protestant Churchman's Union and Tract Society.

Probably Blake's leadership in the Christian Conferences in Toronto in the late 1870s predisposed him to support the Bible and Prophecy Conferences that were held in Niagara-on-the-Lake annually from 1882 to 1897.[44] The conferences were international in character, but the one for 1885 was entirely planned by a Canadian group, which included Blake. It was a vehicle for Bible prophecy, dispensationalism, an expectation of Christ's imminent premillennial second coming, revivalism, anti-modernism, and a soteriological focus on substitutionary atonement. The Niagara conferences are therefore often identified as a precursor to fundamentalism. It seems unlikely that Blake was a premillennialist, a position which his friends Principal Sheraton of Wycliffe and Canon Cody firmly rejected.

Above all, the Christian service with which Blake was perhaps most identified, apart from Wycliffe College, was Sunday schools. For decades he taught Sunday school regularly, at least once a week at his own church, and typically in other parts of the city, often at Central Prison, at King Street and Strachan Avenue. In addition, he taught Sunday school teachers city-wide, drawing three or four hundred teachers regularly to his Saturday afternoon

---

41. Sawatsky, "Howland, William Holmes."

42. Sawatsky, "'Looking for that Blessed Hope,'" 179–215.

43. Young Men's Christian Association of Metropolitan Toronto, *An Historical Sketch*, esp. 33.

44. Sawatsky, "'Looking for that Blessed Hope,'" 38–76.

training classes. He was active in the International Sunday School Committee, which prepared uniform lessons worldwide, and he presided at the third international convention of the International Sunday School Association.

Thus while Blake was immensely loyal to the Church of England, he shared the fundamentally ecumenical Protestant culture of contemporary Ontario to which William Westfall has called our attention.[45] In 1875, addressing a convention in Montreal of the YMCA for Ontario and Quebec, he included this advice: "Let not your Christianity be of that kind which begins and ends by merely pinning your faith to some denomination, but let it be of the stamp which takes the precepts of our blessed Saviour and acts upon them."[46]

FURTHER CONTROVERSIES

In his advocacy and agitation for his causes within the Church of England in Canada, Blake's north star continued to be his Church of Ireland vision. And his adversaries continued to be Roman Catholicism, liberalism, high-churchism, and ritual practices. As he grew older, most Anglican leaders in Canada were increasingly accommodating or endorsing practices, ideas, publications, and institutions that veered away from this vision, and when they did so, he was at the ready. Some of his Anglican friends began to doubt that evangelicals could retain a foothold in their church—W. H. Howland, for instance, joined the new Christian and Missionary Alliance, and in some dioceses the schismatic Reformed Episcopal Church gained traction—but Blake was persuaded that he had more right to call himself an Anglican than his critics.

His most notable disputes in Canadian Anglican thought and practice can be categorized under six themes. One was ritualism. Throughout his life Blake continued to publish tracts and make speeches condemning such practices as processional crosses, altar candles (indeed the very word "altar"), vestments, the eastward position of the priest at communion, fasting communion, prayers for the dead, veneration of the host, incense, bowings (except at the name of Jesus in the Creed), and prostrations. He rebuffed accusations that his condemnations provoked divisions. On the contrary, it was the ritualists who were creating divisions. He pictured ritualists as saying, "Oh, do not bring discord into our Parish by making a party and opposing what we desire to introduce."[47]

45. Westfall, *Two Worlds*.
46. Blake, *Young Men of Canada* (CIHM 01026), 37.
47. Blake, *Anglo-Roman Priesthood*, 51.

A second theme was his opposition to the project, begun by Archbishop Sweatman, to establish a true cathedral for the diocese of Toronto.[48] The oldest church in the diocese, St. James, functioned as a cathedral on special occasions, but it was organized quite like a parish church, and the bishop's authority was restricted. Sweatman wanted a distinct cathedral foundation under his control, staffed by canons who would include theologians, musicians, teachers, and missioners, giving leadership and setting standards for parish life throughout the diocese. Sweatman was following a trend started by Bishop John Medley in Fredericton in 1853, whose lavish and expensive cathedral had caused an uproar among many modest New Brunswickers. Blake was convinced that Sweatman, for whom he seems to have had some personal affection and respect, was misdirecting his energies. Why pay hundreds of thousands of dollars to build a new building if the essential idea was to have a good diocesan leadership staff? Sweatman was able to raise only meagre financial support, and that not without a tinge of scandal, for what was called St. Alban's Cathedral. Only the chancel was ever built. At the end of his life the diocese had amassed such a large and unmanageable debt that its creditors were threatening lawsuits. Blake finally made a contribution to reduce the diocesan debt, but otherwise he refused to give a penny to help St. Alban's Cathedral. On the other hand, he gave many thousands of dollars when it came to building the new St. Paul's, Bloor Street, between 1909 and 1913, to accommodate the crowds who wanted to hear his friend Canon Cody preach.

A third theme was Anglican hymnody. The church party had long favored *Hymns Ancient and Modern* for congregational singing, while the evangelical party had the *Hymnal Companion*. After the Church of England in Canada was formed in 1893, and General Synod was created, it took on the task of trying to reconcile the two parties. At its second session of 1896 it resolved to develop a book that all Anglicans could use. It was twelve years before a committee was appointed, and finally in 1909 the first *Book of Common Praise* was published. It had 795 hymns and an appendix of psalm chants. It included hymns to suit all tastes, liberal, Anglo-Catholic, and evangelical. It was, therefore, widely unpopular. In particular, some hymns of strong Catholic sensibility bothered some of the bishops, including, reportedly, Rupert's Land, Toronto, and Keewatin. They most particularly bothered Sam Blake. He had written several letters to the committee before publication, which apparently were ignored. When the book was published, he prepared for battle. He identified dozens of hymns that were calculated, he thought, to help the Church of Rome swallow up the Church of England,

---

48. Cooke, "Diocese of Toronto," 98–115.

as well as other hymns which weren't exactly unorthodox but were aesthetically impoverished, or as he called it, poor prose with an attempt at rhyme. The examples included hymn 250, which included the phrase "before thine altar kneel" (evangelicals spoke of tables for the Lord's Supper, not altars for sacrifice); hymn 653, "we love the sacred font," which he said taught the heresy of baptismal regeneration; and the hymn "There is a green hill far away," which misrepresented the vegetative character of the drear barren rocky place of skulls. A member of the hymnal committee was incensed that Blake refused to live and let live. Blake, he said, was a "lay pope": "You, Sir, dictate to the whole Canadian Church after the whole matter has been passed upon by the General Synod." Blake replied that if he were really a lay pope, he would certainly have no criticisms of the Book of Common Praise.[49]

A fourth theme was higher criticism.[50] Higher critics, he said, were ridiculing the book of Jonah, refusing to receive the biblical history of creation, denying that Abraham existed, and apparently even denying that sin was punished, or even existed. Blake was scandalized that such teaching had made its way into Knox College, Victoria College, Trinity College, and worst of all University College. The reason University College was worst of all was that Blake argued that, by the University of Toronto Act, it shouldn't be teaching theology at all. He made a complaint to the president of the university, and the governors appointed a committee to investigate. After investigation, the university agreed that its teachers must avoid making theological judgments about Scripture, but Blake wasn't convinced that the university had a broad enough understanding of theology. They might still allow higher criticism under the guise of reading the Bible as literature.

Fifth, Blake was disgusted that church leaders so often poured resources into maintaining unnecessary buildings, ineffective clergy, and declining congregations, instead of funding mission work. In 1910 the rural dean of Toronto, the Rev. John D'Arcy Cayley, the rector of the high-church St. Simon's, had an idea for helping churches with waning attendance. In a pamphlet he argued that what restrained church growth was insufficient seating.[51] Moreover, other denominations in the city were outclassing Anglicans in the size of their churches. He proposed that the wealthier and more successful churches should fund renovations in the churches that

---

49. Blake, *Book of Common Praise, Letter No. 40* (CIHM 72575), and *Reply to an Open Letter* (CIHM 86198). The "lay pope" quotation is in *Reply*, 4.

50. Blake, *Teaching of Religious Knowledge* (CIHM 86847); Blake, *Mr. Blake's Acknowledgment of the Report* (CIHM 75093); and Blake, *The Knife of the Higher Critic* (CIHM 71449).

51. Blake, *Synod of the Diocese of Toronto*.

needed to grow. Blake was always suspicious when clergy had good ideas that the laity were to fund, and it didn't help that Cayley was also an adjunct faculty member at Trinity College. Blake wrote Cayley two private letters that Cayley apparently ignored, and then went public with an open letter, which provoked a reply from Cayley, leading to a rejoinder from Blake. First of all, Blake argued, the diocese should be planning churches according to verified need, not just expanding churches that happened to exist already. Inspecting a map of parish churches in Toronto, Blake thought that it looked "as if chance . . . had blindly played at a game of boundaries."[52] He identified one area of Toronto just a few blocks wide with eight Anglican churches. Whatever the rationale may have been for putting them there when they were built, a more businesslike approach was needed now.

Second, there was actually plenty of space already. Among 42 churches there were 25,000 spaces for an average attendance of 15,000. (Cayley disputed the arithmetic.) Third, building more seating wouldn't fill churches; what was required was good leadership. See how Lawrence Skey at St. Anne's, Gladstone Avenue, had built up his congregation from 200 to 1400! See how Canon Dixon had built up the Sunday school at Little Trinity to 1000! See how packed Canon Cody's St. Paul's was! And that raised a fourth point. The successful churches were evangelical churches. In fact, all the churches that Cayley wanted to support were high-church or ritualistic; all the ones from which he wanted to receive funding were evangelical (St. James, St. Paul, Redeemer, All Saints, St. Anne, St. Peter, Epiphany, Messiah, Little Trinity, and Ascension). The way to grow the church was not by enlarging buildings but by preaching the gospel. Cayley was offended by this remark, because it showed an uncharitable party spirit. "I appeal to you, Mr. Blake," Cayley wrote, "to use your great influence to bring these two great parties together. You, and perhaps you alone, at the present time, can do this."[53] Blake interpreted Cayley as criticizing the partisanship of others without acknowledging his own. He replied that those by whom he himself had long been derided as narrow, unreasonable, and bigoted were in no position to lecture him on charitable speech. And, finally, Blake wondered, why were we so self-centered? Why weren't we sponsoring mission work outside our community, and overseas? The diocese of Toronto, with more wealth than any other in the Dominion, gave a pittance to foreign mission. Could we not "drop little parish politics" and "bring home to each the true conception of the Church as a great missionary organization for the salvation of the

---

52. Ibid., 5.
53. Ibid., 22–23.

world," and work with other religious bodies, and with the business community, to be an advance guard, and do amazing things?[54]

FIRST NATIONS

A final theme, the Church's treatment of First Nations people, is in retrospect perhaps the most important of all; and here, too, Blake's dissent was unproductive. The Church was hell-bent on "civilizing the Indians" (Europeanizing Indigenous peoples), and Blake was unable to counteract its culture-bound assumptions, even from the perch that he occupied for a few years as the chair of the national church's committee on Indian matters.

By way of background, after the General Synod of the Church of England in Canada was created in 1893, it started a Missionary Society (the MSCC) which, though slow to get off the ground, began to assume a general mandate for the Anglican residential schools.[55] Some of these had been run by the Church Missionary Society in England, or by other agencies like the New England Company, or by dioceses. The government provided a large proportion of the operating expenses.

In 1904 the MSCC appointed Blake to chair a committee on Indian residential schools, and Blake took up the challenge with typical focus and energy.[56] At first his main interest seems to have been good financial stewardship. The residential schools were immensely expensive and could easily eat up the entire budget of the MSCC. So his initial interest was to increase government funding, improve conditions, and strengthen educational resources in the schools. To that end he prepared questionnaires for the bishops and entered into wide correspondence with school principals and the leaders of the Women's Auxiliary, who sponsored some of the teachers.

As he began reading the responses to his questionnaires, however, and listening to western bishops, his lawyer's skeptical intuitions snapped into action. He readily recognized the vague generalities and evasive answers that people give when they don't really know what they're doing. In the

---

54. Ibid., 44.
55. Hayes, *Anglicans in Canada*, 29–35.
56. Records of the Special Indian Committee that Blake chaired are in Anglican Church of Canada, General Synod Archives, Missionary Society of the Church of England in Canada, series 2–14, GS 75-103 and GS 75-104. Many of the documents found there are published in Blake, *Memorandum on Indian Work*. See also Blake, *To the Members of the Board of Management* (CIHM 86242); Blake, *Call of the Red Man*; and Blake, *Missionary Society* (CIHM 86243). A reply to Blake is Tims, *Calgary's Appeal*, in the Missionary Society archives. See also the discussion by Grant, *Moon of Wintertime*, 192–96.

operations of the residential schools there was no whiff of educational quality assurance, no evidence that the schools were doing children any good at all. On the contrary, some teachers were clearly inept, and seemed to be there because they weren't wanted elsewhere. He began to suspect that the system of residential schools had been developed as an instrument to get eastern money into the hands of western bishops.

His biggest initial shock was the appallingly unsanitary conditions at the schools. At the Old Sun school on the Blackfoot reserve in Alberta, for instance, he counted 99 students who had entered between 1894 and 1904, of whom 41 had died. When he challenged the supporters of the school, they offered the explanation that the Indians themselves lived in unsanitary conditions on their reserves, and the death rate was actually worse there at their homes than in the schools. Blake knew something about defendants inventing self-exculpatory facts, and he checked with the Indian Department whether Indian children were dying at home in large numbers. The Indian Department replied that it knew of no statistics whatever on death rates on the reserves. The anecdotal factoid that numbers of Indian children were dying on the reserve was a convenient fiction. Blake suspected bigotry and self-interest.[57]

By 1906 Blake was doubting the very notion of Indian residential schools. The historian John Webster Grant suggests that Blake stood alone against an almost unanimous opinion of the missionary establishment, but actually there are signs in his correspondence that several others shared his suspicions, or were beginning to do so. He quoted the general secretary of the most important Church of England missionary society, the Society for the Propagation of the Gospel: "An Indian boarding school . . . if it is to succeed, would appear to be a place full of children taken away for ever from their parents . . . . But is it right to go to a mother and say, 'Give me your child, you shall never see him again!'"[58]

And the principle of compulsory attendance bothered him. First Nations children were being taken involuntarily from their families to remove them from what was derisively called their blanket life. Blake wrote one of the bishops,

> I cannot but feel that the increase of the attendance of children at the schools must depend very largely upon the legitimate attractions that are presented by those who have the work of

---

57. Blake, *Memorandum on Indian Work*, 9; Address of Canon Murray to the Board of Management of the MSCC, October 1910, among the Missionary Society documents cited.

58. The original source of the quotation is Montgomery, "Canada," 5.

supervision and teaching. I have never been able to see that we can reasonably say to the Department—compel children to attend these schools. It seems to me to be a dangerous power to leave in the hands of [Indian] Agents in the locality.[59]

Schools should build their enrolments by the attractions of excellence, not compulsion.

Most radically, Blake began to challenge the underlying rationale of Anglican missions to the First Nations, the conviction that Christianization was dependent on civilization, that is, Europeanization. Missionaries in the Arctic, far from residential schools, had verified that Native people could live as Christians, differently of course from white people in the cities, but in a way consistent with their profession. One wonders whether Blake's experience as an Irishman, with a national history of being culturally disrespected by the English, had educated his sympathies.

Blake did achieve a small victory, but it was short-lived. In 1907 he succeeded in having the MSCC declare that it was going to get out of the business of Indian schooling, leave the task to the government, and concentrate its efforts on good old-fashioned missionary work: preaching, teaching in local churches, pastoral care, social service, prayer. The western bishops and the missionary establishment were outraged. How could a Toronto layman presume to know how things worked in the Canadian Northwest? They succeeded in outmaneuvering Blake, and in 1910 the MSCC rescinded its decision to abandon the Indian residential schools. These continued for another seventy years, and, as most people would now acknowledge, accomplished far more harm than good.

CONCLUSION

Sam Blake maintained his sense of Irish roots throughout his life, but he also recognized that Canada had a national identity, too, which he had happily embraced. A year and a bit before his death, in an address to the Canadian Club, he built up to a peroration on this theme. From the printed text, which includes interpolations like "Applause," "Laughter," and "Long Applause," it's easy to see how even at the age of 76 he could hold an audience in his hand. At the end, he acknowledged the warmth in his heart for the Irish Protestant Benevolent Society (laughter form the audience). Indeed, he had been a loyal member and a sometime president of that group. But he went on to say,

59. Blake to Bishop of Calgary, 4 Jun. 1906, among the Missionary Society documents cited.

> Some man will say St. Andrew's Society stands first—let him have it. Some St. George's Society—very well. But I would like to see a strong, national, Canadian Club that knows no nationality except as we Canadians are a nation, with our own standard of patriotism, of right, of kindness, of consideration for others, endeavoring to have that standard raised throughout the whole of this land.

He could hardly have guessed how much more multicultural Canada would become over the next century, but this speech at the end of his life clearly discloses a leitmotiv of his life: he was loyal to his Irish spirit, and he had contributed it to the rich association of cultures of this new great nation. True to his Irish roots and sensitive to the realities of his Canadian context (or, really, his British Canadian context), he recognized the common values that all settler Canadians brought from the Old World: right, kindness, justice.

I suggest that the same is true of Sam Blake's Christian vocation. He remained loyal to his Church of Ireland roots and his Church of Ireland vision, but he carried its riches into the larger treasury of Protestantism in Canada, a country where, perhaps more than most places, people with different religious convictions could embrace their common values and together pursue their common goals.

But if his Church of Ireland vision was compatible with other types of Protestantism, it wasn't consistent with the Romanizing, or the higher-critical, or the liberal trends that were also afoot, most irritatingly and shamefully in his own denomination. So while one dimension of Blake's vocation was primarily constructive, working both with other Anglicans and ecumenically in projects and ministries of education, evangelism, and social service, the other was primarily critical, attacking everything fundamentally inconsistent with his vision. However, Blake wouldn't likely have divided the constructive from the critical in this way. Many of his constructive projects were designed as rivals to theologically impure ventures, and many of his criticisms couched invitations to constructive alternatives.

Whether constructively or critically, Blake helped shape the Church's life in his day by invigorating its discussions, exercising ministry, organizing events and projects, promoting institutions, and advancing philanthropy, all consistent with his Church of Ireland vision of a scripturally resonant, Calvinistically charged, evangelical faith united with an intellectual culture in the service of God in church and community. To this end, his most astounding resource was his energy. He seemed to be able to give his undivided attention to a great many projects at once. Whatever he took on, he brought to completion. When Blake died in 1914, Canon Cody had no trouble choosing a text for his funeral: "I have fought a good fight, I have finished my course, I have kept the faith" (2 Tim 4:7).[60]

He died, I believe, as the last great voice in his spiritual line. In his closing years, the fundamentalist-modernist controversy was seriously reducing the space where one could stand as a conservative evangelical who valued intellectual culture, felt at home in the modern world, and was committed to working with others to build a just and compassionate community. That place to stand would need to be rediscovered by a later generation in a different way.

BIBLIOGRAPHY

Akenson, Donald Harman. *The Church of Ireland: Ecclesiastical Reform and Revolution, 1800–1885*. New Haven, CT: Yale University Press, 1971.

———. *The Irish in Ontario: A Study in Rural History*. 2nd ed. Montreal: McGill-Queen's University Press, 1984.

Backhouse, Constance B. "'To Open the Way for Others of My Sex': Clara Brett Martin's Career as Canada's First Woman Lawyer." *Canadian Journal of Women and Law* 1 (1985) 1–41.

Beattie, Kim. *Ridley: The Story of a School*. 2 vols. St. Catharines, ON: Ridley College, 1963.

Blackwell, John D. "Blake, Samuel Hume." In *DCB* 14. Toronto: University of Toronto Press, 1998.

Blake, Samuel Hume. *An Anglo-Roman Priesthood Versus an Anglo-Protestant Laity. Is There Not a Cause?* Toronto: Haynes, 1910.

———. *The Book of Common Praise, Letter No. 40*. Toronto: L. S. Haynes, 1909.

———. *The Call of the Red Man as Answered by the Commissioner of Indian Affairs of the United States of America; What Will Be the Answer of the Dominion of Canada?* Toronto: Bryant, 1908.

———. *The Knife of the Higher Critic: The Judgment of the Lord, the Burial of an Ass*. Toronto: Haynes, 1907.

———. *Memorandum on Indian Work*. Toronto: Bryant, 1909.

———. *Missionary Society of the Church of England in Canada: Memorandum for the Rev. Dr. Tucker*. Canada?: [s.n.] 1907.

———. *Mr. Blake's Acknowledgment of the Report of the Board of Governors on "The Teaching of Religious Knowledge in University College Ultra Vires" and Other Matters*. Toronto: Haynes, 1910.

———. *Reply to an Open Letter of W. B. Carrol*. Toronto: Haynes, 1910.

———. *Report of Special Committee to the Board of Governors, University of Toronto*. Toronto: University of Toronto Press, 1909(?).

———. *Standards: An Address to the Canadian Club, November 11th, 1912*. Toronto: [s.n.] 1912.

---

60. Masters, *Henry John Cody*, 96.

———. *Synod of the Diocese of Toronto, 1911: A Promise Fulfilled.* Toronto(?): [s.n.] 1911?

———. *The Teaching of Religious Knowledge in University College Ultra Vires.* Toronto: [s.n.] 1909.

———. *To the Members of the Board of Management of the Missionary Society of the Church of England in Canada.* Toronto: Anglican Church of Canada, 1907.

———. *Wycliffe College: An Historical Sketch.* Toronto: Wycliffe College, 1910.

———. *Young Men of Canada: A Lecture.* Toronto(?): printed and published by B. J. Hill, 1876.

Bonham, James W. *The Church Revived: A Sketch of Parochial Missions.* New York: Whittaker, 1886.

Bradley, Richard A., and Paul E. Lewis. *Ridley, A Canadian School.* St. Catharines, ON: Ridley College, 2000.

Brown, Elizabeth. "Equitable Jurisdiction and the Court of Chancery in Upper Canada." *Osgoode Hall Law Journal* 21 (1983) 274–314.

Byers, Mary. *Havergal: Celebrating a Century, 1894–1994.* Toronto: Boston Mills, 1994.

Charlesworth, Hector. *Candid Chronicles: Leaves from the Note Book of a Canadian Journalist.* Toronto: Macmillan, 1925.

Cody, Henry J. "Samuel Hume Blake." *University of Toronto Monthly* 15 (1914–15) 14–17.

Cooke, William G. "The Diocese of Toronto and its Two Cathedrals." *JCCHS* 27 (1985) 98–115.

Cronyn, Benjamin. *Bishop of Huron's Objections to the Theological Teaching of Trinity College.* London: Thomas Evans, 1862.

Dent, John Charles et al. *The Canadian Portrait Gallery.* 3 vols. Toronto: Magurn, 1881.

Edinborough, Arnold, ed. *The Enduring Word: A Centennial History of Wycliffe College.* Toronto: University of Toronto Press, 1978.

Ford, Alan. "Ussher, James (1581–1656)." *Oxford Dictionary of National Biography.* Oxford: Oxford University Press, 2004.

Friedland, Martin L. *The University of Toronto: A History.* 2nd ed. Toronto: University of Toronto Press, 2002.

Grant, John Webster. *Moon of Wintertime: Missionaries and the Indians of Canada in Encounter Since 1534.* Toronto: University of Toronto Press, 1984.

Griffith, Gwyn. *Weaving a Changing Tapestry: The Story of the Centre for Christian Studies and its Predecessors, 1892–2005.* Toronto: Self-published, 2009.

Hague, Dyson et al. *The Jubilee Volume of Wycliffe College 1877–1927–1937.* Toronto: Wycliffe College, 1938.

Haldenby, Grace. *Anglican Women's Training College: A Background Document.* Toronto: AWTC History Committee, 1989.

Hayes, Alan L. *Anglicans in Canada: Controversies and Identity in Historical Perspective.* Chicago: University of Illinois Press, 2004.

———. "Repairing the Walls: Church Reform and Social Reform 1867–1939." In *By Grace Co-Workers: Building the Anglican Diocese of Toronto, 1780–1989,* edited by Alan L. Hayes, 43–96. Toronto: Anglican Book Centre, 1989.

———. "The Struggle for the Rights of the Laity in the Diocese of Toronto, 1850–1879." *JCCHS* 26 (1984) 5–17.

———. "Sweatman, Arthur." In *DCB* 13. Toronto: University of Toronto Press, 1994.

Headon, Christopher. "Whitaker, George." In *DCB* 11. Toronto: University of Toronto Press, 1982.

"Hon. Samuel Hume Blake, K. C." *Canada Law Journal* 50 (1914) 450–52.

Livermore, J. Daniel. "Hume, Catherine Honoria." In *DCB* 11. Toronto: University of Toronto Press, 1982.

Magocsi, Paul R. *Encylopedia of Canada's Peoples*. Toronto: University of Toronto Press, 1999.

Masters, Donald C. "The Anglican Evangelicals in Toronto, 1870–1900." *JCCHS* 20 (1978) 51–66.

———. *Henry John Cody: An Outstanding Life*. Toronto: Dundurn, 1995.

Melville, Henry. *The Rise and Progress of Trinity College*. Toronto: Rowsell, 1852.

Milton, Anthony. "Laud, William (1573–1645)." In *DNB*. Oxford: Oxford University Press, 2004.

Montgomery, H. H. "Canada." *A Quarterly Review for the Study of Missions* 5 (1907) 1–13.

Nockles, Peter B. "Church or Protestant Sect? The Church of Ireland, High Churchmanship, and the Oxford Movement, 1822–1869." *Historical Journal* 41 (1998) 457–93.

Power, Thomas. "'Of No Small Importance': Curricular Change in the School of Divinity, Trinity College Dublin, 1790–1850." In *Change and Transformation: Essays in Anglican History*, edited by Thomas Power, 140–83. Eugene, OR: Pickwick, 2013.

Rainsford, William S. *The Story of a Varied Life: An Autobiography*. Garden City, NY: Doubleday, 1922.

Rawlyk, George. *Aspects of the Canadian Evangelical Experience*. Montreal: McGill-Queen's University Press, 1997.

Rose, George Maclean, ed. *A Cyclopaedia of Canadian Biography: Being Chiefly Men of the Time*. Toronto: Rose, 1886.

Sahlins, Marshall. *Culture in Practice*. New York: Zone, 2000.

Sawatsky, Ronald G. "Howland, William Holmes." In *DCB* 12. Toronto: University of Toronto Press, 1990.

———. "'Looking for that Blessed Hope': The Roots of Fundamentalism in Canada, 1878–1914." PhD diss., University of Toronto, 1985.

Schull, Joseph. *Edward Blake*. 2 vols. Toronto: Macmillan, 1975–76.

Swainson, Donald. "Blake, William Hume." In *DCB* 9. Toronto: University of Toronto Press, 1976.

"Sweatman, Arthur." In *DCB* 13. Toronto: University of Toronto Press, 1994.

Talman, James J. "Cronyn, Benjamin." In *DCB* 10. Toronto: University of Toronto Press, 2003–. http://www.biographi.ca/en/bio/cronyn_benjamin_10E.html.

Tims, John William. *Calgary's Appeal on Behalf of Calgary's Children of the Prairies: Being a Criticism and Reply to the* Memorandum on Indian Work, *Addressed to the Board of Management of the M.S.C.C. by the Hon. S. H. Blake, K.C.* Calgary(?): 1909?

Westfall, William. *The Founding Moment: Church, Society, and the Construction of Trinity College*. Montreal: McGill-Queen's University Press, 2002.

———. *Two Worlds: The Protestant Culture of Nineteenth-Century Ontario*. Montreal: McGill-Queen's University Press, 1989.

Young Men's Christian Association of Metropolitan Toronto. *An Historical Sketch of the Toronto Young Men's Christian Association*. Toronto: YMCA, 1913.

11

Anglican Deaconesses in Canada 1889–1969

Two Operational Models of a Gendered Order of Ministry

ALAN L. HAYES

CANADA'S FIRST ANGLICAN DEACONESS was set apart on a Sunday in July 1889 by Bishop John Medley of New Brunswick. No Canadian woman before her had been admitted by a bishop to an order of public ministry in the Anglican Church. The service of ordering took place in a cathedral and involved prayer and laying-on of hands in a manner analogous to the ordination of priests and deacons, who were always male.[1] Medley was acknowledging, as many of his contemporaries did, that women could have the gifts and calling for ministry, and people who did ministry in the name of the church should be duly authorized and accountable.

The term "deaconess" seemed ideal for an ordered public ministry for women, since it was a word (or rather the contested translation of a word) that had been used for what appeared to be a similar purpose in the early

---

1. The story of Canada's first Anglican deaconess is told in two articles in *The New Brunswick Anglican*, available online at http://fredericton.anglican.org/nb_ang.html: Liebenberg, "Remembering an Extraordinary Woman," 8; Edmonson, "Fifth Annual Commemoration," 9.

church, perhaps even in the time of St. Paul. And since deaconesses had for many years been set apart in the Church of England, the Protestant Episcopal Church in the United States, and elsewhere, a Canadian bishop need not fear being accused of radical innovation. Over the next eight decades hundreds of single or widowed Anglican women were ordained, ordered, commissioned, consecrated, set apart as, admitted as, or made deaconesses. (Different terms were used.) The order of deaconess was terminated in 1969 by the General Synod, the highest governing body of the national denomination, when the principle of gendered ministry had lost favor. No new deaconesses would be commissioned, and existing deaconesses would ideally be recognized as belonging to the order of deacon, previously reserved to men.

Generally speaking, there were two different operating models for the office of deaconess, the model of the gendered ministry professional and the model of the gendered ministry helper. In the first model, the deaconess's gender was an asset that allowed her, in at least symbolic collegiality with her fellow deaconesses, to do ministry as a woman, especially in spheres where women, in the understanding of the day, could work more suitably: for instance, with vulnerable populations. The deaconess need not fit herself to the conventional expectations and social constraints attached to male priests and deacons. She took pride in her distinctively female vocation, and appreciated the opportunities, sometimes not entirely open to male clergy, to specialize in ministries to the marginalized, the impoverished, the sick, immigrants, people in isolated communities, Indigenous peoples, and women and children in urban parishes. She could be independent, creative, and resourceful, and she was not required to channel patriarchy. In the second model, by contrast, the deaconess's gender condemned her to be always the submissive assistant to a male authority. Her role was to labor at the subordinate and sometimes menial tasks that were assigned to her by a clergyman whose attitudes were saturated with sexism, as part of an institution that frankly devalued her work, as was painfully obvious in the meagre salary it accorded her. Many deaconesses moved from one model to the other in different parts of their career, or, indeed, sometimes from day to day, or even from hour to hour.

THE SOURCES

The documentation for the work of deaconesses is by no means full. Being institutionally marginalized, deaconesses make little impact on the obvious sources for the study of Canadian Anglicanism—synod journals and committee reports, vestry minutes, the church press, episcopal correspondence, memoirs of and by clergy. The committees that did consider the ministry of deaconesses were, even as late as the 1950s, exclusively or overwhelmingly male. And personal records, where they have been preserved at all, are scattered. It is a frustration for the historian to see so regularly in the Anglican historical documentation men, men, and more men, and the occasional chivalrous vote of thanks for some assistance from "the ladies."

The single most important source is the records of the Church of England Deaconess and Training Missionary House in Toronto, later called the Anglican Women's Training College (AWTC). These records are in the General Synod Archives (GSA) at the head office of the Anglican Church of Canada (ACC).[2] They cover only graduates of the institution, and so ignore woman church workers who were trained in England, British Columbia, the United States, or elsewhere, or whose training was more informal. But most Canadian Anglican deaconesses came from the Toronto school. The AWTC liked to stay in touch with its graduates, making it the only institution that was intentionally maintaining some contact with deaconesses across the national Anglican Church. A prosopographical study of AWTC alumnae would certainly yield telling results. What social backgrounds did they represent? What brought them to the Deaconess House? How long did graduates, on average, remain in ministry? What kinds of ministry did they choose? At the present, however, our information about graduates is largely anecdotal rather than systematic.

Among the AWTC materials in the GSA is a box of transcripts of interviews of graduates conducted in the 1990s by Gwyn Griffith,[3] a principal of the Centre for Christian Studies, a successor institution, as data for her *Weaving a Changing Tapestry: The Story of the Centre for Christian Studies and its Predecessors*.[4] The records of the national Women's Auxiliary (WA), which sponsored most woman missionaries in the ACC, are also in the GSA. The archives for some dioceses do have important resources for the subject as well, but I have only scratched the surface there.[5]

2. ACC, GSA, AWTC fonds, which is categorized into seven series and has a very useful finding aid.

3. The finding aid reports that "Gwyn Griffith undertook this project following her term as Principal of the Centre for Christian Studies (formerly AWTC)" from 1992 to 1994. For the oral histories which she conducted, GSA has tapes, transcriptions, and slides of the participants. ACC, GSA, AWTC fonds, box AV95-11. These will be cited as "Griffith, interview."

4. Published by Griffith herself, 2009.

5. I'm very grateful to researchers, archivists, former deaconesses, and others who have pointed me to resources, or shared memories, or helped me understand things. I am particularly grateful to Melanie Delva, formerly archivist for the diocese of

In the historical records it is not always easy to distinguish deaconesses from other salaried women church workers. Not all women who trained as deaconesses became deaconesses; not all women who functioned as deaconesses or were called deaconesses were trained as deaconesses or formally admitted as deaconesses; not all women who were admitted as deaconesses remained as deaconesses. Until 1960 there was no central authority keeping an official record of Canadian Anglican deaconesses. Most salaried women church workers were not deaconesses. These included parish assistants, parish social workers, Christian education directors, youth workers, girls' workers, overseas and domestic missionaries, church secretaries, matrons or teachers or administrators at Indian residential schools or Inuit hostels, settler workers in the west, nurses and other health care workers, diocesan staff members, Women's Auxiliary field secretaries or bookroom managers or staff members, national church staff, camp counsellors, Church Army ministers, staff members at various church agencies such as homes for unwed mothers or orphanages or shelters for homeless people or homes for the aged, and administrators of Sunday School by Post. Also, there were women who had formally recognized but non-salaried ministries, notably Anglican nuns and religious sisters, and clergy wives. Beyond all of these, there were thousands upon thousands of women who served the church in volunteer capacities. These other women in ministry are of just as much historical interest as deaconesses, but my intention here is to focus on those we can recognize as deaconesses, while referencing other women church workers where their experience might be apposite.

THE ANGLICAN ORIGINS OF DEACONESSES

The origins of an episcopally authorized public ministry of women that was explicitly inferior to the holy orders of priest and deacon had its origins in the nineteenth century. The office of deaconess was created to address three main issues. First, women were already doing ministry, but not always within the accountability structures of the church. Second, the church's agenda for mission was becoming greater than what men alone could accomplish. Third, the expanding role of women in society challenged the patriarchal

---

New Westminster, now animator for reconciliation for the ACC; Karen Evans, formerly the librarian of General Synod; Gwyn Griffith, whose book is frequently quoted here; Karen Heath, who worked on this topic for an exhibition at Wycliffe College in 2006; Nancy Hurn and Laurel Parson of GSA; Mary-Anne Nicholls and Caese Levo of the diocese of Toronto archives; Tom Power, librarian of the Graham Library of Trinity and Wycliffe Colleges and a faculty member in history; and the late Margaret Stackhouse, an AWTC graduate and a friend of forty years.

assumptions that had excluded women from formally recognized public ministries. In the 1850s and 1860s in England, a little later in the United States, and later still in Canada, Anglican pastors, scholars, and bishops came up with the theological categories, the pastoral models, and the institutional structures that were required to define an office of deaconess, and shape it to meet contemporary needs.

First, then, by the 1850s Anglican women were already exercising functions of ministry. In England they taught children and others in Sunday schools; they did charity work; they participated in guilds and clubs; they advocated for justice and social change in anti-slavery societies and temperance organizations; they administered pastoral care in their societies of district visitors; they supported family life through mothers' meetings; they wrote hymns, religious tracts, and articles for periodicals like the *Christian Lady's* magazine; some were clergy wives; after 1845, a few were nuns or religious sisters. These activities appeared consistent with women's Christian gifts and discipleship, since, in the Victorian construction of gender, women in their proper nature were specially attuned to the religious dimension of existence, had maternal instincts, cared for others, disciplined their emotions, and were morally virtuous. A broad consensus was developing that women could properly do Christian work in the public sphere in a part-time, voluntary, and independent way. If that were so, surely they could do Christian work in a full-time, formally recognized, and accountable way!

Second, the missional agenda of the English church was expanding. Abroad, the colonies needed clergy and teachers, religious libraries, and funding for buildings and other purposes; at home, social reformers were tackling such evils of the factory system as child labor, pauperism, and slums. Among numerous church, para-church, and philanthropic organizations which involved women were the Church Missionary Society (1799), the British and Foreign Bible Society (1804), the London City Mission (1835), the YWCA (1855), and various "ladies' societies" such as the Friendly Female Societies. In short, laborers were needed for the field, well beyond what a male clergy and a male laity could supply.

Third, English women were challenging their exclusion from the social spheres that mainstream Victorian culture conventionally restricted to men. Challenging the assumption that a woman should remain "the angel in the house" was no longer confined to irreligious radicals like Mary Wollstonecraft; even conservative evangelicals like Charlotte Elizabeth Tonna (1790–1846) were urging women to exert their influence for good in the social sphere.[6] Women were breaking barriers in education; Queen's

---

6. Gleadle, "Charlotte Elizabeth Tonna," 97–117.

College in London, which opened in 1848, was the first school in England where young women could earn academic certifications. Paid work was common for working-class women, and many middle-class women had roles in business, often behind the scenes in bookkeeping and correspondence. Women were also beginning to break into some of the professions. Florence Nightingale (1820–1910) famously took thirty-eight nurses whom she had trained to Istanbul, where they tended the sick and the wounded during the Crimean War.[7] Nightingale came from a wealthy family and had the means to clear paths for other women. As women began to move into the professions and positions of leadership, many Christian leaders saw the value of enlisting them in Christian service, rather than lose them to secular employment.

These diverse streams—women working effectively in service, an expanding agenda for Christian mission and ministry, and an increasingly educated and skilled female population that was challenging gender assumptions—converged in a new form of church feminism.[8] What was required for the church to define a formal role for the ministry of women was a theological rationale. The key figure for this task in England was the Anglican evangelical scholar John Saul Howson (1816–1885), who argued that there was biblical warrant for the ministry of women. He was able to cite an impressive array of examples of women's leadership in New Testament times and in the early church. In 1857 he published the first of two influential papers advocating an order of deaconesses for the Church of England. The New Testament clearly identified women in the role of "diakonos" or "diakone," which the evangelicals translated as "deaconess." (The translation was tendentious, as the original Greek word was not specific as to gender, and also was a common word that did not necessarily connote a defined church office. In other words, alternative translations for the Greek word include "deacon," "helper," "servant," and "minister.") He concluded that the evidence for deaconesses in the New Testament was as strong as its evidence for bishops.[9]

---

7. Nightingale's collected works are available in sixteen volumes under the general editorship of Lynn McDonald of the University of Guelph and published by Wilfrid Laurier Press. The materials are available online at http://www.uoguelph.ca/~cwfn/archival/index.htm.

8. Blackmore, *Beginnings of Women's Ministry*, gives a summary of the deaconess movement in England, from which some of the material in the following paragraphs is taken; this book is reviewed by Peter Sherlock, who picks up the term "church feminism." See also Jurisson, "Deaconess Movement," 821–33.

9. Blackmore, *Beginnings of Women's Ministry*, xlv.

Conversations in 1858 in the Convocation of Canterbury, a high deliberative body in the Church of England, demonstrated a warm receptivity to the Christian service of women, always with the assumption that it did not unsettle existing male power structures. Where Anglicans disagreed was on what form the ministry of women might best take. The wars of "churchmanship" or theological partisanship, which touched most dimensions of Anglican life from the 1840s on, found a battlefield in the ministry of women. One party, often called Anglo-Catholic, promoted monastic and religious sisterhoods in the Church of England, ordered communities for women who were bound to God and to one another by life vows. Religious orders had been suppressed in the sixteenth century, but were now being revived. The other party, often called Anglican evangelical, wanted a biblical warrant for church doctrines and practices. They opposed sisterhoods as non-biblical, grounded in an atavistic medieval ethos of works-righteousness, and likely to strengthen the spirit of dreaded Roman Catholicism. Instead, the evangelical party rallied around Howson's call for deaconesses, as a ministry for women that claimed a biblical foundation.

Deaconesses had disappeared from mainstream Christianity in the Middle Ages, and at the English Reformation they were not recognized in the *Book of Common Prayer*, the foundation of Anglican church polity and liturgical observance. However, John Wesley, an Anglican priest who launched the revival movement that later crystallized into world Methodism, and who was not always fussy about the details of Anglican church order, appears to have trained some deaconesses in the 1730s and 1740s.[10]

Anglicans found a recent precedent for the training and commissioning of deaconesses in contemporary Germany. In the 1830s a German Lutheran pastor at Kaiserswerth, now part of Düsseldorf, had established a school for deaconesses. The students lived in community without distinction of class or rank, took no life vows (as nuns did), and trained for service as teachers, nurses, and charity workers. The school had already attracted several Anglican visitors. Two of these visitors who would bear particular influence on the development of the Anglican office of deaconesses were Florence Nightingale and Elizabeth Ferard (1825–1886).[11] Nightingale took her basic nursing education at the Kaiserswerth institute in 1851, and published a thirty-two-page account of it for English readers.[12] Ferard, the daughter of a London solicitor, studied at Kaiserswerth in 1856, and although she was put off by its narrow vision and austerities, she was inspired by its general direc-

---

10. Hammond, *John Wesley in America*, 136–39.
11. Bonham, "Ferard, Elizabeth Catherine (1825–1883)."
12. Nightingale, *Institution of Kaiserswerth on the Rhine*.

tion. Within a few years she was the head deaconess at a young English institution called the North London Deaconesses' Institution, which had been established by a relative of hers, the Rev. Thomas Pelham Dale (1821–1892), with the approval of the bishop of London. In 1862 Ferard was set apart by the bishop as the first deaconess in the Church of England.

The preceding narrative will give the erroneous impression that the route to deaconesses was a tidy process. Actually through the 1850s and 1860s there was a host of conversations, decisions, events, models, projects, and patterns of training. The very first deaconesses in the Anglican world appear to have been appointed by the Episcopal bishop of Maryland in 1855; they lived in community in Baltimore.[13] In 1860 an Anglican evangelical priest, celebrated mission preacher, and social reformer in London, the Rev. William Pennefather (1816–1873), established a deaconess institute which, when he was appointed to a church near Mildmay Park in London a few years later, was renamed Mildmay Deaconess House. Because it was not approved by the bishop, and mixed non-Anglicans with Anglicans, it had no official standing, but its influence was wide, not least in Canadian Anglicanism.

As the deaconess movement gained traction, a group of Church of England bishops met in 1871 and promulgated a set of principles and rules for deaconesses. Their definition of a deaconess, "a woman set apart by a bishop under that title for service in the church," was wonderfully general without quite being empty, and was widely used or adapted. The Convocation of Canterbury that year favorably discussed the bishops' statement, and the upper house (the bishops) advised that deaconesses "should be admitted in solemn form by the bishop, with benediction, by the laying on of hands." By the turn of the century, a number of English and American dioceses had deaconesses and houses for the training of deaconesses. In 1889 the General Convention of the Episcopal Church approved a canon (that is, a church law) on deaconesses.

THE OFFICE OF DEACONESS IN CANADIAN ANGLICANISM

Canadian Anglicans in the Victorian era kept themselves well informed of developments and controversies in other parts of their global communion, thanks to their networks of correspondence and their numerous denominational publications. In 1862, for example, the *Church Chronicle for the*

---

13. For the Episcopal Church movement for deaconesses, see Donovan, *Different Call*, especially 88–122.

Diocese of Montreal published a lengthy article on deaconesses, as an example of "one of the cheering signs of the increased vitality of the Church of England."[14] It summarized conversations about women's ministry in the Convocation of Canterbury in 1858, quoted at length from a statement on deaconesses by the bishop of London, and recognized numerous practical initiatives that had already been launched. Anglicans followed these developments, but no momentum would develop for Canadian deaconesses for another three decades.

In 1883, the synod for the Anglican ecclesiastical province of Canada (which then comprised Ontario, Quebec, New Brunswick, Nova Scotia, Prince Edward Island) formed a committee of bishops, clergy, and laity (all men of course) to discuss "the employment of Christian women." It recommended a canon, or church law, allowing women to be admitted as deaconesses, or to be professed as members of sisterhoods, in any diocese where the bishop approved.[15] The recommendation was laid over to the next session of provincial synod in 1886, where it was hotly debated at length in both the "houses" of the synod (the house of clergy and laity, and the house of bishops). The synod journal does not report the substance of the debate, but in general the Anglicans of a catholic disposition who were promoting sisterhoods maintained that the only proper role for women with strong religious convictions was a consecrated life insulated from the ways of the world. Evangelicals retorted that Christian disciples were to serve the world, not withdraw from it into a round of liturgical observances; moreover, they argued, religious vows violated the principle of the freedom of the gospel and led to legalism, and perhaps even to Roman Catholicism. But Anglican catholics were equally hostile to the evangelical proposal for deaconesses as a public ministry of Christian service, which they condemned as an innovation of worldly Protestant or even secular spirit, defying the apostolic rule and church tradition that women were to be modest, deferential, and quiet. In addition, they argued that church tradition connected pastoral authority to liturgical leadership, and women could not lead the public worship of the church. In the end the synod resolved "that considering the difficulties surrounding any definite regulations in regard to Sisterhoods and women's work generally, the further discussion of the Canon proposed be deferred until the next Session of the Provincial Synod,"[16] that is, until 1889. In fact, the provincial synod did not return to the matter in 1889, presumably be-

14. "Church Deaconesses," 184–87.

15. *Church of England in Canada* (1883) 71, 75, 91–92. For material in this section I have used, with a few corrections in detail, Kemper, "Deaconess as Urban Missionary," 171–90.

16. *Church of England in Canada* (1886) 46, 53, 54, 56, 57, 62, 82, 88, 91–92.

cause there was still no prospect of agreement. The issue was still a live one, however; an Anglican newspaper asserted that "the permanent diaconate of women is . . . one of the questions of the day."[17]

The Christian leadership of women was being widely recognized in the 1880s. Maurice S. Baldwin, the bishop of Huron, an "evangelical of evangelicals" as he was called, declared in his charge to the annual meeting of his diocesan synod in 1885, "This is the age for the ministry of woman," and he strongly commended the order of deaconesses as scriptural.[18] In the same year the Women's Auxiliary to the denominational mission society (the "WA") was founded. It functioned at first as a kind of handmaiden to the male-controlled mission society, but it quickly grew into a powerful independent force where women exercised significant leadership. It would become by far the most significant women's group in the Anglican Church. And in 1884 the first Anglican sisterhood in Canada, the Sisters of St. John the Divine, was formed.

The appointment of the first deaconess came from a surprising direction. John Medley, the bishop of Fredericton (his diocese was coterminous with the province of New Brunswick), was by no means in the evangelical camp, but he recognized the legitimacy of the office of deaconess as rooted in the biblical witness and the tradition of the early church, and he was a practically minded chief pastor in an under-resourced territory. In his diocese a faithful, committed, reliable Christian woman in her sixties had been working for several years with struggling or abandoned country missions, sometimes with the support of the diocesan Women's Aid Association. Mary Nameria Jacob (1820–1904) had a heart for little places like Ludlow, where the church would have disappeared except for her exertions. She visited parishioners, taught Sunday school, encouraged choirs, raised funds for painting and rebuilding and organs, organized summer picnics and Christmas festivities, and administered charity. In July 1889 Medley made her a deaconess at a ceremony in the cathedral, and in the years after he took obvious pleasure in reporting to his meetings of the diocesan synod on the work of his deaconess.

This was a fine initiative, but it was more a recognition than a commissioning. Anglican evangelicals envisioned a system which would recruit, train, and deploy deaconesses in significant numbers. The *Evangelical Churchman*, the weekly Anglican party newspaper published by a group closely connected with Wycliffe College, Toronto, was now publicizing news of English and American progress in the deaconess movement, promoting

---

17. *Canadian Church Magazine and Missionary News* 2.22 (Apr. 1888) 92.

18. Diocese of Huron, *Journal of the Synod* (1883). See also Hayes, "Baldwin, Maurice Scollard."

similar initiatives for Canadian Anglicanism, proposing a school for deaconesses (partly as an answer to monasteries of women), and announcing meetings on the subject.

No bishop was taking on the project, and so the alumni association and supporters of Wycliffe College claimed it for themselves. Over the previous fifteen years Anglican evangelical leaders in southern Ontario, recognizing needs and impatient for action, had succeeded in founding several institutions, including Wycliffe College itself, Ridley College for boys, and Havergal College for girls, as well as a society for foreign missions. In 1890 the alumni association appointed a committee to lay plans for a deaconess school. In 1891 the committee reported back optimistically, in January 1892 they examined proposals, and in February they made recommendations. In June 1892, they organized a public meeting. For the keynote speaker they first invited Bishop Maurice Baldwin, but Baldwin persuaded them that it would be more proper and more strategic to persuade the bishop of Toronto to speak.[19] Wycliffe, after all, was in the Toronto diocese, and, besides, the endorsement of the bishop of Toronto, who avoided aligning with church parties, would have wider credibility than the more partisan Baldwin's. At the June meeting, a resolution was passed to establish a home for the training of deaconesses, under the presidency of the bishop of Toronto. The chief figure in the governance of the school would be the chair of the board of the projected home, Newman Wright Hoyles (1844–1927), a Wycliffe trustee and a director of the *Evangelical Churchman*. (Hoyles, as the head of the law school for Ontario at Osgoode Hall, also led the way for women to enter the legal profession in the province.)[20]

For these evangelical men, the operational model of the office of deaconess that dominated their thinking was the ministry helper. In February 1892, their committee defined its expectations of deaconesses in a list:

> General assistance of clergy in parishes in district visiting (especially spiritual work). 1) Bible reading and personal evangelistic work amongst the poor and rich; 2) Care of poor and sick. Soup kitchen and making and selling old clothes; 3) Care of young women in homes; 4) Care and correction of children; 5) Creches, etc.; 6) Prison work; 7) Training church workers; 8) the fostering and development of a foreign missionary spirit.[21]

19. ACC, Diocese of Huron archives (Huron College, London, ON), Baldwin's episcopal letter-book, 11 Mar. 1892.

20. Moore, "Hoyles, Newman Wright."

21. The records of the committees that founded the deaconess training school are in ACC, GSA, AWTC fonds, series 1. This passage is quoted in Kemper, "Deaconess as Urban Missionary," 177.

Few of these expectations required professional skills, decision-making authority, or gifts for leadership. Indeed, for many founders, the specific tasks that deaconesses might be capable of executing were less important than their character, moral virtue, faithfulness, and sense of discipleship. Nevertheless, there was potential that a more independent and professional role, akin to a social worker's, might grow out of doing ministry among the poor and in prisons, and training church workers pointed to the possibility of greater responsibility as well. Nevertheless, the founders were determined to avoid establishing a professional model. The deaconesses were to understand their vocation as no higher than that of a wife and mother, who was herself seen as a type of consecrated household assistant, not someone with formal training or independent of male authority.

The next step was to recruit a head deaconess to teach the students. After some failed efforts in other directions, the Wycliffe group appointed Sybil Wilson, the unmarried daughter of the late Sir Daniel Wilson, who had been the president of the University of Toronto as well as a Wycliffe trustee. Sybil Wilson had the advantages of high social standing, independent wealth (she would not require a salary), and a willingness to mingle with the lower classes. She was not herself, however, a deaconess. So, the school was put on hold while she went to the Mildmay Deaconess House in London for training. She returned a year later to open the Deaconess House in her own home on St. George Street, at the heart of the University of Toronto. The grand event was attended with great fanfare and the distinction of an address by the bishop.

There were, however, no students. Also, there were almost no funds. Recruitment and fundraising were no easy things for an office of church ministry which existed nowhere in Canada except rural New Brunswick, where there was only one seventy-three-year-old example. Moreover, the prospects for attracting students were the less propitious given that the founders of the training school, all of them men, envisioned that deaconesses would serve without salary. Since the women also had to be single or widowed—a married woman had a vocation to serve her husband, and could not possibly accept a second vocation on top of that—the office of deaconess would have been limited to women of considerable independent wealth. For the evangelical men, the principle at stake was that "this work may remain wholly a service of love and mercy." Moreover, it was essential that deaconesses not be seen as a variety of "working girl," a morally questionable breed, as historian Alison Kemper has pointed out.[22]

---

22. Ibid., 179.

The founders did relent on the point of salary, and in the winter of 1894 two women finally enrolled. But by the spring, the strain had broken Sybil Wilson's health, and she resigned. Since the Deaconess House was Sybil's own house, temporary substitute quarters had to be found; a Wycliffe professor volunteered his home. An interim head deaconess was appointed, and then another. Notwithstanding these setbacks, the whole project must have seemed to have succeeded when in December 1894 the bishop of Toronto set aside Annie Rae of Watford, Ontario, and Suzanne Lucinda Sandys of Chatham, Ontario, as deaconesses in a ceremony at St. James Cathedral.[23] It was now formally affirmed that women could and should be theologically trained for a formally recognized public ministry in what was then called the Church of England in Canada.

As is often the case in Canadian Anglicanism, where bishops maintain their authority jealously, there were no uniform processes across the country for recognizing, appointing, remunerating, regulating, and keeping track of deaconesses. These varied from bishop to bishop, diocese to diocese. The earliest national effort to bring some measure of consistency was a canon on deaconesses passed by General Synod, the highest instrument of governance in the denomination, in 1921.[24] General Synod was responding to a recommendation the previous year promulgated by a committee of Lambeth Conference (the gathering of bishops in the worldwide Anglican Communion every ten years or so, which carries some moral weight but no juridical authority). The Lambeth committee recognized the office of deaconess as an "order of the ministry" with the stamp of apostolic approval, advised national churches to produce a form for the "making of deaconesses," and identified a few functions that deaconesses might serve.[25] General Synod's new Canon XVII began by affirming that "the time has come when this office should be canonically recognized." Communicant women at least twenty-five years old, unmarried or widowed, were eligible for the office. They required certain virtues of character that the canon enumerated. The House of Bishops was asked to devise a liturgical form by which bishops could set apart deaconesses. Deaconesses must be licensed by the bishop, and were to serve under the authority of the parish priest. The position of deaconess would be vacated by marriage, or by resignation; but no deaconess could be removed without cause. The canon thus gave formal national recognition to an office of ministry which had in fact already existed for

23. Griffith, *Weaving a Changing Tapestry*, 169.
24. The text is given in Hayes, *Anglicans in Canada*, 295–96.
25. https://archive.org/stream/conferenceofbishoolamb/conferenceofbishoolamb_djvu.txt.

thirty years in many Canadian dioceses, and established some standards of permanence and professionalism for it.

Specific policies, procedures, and standards for deaconesses remained untidily inconsistent across the country over the next thirty years, despite a few desultory attempts by General Synod and the House of Bishops to review the ministry of deaconesses and to have creative thoughts about "women's work" in general. Between 1928 and 1931 an Anglican National Commission studied the state of the church, with all its resources and problems. It sent a little group of field commissioners across Canada to have wide-ranging conversations, who reported concisely that "few direct references were made to the ministry of women," but that "in practice their ministry is most acceptable."[26] In 1930 Lambeth Conference passed a resolution suggesting ceremonial forms for ordaining deaconesses, and in 1931 General Synod considered it ever so briefly and referred it to the House of Bishops. The latter appointed a committee on women's work that met between 1932 and 1935 and produced a report which contained a few modest recommendations; for instance, from time to time a bishop and interested clergy might talk with groups of churchwomen involved in professional or institutional work. In 1937 the primate appointed a committee with bishops, clergy, and laymen and women, which submitted brief reports when General Synod met every three years or so.[27] In 1943, for instance, it recommended more trained women church workers, and suggested that financial support for students at Deac House and better salaries for workers would help recruitment. Their report was adopted by General Synod with amendments, and referred back to the committee.[28]

The most glaring inconsistency among dioceses in their oversight of deaconesses was how they understood the ordering of deaconesses. Was it analogous to the ordination of male deacons and priests? In that case deaconesses should be considered clergy. Or was it a commissioning of laypeople? Or was it something else? Resolution 68 of the Lambeth Conference of 1930 referred to "the ordination of deaconesses," not a mere "setting apart."[29] The first national Canadian form for setting apart a deaconess, promulgated by the House of Bishops in October 1921, directed the bishop to lay hands on the candidate and say, "Take thou authority to execute the office of a deaconess in the Church of God, whereunto thou are now set apart." This construction sounded very parallel to the ordination of a deacon. Af-

26. Anglican National Commission, *The Report of the Field Commissioners*, 34.
27. *General Synod Journal* (1937) 108–10.
28. *General Synod Journal* (1943) 54, 329.
29. *Lambeth Conference*. Resolution 68.

ter ordination, just as clergy received a formal document of their status, called "letters of orders," so did deaconesses. The letters of orders used in New Westminster, for instance, in 1951, declared, "We Godfrey do make it known . . . that we solemnly ordered to the office of deaconess . . ."[30] In 1922 the strongly evangelical bishop of Saskatchewan, George Exton Lloyd, scrutinized the letters of orders of deaconess Mabel Jones, decreed that they "constituted her clergy," and gave her a seat in the diocesan synod.[31] But almost no one followed his example.

In Toronto, the phrase "setting apart" was normally used instead of "ordination." However, Derwyn Owen, who was primate of the national church from 1934 to 1947, approved speaking of a deaconess as being "in the diaconate," the term also used for male deacons. As a fellow bishop recalled later about Owen's views,

> He also held that the word "ordained" was a proper use in that it may be used for the ceremonial admission to the ministry not only of men but also of women in the service of the Church, and that it has not been the restricted use for the priesthood or for the office of deacon.[32]

If "ordination" means admission to an order, and if orders include what medieval Christians called "minor orders" other than the holy orders of deacon and priest (or presbyter), and if it was proper to talk of an "order of deaconesses," then speaking of the ordination of deaconesses was not wrong. But many resisted the term as implying too close an analogy with the *real* ordinations of male deacons and priests.

Aside from the eccentric diocese of Saskatchewan, deaconesses did not have full membership in their diocesan synod. Some dioceses gave deaconesses seating, typically as a group in an isolated section of the room, but did not allow them to speak. Some allowed them to speak if invited, but not vote. Still others did not invite them to synod at all. Should they be included in the procession at diocesan liturgical events? In 1971, when David Somerville was installed as bishop of New Westminster, it was apparently decided that deaconesses could process, but no one told deaconess Anne Crookes. She wrote the new bishop afterwards apologizing for the snub of not knowing that she was invited.[33]

---

30. ACC, Diocese of New Westminster [DNW] Archives (Vancouver), D373/13, services ordering deaconesses.

31. Hayes, *Anglicans in Canada*, 175-76.

32. ACC, DNW Archives, Deaconesses D2008-19, Bishop of Diocese to A. Edgar, 21 Nov. 1951, d2008-19.

33. ACC, DNW Archives, clergy files, Anne Crookes, 26 Jul. 1971.

In the 1950s the old General Synod committee on women's work, the one established in 1937, finally showed some life. Cultural influences, such as the expanding role of women in society, no doubt played its part, but I suspect that the activation of the committee had a great deal to do with a very influential couple in the diocese of Toronto. Reg Soward (1907–2001) was a long-time chair of the board of the Anglican Women's Training College (AWTC), the successor institution to Deaconess House, and also the chancellor (the chief legal officer) of the diocese of Toronto, and he was a fervent supporter of the ministry of women. In fact, he was already arguing publicly for the ordination of women to the priesthood in the 1940s. Ruth Cornish Soward (d. 1994) was a graduate of Deaconess House who devoted considerable time to its support later, for a while as a board member.

Ruth Soward was chair of a subcommittee of the committee on women's work; its task was to report on "the future pattern of women's work in the Church." Her subcommittee canvassed a variety of interested parties and circulated questionnaires. The subcommittee reported to General Synod in 1955.[34] It argued that deaconesses should be considered ordained ministers, and cited the example of the Church of England in support. It regretted that in some dioceses deaconesses did not hold a bishop's license, as required by the canon of the national church. It noted a wide variety of educational standards for deaconesses: some had university degrees, while others depended on "sanctified common sense." It concluded, however, that "on the whole we must recognize that professionalism has come to stay." It recommended that deaconesses should have full membership in their diocesan synods, that an ecclesiastical authority should be commissioned for deaconesses to ensure their fair and consistent treatment and to receive appeals in case of problems, and that deaconesses should be allowed to continue in their office after marriage. The last recommendation was accepted in 1959.

A long-standing injustice suffered by deaconesses was that they typically retired without a pension. In 1955, on a motion by Reg Soward, General Synod authorized a pension fund for woman church workers, which could include graduates of AWTC or similar schools, and deaconesses employed full-time in the work of the church.[35] However, even after the fund was established, the dioceses did not all consistently enroll their deaconesses in the fund.

---

34. *General Synod Journal* (1955) 40, 390–401; excerpted in Hayes, *Anglicans in Canada*, 298–301.

35. *General Synod Journal* (1955) 63–64.

THE TRAINING OF DEACONESSES

The never resolved tension between the deaconess as gendered ministry professional and the deaconess as gendered ministry helper was embodied in the training of deaconesses. If one had to generalize, one might say that the curriculum tended to emphasize the model of ministry helper from the 1890s to the 1930s, and the model of ministry professional from the 1940s to the 1960s. For instance, in the earlier period residential rules and narrow standards of theological orthodoxy were more rigidly enforced than in the later period, and field placements were generally more closely supervised in the earlier period as well. But in both periods the theological coursework taken by the deaconesses was to a large extent the same as that taken by men training for ordination, and specialized field training was available for specific vocational paths.

In 1895, after Sybil Wilson's resignation as head deaconess, and two interims, the next head deaconess, Frances ("Fanny") Cross, brought stability and momentum to the school for a while. More students enrolled, and revenues increased. A broader purpose for the school was added when the Missionary Society of the Church of England in Canada enlisted the Deaconess House as a training school for women missionaries to the Canadian North West. Accordingly, in 1899 the Deaconess House became the Deaconess and Missionary Training House. But it was usually simply called the Deac House.

Fanny Cross's health broke in 1901; she entered a sanitarium with tuberculosis and died two years later. She was followed as principal by Emma Naftel (1901–1907); by the end of her principalship, the bishop of Toronto had set apart fifteen graduates as deaconesses. Following Naftel were Thomasina Connell (1907–1933), Harriet Emery (1933–1942), May Watts (1942–1947), Annie Edgar (1947–1955), Ruth Scott (1955–1966), and Marion Niven (1966–1969).

Some Canadian deaconesses trained in other institutions, including the Mildmay Deaconess House in London and in the Episcopal Church schools for deaconesses in New York and Philadelphia. Anglican Theological College in Vancouver also trained some deaconesses for a period. But most deaconesses were graduates of Deac House.

Deac House moved twice. In 1903, it moved from the University of Toronto area to 179 Gerrard Street East, across from Allan Gardens, then "a healthy part of the city." The property cost $8000, of which $2000 was paid by Samuel Hume Blake, a high-profile Toronto lawyer who had been the chief founder of Wycliffe College. The overseers of Deac House at the time regretted that the building was situated so far from the university, but took comfort that an inner-city location was very appropriate for students seeking practical experience in urban ministry. As that neighborhood deteriorated in course of time, however, and became a center for prostitution, concerns arose. In 1946, under the leadership of Reg and Ruth Soward, the school was moved to 217 St. George Street, north of Bloor, near the University of Toronto. Two years later the house next door was purchased as well, and in 1955 a wing was built between the two buildings. The second house was rebuilt in 1965.

In addition to prospective deaconesses and missionaries, the Deac House began to serve women engaged to be married to clergymen, who took a short-course "diamond ring program." It accommodated women considering other forms of Christian service as well. In 1947, partly to reflect this broader institutional mission, partly to appeal to a broader national market, and partly to signal that it wanted to leave church partisanship behind, Deac House began to be called the Anglican Women's Training College.

At first, the program of study at Deac House required two years of study. In 1924 it was extended to three years. From the beginning the curriculum can be seen as guided by four principles: evangelical formation, socialization into the values of the profession, academic education, and professional training.

Evangelical Formation

As for evangelical formation, the consistent undercurrent in all the life and work of Deac House until World War II was the reinforcement of Protestant orthodoxy. This was defined by a statement of principles borrowed from those established for Wycliffe College, centered on biblical authority, justification by faith alone, and a Protestant sacramental theology. These principles were intended to reflect the Protestant doctrine of the Thirty-nine Articles of Religion of the Church of England. The subtext of these principles was the rejection of Anglo-Catholic error.

Evangelical and low-church (non-ritualistic) orthodoxy was taken seriously. As early as 1897 a student was expelled for her doctrinal deviations.[36] In the 1930s Principal Harriet Emery wrote several evangelical rectors in Toronto warning them that many "Ritualistic Churches rather than Churches of the Evangelical standing" were asking for deaconesses. The board had struggled with this threat, and "it was keenly felt that the Students should not be under this influence when we desire them to be true

36. Griffith, *Weaving a Changing Tapestry*, 156.

to the principles for which the House stands."[37] Emery concluded by urging the evangelical rectors themselves to take on some Deaconess House students. If the Deac House was suspicious of high-church Anglicans, high-church Anglicans in turn were suspicious of the Deac House. A student named Beth Ann Exham, whose home congregation was in the high-church tradition, was warned by her fellow parishioners when she was contemplating going to AWTC that it would "have me United Church before I got out of there."[38] As late as 1952 Howard Clark, the dean of Ottawa, and later the primate, sent a scorching letter to Reg Soward, the chair of the AWTC board, complaining that the school's principles were too evangelical. Clark was particularly grieved with one statement allowing that non-episcopal churches were really churches, and another one defining Christ's real presence in Holy Communion as being in the hearts of believers and not in the elements of bread and wine. "I personally dissent most strongly from both opinions and would feel some difficulty in sending any young woman from my parish to a College where they were taught," he complained.[39]

The partisan antagonism between advocates of religious sisterhoods and advocates of deaconesses long continued. In 1938 Margaret Steel was the first Deaconess House student from the high-church diocese of Qu'Appelle; she recalled in 1992, "Of course anyone that heard I wanted to go into church work tried to persuade me to go to the Convent."[40] When a former student named Miss Peters (her name does not appear on Gwyn Griffith's list of graduates) began wearing a pin signifying the Sisters of St. John the Divine, Principal Emery was obliged by the Executive Committee in 1933 to write her an uncomfortable letter:

> I know that your sympathies have never been absolutely one with the principles of churchmanship of our Deaconess House and it seemed to me that your position was more intensified than ever when you were here in the Autumn . . . Would you mind not wearing your S.S.J.D. cross when here and would you try not to influence the students towards that type of churchmanship. Miss Connell's last year here was made miserable for her because three of the students, who, though taking their training here were spending any spare time they had at the Sisterhood

---

37. ACC, GSA, AWTC fonds, correspondence, from Emery to Rev. W. R. R. Armitage, 18 Sept. 1934.

38. Griffith interview, Exham.

39. ACC, GSA, AWTC fonds, Box M75-27, 2-a-3 Executive Committee correspondence, Clark to Soward, 4 Mar. 1952.

40. Griffith interview, lunchtime conversation with graduates in the Vancouver area, 18 May 1992.

and I respect the Reverend Mother very much because just as soon as she noticed it she forbade them coming without Miss Connell's permission. Of course this could not go on for at least we must be loyal to what we believe and what the House stands for but Miss Connell had no end of trouble about it. The outcome has been that one of the three is entering the Sisterhood and the other two have withdrawn from their position.[41]

Theological partisanship did mellow after World War II. A liberal evangelicalism that did not stress propositional precision grew in prominence, associated with such Wycliffe College leaders as Principal Ramsay Armitage, Reg and Ruth Soward, and Canon Henry Cody of St. Paul's Church, Bloor Street, the flagship preaching church for the denomination. And as the AWTC sought to cast its net wider, the statement of principles was dramatically reduced in 1953 to just two points, an affirmation of the Bible as the rule of faith, and the acceptance of the Book of Common Prayer. Both of these statements were sanctioned by the *Book of Common Prayer* and had no partisan edge. By the 1950s the provost of Trinity College, the rival of Wycliffe College, was a vice-patron of AWTC, and Trinity was represented on the school's curriculum committee.

Socialization into Professional Values

Second, Deac House sought to socialize students into the professional values, manners, and standards of comportment of the office of deaconess. The residential character of the program was a key strategy for this educational outcome. Students and some staff lived together in a large old house, joining in morning and evening prayer, sharing household chores, and entertaining visitors. Typically, a dozen or two students were enrolled at a time, fewer during the Depression. The most enrolled at the same time (in 1958) was forty-six. In this family model, the staff were the mother, and the students were the daughters. There were sheets of written and unwritten rules, and the staff had many opportunities to watch and correct their charges. Students wore uniforms, with exceptions as determined by rules, to help cultivate a sense of community and identity, and to minimize expressions of social distinctions. In the early years the uniforms were green; later students wore a grey dress with turned down collar and white cuffs, a black or grey coat with a silver pin identifying them as deaconess students, and a distinctive hat which many disliked. Skirts had to be not too short and not too long.

41. ACC, GSA, AWTC fonds, correspondence, from Emery to Miss Petra at request of Executive Committee, 13 Dec. 1933.

For many years there was a rule about how far window-shades should be pulled down, the story being that Lady Gooderham, when she drove by the Deaconess House in her carriage, liked the window-shades to be uniform.[42] Table manners were enforced strictly. The women had practice pouring tea at social events. One student called the Deac House a combination kindergarten and finishing school. June Bradley, who graduated in 1951, recalled that "in many ways it was a very oppressed community."[43]

In the world of Deac House, it was an article of faith that middle-class manners would prove useful in ministry. Those outside sometimes saw things more ironically. In 1943 a male correspondent named Trever Jones, who was familiar with women church workers in northern Canada, described

> two graduates of the Deaconess House who sent formal written invitations for a Hostess Tea to a number of Indian women, many of whom could not read English. When the women assembled in their ragged clothes and shawls, the two staff members formed a reception line arrayed in formal attire. They then talked to each other, while sipping tea, and the Indian women sat around in bewildered silence.[44]

Similarly, the white middle-class norms that ruled at Deac House included racist attitudes towards Asians, Indigenous peoples, and Jews. Just one expression of these prejudices was the conviction that "those preparing for work in Indian residential schools required lower qualifications and less training."[45] Joan Lew, an Asian Canadian from Vancouver who studied at AWTC in the early 1950s, experienced what she called a "condescension" on account of her race, "especially from the WA people." She explained, "The people who were helping us want to feel that they were the superior ones. That was the feeling I got, but it wasn't discrimination as such."[46]

Theological Education

Third, in the area of theological education, the curriculum from the beginning included instruction in Bible, church history, missiology, Prayer

---

42. Griffith interview, Frances Lightbourn.
43. Griffith, *Weaving a Changing Tapestry*, 127.
44. ACC, GSA, AWTC fonds, correspondence, Trever Jones to Dr. Taylor, 23 Nov. 1943.
45. Griffith, *Weaving a Changing Tapestry*, 158.
46. Griffith interview, Lew.

Book, apologetics, and social sciences. Many of these courses were taught by Wycliffe College instructors; in the 1930s some students were taking Trinity College courses, and after World War II both Trinity and Wycliffe participated in AWTC programs. The evident assumption was that women were as intellectually capable as men, and that ideally their ministry should be just as theologically formed as the men's. It evidently surprised some contemporaries that the women frequently achieved a higher standard than the men. (In fact, it was cause for comment that some men borrowed some women's class lecture notes.) In 1931 Mabel Jones was the first person to graduate from Wycliffe in the regular program; this is the Deaconess Jones who was recognized as a clergyperson in Saskatchewan.

The theological instruction was definitely correlated to the goal of evangelical formation. Critical thinking was not a priority before World War II. Deaconesses should be sufficiently formed in their biblical knowledge and theology that they could resist high-church thinking, champion orthodoxy in their Sunday school teaching, and, perhaps, give an account of their faith to adherents of other religions in foreign missions, and to the lapsed and the religiously tepid in Toronto.

Field Work

Finally, the practical side of the training focused on field work. In 1912 two streams were created, one for deaconess nurses and one for deaconess teachers. One senses here a step towards professionalizing the curriculum. In the three-year program that became standard, the women had a part-time placement during their second and third years, and a full-time ministry during their two summers. (In the 1950s, some took a two-year academic program followed by a third year in placements.) Placements reflected the prospective vocations of the students. In general, in the first five decades, Deac House was training overseas missionaries, Indian Residential School teachers, church assistants, and Christian social workers. At least one social services placement was almost inevitable for everyone. In fact, the Deac House ran its own social service in the coach house in the back of 179 Gerrard St. East. This facility came to be called the Mildmay Institute, in honor of the Mildmay Deaconess House in England, where Principal Thomasina Connell had studied. Mothers from the lower classes came there for meetings while their children were being tended by deaconess students, and for many years a dispensary was administered there as well. From the 1930s, the vast majority of students spent at least one summer as "vanners" or "van ladies," driving with the Sunday school vans among the rural outposts in western Canada. The van program was run by a wealthy, strong-willed English lady named Eva Hasell and her companion Iris Sayle.[47] Some bishops who did not like to kowtow to Eva Hasell set up their own diocesan van programs. The format was consistent over the decades: pairs of young women lived in the vans, using them as mobile bases for Christian education programs, driving hundreds of miles over bad roads to visit people in isolated places. Through the summers they washed their laundry in lakes, cooked meals over campfires, and made no money at all. It sounds a little hokey, perhaps, but almost all the young women loved it.

During the 1940s, the war closed off most overseas missions; Indian residential schools began their journey to disfavor; and social services were increasingly assumed by governments. As a result, from this point, the role of the Mildmay Institute came to be questioned. In 1942 a WA field secretary, Ruth Carruthers, worried that the Deac House was being used to serve the Mildmay rather than the other way around, and that in any event this kind of placement was too narrow an educational foundation for the deaconesses' future work: "too much stress is laid on work amongst one class of people only."[48] (She meant that students were doing too much to help the inner-city poor, and not spending enough time with middle-class Anglican parishioners.) After 1947 the Mildmay was much less used, and in 1954 it was closed. Instead, field placements focused more on general ministry in northern parishes, and on Christian education and pastoral work in southern parishes. Popular placements included teaching Sunday school, training Sunday school teachers, and overseeing youth groups in Anglican evangelical churches in Toronto, such as St. Paul's, Redeemer, St. Peter's, and Little Trinity.

A question that continually recurred for the leaders and teachers of Deac House was whether it should focus on practical training or academic study. Mary Sudman Donovan, in her penetrating history of women's work in the Episcopal Church, has identified this question as key. Most of the difficulties which deaconesses faced in these years, she points out, stemmed from a dichotomy in how the deaconess was understood. The clergy most frequently saw the deaconess as "a religious extension of the ideal of true womanhood," pious and submissive; many deaconesses, by contrast, preferred to see themselves as theologically and practically trained professional church workers.[49] Thus in 1943, surveyed for a curricular review, many

---

47. Fast, *Missionary on Wheels*.

48. ACC, GSA, AWTC fonds, M75-57, box 15, Ruth Carruthers to Mrs. Coggan, 1942.

49. Donovan, *Different Call*, 90.

male clergy said they wanted deaconesses to be trained to provide practical female help. From John House, the principal of Old Sun School, an Indian Residential School in Gleichen, Alberta, came this advice: "Since the niceties of religion are practically useless here, a course in theology for women workers is very much a waste of time." The skills he needed in his female staff were cooking, dressmaking, laundering, and dairying—the work of a proletariat that knows its place.[50] Similarly, Gilbert Thompson, of The Bishop Horden School in Moose Factory, warned that "the average candidate for school work was wasting her time by attending so many theological lectures." Some deaconess students before the 1950s sensed that the menial understanding of servanthood was embodied in the curriculum; Rosemary Anne Benwell, who graduated in 1940, recalled, "I suppose I was being groomed to be a helper more than a leader . . . . I was . . . taught to try to carry out the wishes of the rector, perhaps not to be too full of original ideas myself."[51] But the views of professors at Wycliffe (and later Trinity) provided a counterweight, and many students and staff at the Deac House valued a theological education. Marion Niven, at her installation as principal in 1966, said that the purpose of AWTC was not narrow specialization for a career but "basic education in theological thinking and Christian communication" that aimed to equip students for whatever possibilities of service arose where a woman found herself.

THE MINISTRIES OF DEACONESSES

From the beginning, a deaconess was a single or unmarried woman set apart by prayers and the laying-on of hands by a bishop for the service of Christ in the church. The deaconess did not take life vows, and was free to resign at any time, or to enter marriage, by which she would vacate her position. The ministry helper model of deaconess predominated at first. Deaconesses would serve as parish visitors and assistants to parish clergy, or as urban missioners and charitable relief workers on behalf of churches. As parish assistants they might visit parishioners and the sick, prepare families for baptism, teach confirmation classes, lead study groups, work with women in such ways as supporting mothers' meetings and sewing circles and counseling, work with children and youth, and perhaps do some nursing. In fact, in course of time, the ministries of deaconesses became more varied than

---

50. ACC, GSA, AWTC fonds, M75-57, box 15, to J. S. S. Clarke from John House; the second quotation from House is from the MSCC report, 17 May 1938, same location.

51. Griffith, *Weaving a Changing Tapestry*, 128.

that, and often took on a more professional and independent character. In particular, deaconesses proved their use in situations that were too arduous or too ill-paid for men, such as in isolated areas, and there they might function as parish priests in all ways except presiding at Holy Communion. Many undertook activities that could look like social work for minorities and the marginalized, and advocacy for justice.

Gwyn Griffith, in her history of Canadian schools for deaconesses, identified about 450 graduates of Deac House/AWTC. Principal Ruth Scott in 1963 reported 800 graduates; she may have been including women who attended as diploma students or special students but did not graduate.[52] Principals occasionally produced lists of graduates, such as one dated 1932 which identifies sixty-two "set apart deaconesses" who were graduates of the Deac House.[53] At this midpoint of the period of deaconesses, about one in four were working in social services or urban missions; a like number were working overseas (China, Japan, India, Chile, Egypt, South Africa); about a dozen were doing parish work in city churches, and seven in northern or remote churches. Other ministries, involving one or two deaconesses each, were a mission to the Jews, an "Oriental" mission in Vancouver, the Deaconess House staff itself, a diocesan staff, a deanery, and ministries identified simply but imprecisely by the name of a place (for instance, Lachine, Toronto, Winnipeg). These lists were compiled informally from available data; there was no central authority keeping track of Canadian Anglican deaconesses until 1960, when an official list began to be compiled for the annual Anglican *Year Book* that included a directory of clergy.

Not entirely differently from male clergy, deaconesses could serve a very diverse set of pastoral, liturgical, administrative, educational, and missional functions, in a wide variety of ecclesiastical, social, and cultural contexts. At one end of a spectrum, some deaconesses, especially those in isolated areas, or else working on the staff of a diocese or General Synod, enjoyed a fair degree of independence with a wide scope of action. At the other end, some functioned as a kind of ecclesiastical proletariat, undertaking specific, narrowly conceived, sometimes menial tasks assigned by a supervisor; many of these were in urban parishes. Some deaconesses wanted to share in liturgical ministry; others had very little interest in that.

To begin with parish deaconesses, their activities might typically include Christian education work, such as teaching Sunday school, training Sunday school teachers, administering Girls' Auxiliary, Junior Auxiliary, and

---

52. *Rupert's Land Diocesan* (Apr. 1965), news clipping, AWTC Series 5: Printed and Miscellaneous Material: Scrapbooks, 1961–1965.

53. ACC, GSA, AWTC fonds, Miss Connell's correspondence, November 1932.

Little Helpers groups; leading mothers' groups, conducting junior choirs, and producing plays and pageants. Many also did some basic social service work, such as giving meal tickets to the homeless, intervening with welfare agencies, and working with orphanages. Parish deaconesses noted that additional side jobs just seemed to accumulate. Among those who found great satisfaction as a parish deaconess was June Bradley, who served at St. Mary's, Kerrisdale, in Vancouver, in the late 1960s. She later recalled how "life opened up for me" there. With a Sunday school of a thousand children, and people lining up to teach them, she embraced the challenge of introducing the controversial liberal "new curriculum" that the national church staff had developed. As she recalled later, "We had a ball with it. I know the [wider] church hated it and it flopped, but we had a wonderful time with it."[54]

Some Deac House graduates were appointed to remote sites. Not being under direct supervision and being the only ministers on the ground, these deaconesses enjoyed considerable independence and scope of action. The main exclusion was they could not preside at Holy Communion, which, however, was not frequently celebrated in most Anglican churches before the 1970s. Deaconess Margaret E. Robinson served from 1938 to 1944 in Clinton, BC, in the diocese of Cariboo, and when Bishop George Wells installed her, she records the following conversation:

> He said: I wish you to baptise, so I said "I suppose you mean in an emergency." He said "No I mean normally." He saw that the situation in which he placed me *was* an emergency.[55]

In the diocese of Brandon (Manitoba), the name "Bishop's Messengers" was used, rather than "deaconesses," for women in charge of remote parishes.[56] The Bishop's Messengers were founded by an English woman named Marguerita Fowler and her companion Muriel Secretan in 1928; at first it was "a little piece of England," but it increasingly attracted Canadian workers. These worked without salary, but had free use of a vicarage. One Bishop's Messenger was Helene Hannah, an AWTC graduate of 1962 who served for seven years. She recalls her first mission parish as having a vicarage without insulation, punky firewood that burned poorly, a little toilet pail with a pipe that had to be carried out every day, and a laundry tub for melted snow. She and her partner took services, ran the youth group,

---

54. Griffith interview, Bradley.

55. ACC, Provincial Synod of BC and Yukon Archives (Vancouver), Synod of the Diocese of Cariboo fonds, Clergy files, Deaconess Margaret Robinson, C24/7.

56. Barnett-Cowan has written an excellent summary of its work in Ferguson, *Anglican Church and the World* ("The Bishop's Messengers," 176–87).

administered funerals, and helped with the women's fundraising sales.[57] The name Bishop's Messengers, though strictly referring to Fowler's group in Brandon, was sometimes also used generically in other western dioceses for women in remote parish ministry. In rural Saskatchewan, for example, Ina Caton, a 1958 graduate, lived in one vicarage that was so dilapidated that the bishop would not countenance letting a male clergyman live in it, since that would have been unfair to his family.[58]

It is a recurrent theme that deaconesses and other women church workers were commonly deployed to placements that men refused to accept. It was "owing to the great lack of men for the ministry and the unlimited field for workers in the territories and western provinces," declared the first secretary of the Missionary Society of the Church of England in Canada in 1904 in a much-quoted passage, that the necessity had arisen "that trained, God fearing women should stand in the gap."[59] Mary Rendell, a 1954 graduate of AWTC, recalled that in the 1950s, similarly, "if you couldn't get anybody else to do a job, you went to the Dominion Board of the WA and persuaded them to send you a WA candidate and provide you with some enormous sum like $900 a year, from which to pay her," along with one or two extra concessions, such as firewood.[60]

Accordingly, a deaconess in charge of a parish in a more affluent diocese was very much rarer. But there were examples. When the rector of the parish at Midland, Ontario, died, Derwyn Owen, the archbishop of Toronto, abruptly placed the parish deaconess in charge; she was Frances Gray, a 1944 graduate of the Deac House. The decision was particularly unexpected since, as it happened, the organist of the church was a priest. Gray may have seemed the more suitable since she was the daughter of the bishop of Edmonton. She remained in charge for a year and a half. She exercised no sacramental ministry, of course; "in those days you didn't even administer the cup." And, she added, "Certainly no change in salary!"[61]

Deaconesses in social work were associated with a variety of organizations, which in Toronto included the Downtown Churchworkers' Association, St. Faith's Lodge (a home for delinquent girls), the Women's Welfare League, and the Mildmay Institute that was attached to the Deaconess House itself. Travelers Aid in Hamilton was also a placement for social service.

---

57. Griffith interview, Hannah.
58. Caton, *Reflections on a Life of Mission*.
59. Rutherdale, "I Wish the Men Were Half as Good," 32–58 at 33.
60. Griffith interview, Rendell.
61. Ibid., Frances Lightbourn.

Some deaconesses served in Indian residential schools. A Deac House graduate named Ruth Snuggs served at Fort George, Quebec. Among the other women staff there was a WA missionary named Bessie Quirt, whose journal for 1944 includes this dismaying report:

> I notice when I walk through the village with Miss Snuggs she does not speak to the Indians as she meets them on the trail. Her general attitude seems to be that they are just Indians, while Lily, Miss Scott and I are all anxious to get to know them.

Similarly, when a Cree baby died, and Quirt and others started off to visit the family to offer sympathy and prayer, "Ruth . . . just snorted—she was so surprised. It evidently is not done here—to visit the people in their houses and tents." Quirt also discovered that she was breaking with convention when she went to a Cree worship service.[62] Quirt's experience reminds us of the strictly Eurocentric education that Deaconess House dispensed, quite in common with the practice of the times and long after.

Ministries in overseas missions were varied.[63] In China, deaconesses might be attached to an orphanage, a hospital, or an organization for the rescue of abandoned infants. The mission field in Japan included a school for the blind, parish ministry, a mission among factory girls and women, and a training center for kindergarten teachers. In India deaconesses worked with several schools, and in the Punjab was perhaps the best known mission of the ACC, the Maple Leaf Hospital at Kangra. From 1956 to 1972 Joan Lew worked at the Maple Leaf Hospital on the top of a hill in Kangra, India, as a lab technician, but was uncomfortable with the Canadians' isolation from the people. "The only Indian people were our patients and our workers," she recalled in 1992. "We controlled the situation . . . [We were] king of the castle." Because, as an Asian by ancestry, she could pass as an east Indian, she sometimes went into the town below, which white Canadians seldom did. There she discovered that the locals regarded the mission staff as "the scum of the earth . . . . It's their land."[64]

The main Jewish mission was the Nathanael Institute, established in 1911. It was not, of course, much welcome in the Jewish community.

---

62. She left a significant journal which is now in the GSA; it was used by Rutherdale, *op. cit.* In addition, a very sizable collection of Quirt's correspondence has been accessioned by the Wycliffe College archives.

63. The character of these various ministries is described in much greater detail in a very helpful study by Haldenby, *Anglican Women's Training College*, which was commissioned but not published; a mimeographed copy is in the Graham Library of Trinity and Wycliffe College and in the AWTC fonds.

64. Griffith interview, Lew.

It primarily taught English to immigrants and did settlement house work. Other deaconess graduates served as prison or hospital chaplains, probation and parole officers, and ministers to immigrants.

During World War II, several missionaries, many of whom had returned from service in Japan, worked among Japanese-Canadian evacuees in internment camps, and with their resettlement after the war.[65] They included Margaret Foster, Frances Hawkins, Hattie Horobin, Aya Suzuki, Grace Tucker, and Mae Walker. Tucker, set apart as a deaconess in 1938, was awarded the Order of Canada in 1987, having been nominated by Japanese congregations.

A few deaconesses became so widely known for their faithful effective work and their strong personalities as to become ecclesiastical celebrities. Perhaps the best known Anglican deaconess was Hilda Hellaby (1898–1983) of British Columbia, who through her career garnered numerous awards and distinctions and was profiled in many articles in the church and popular press.[66] She was also admitted to the Order of Canada in 1971, and is featured in her own stained glass window in the cathedral of the diocese of Yukon, in Whitehorse. She began her ministry in 1920 working in Vancouver's Chinatown under the auspices of the Anglican Provincial Board of Missions to Orientals.[67] In a context of virulent anti-Asian agitation among the whites, Hellaby built trust by being a person of compassionate character and particularly by becoming fluent in Cantonese.[68] She worked mainly with immigrant women and children, teaching them English, helping them adjust to their new situation, and holding lectures. In July 1928 the archbishop of New Westminster admitted Hellaby to the order of deaconess. She took a furlough to study theology at the Anglican Theological College in Vancouver, and in 1930 became the first Anglican woman in Canada to receive an academic title in theology. During the Depression, she organized a soup kitchen; her helpers made a daily round of restaurants and grocery stores to scrounge scraps and bones from which to make a hearty soup, and she fed up to 1200 people twice a day. In 1936 she adopted a Chinese girl, Felicity, an unheard of event for a single woman. To the limited extent possible, she sought to interpret the situation of the Chinese immigrants to the white majority population and instill sympathy.

---

65. James, "'An Opportunity for Service.'"

66. ACC, DNW Archives, clergy files, Hilda Hellaby; Hellaby, *Hilda Hellaby*.

67. ACC, BC&Y Archives, Series 4, Oriental Missions, administrative committee of Board, regular and special meetings, 1925–1933, PSA 4/2.

68. Wang, "Organised Protestant Missions," 691–713.

In 1942 she moved to Vernon, BC, again working in the Chinese community. The explanation for her move probably lies in a private letter she wrote to her bishop several years later, where she appears to refer to the director of the Chinese mission that she had had to endure. "Subordinating oneself to a jealous and small minded man" had become unsupportable, she wrote. "If one remains in the background, one is 'refusing responsibility'; if one shows initiative, one is 'trying to take over.'"[69]

In 1951, realizing a childhood dream to serve in the north, she moved to Dawson City to run a hostel sponsored by the Anglican Church that was intended for Indigenous teenagers who had come from their own communities to take high school courses. She became acutely aware of the social issues of Indigenous people and their exploitation by racist settler whites, and she gained a reputation for boldly advocating for the just treatment of Indigenous peoples in ways that challenged ecclesiastical, governmental, and corporate assumptions and interests. She was then asked to take charge of the church at Mayo, Yukon, a base for silver-lead-zinc mining. She found that Indigenous workers were employed at hard labor for long hours underground, and she advocated for their fair treatment and proper nutrition. She also taught school in the Native village nearby. After nine years, an ordained rector arrived for Mayo and nearby Elsa, and Hellaby moved to a church at Carmacks, where she ministered to Indigenous peoples whose traditional ways had been disrupted by the construction of the north Klondike Highway.

She finally retired to a seniors' residence in Yellowknife. Her Indigenous friends came to visit, but she had to find an off-site place to meet them since "this of course is not feasible at the Home," as she explained with some irony. In her retirement she worked part-time as the bishop's secretary, edited the diocesan magazine, assisted in her parish, and wrote stories, memoirs, and poetry.

In Hellaby's support and advocacy for Indigenous people, Chinese immigrants, and other marginalized persons, she was often accused of being naïve. "Of course I've been taken for a ride," she admitted. But her principle, as she often said, was "When in doubt, take the losing side. The winners don't need you—they're doing O.K."

Although, unlike professed religious, deaconesses did not take vows of celibacy, they could not (until 1959) continue to serve if they were married. Some early Deac House principals seem to have regarded it as a loss if a promising student married. An alumnae newsletter of 1934 was probably

---

69. ACC, DNW Archives, Clergy files, Hilda Hellaby, Hilda Hellaby to Bishop, 27 Apr. 1955.

only half joking when it reported, "Two of our Graduates have succumbed to the lure of wedded life." As deaconesses paired off with Wycliffe or Trinity students, Principal Ruth Scott (1955–1966) was reported to have said, "This is not a marriage bureau!" She spoke of losing many of her students to the MRS degree (i.e., they had become "Mrs.").[70] But, indeed, many of the husbands for these women were clergy, and, in the manner of the day, the women did exercise a significant though unpaid ministry as clergy wives. They might serve as honorary chairs of church groups, address gatherings of men and women, teach, lead prayers, sponsor activities and events, and represent the congregation at community organizations. "Some of our Deaconesses who have married are a tremendous help to their husbands in their work," Principal Harriet Emery acknowledged in 1939.[71]

In fact, some students came to the Deac House for "the diamond ring program." This pattern began with Sarah Ann (Sadie) Alexander (1869–1955) in 1895. After a little theology at the Deaconess House, she married her childhood sweetheart, Isaac Stringer (1866–1934), a missionary to Herschel Island in the Beaufort Sea. There she ran a day school for Inuit children and a night school for whalers. Stringer went on to become bishop of Selkirk (Yukon). Some women felt that the program gave them an independent theological outlook and kept them from being simply submerged into their husband's identity. Beth Ann Exham, a 1960 graduate, married a man whom she had first met as a student at a dance at Trinity. "There was a time when I said that I was the unpaid curate, unpaid secretary and unpaid everything else, but I don't think that was entirely bad. For me that was an opportunity." If her husband was ill, she took the service.

Several clergy husbands besides Stringer went on to significant careers in the church, and as a result they and their wives were in a position to be great friends to the Deaconess House. The first student enrolled in the school in 1893, Annie Ray, is an example.[72] She was made deaconess by Bishop Sweatman at the end of 1895, served a while at Little Trinity Church, became engaged to a missionary to China named William Charles White, married him in Shanghai, and served with him until he was forced home in 1934. White was made bishop of Honan (now Henan) in 1909, and was one of the most widely respected clergy the ACC has had. Annie died soon after their return to Canada, and a year later White married another Deaconess House graduate whom he had known in China, Daisy Masters. In these

70. Griffith interview, Niblock.

71. ACC, GSA, AWTC fonds, correspondence folder 1930 3-I, Emery to Thomas, 9 Aug. 1939.

72. Griffith, *Weaving a Changing Tapestry*, 169; ACC, GSA, William White fonds; Walmsley, *Bishop in Honan*.

years, White was a professor of archaeology at the University of Toronto, the first curator of the Chinese collections at the Royal Ontario Museum, and the founder of the university library's east Asian studies collection, and he and his second wife were both active in the work of the Deaconess House. In fact, she occupied the extremely influential position as Candidates Secretary of the WA.

A few other deaconess candidates or graduates who married clergy are Margaret Allman '51 (Reg Stackhouse), Gertrude Baldry '19 (F. H. Gibbs of Cheshire), Edna Cecilia Bailey '36 (Rev. Mr. Sinclair), Mary Bayly '44 (Coster Scovil), Verna Bennett '30 (W. E. Taylor), Dorothy Bradley '63 (Michael Peers, later primate of the denomination), Frances Clute '00 (William Simpson), Betty Coolen '66 (Wilbur Way), Dora Ann Crabtree '66 (Harold Hinton), Helen Curwood '49 (Lloyd George McFarlane), Gwyneth Faulkner (L. Phillips, a military chaplain), Ruby-Maude Gandier '16 (H. Alderwood), Ruth Gardner '33 (Lionel Rowe), Frances Gray '44 (Gilbert Lightbourn), Mary Elizabeth Harrison '04 (Elias William Gardiner), Dorothy Hay '49 (Rev. Mr. Chabot), Mary Holtby '29 (F. J. Coleman), Elsie McGee '42 (Norman Gore), Pamela Robinson '58 (Rev. Mr. Niblock), Muriel Stanley '30 (T. W. Isherwood), and Florence (Flossie) Weymouth '38 (H. Surdivall).

Deaconesses typically wore uniforms in public. The uniforms seem to have varied somewhat from place to place and across the years, although a gold deaconess pin seems to have been standard. In 1961 Toronto deaconesses had conversations about moving from a "uniform" to a "deaconess dress," reflecting, perhaps, a desire for a more professional public profile. Some envisioned the new look as "a jacket dress with straight skirt of six panels, plain fitted with round neck, navy blue lightweight material, straight cut jacket." There was more disagreement about the collar.[73]

SATISFACTIONS AND FRUSTRATIONS IN DEACONESS LIFE

Many deaconesses felt fulfilled in a calling from God to help people in need. Many also sometimes experienced a demoralizing sense that their ministries were being obstructed by institutional constraints and personal conflict. To a great extent the deaconesses who felt most fulfilled were those who functioned as gendered missionary professionals, often in remote situations or on diocesan staffs; the ones who were more frustrated were those who functioned as gendered ministry helpers, often assisting a rector in

---

73. ACC, Diocese of Toronto [DT] Archives, Women Workers General Correspondence 1959–1966, report on deaconess conference, 26–27 April 1961, Aurora.

his management (or mismanagement) of parish projects and routines. But there were many exceptions. There were parish deaconesses who got along splendidly with their rectors, as we have seen with June Bradley in Kerrisdale. And some remote ministries could be lonely, and some staff positions had their own frustrations.

Ministry presented many attractions to a single young woman if she loved Jesus Christ, craved adventure, enjoyed good physical and mental health, had simple tastes, and accepted sacrifice. Betty Cox in 1941 was in Saskatoon handling Sunday School by Post, corresponding with hundreds of children, and sometimes visiting them: "We touched many, many lives," she said.[74] Beth Ann Exham recalled being at a girl's birthday party in Whitehorse in the 1960s and having a high time of it playing 45s (the vinyl records that were played back on turntables rotating at 45 rpm) and teaching the children to dance the twist. She was delighted when one of the girls exclaimed, "I never knew missionaries did this sort of thing!"[75] Griffith's interviews with deaconesses are peppered with such comments as "loved the work" and "wouldn't give up any of it."

Women church workers were surveyed about their ministries in 1960, and their replies are intriguing. The questionnaire, called "Your Vocation in the Church," was administered by a committee of the national church—the "Needs and Recruiting Sub-Committee" of the "Commission on the Training of Women."[76] It garnered 150 replies. It should be kept in mind that most of the respondents were not deaconesses, but the compilation of results does not allow us to separate out the deaconesses. The replies are nevertheless useful in giving us a snapshot of how women church workers claimed their ministry, responded to training, found encouragement, and dealt with adversity. They summarize the many satisfactions that women found in salaried ministries, and some of the frustrations they had to endure.

Most came from Anglican families (about 80%). Asked how they decided to enter this work, they answered diversely: the influence of specific individuals, experience in Christian groups, a sense of divine calling, a missionary appeal, "the happiness of a deaconess friend," a drowning accident, dissatisfaction in secular work, and "greed, hate, drunkenness and immorality around me." As to the influences they experienced in opposition to choosing church work, they variously answered scoffing friends, the discouragement of parents, a sense of inadequacy, finances, embarrassment

74. Griffith interview, Cox.
75. Ibid., Exham.
76. ACC, Commission on Church Vocations, "Analysis of Women's Questionnaire: 'Your Vocation in the Church,'" April 1961, in DT Archives, Women Workers General Correspondence 1959–1966.

with their family situation, and their race. Among discouragements they faced in training, they noted academic difficulties, lack of freedom, bad personal relationships, family illness, and their decision to marry. One said that the "extreme evangelism of some students made me feel I did not belong." But, another said, "Difficulties caused by some were compensated by others." Encouraging features of their training included their coursework, community life, support from friends and staff members, an assurance of their calling, the knowledge that they would be serving people's needs, and the desire to serve.

Among the greatest satisfactions they reported in the survey were a sense of the fulfilment of their vocation, meeting challenges, the sense that their work was worth dong, a sense of being used by God, helping others, "watching children grow up," fellowship with other church workers and leaders, making friends, and developing programs. Frustrations included the image and sometimes the reality of dowdy, dreary women church workers, constraints on their ministry imposed by superior authorities, apathy and indifference, the words "we do it this way," difficulties finding volunteers, uncommitted congregations, problems with church authorities (or ill-defined authority), personal difficulties, changes in clergy, changes of policy. One respondent, unhappily, named "husband and family" as her greatest discouragement.

To the extent that we can generalize from decades of women church workers, we sense that missionaries for the WA (who were mostly not deaconesses) felt the greatest support and had the best working conditions. It probably helped that their direct or indirect supervisors were generally women. The WA was relatively generous in its financial support. In the 1960s, working in Port aux Basques, Newfoundland, as a youth worker, Margaret Treadwell fell sick, and the WA cheerfully paid a $5000 medical bill for her.[77] Moreover, the WA paid travel expenses to and from the mission field, granted furloughs, and, unusually among employers of woman church workers, gave a retirement pension. Moreover, the WA was usually (though not always) willing to intervene with the male church establishment on behalf of women workers in exploitive or abusive situations. Such situations commonly arose in the Indian residential schools, where the administration reported to the male-managed denominational mission society while the "female native agents" were the responsibility of the WA. Thus at the Shingwauk Indian Residential School at Sault Ste. Marie, Ontario, a principal lashed out at WA missionaries who refused to make the children wear substandard clothing. The missionaries complained to the WA; the

77. Griffith interview, Treadwell.

WA complained to the head of the denominational mission society; and the latter required the principal to apologize. James Miller, in reflecting on this incident, suggests that the "gushing comments" which can be found in letters written by female workers in the schools when WA presidents came to visit make sense in the context that the WA executive was the women's "confidant and ally in contests with insensitive and unsympathetic males."[78]

The Bishop's Messengers and the deaconesses working in remote areas without close supervision seem to have been generally satisfied with their ministries, despite (or perhaps because of) low pay, harsh weather, and austere living conditions. It is true that in the 1960 survey several women mentioned the difficulties of isolation, and not a great many women remained in these situations for their careers, but after they left, they often recalled them fondly. Deaconesses who worked on diocesan staffs or on General Synod staff also generally reported considerable job satisfaction. Deaconess June Bradley was appointed in 1965 to a position in adult education at the Department of Religious Education at the national denominational headquarters in Toronto. It was the first job she had ever had where men and women were paid on the same scale. For thirteen years she had worked in parishes where, she recalled, "I had this mindset from somewhere that you never asked what you were going to be paid. You were just grateful for whatever pittance people doled out to you for working seven days a week." When she came to General Synod she was told that she would be paid $5500. "I thought that was riches," she recalls. Then there was a restructuring, and her salary immediately soared to $9000![79]

Deaconesses who worked in busy parishes or urban ministries under the supervision of men sometimes flourished, but perhaps more often reported frustrations. The status of a parish deaconess was always much lower than a clergyman's, as was her salary. Indeed, the very decision to hire a woman typically reflected the church's inability to afford or attract a man for the work. The parish deaconess was there typically to assist, not to initiate, lead, reform, or advise. She was to remain in the background and not attract attention, and she had best not expect much public appreciation. Ruth Pogson, an AWTC graduate who worked on the diocesan staff in Toronto, described the common situation of the urban and suburban parish deaconess at a consultation on women's work in the church in 1963.[80] The

---

78. Miller, *Shingwauk's Vision*, 246.
79. Griffith interview, Bradley.
80. ACC, DT Archives, Women Workers General Correspondence 1959–1966, Minutes of a consultation on women's work in the church, 21 May 1963.

deaconess, Pogson said, often experienced a painful lack of respect from staff and congregation:

> Many people have never been conditioned to take direction from "a young nip of a girl." Their life is often a misery because of lack of acceptance by the congregation. This is partly her position and partly her person. Both rejections are hurtful but the latter wounds more deeply.

Some clergy refused to employ deaconesses on the grounds that their recognition by the church might make them uppity. Principal Emery, in a letter to the bishop of Brandon, noted "a disinclination on the part of some of the clergy to recognize the Deaconess Order. This is due, I feel, to suspicion that women are desiring to usurp more than their proper province."

The salary of deaconesses was usually unconscionably low, reflecting not just budgetary constraints in the church but also the disparagement of women's ministry. Indeed, some male clergy could not fathom why a woman should be paid at all. An Anglican minister in the Parkdale area of Toronto named Bernard Bryan, in correspondence of about 1930, acknowledged that parish visiting, nursing, and assisting mothers' meetings were valuable activities, but he seemed bewildered to understand why women should be paid to do them. "It would be a good thing if we could encourage a large class of *volunteer* helpers from our city parishes to attend the course of training without charge in order to fit them better for *voluntary* work in our parishes."[81] Principal Emery wrote the bishop of Brandon in the 1930s that if a woman was thinking of being a deaconess,

> she must be content to know that when she is ready for service, she will receive the lowest possible remuneration: some of our Deaconesses at the present time are working in isolated places at from Ten to Fifteen Dollars a month, with maintenance. In our cities the salaries range from Six Hundred to One Thousand Dollars a year. There are two or three Deaconesses in Canada who receive Twelve Hundred Dollars, or a little more, a year.... There is no sense of security for the future, for in Canada there is no pension scheme such as prevails in England.[82]

When Betty Cox graduated in 1942, she was offered a position in New Brunswick, but "I was to pay the way down. . . . Had that been a man, a Wycliffe man, he would have had his fare paid, he would have had a proper

---

81. ACC, GSA, AWTC fonds, box M75-57, folder 3-I, replies of clergy, Bernard Bryan.

82. Ibid.

place, but to offer $32 a month and they didn't say how I was to get there—I wept."[83] Marion Niven, after earning an MA from Union Theological Seminary in 1959, was invited to join the staff of AWTC, and although thirty-three years later she had forgotten her precise starting salary, she recalled, "I remember my dad was absolutely horrified . . . He didn't have a clue about the feminine side of life."[84] Margaret Steel, a 1938 graduate, spent seven years as superintendent of an Anglican home for elderly ladies in Vancouver called St. Jude's, and never got a raise. Her successor started with double her salary. The treasurer explained, "You didn't ask for any more."[85] Mary Biddle worked as a teacher for five years before going to AWTC, and after graduating in 1962 she could afford to work at St. Stephen's, Calgary, and St. Christopher's, West Vancouver, only because she had saved money from her previous career:

> I did not get the pay that the men did. I don't remember the amount but it was close to half what I was making teaching . . . . It was an understanding that women would be looked after, but men had wives and family, so, "Hey, Mary, you can understand that the men would have to be paid more." . . . In a sense it made me feel that in a sense I should be volunteering my time anyway . . . . It was just ingrained in us, wasn't it? . . . I should have fought for others, and I didn't.[86]

Not only were deaconesses frugally paid while they were active, but they typically had no pension when they retired. Audrey Forster, a 1938 graduate who worked for about a quarter of a century at the Nathanael Institute, received an annuity from them when she retired which in 1992 was paying her $13.39 a month.[87] One idea for retired deaconesses who had no pension was simply to go back to work. In 1936 Bishop Derwyn Owen wrote Principal Emery on behalf of Ida Collins, an 1897 graduate: "She seems to be in a rather desperate position, in need of work or pension. Is there anything you can suggest that could be done in regard to her?" Emery replied to the bishop that she knew something of Collins' situation. Collins did have the old age pension, "which I know is very inadequate if one is depending on it solely . . . . It seems a pity that one who has done as much missionary service as Miss Collins, is depending on that fund for her later days."[88] In

83. Griffith interview, Cox.
84. Ibid., Niven.
85. Ibid., Steele.
86. Ibid., Biddle.
87. Ibid., Forster.
88. ACC, GSA, AWTC fonds, box 5, Derwyn Toronto, 13 Nov. 1936.

1967 the Anglican Church Women's association for the diocese of Yukon felt "concerned about Deaconess Hellaby's retirement, knowing that she is not on a Church pension or a WA pension." They wrote the diocese of New Westminster, where she had spent most of her career, imploring the bishop to do something to help her.[89]

Some woman church workers were never bothered by their low status. It was what they signed up for, and it was how the world worked. Others were not bothered at the time, because it did not occur to them that things might be different, but in later years, looking back, they wondered how they put up with it. Even the low salary did not trouble all deaconesses. Beth Ann Exham '60 said that money was not an issue for her "as long as I had enough to eat. Money for me was just something that got you through. It always had, in our family. We never had very much. We got through from one month to the next."[90]

As female subordinates in a male-dominated system, deaconesses sometimes found that they were scapegoated when problems arose, ignored when they suggested improvements, and overlooked when praise was passed out for the programs that were fruitful. June Bradley, who later had a marvelous time at St. Mary's, Kerrisdale, began as a deaconess at age 23 at St. Timothy's, North Toronto, where the rector's style was "to make all the decisions and lay out what was to be done, and we did it!" She earned $100 a month, depended for clothing on her sister's cast-offs, and had always to wear the deaconess uniform at church. She recalls being "desperately lonely"—a frequently recurring theme in many of Gwyn Griffith's interviews. From there Bradley went to St. Thomas', St. Catharines, where the rector, in her recollection, was a heavy drinker and in difficulty in the parish. When he was criticized by his parishioners, he "developed a habit of setting me up so that I was responsible." She was not allowed to see him unless she made an appointment in advance with the secretary.[91]

Norma Soules, not long after graduating from AWTC in 1956, was hired in Christian education at St. Jude's, Oakville, "the cocktail circuit type of thing and very high class," where she was painfully aware of her own low social status. Her office, as she recalled it, was a cupboard with no windows. After a few months she quit and bought a one-way ticket to Edmonton, her home town, and never again worked in a church.[92] Edith Shore, who

89. ACC, DNW Archives, Mrs. H. C. M. Grant, Diocesan President, Anglican Church Women, Diocese of Yukon, to Bishop Gower, diocese of New Westminster, 8 Dec. 1967.

90. Griffith interview, Exham.

91. Ibid., Bradley.

92. Ibid., Soules.

had given her life to Jesus at a Brian Green mission when she was 16 and enrolled at AWTC at age 19, found herself at age 22 as director of Christian education at St. George's, St. Catharines. The staff had morning prayer together every day; the three men took their place in the chancel, and Shore sat in the first row of the nave. They had their office in the main building; she had hers in the parish hall. They had secretarial assistance, she did not. "I came out just really, really hurt by that experience," she recalled in 1992, by which time she was no longer attending church. "I don't miss it a whole lot," she said.[93]

The deaconess' total powerlessness is tellingly revealed in an article by Norman Knowles that gives the case study of Mary Alice Tamkin, who graduated from the Deac House in 1918 at the age of 23, and was sent to a church in Halifax on probation.[94] She was housed in the rectory. The rector, a man old enough to be her father, "often called Mary down to his study," Knowles reports on the basis of numerous WA and Deaconess House records in the GSA, "where embraces soon became kisses on the cheek and then on the lips." Not knowing how to respond, Mary attempted to "laugh off the incidents," but her inner turmoil increased. In October the rector pulled Tamkin onto a couch, and "kissed me again and again . . . . He was feeling my breast and saying, 'Isn't it beautiful? Isn't it beautiful?'" She wrote her best friend, "That man has blighted my life." At length, the upshot was that the male leaders of the denominational missionary society investigated and determined that Tamkin had lacked sufficient moral vigilance. She was required to resign. The archbishop of Nova Scotia was advised of the rector's "indiscretion," and, to check any suspicion of scandal, honored him by appointing him examining chaplain. Ten years later Tamkin was the superintendent at a home for blind girls.

In the late 1950s some deaconesses in the more populated areas of the country, notably southern Ontario, began meeting together regularly as an antidote to the loneliness, sense of isolation, and marginalization that they so often felt. A Fellowship of Deaconesses was formed in 1959, "to deepen the spiritual life of Deaconesses," and for purposes of advocacy.[95] In the 1960s women church workers in the diocese of Toronto were meeting four times a year at a downtown church, and in addition organized an annual retreat and a full-day conference that might draw a crowd of sixty.

In 1964 a survey was conducted in the diocese of Toronto which gives us an unusual opportunity to see deaconesses through the eyes of their

---

93. Ibid., Shore.
94. Knowles, "The Rector and the Deaconess," 97–114.
95. ACC, GSA, AWTC fonds.

supervising male clergy. David Jones, the diocesan director of leadership training at the Anglican conference center, asked the clergy about their working relationships with their deaconesses, and the replies make for fascinating reading.[96] On one end of the spectrum, one or two male clergy reported that trained and skilled women church workers were the parish's greatest asset. On the other end, some clergy indicated that the problems that a woman worker created were too great to allow them ever to make further such appointments. Overall it is clear, unsurprisingly, that relations between male supervising clergy and a subordinate female worker-class often generated friction. This finding agrees with the 1960 national survey where a dozen women reported discouragement in working with their male bosses, and with a recommendation to General Synod in 1955 that deaconesses should have a recourse of appeal to a higher level in case of conflicts in the parish.

One priest answering the 1964 Toronto survey seemed genuinely to appreciate working with deaconesses: "As far as my own work is concerned," he said, "I find women easier to work with than many clergy." But many others offered generalized affirmations that ring as clichés, as with those men who spoke of "sharing responsibilities" with their deaconess and working as a team. "We work together very closely," one said vaguely. But when these descended to specifics, many identified niggling annoyances with the women that got on their nerves. One complained that some parish workers had "a tendency to waste time in superfluous telephone conversations." Another complained of "lack of proper communication." Another was unhappy that women workers sometimes picked up "worship or teaching fads which they may try to impose or suggest to clergy"; another similarly complained of women workers following "religious fads." Still another was exasperated with "the unnecessary details with which they [the clergy] are beset on the part of the workers." Along the same line was a comment that with a deaconess "continuous consultations are necessary throughout any new project." Another respondent thought that women workers could become so emotionally involved in a particular pastoral case that they lost perspective and good judgment. One suspected that women workers felt that "their full talents are not being used," but added, "This is usually unwarranted." Deaconesses were seen as lacking a sense of the whole: a priest complained of a deaconess with "a sense of the importance of one's own areas of responsibility to the exclusion of other parts of the Church's ministry." A priest was dismayed that he felt obliged to use "tact" in speaking with women;

96. ACC, DT Archives, Women Workers General Correspondence 1959–1966, Replies to a questionnaire sent out by parish workers, 31 Jan. 1964, collated by the Rev. David E. Jones, director, Anglican Conference Centre and Leadership Training.

"male–female communication . . . cannot be used as well as with another man." Even an apparent compliment to deaconesses veiled the respondent's disparagement: one clergyman preferred deaconesses to male assistant curates partly since "there is no likelihood of rivalry." But another respondent recognized that this structural subordination was a problem rather than an advantage: "the knowledge of always being second in command presents the parish worker with a problem on some occasions."

Deaconesses were given to understand that they were not full colleagues in ministry in the eyes of male clergy. At a women church workers' conference in 1968, Ruth Pogson recognized that "many women workers are afraid to disagree with their rectors, to be really honest with them, because they feel they are 'second-rate citizens' as it were." For their part, she said, clergy were threatened by challenges to "traditional ways," apparently referring in part to the status of women.[97] In the diocese of Toronto in 1966, when the archdeacons and the rural deans were planning a retreat, the executive archdeacon advised that "the general feeling was that full-time Women Workers should not be invited to the Quiet Day since the unity of the clergy might be somewhat impaired."[98] Remarkably absent in these discussions, both from the deaconesses and from the male clergy, is reference to patterns of common study or prayer.

THE TWILIGHT OF THE OFFICE OF DEACONESS

The office of deaconess, and indeed the role of women in church in general, generated a flood of conversations, meetings, reports, debates, and initiatives in the 1960s. From one point of view, the church was finally moving from a model of deaconess as ministry assistant to a model of deaconess as ministry professional, as it revalued women's work in the church in general. It was aiming to establish fair and consistent policies for deaconesses in their salaries and pensions, canonical authority, working conditions, and professional identity. From another point of view, however, the church was making the ultimately futile attempt to preserve a place for a gendered ministry at a time when Canadians were increasingly regarding gender distinctions as inherently gender discrimination. And the more a deaconess was made to look like a ministry professional, the more she looked like a

---

97. ACC, DT Archives, Report of the annual St. Luke's Day Conference for diocesan women workers, 18 Oct. 1968.

98. ACC, DT Archives, Women Workers General Correspondence 1959–1966, G. H. Johnson to Bishop Hunt, 24 Nov. 1966.

female deacon, making a gendered differentiation unnecessary. Finally in 1969 General Synod decided that the time for deaconesses had passed.

A major piece of reinvigorating the office of deaconess during the early 1960s was expanding its liturgical role. Bishop Robert L. Seaborn of Newfoundland, who chaired a bishops' committee on the status of deaconesses, assumed leadership in this area. (He was the nephew of Annie Edgar, the principal of AWTC from 1947 to 1955.) In 1960 the House of Bishops agreed in principle that deaconesses could be authorized by their bishop to preside at services of morning and evening prayer, litany, baptisms, and funerals, omitting those parts reserved to priests. Given the lumbering machinery of the church, a revised canon incorporating this change had to be approved by General Synod in 1962 and then confirmed in 1965.[99]

The decision that women might lead services led in turn to the kind of question that Anglicans love to be vexed by: what ecclesiastical garb should a deaconess wear in the chancel when leading or assisting at these services? The Toronto deaconesses had a lengthy discussion of the matter at a conference in 1961.[100] They wanted garb that expressed the dignity of the office, but that would not look too clerical, as a cassock or Geneva gown would. One idea was a double-breasted black gown of light weight, ankle length, loose sleeves, white ruching at the neckline, worn with either a surplice or a tippet with a deaconess pin. The bishops devoted further conversation to the matter. But it was never quite settled.

In 1959 the bishops decided that deaconesses could be set apart for "life-long service," which, decoded, meant that they could remain deaconesses if they married. This change, when added to the new provision that deaconesses could be authorized to lead services, required a revision of the order of service for setting apart a deaconess. The process for accomplishing this task was also fraught, requiring considerable discussion in General Synod and the House of Bishops, and referrals to a revising committee. The new service of ordering was finally agreed and printed in 1963, and offered for sale at the Anglican Book Centre.

The bishops and others had some other tidying in view. The bishops wanted consistent standards of training for the deaconesses, and in 1960 they agreed on phrasing: deaconess candidates required "adequate training at a recognized training school followed by at least one year of practical experience." This provision also was incorporated into the revised canon that was confirmed in 1965. Likewise, the bishops appear to have been

99. ACC, GSA, House of Bishops, Minutes, 25–27 Aug. 1960; *General Synod Journal* (1961) 107, 340.

100. ACC, DT Archives, Women Workers General Correspondence 1959–1966, Report of the Deaconess Conference, 26–27 Apr. 1961, Aurora Conference Centre.

concerned that some deaconesses were acting too much as free agents in accepting appointments without episcopal authority. They stressed that deaconesses required a license from the bishop wherever they served, as well as written permission from the bishop to accept a position in another diocese. Another piece of tidying, as we have noted, was to make an official compilation of the names of all the active deaconesses.

While all this energy was being devoted to developing and regulating the office of deaconess, the times were changing. By 1964, across Canada, there were only thirty-nine Anglican deaconesses in active service.[101] At AWTC, enrolment numbers were declining dramatically. Residence rooms were going empty, and the college's operating revenues were being strained. In fact AWTC could not survive. In 1969 it merged with Covenant House, which trained deaconesses for the United Church of Canada, creating the Centre for Christian Studies. This school still exists, having moved to Winnipeg in 1998.

The demand for deaconesses was declining partly because the work that many of them had traditionally done in health care and social services had been taken over by the government. By the same token, women who wanted to work in social services or health care would be better advised to seek employment with a government or agency, where they would be assured of better salaries and better working conditions than the church could offer, and probably more respect as well. A deaconess who replied to a question on the 1960 "Your Vocation in the Church" about her greatest discouragement said that her parents tried to persuade her to become a civil servant rather than a deaconess, "since a government job is considered important and significant, and a Church job outside the main stream of things." Principal Ruth Scott traveled to Vancouver in the 1960s hoping to raise funds and recruit students, but what she found made her think twice about traditional women's ministries.

> In Vancouver, I spoke to one congregation and, afterwards, in chatting with the president of the Young People's group of that Church, a young lawyer, I learned that all the young people, including many of the teenagers, drove their own cars, and had membership, through their families, in exclusive social clubs where every recreation facility was available to them. The kind of service usually rendered by the run-of-the-mill Church group or club was neither needed by them, nor do they appeal to them.[102]

101. ACC, GSA, Executive Council minutes, 31 Aug.—3 Nov. 1964, 125, Report of Bishop Seaborn.

102. ACC, GSA, AWTC fonds, M75-27 2CQ, Report of Executive Committee, July 196[?].

The comment reveals that the Anglican Church had become an institution serving the middle class; the lower classes, immigrants, and Indigenous peoples were no longer squarely within its field of vision.

It was not just social service and health care jobs that beckoned women away from church work. Women were aware that Canadian society at large was opening opportunities to them, and valuing their contributions, much more warmly than the Anglican Church was doing. By 1936 the United Church of Canada had a female minister; by 1942 the CBC had a female broadcasting personality; by 1951 Ottawa had a female mayor; by 1958 Canada had a female cabinet minister; in 1960 the Voice of Women was established. The Anglican Church, by contrast, kept women in their place. Rosemary Draper, a 1959 graduate, tried working at St. Paul's, Bloor Street, but she found her scope for initiative and action very severely limited, as Grace Haldenby relates:

> The prevailing attitude on Parish Council was autocratic. She was told, "We leave the decisions to the men . . . " After six years Rosemary decided to return to teaching, going to the Duke of York School in downtown Toronto, a pilot project involving social work as much as teaching. She feels her 25 years since in this kind of teaching have been of more significance in the lives of others . . .[103]

It is not that a great number of deaconesses considered themselves feminists; most did not. But fewer women, having other choices, were interested in serving in contexts where they knew they were unlikely to feel valued.

All discussions of deaconesses were abruptly and dramatically displaced when, to widespread surprise, the prospect of ordaining women as deacons and priests came sweeping onto the Canadian Anglican agenda. The Lambeth Conference in 1968, attended by 460 Anglican bishops from around the world, recommended that the diaconate be open to both men and women, and that "those made deaconesses by laying-on of hands with appropriate prayers be declared to be within the diaconate."[104] It even envisioned that women would soon begin to be ordained priests, asking only that the advisory Anglican Consultative Council, representing churches across the Anglican Communion, should be consulted first. In 1969, the General Synod embraced the recommendation that deaconesses were to be regarded as members of the diaconate, and that in future women could be ordained

---

103. Haldenby, *Anglican Women's Training College*, 93.

104. *Lambeth Conference* (1968). Resolution 32, available online at http://www.anglicancommunion.org/media/127743/1968.pdf.

as deacons on the same basis as men. It was also organizing itself towards the ordination of women as priests, which received final authorization from General Synod in 1975.

The recommendation of the Lambeth Conference, echoed by the decision of General Synod, that some deaconesses were deacons was more complicated than it looked at first. Not all deaconesses, but only those admitted with laying-on of hands and "appropriate" prayers, were within the diaconate. Whether a specific deaconess was now a deacon, might have to be decided on a case-by-case basis by the deaconess's bishop. Moreover, not all deaconesses wanted to be deacons. For one thing, ministering collegially with other women was more attractive to many than being submerged into an overwhelmingly male order in an overwhelmingly patriarchal institution, and having to prove to skeptical men that they were their equal.

Accordingly, the agreed process for deaconesses was this. Deaconesses would indicate to their bishop if they desired to be deacons. The diocese would seek to determine whether the deaconess met the criteria for being a deacon. If she did, she should be received. If she did not, she should be ordained. If it was unclear, she could be conditionally ordained. Once accepted as deacons, the women would be licensed, as deacons, be placed on the same salary scale as deacons, join the same pension fund as deacons, and take their place in diocesan synods as deacons.

In the diocese of Yukon, Bishop John Frame was satisfied that Hilda Hellaby's admission as deaconess was a valid ordination, and ratified it by a declaration in the context of a service in Christ Church Cathedral, Whitehorse.[105] In the diocese of Toronto, which likely had the greatest number of deaconesses, Bishop George Snell declared that "in order to avoid any misunderstanding, now or in the future, the regularity of their [the deaconesses'] status shall take place by conditional ordination."[106] Several women took the opportunity to retire, or resign. Some women did hope to be recognized as deacons, but their bishop demurred.

No new deaconesses would ever be set apart. As late as 1974 a woman church worker in the diocese of Toronto asked to be consecrated a deaconess, but was told that that opportunity was no longer available.[107] In fact, the diocese of Toronto and other dioceses no longer licensed continuing deaconesses to any church appointment. They simply ceased to be recognized as existing.

---

105. ACC, DNW Archives, clergy files, Hellaby.

106. ACC, DT Archives, Status of Women in the Church, George Snell, bishop of Toronto, statement for the diocesan synod, typewritten double-spaced, 1 Jun. 1971.

107. ACC, DT Archives, Status of Women in the Church, Letter to Bishop Allan Read, 26 Apr. 1974.

Some deaconesses preferred to remain deaconesses, such as Edith Shore of Toronto and June Bradley of Vancouver. Being incorporated into a privileged clergy establishment was not their style. Bishop Snell of Toronto, who supported the ordination of women and saw "definite benefits in being recognized as a deacon," added, in a statement to the House of Bishops, that incorporating deaconesses into the diaconate "may mean a step backward as far as the working out of their professional standing is concerned."[108] What looked like progress in one light could look retrograde in another.

In 1975, when the opportunity for women to be priests opened, the women deacons had a new decision to make. Without a great deal of bother, perhaps only several extra theological courses, or even less than that, they could be ordained priest, which would confer on them a fully recognized professional status, authorization to preside at Holy Communion, stronger institutional support, and an improved salary scale. Some deaconesses who had become deacons decided that their vocation really was diaconal and not priestly or presbyteral, and they did not proceed: these included Audrey Forster and Frances Gray Lightbourn. A number of deaconesses, however, did become priests. Bev Shanley, who had been a parish deaconess in Cobourg and in the two-point parish of Lowville and Nassagaweya, Ontario, was one of the first six women who were ordained priest in the ACC on 30 November 1976. Margery Pezzack, a parish deaconess at St. John's, York Mills, was the first woman to be ordained priest in the diocese of Toronto; she remained at York Mills, where she spent a total of fifty years. Others who accepted priest's orders, either very soon, if their diocese were progressive, or after many years, if it were not, included Sister Rosemary Ann (Benwell), Mary Biddle, Dorothy Daley, Ruth Matthews, Mary Rendell, and Thora Wade Row.

Wendy Fletcher-Marsh has called the ordination of women as Anglican priests in Canada "a revolution from above." It was not driven from below by radicals and feminists, but led by a predominantly male establishment. The women who were priested in the early years, Fletcher-Marsh points out, rejected the label of feminism with virtual unanimity.[109] By contrast, my impression is that the deaconesses who declined to become priests were much more likely to be feminists who did not want to feel like honorary men in a clerical elite. From this point of view, Fletcher-Marsh's "revolution from above" was not unambiguously a process for enabling the ministry of women. Because the ordination of women as priests was combined, as it did

---

108. ACC, DT Archives, Status of Women in the Church, Letter from Bishop George Snell to House of Bishops, Oct. 1970.

109. Fletcher-Marsh, "Revolution from Above." Her book-length study is *Beyond the Walled Garden*.

not logically need to be, with a suppression of the order of deaconesses, it can be seen partly as a way of preventing women from having a corporate gendered professional identity and authority that was untidily independent of male control.

CONCLUSION

Over the eighty years from 1889 to 1969 only a few hundred Anglican deaconesses were set apart. For their number, they made a significant impact on Anglican church life and on many parts of Canadian society, from sea to sea to sea.

We have noted a dichotomy in how deaconesses were understood. Sometimes they were seen as an order of carefully selected, theologically trained, professionally qualified leaders in ministry who could undertake work particularly suited to women. But sometimes they were seen as a pool of cheap labor on a low rung of the ecclesiastical ladder, willing to take on specific minor tasks as directed by their male managers.

Perhaps paradoxically, deaconesses could be seen in both ways at the same time. That is, even when they were in responsible positions with considerable autonomy to make professional judgments, they were still widely seen as inferior in status to clergy, doing things it was not worthwhile to pay men to do. This devaluing of deaconesses may have kept the order pure. In the period occupied by the deaconesses, which was the last century of Christendom, the office of priest was still one that could command social prestige, institutional authority, community respect, and opportunity for advancement. The office of deaconess commanded nothing of the sort. One senses, reading the documents, that very few women had self-serving motivations for entering this ministry. The chief attractions—self-sacrifice, faithful discipleship, and being helpful to others—were spiritual, and did not unduly impress the world.

One cannot measure these things, but I have the impression that deaconesses as a group were at least as effective in their sphere as the clergy were in theirs. One reason why the matter is hard to measure is that almost all the work deaconesses did with parish women and children, the inner-city poor, immigrants, ethnic communities, Indigenous peoples, delinquent adolescents, and the sick, is not documented. But the evidence is that the deaconesses worked hard, faithfully, and with caring hearts and good intentions. I suspect that if we knew a great deal more, we might be embarrassed at the Eurocentrism and the ideological rigidity of many of the deaconesses. But we would likely find the same about the clergy. At least, though, as we complete this study, we can reject easy stereotypes of the deaconess as a prim, uniformed, conservative, unimaginative church lady whom marriage eluded.

Sadly, even today it is the model of deaconess as the submissive assistant who looks after matters of inferior importance that endures, rather than the model of deaconess as the specially gifted, theologically qualified, professional leader. That is in large part a result of the breakthrough of the ordination of women in 1976, which our historical metanarrative values by trivializing or simply forgetting the ministry of the saintly faithful women who came before. But an alternative narrative is possible, one that was favored by some of the deaconesses who in the 1970s refused to become deacons and priests. When deaconesses could be used as low-paid ministry helpers who served under the supervision of men and did not threaten patriarchy, the church found them very useful. But when increasingly they were functioning as ministry professionals, but outside the orders of clergy, they became an organizational anomaly, if not a threat. The church did not want a group of collegially organized, mission-minded, professionally skilled women with a heart for the marginalized, and it especially did not want such a group when it was demanding better treatment and greater respect. It made managerial sense to co-opt them into a male-dominated clergy. Nevertheless, today, as the church looks for new models of ministry and service, the order of deaconesses, in all its powerlessness, humiliation, and responsiveness to need, may be a precedent of interest.

BIBLIOGRAPHY

Anglican National Commission. *The Report of the Field Commissioners.* Toronto: Church of England in Canada, 1931.

Barnett-Cowan, Alyson. "The Bishop's Messengers: Women in Ministry in Northwestern Manitoba, 1928–1979." In *The Anglican Church and the World of Western Canada, 1820–1970*, edited by Barry Ferguson, 176–87. Regina, SK: Canadian Plains Research Center, University of Regina, 1991.

Blackmore, Henrietta, ed. *The Beginnings of Women's Ministry: The Revival of the Deaconess in the Nineteenth-Century Church of England.* Church of England Record Society 14. Woodbridge, UK: Boydell, 2014.

Bonham, Valerie. "Ferard, Elizabeth Catherine (1825–1883)." In *DNB* (online edition). Oxford: Oxford University Press, 2004. http://www.oxforddnb.com.myaccess.library.utoronto.ca/view/article/39512.

Caton, Ina. *Reflections on a Life of Mission and Service in the Anglican Church of Canada.* Toronto: Little Trinity Church, 2000.

"Church Deaconesses." *Church Chronicle for the Diocese of Montreal* 2.12 (April 1862) 184–87.

Church of England in Canada. Hamilton: Spectator, 1883–1900.

Diocese of Huron, Church of England in Canada. *Journal of the Synod*. London: Diocese of Huron, 1883.

Donovan, Mary Sudman. *A Different Call: Women's Ministries in the Episcopal Church, 1850–1920*. Wilton, CT: Morehouse-Barlow, 1986.

Edmonson, Debbie. "Fifth Annual Commemoration Service for Deaconess Mary Nameria Jacob Celebrated at King's Landing." *The New Brunswick Anglican* (Sept 2013) 9.

Fast, Vera. *Missionary on Wheels: Eva Hasell and the Sunday School Caravans*. Toronto: Anglican Book Centre, 1979.

Ferguson, Barry, ed. *The Anglican Church and the World of Western Canada, 1820–1970*. Regina, SK: Canadian Plains Research Center, University of Regina, 1991.

Fletcher-Marsh, Wendy. *Beyond the Walled Garden*. Dundas, ON: Artemis, 1995.

———. "Revolution from Above: Women and the Priesthood in Canadian Anglicanism, 1968–1978." Canadian Society of Church History Series: Historical Papers 1995. http://historicalpapers.journals.yorku.ca/index.php/historicalpapers/article/viewFile/39439/35764.

General Synod Journal (1893–1952). [S.l.]: General Synod of the Church of England in Canada, 1893–1952.

General Synod Journal (1955–1980). Toronto: Anglican Church of Canada General Synod, 1955–1980.

Gleadle, Kathryn. "Charlotte Elizabeth Tonna and the Mobilization of Tory Women in Early Victorian England." *The Historical Journal* 50 (2007) 97–117.

Griffith, Gwyn. *Weaving a Changing Tapestry: The Story of the Centre for Christian Studies and its Predecessors, 1892–2005*. Toronto: Self-published, 2009.

Haldenby, Grace. *Anglican Women's Training College: A Background Document*. Toronto: AWTC History Committee, 1989.

Hammond, Geordan. *John Wesley in America: Restoring Primitive Christianity*. Oxford: Oxford University Press, 2014.

Hayes, Alan L. *Anglicans in Canada: Controversies and Identity in Historical Perspective*. Chicago: University of Illinois Press, 2004.

———. "Baldwin, Maurice Scollard." In *DCB* 13. Toronto: University of Toronto Press, 2003–. http://www.biographi.ca/en/bio/baldwin_maurice_scollard_13E.html.

Hellaby, Hilda. *Hilda Hellaby: A Life in Story, Poems and Prayer*. Whitehorse, YT: Willow Printers, 2000.

James, Cathy L. "'An Opportunity for Service': Women of the Anglican Mission to the Japanese in Canada, 1903–1957." MA thesis, University of British Columbia, 1990.

Jurisson, Cynthia A. "The Deaconess Movement." In *Encyclopedia of Women and Religion in North America*, edited by Rosemary Skinner Keller and Rosemary Radford Ruether, 821–33. Bloomington, IN: Indiana University Press, 2006.

Kemper, Alison. "Deaconess as Urban Missionary and Ideal Woman: Church of England Initiatives in Toronto, 1890–1895." In *Canadian Protestant and Catholic Missions, 1820s–1960s: Historical Essays in Honour of John Webster Grant*, edited by John S. Moir and C. T. McIntire, 171–90. Toronto Studies in Religion. New York: Peter Lang, 1988.

Knowles, Norman. "The Rector and the Deaconess: Women, the Church, and Sexual Harassment in Early Twentieth-Century English Canada, a Case Study." *Journal of Canadian Studies* 31.2 (1996) 97–114.

Lambeth Conference: Resolutions Archive from 1930. http://www.anglicancommunion.org/media/127734/1930.pdf.

Lambeth Conference: Resolutions Archive from 1968. http://www.anglicancommunion.org/media/127743/1968.pdf.

Liebenberg, Gillian. "Remembering an Extraordinary Woman in Our Early Church." *The New Brunswick Anglican* (Dec. 2004) 8.

Miller, James. *Shingwauk's Vision: A History of Native Residential Schools*. Toronto: University of Toronto Press, 1996.

Moore, Christopher. "Hoyles, Newman Wright." In *DCB* 15. Toronto: University of Toronto Press, 2003–. http://www.biographi.ca/en/bio/hoyles_newman_wright_1844_1927_15E.html.

Nightingale, Florence. *The Institution of Kaiserswerth on the Rhine, for the Practical Training of Deaconesses*. London: Colonial Ragged Training School, 1851.

Rutherdale, Myra. "'I Wish the Men Were Half as Good': Gender Constructions in the Canadian North-western Mission Field." In *Telling Tales: Women in Western Canada*, edited by Catherine Cavanaugh and Randi Warne, 32–58. Vancouver: University of British Columbia Press, 2000.

Sherlock, Peter. Review of Blackmore, *The Beginnings of Women's Ministry*. *Anglican and Episcopal History* 77 (2008) 94–95.

Walmsley, Lewis Calvin. *Bishop in Honan: Mission and Museum in the Life of William C. White*. Toronto: University of Toronto Press, 1974.

Wang, J. "Organised Protestant Missions to Chinese Immigrants in Canada, 1885–1923." *Journal of Ecclesiastical History* 54 (2003) 691–713.

12

From Trinity College, Dublin, to *Terra Australis*

Trinity-educated Clergymen in Colonial Australia

MICHAEL GLADWIN

THIS CHAPTER CONSIDERS THE colonial and imperial experience of clergy who trained at Trinity College, Dublin (hereinafter Trinity). More specifically, the focus is on the experience of Trinity men who served in the Australian colonies' formative decades between the first colony's founding in 1788 and the beginnings of semi-representative government in 1850. Irish clergymen made up nearly a quarter (23 percent) of the 235 Anglican clergymen who served in the Australian colonies before 1850.[1] A quarter of Tasmanian clergy and nearly a third of Western Australian clergy were Irish. While the majority of Australian Catholic priests studied at the Missionary College of All Hallows, Drumcondra (Dublin), or the more austere St. Patrick's College, Maynooth, the vast majority of Australian Anglican clergymen were products of Trinity College: out of all the Irish Anglican clergymen who served in Australia before 1850, 87.5 percent were educated at Trinity.[2]

---

1. *Viz.*, forty-eight clergymen out of a total of 235.

2. Forty-two out of forty-eight Irish clergymen were educated at Trinity College, Dublin; three were educated at Oxford and one at Cambridge.

It has been argued elsewhere that Irish Anglican clergymen played an important role in the creation of a nineteenth-century "Greater Ireland."[3] Here the term "Greater Ireland" denotes a diasporic movement in which the Irish transformed into a global people, actively participating in British imperial expansion and colonial nation-building in Australia, Canada, India, South Africa, South America, New Zealand, and the United States.[4] As recent work on the colonial missionary movement and Greater Ireland has pointed out, this was a period of growing missionary interest, coupled with a massive rise in Irish migration to British settler colonies in the same period (sometimes denoted as "Greater Britain," as distinct from dependent colonies such as India).[5] While the focus of my own research has been on clergy in the Australian colonies, others have analyzed the role of Irish clergy in the British settler colonies of Canada, New Zealand, and the Cape.[6] Although these accounts have paid useful attention to the clergy's recruitment, training, and education, there has been relatively little recognition of the specific and important role played by Trinity College.[7] Among historians of the Irish in Australia, Jarlath Ronayne has highlighted the influence of the Anglo-Irish and their extensive Trinity College connections. Nevertheless, his focus has been predominantly on Trinity men in the legal professions, the civil service, and politics.[8]

---

3. Gladwin, "'Mindful of Her St. Columbas,'" 297–318.

4. For an exhaustive study of the backgrounds, recruitment, and careers of Anglican clergy in Australia, see Gladwin, *Anglican Clergy in Australia*.

5. Strong, *Anglicanism and the British Empire*; Carey, *God's Empire*; Hardwick, *Anglican British World*; Barr and Carey, *Religion and Greater Ireland*; Gladwin, *Anglican Clergy in Australia*.

6. Hardwick, *Anglican British World*, ch. 1; Carey, *God's Empire*, ch. 8. For a helpful discussion of the religious dimensions of the concept of "Greater Britain," see Wolffe, *God and Greater Britain*; and Carey, *God's Empire*, 243, 378–79. For the broader phenomenon of "settlerism" in the "Anglosphere," see Belich, *Replenishing the Earth*, 1–14.

7. In Carey's ground-breaking *God's Empire*, for example, Trinity College is not listed in the index, while the main discussion of Trinity in Barr and Carey, *Religion and Greater Ireland*, is my own chapter on Australian Anglican clergymen. This is no doubt due to the broad scope of these works and the consequent need for selectivity, as well as the fact that Irish Catholics migrated in greater numbers and have received more historiographical attention. Hardwick, *Anglican British World*, ch. 1, however, pays more attention to Trinity connections, as does Grant, *Victoria's Debt to the Irish Church*.

8. Ronayne, *Irish in Australia*, focuses on links between Trinity College and colonial Australia. See also Ronayne, *First Fleet to Federation*; and Ronayne et al., *Irish Imprint in Australia*. Ronayne does, however, acknowledge the influence of key clergymen such as Hussey Burgh Macartney and Henry Fulton.

These historiographical oversights are significant because, as this chapter will demonstrate, Trinity-educated clergy exerted an influence on colonial Australian life disproportionate to their numbers. Trinity men were among Australia's leading churchmen, educators, scholars, journalists, humanitarian advocates, and builders of cultural institutions. In short, they played a key role in creating civil society in Australia. Trinity men's theological commitments and recruitment for colonial service also reveal significant theological diversity among Trinity College students at a time of heightened sectarian division, while their writings and preaching reveal a vision of a liberal and humane empire that was informed by their Irishness. These contributions, as well as the formative shaping influence of Trinity College, are the focus of this chapter.

BACKGROUND, RECRUITMENT, AND MOTIVATION

Growing overseas missionary interest occurred against a metropolitan Irish backdrop of Protestant mobilization—both elite and plebeian—against the threat posed by an increasingly politicized Catholicism during 1820–1850. An evangelical "revival" (or "crusade" as some historians have called it) in early nineteenth-century Ireland issued in the expansion of voluntary religious societies in an effort to convert both the "heathen" overseas (non-European and settlers) and Catholics closer to home. Nevertheless, the Protestant cause in both Ireland and the colonies was complicated by tensions between evangelicals and high churchmen, as well as differences between elite, middle-class, and plebeian expressions of Protestantism, with a generally brighter Orange tint on the lower rungs of the social ladder.[9] These political, theological, and ecclesiological tensions, as we shall see, were also evident among Trinity-educated men who served as Anglican clergy in the Australian colonies.

In terms of their social background, the majority (88 percent) of Irish Anglican clergyman in Australia can be located firmly in the substantial middle class, gentry, or upper ranks of the Anglo-Irish elite—which Roy Foster has labelled the "Ascendancy."[10] The relatively high percentage of

9. Wolffe, *Protestant Crusade in Great Britain*; Hardwick, *Anglican British World*, 152–61. See also Carey, *God's Empire*.

10. The following paragraphs on background and recruitment expand on the discussion in Gladwin, "Mindful of Her St. Columbas," but with a focus on Trinity men. Analysis of their fathers' occupations and university education suggests forty-two out of forty-nine clergymen as having middle- to upper-class social backgrounds. Fathers' occupations are not known for nine out of forty-nine clergymen, but their social location can be pieced together from university attendance, especially through entries in

Anglo-Irish among the Anglican clergy in colonial Australia is striking, especially given that the Anglo-Irish never constituted more than about 5 percent of Australia's nineteenth-century non-Indigenous population. In terms of the Irish born in mid-nineteenth-century Australia, only about 10 percent were Anglo-Irish and Protestant (the other 90 percent were Irish Catholics).[11] Those figures need to be qualified, however, by the fact that the bulk of unassisted Irish migrants were Protestants. Moreover, by 1911 Protestants made up a quarter of the Irish-born population in Australia. On the whole, a higher percentage of Irish migrants were Protestant in comparison with immigrants in Britain and the United States.[12]

This reality raises the questions of how and why these Trinity men made the sea journey of 10,000 miles to serve as Anglican clergy in the antipodes of the British Empire. It is well known that economic push factors drove Irish clergy migration to northwest England in significant numbers in the wake of the Church Temporalities Act (1833). Even more clergy migrated with the refusal of many Roman Catholics to pay legally imposed tithes and the devastating onset of the famine during the 1840s. It is only recently, however, that scholarly attention has turned to their migration to the settler colonies of the British Empire generally, and the Australian colonies specifically.[13]

There is little doubt that the push factors driving Irish clerical emigration to England were also driving clergy to the settler colonies, not least those in Australia. Among the Irish-born clergy who served in Australia, only seven migrated to Australia before the passing of the Church Temporalities Act in 1833; forty-one clergymen (85 percent of all Irish Australian clergymen) migrated during 1833–1850. The Irish famine appears to be a major factor: twenty-four clergymen (half of all Irish clergymen) arrived

---

Burtchaell and Sadleir, *Alumni Dublinenses*, and other assorted sources of evidence. Some were sizars, suggesting a humbler background than those of the substantial middle class. See Gladwin, "Australian Anglican Clergymen," ch. 1, section 6, for a detailed methodology and categories of social background. For the Anglo-Irish "Ascendancy" in Australia during our period, see Ronayne, *First Fleet to Federation*, 3–7; and Ridden, "National Identity, Religion, and Liberalism." For the Anglo-Irish in Ireland, see Foster, *Modern Ireland*, ch. 8. For the metropolitan Irish Church, see Acheson, *History of the Church of Ireland*; Hempton, *Religion and Political Culture*; and Yates, *Religious Condition of Ireland*. For Irish clergy generally, see Barnard and Neely, *Clergy of the Church of Ireland*.

11. Ronayne, *First Fleet to Federation*, 12–13.
12. Ronayne, "Who Was Who among Irish-Australians?," 33.
13. For the Australian colonies, see Gladwin, *Anglican Clergy in Australia*, chs 1, 3. For a useful précis of the settler colonies of British North America (Canada) and the Cape, see Hardwick, *Anglican British World*, ch. 1.

in Australia during the height of the famine between 1845 and 1850. In terms of economic drivers, it is also worth noting that of the 76 percent of Australian Trinity men whose family size is known, the average number of children per family was around seven. Nine Trinity men had families of eleven or more children, and several were subsisting on meagre curate's stipends (often £50 per annum or less) prior to their Australian careers. Among such men was William Stone, a native of Kilkenny who took his BA from Trinity in 1809 and was ordained in the same year. Stone served in three Irish curacies for over seventeen years before taking up his Australian post. He arrived in Sydney in 1841 with a wife, Susan, and six children in tow. Prior to his Australian service, William Singleton, who took his BA in 1826, was working in four private asylums in Finglas to support a wife and ten children on £60 per annum.[14] All of this suggests the attractiveness of economic opportunities abroad for these colonial Quiverfulls.

Family connections in the colonies were also a factor. Many clergymen already had relatives or friends in Australia prior to their departure, in several cases displaying the classic characteristics of chain migration. In Ireland the effects of the famine were pushing up into the middle classes during the 1840s, encouraging the migration of Trinity-educated lawyers and doctors to Melbourne and Port Phillip (later renamed Victoria). One result of this was that an elite circle of blood relations called the "Irish cousinage" dominated the bar, bench, and early public life in Port Phillip. This circle included Attorney General William Stawell, Charles Griffith, Redmond Barry, and the later Dean of Melbourne, the Rev. Hussey Burgh Macartney. Macartney was a Trinity graduate and son of an Irish MP with baronets in both family lines (named after his ancestor Walter Hussey Burgh, chief baron of the Irish Exchequer, whose portrait hangs in Trinity's Dining Hall). Macartney's cousin, Charles Griffith, doyen of the "Irish cousinage," urged Macartney to migrate to Melbourne in 1848 with several eminent Irish relatives. Macartney's nephew, John Cheyne, followed him to Australia in 1848 and then to holy orders after ten years' farming in New Zealand.[15] It is worth noting that all of these men either studied at Trinity or came from families who had long associations with the college.[16] The Rev. Henry Phibbs Fry

---

14. Disney to Ernest Hawkins, 15 and 17 Mar. 1849; Chaplain, Archbishop of Dublin to Ernest Hawkins, 17 Mar. 1849; Cooper to Ernest Hawkins, 22 Mar. 1849; William Singleton to Ernest Hawkins, 3 and 28 May, 5 Jun. 1849; National Library of Australia (hereinafter NLA), USPG, Home, Australian Papers, including Candidates' Papers, 1821–1898, AJCP Mfm M1222.

15. Ronayne, *Irish in Australia*, 107. Cheyne was ordained by Bishop Perry in December 1849: see Hassall, *In Old Australia*, 24.

16. Ronayne, *Irish in Australia*, 105.

of Sligo was another clergyman who had family already in the colonies, in this case a brother (Oliver) who was a Crown Land Commissioner in New South Wales.[17]

Friendship and collegial networks at Trinity were important. The Rev. Rowland Davies migrated to Tasmania on the strength of enthusiastic letters from his friend, the Rev. William Browne. Both men were Trinity graduates with connections to Mallow, Co. Cork. Browne's efforts to recruit his brother (also a clergyman) were, however, unsuccessful, despite three applications to the United Society for the Propagation of the Gospel (hereinafter USPG), the main agency for sending Anglican clergymen to the colonies of the British World.[18] The Rev. C. R. Elrington, Regius Professor of Divinity in Trinity College, Dublin, exploited high church networks through his friendship with Hackney Phalanx leader Joshua Watson. In 1840 Elrington asked Watson to press the London-based USPG Committee to supply clergy for Western Australia. Elrington had been alerted to the need by the sister of a former pupil.[19] Elrington knew personally of eight or nine expatriate Irishmen of high character, and at least one of considerable fortune, who would warmly support the church in WA.[20] One of the most influential Trinity men in the Australian colonies, Henry Phibbs Fry, was well acquainted with the Rev. Dr. J. H. Todd (a fellow and later Regius Professor of Hebrew at Trinity College) and several Irish MPs.[21]

The preaching and missions advocacy of the Anglo-Catholic Rev. Dr. Samuel Hinds, a former West Indian missionary himself, electrified several Trinity undergraduates. In his audience at Trinity was Francis Russell, an honours law student and committed evangelical with missionary aspirations. Russell's zeal was directed towards the Australian colonies, where he served with distinction as a pioneer bush clergyman and church planter for over thirty years. Russell also recruited several fellow undergraduates,

---

17. For Oliver Fry, see *Sydney Gazette* (28 Aug.) 1841.

18. For Davies, see Hart, "Davies, Robert Rowland," 291–92. See also Browne's brother's several letters to the USPG seeking a Tasmanian post for his brother (Bodl., Rhodes House Library, USPG, Miscellaneous, X Series).

19. C. R. Elrington to Joshua Watson, 26 Jun. 1840 (NLA, USPG Unbound Australian Papers, Dio. Sydney, Western Australia, Letters Various 1837–42, AJCP Mfm ML1222).

20. John Hutt to Mr. Phillips, 19 May 1842 (NLA, USPG, Unbound Australian Papers, Unbound Australian Papers, Spiritual needs of WA 1837–41, Box 16, AJCP Mfm ML1222). For the broad context of Western Australian Anglicanism in this period, see Strong, "Church and State in Western Australia," 517–40.

21. See Candidates' Testimonials 1837–44 (Bodl., Rhodes House Library, USPG, X-Series, Miscellaneous, X/114), fols. 36–37.

including his best friend Peter Beamish, for missionary service in the colonies.[22]

Evangelical networks were also important. The second senior chaplain in South Australia, James Farrell, was a product of evangelical networks known as the Dublin Rotunda School, an Irish equivalent of London's Exeter Hall that was so named for its meetings in a rotunda of the Dublin Lying-In Hospital.[23] In 1835 the military commander of Western Australia, Colonel Frederick Irwin (son of a Co. Donegal clergyman) was one of the driving forces behind the creation of the first evangelical society for colonial clergy, the Western Australian Missionary Society, later renamed the Colonial Church Society (CCS).[24] The society was formally founded in Dublin in 1836. The society's minute books reveal how Irwin utilized his Irish connections for clergy recruitment.[25]

Trinity men were also recruited from among settlers already in Australia. John Whitelaw Schoales was an Irish settler in Western Australia who returned to Dublin on a government mission to secure laborers and artisans. He wrote several circulars regarding Western Australia and became a key adviser to the USPG during the 1840s on matters West Australian. In this capacity Schoales nominated clerical friends as men who might be approached. In 1850 he answered his own prayers by offering himself as a candidate for South Australia. Another Trinity graduate, William Gore of Co. Wexford, was the younger brother of an Irish baronet. William arrived in the colony after his parents died, joining two brothers already in Australia. With brothers in the law, army, and navy, Gore's entry into the church was typical of the younger sons of well-connected gentry. Francis Hales was another Irish settler who entered the ministry. The son of a military officer, he had sailed with his parents to Sydney in 1826, Hobart in 1827, and Bombay in 1829, which provided him with plenty of colonial experience. His father died in 1832, leaving him a Hobart estate worth £144. Hales subsequently

---

22. F. T. C. Russell to USPG, 16 Dec. 1848; Charles Strong to USPG, 27 Aug. 1846; F. T. C. Russell Candidate Papers (NLA, USPG, Australian Papers, Candidates' Papers, 1821–1898, AJCP Mfm M1223).

23. South Australia's second colonial chaplain, James Farrell, was a product of this school.

24. See CCSS, *Annual Report of the Colonial Church* (1851).

25. For the activities of Irwin and his metropolitan associates, see the society's annual reports, the Committee Minute Book 1839–42, and the General Committee Minute Book 1850–55 (Guildhall Library London, Colonial Church Society, CCS/MS/15673 and 15674). The minute books cover the periods 1839–42 and 1850–55 onwards, with gaps apparently due to bomb damage during the Second World War. For the society's early history, see *The Record* (12 Oct. 1835) for an early advertisement outlining the society's intentions; Mullins, *Our Beginnings*, 3–20.

sailed to Britain for education at Trinity College, Dublin, and returned to Australia in holy orders with the new bishop of Melbourne, Charles Perry, in 1847.

Economic push factors and personal networks were clearly important, but there is evidence to suggest that for many the motivation for Australian service was also more than merely economic or personal. One of the key findings of scholars who have analyzed the social location and formation of overseas missionaries during this period is that the quest for economic security and social status "was not thought incompatible with religious belief and mission."[26] The same might be said of many Irish Australian clergymen. Several clergymen had expressed an early missionary vocation in a milieu where intense popular interest in the Protestant missionary movement had burgeoned since the 1790s. John Newton and other English evangelical patrons of first-generation Australian clergymen envisioned their protégés' mission as nothing less than "the opening for the propagation for the gospel in the Southern Hemisphere."[27] By the 1830s there was similar interest in Ireland, perhaps most strikingly evident in the creation of the CCS. In the 1840s there appears to have been something of a missionary awakening at Trinity, as evidenced by the influence of figures such as Hinds and Elrington. Francis Russell, for example, had excellent prospects in Ireland but had "fixed his heart on going to China." He contemplated applying to the Church Missionary Society (CMS), but eventually settled for New South Wales, as did his Trinity friend Peter Beamish, who had equally good prospects at home but trusted that an "earnest desire for the glory of our Blessed Lord and Saviour led me first to think of missionary labor." Both men had outstanding testimonials and were much vaunted as superior men.[28]

Also striking is the extent and depth to which Irish clergymen exhibited a genuine vocation for the ministry.[29] Analysis of the clergy's candidates'

---

26. Piggin, "Social Background, Motivation, and Training," 2, 16–18.

27. John Newton to William Wilberforce, 15 Nov. 1786, quoted in Macintosh, *Richard Johnson*, 26.

28. Samuel Hinds to G. H. Fagan, 4 Jan. 1847 (NLA, USPG, Home, Australian Papers, including Candidates' Papers, 1821–1898, AJCP Mfm M1223); Peter Beamish to USPG, 24 Dec. 1846 (NLA, USPG, Home, Australian Papers, including Candidates' Papers, 1821–1898, AJCP Mfm M1223); W. G. Broughton to Ernest Hawkins, 2 Oct. 1847 (NLA, USPG, SPG/C/MSS, Australian Papers, Bishop Broughton's Letters 1844–49, Box 13, M1465).

29. Care needs to be taken with assessing missionary motives, not least because of the ubiquity of pious formularies and sentiment during the period. Nevertheless, a wide range of extant evidence—including correspondence, obituaries, application forms, and multiple testimonials for many USPG clergymen—cautions against too cynical or suspicious a hermeneutic. See Gladwin, *Anglican Clergy in Australia*, ch. 3,

papers and self-understanding reveals that many Australian clergymen were imbued with a desire to fulfil their ordination promise, as the Prayer Book puts it, to be "apt and meet" for "learning and godly conversation," and "to exercise their Ministry duly, to the honour of God, and the edifying of his Church."[30] The Rev. Henry Phibbs Fry devoted a third of his well-received 1843 theological monograph, *Apostolic Ministry*, to a thoroughgoing exposition of the priesthood in a moderate Tractarian key, saturated in scriptural and patristic sources, and arguing earnestly for the veracity of apostolic succession. In Fry's view the separation "to the holy office by the hand of our Lord's Apostles bore a sacred obligation of the highest character" and gave clergymen "the sanction and authority of the Divine Being for the exclusive performance of the ministerial offices of worship."[31] The seriousness with which Trinity men took their vocation is also borne out in analysis of their colonial careers.

CONTRIBUTION TO THE AUSTRALIAN COLONIES

Trinity-educated clergy punched above their weight in terms of their influence on colonial Australia's fledgling religious, cultural, intellectual, and political life. The contribution of Irish clergy (including non-Trinity men) has been discussed elsewhere, but it is helpful to summarise some salient contributions of Trinity men here.[32] In the first place, their influence might be considered in terms of length of service alone. Trinity men averaged a remarkable twenty-five years of Australian service each. Five men served for more than fifty years each; three for more than forty years; seven for more than thirty years; and nine for more than twenty years. Several Trinity men held key posts as archdeacons and rural deans in Port Phillip (Victoria) and Van Diemen's Land (Tasmania). In South Australia, founded in 1836 as the first Australian free colony, the first two clergymen were Trinity-educated evangelicals, dominating the church as senior clergy until the arrival of a bishop in 1847. English-born Australian bishops occasionally expressed misgivings about Irish clergy. "Although they possess many valuable quali-

---

and Piggin, "Social Background, Motivation, and Training," 153, for a similarly critical but optimistic approach to the motives of Indian missionaries.

30. "Form and Manner of Ordering of Deacons," 732–33.

31. Fry, *Scriptural Evidence*, 30, 33. For the warm metropolitan reception of this work, see the review in *Church of England Quarterly Review*, vol. 16, 262–72.

32. See Gladwin, "Mindful of Her St. Columbas." See also Gladwin, *Anglican Clergy in Australia*, chs 1, 2, 5, 7; Gladwin, "Flogging Parsons?," 1–18; Gladwin, "Journalist in the Rectory," 56.1–56.28.

ties," wrote Charles Perry, bishop of Melbourne, to William Grant Broughton, bishop of Sydney, in 1850:

> There is in almost all of them more or less of wrongheadedness ... which is continually bringing them into difficulties, and putting them into a false position. I ... feel very thankful when I can secure the services of a sound, sensible, sober minded Englishman.[33]

Nevertheless, Perry's most valuable clergyman and choice for archdeacon was Hussey Burgh Macartney, while his clerical roster included long-serving Trinity men such as Francis Russell, Peter Beamish, John Cheyne, Francis Hales and William Singleton. Both Perry and other bishops, especially Francis Russell Nixon in Tasmania, continued to accept significant numbers of Irish clergymen, the latter bishop to a diocese in which a quarter of the clergymen were Irish born. Several other Irishmen held senior clerical posts as archdeacons and rural deans.

Trinity-educated clergymen were among the early Australian colonies' foremost scholars and educators. The first Irish Anglican clergymen (and second Trinity graduate) in Australia, the Rev. Henry Fulton, is a case in point.[34] Fulton's academic career began as a pensioner at Trinity in March 1788, the same year the Australian colonies were founded. After taking his BA in 1792, his first known clerical positions were as curate of Kilmore Union and Vicar of Monsea, both in County Tipperary, which he took up in 1796. In 1797 he is listed as one of several evangelical clergymen in nearby Silvermines. Fulton was connected, however, with the United Irishmen cause and was caught administering the "Defender's Oath" to local men, an outlawed practice that resulted in a conviction of sedition and a sentence of transportation to New South Wales for life. He was the only licensed Anglican clergyman before 1850 to come to Australia at His Majesty's pleasure. Fulton's impeccable behavior and a desperate shortage of clergy led to his appointment as a colonial chaplain shortly after his arrival in the colony. Finding himself in an outlying rural area with no educational facilities, in 1814 Fulton established the Castlereagh Classical Academy (one student described it as "Castlereagh Seminary").[35] The school was held in the local glebe house:

33. Charles Perry to W. G. Broughton, 7 Jun. 1850, quoted in Hardwick, "Anglican Church Expansion," 374.

34. For an overview of Fulton's background and career, see Cable, "Fulton, Henry," and Melbourne, "Unexpected Chaplain."

35. Melbourne, "Unexpected Chaplain." Tompson, "Retrospect," describes the academy as a seminary.

for the accommodation of a few young Gentlemen not exceeding twelve; wherein are taught the Latin and Greek classics, French and English grammatically, Writing, and such Parts of the Mathematics, both in Theory and Practice, as may suit the Taste of the Scholar, according as he may be intended for Commercial, Military or Naval Pursuits.[36]

The fees of £50 per annum (excluding books and bedding) suggest an education pitched at the elite level—prosperous young colonial men rather than those of humbler origins.[37] This was the first secondary school in the Australian colonies. An inventory of some of the volumes in Fulton's library reveals the range of learning that students probably had access to, as well as something of the breadth of Fulton's reading in the classics, languages, philosophy, history, and theology:

> Latin, Greek and Hebrew bibles, Cook's *Voyages*, Locke's *Essays on Human Understanding*, Virgil, evangelical magazines, the *History of Greenland*, Cicero's *Orations*, Calvin's *Life*, Goldsmith's *England*, the *Life of Charles XII*, Roman History (5 vols), Aristotle's *Ethics*, Tacitus (3 vols), St. Augustine's *Confessions*, Soame's *History of the Reformation*, Oteaheiti *Testaments*, *Letters of Clement XIV*, a *New Zealand Grammar*, *A Portuguese Grammar*, *A Spanish Grammar*, Jamison's *School Dictionary*, Foxe's *Martyrs*, *Psalms in Latin*, and Wesley's *Hymns*.[38]

Fulton's academy quickly gained an excellent reputation, providing local men with what was at that time the most rigorous and advanced education in the colony. It is worth noting in this regard that one of Fulton's protégés, Charles Tompson, was among Australia's most important early poets and proto-nationalists (as well as being a son of convicts). Moreover, Tompson's *Retrospect*, the first collection of poems to be published by an Australian-born poet, commenced with a panegyric to Fulton: "O FULTON! tutor of my early hour, / Nurse of its shoot—its bud—its op'ning flow'r."[39] Tompson's poem went on to describe the lived experience of Fulton's academy, evincing Fulton's passion for the education and Christian formation of his young charges:

> The welcome hour arrives,—then all repair
> To join their tutor in th' unstudy'd pray'r.

36. *Sydney Gazette* (18 Jun. 1814).

37. Melbourne, "Unexpected Chaplain," 16.

38. Ibid., 17. Melbourne adds that the inventory of Fulton's is no longer extant and has to be pieced together from earlier scholars' descriptions of it.

39. Tompson, "Retrospect," 1.

> (To him, kind pastor! was the blessing given,
> To ask the boon and to be heard in heaven,—
> ... The pastor's sacred tongue diffuses round
> The Gospel truths with holy precepts crown'd;
> For him bright hands prepare, in realms above,
> A wreath of glory and a crown of love!
> For, pious in himself, his lips impart
> Those conscious truths that live within his heart;
> Cheerful in life, and to his calling true,
> He knows the Word by books and practice too![40]

Fulton continued to serve with distinction in NSW until his death in 1840. In addition to his extensive educational, parish, and pastoral work, he acted as a magistrate, advocate for convicts and local workers, itinerating convict chaplain, and anti-Catholic controversialist.[41]

A subsequent educator of similar stature was the Rev. David Boyd, who arrived in Sydney in 1848, aged 34. Boyd influenced a generation of young colonial men as a teacher at the prestigious Sydney College and later in various boarding and grammar schools. One of Boyd's most famous students, Rolf Boldrewood, author of one of the first great Australian novels, *Robbery under Arms* (1888), recalled his Irish tutor fondly:

> He was an accomplished person ... [a] first-rate classical scholar, with a fair knowledge of French, German and Italian—possibly Hebrew for he knew pretty well everything, from astronomy to single-stick fencing to comparative philology. He rode, drove, shot, fished, painted, was musical, mathematical—a mesmerist, doubtless ... We boys looked upon him as a successor of the Admirable Crichton [the famous sixteenth-century Scottish polymath and athlete], and revered him accordingly.[42]

Other clergy such as Macartney were involved in founding grammar schools and university colleges such as Trinity College in the University of Melbourne.[43] The Rev. Francis Russell's name was perpetuated after his death in a Trinity College (Dublin) scholarship.[44] Obituaries of these

---

40. Ibid., 3, 11.

41. Gladwin, "Mindful of Her St. Columbas," 302; Cable, "Fulton, Henry."

42. Thomas Alexander Browne (also known as Rolf Boldrewood), quoted by his daughter in the *Argus* (18 Apr. 1925). For Boyd, see the *Newcastle Morning Herald* (9 Apr. 1892) obituary.

43. Ronayne, *Irish in Australia*, 163 and ch. 7 for Trinity men's contribution to education in colonial Australia.

44. "Rev. Dr. Francis Thomas Cusack Russell."

pioneer clergy often stressed the scholarly and educational attainments, not least Trinity connections. Consider this obituary for the Kilkenny-born Rev. William Stone:

> During a long and blameless life the Rev. Mr. Stone was remarkable for his fearless independence, high-minded principle, urbanity of manner, and cheerful and kindly disposition—qualities which caused him to be universally esteemed and respected. Unaffectedly and deeply pious, he was neither ascetic nor fanatical but always ready to make every reasonable, allowance for the views of those who conscientiously differed from him in religion. His memory, well stored with many a passage from his favourite Greek and Latin authors, remained bright and clear up to the time of his decease. His conversational powers were unusually great, full of a wise and gentle satire upon follies and faults, that pleased, whilst it improved, all who felt the lambent flame . . . the Christian warfare of the fine old Irish clergyman and talented Trinity scholar is over at last.[45]

Stone's obituary hints at the importance of a university education for clerical claims to gentility, that key criterion of social worth and standing for nineteenth-century Britons. As the novelist Anthony Trollope put it, "Trust was put more or less by all classes, that the parson of the parish was at least a gentleman."[46] In the colonial context, no less than in the metropole, gentility was a means of establishing social position, defining prestige, and legitimizing social leadership.[47] "What is of much importance here," observed one Australian bishop:

> [is] gentlemanly manners and feelings. Many of the settlers are men of family and education, and though their worldly circumstances are now in many cases low, many of them working like common men in the cultivation of their own little portions of land, yet they are gentlemen still, and require that their teachers also should be like them.[48]

45. Obituary, *Sydney Morning Herald* (25 Aug. 1870).
46. Trollope, "Parson of the Parish," 58–59.
47. Russell, *Wish of Distinction*, 1–2. See also Russell, *Savage or Civilised*, ch. 4.
48. USPG, *Annual Report* (1849), clxvii. See also Le Couteur, "Brisbane Anglicans," 120–22; and William Tyrrell to USPG, 22 Aug. 1848 (NLA, USPG, SPG/C/MSS, Unbound Australian Letters, Box 16, AJCP Mfm ML1222). Tyrrell wrote of northern New South Wales that "[t]he districts committed here to the care of a clergyman are immense, isolated, settled over by a fastidious, tho' impoverished class of proprietors, who are most keen-sighted to all defects of common scholarship and gentlemanly bearing." Cf. Trollope, "Parson of the Parish," 58–59 (quoted above, note 46).

Gentility in Australian cities and towns consisted of the principal officers of government and the clergy, and at a lower level the leading professional men and merchants. In the country, however, gentility could reach down into the ranks of a Clerk of Petty Sessions, the better educated medical man, or perhaps a "superior tradesman."[49] It was important for clergy because it ensured that they could move easily among and influence the middle and the higher echelons of society as well as the low.[50] Gentility provided local clergy with significant community standing and social/cultural capital, which, as we shall see, several Trinity men used to good effect.

CULTURAL AND INTELLECTUAL LIFE

Apart from their work as educators, one of the most striking features of Trinity graduates' experience is their contribution to the Australian colonies' fledgling cultural and intellectual life. Several were journalists, scholars, controversialists, or builders of cultural institutions.[51] In Adelaide, for example, the Rev. Charles Howard was a founding member of the Adelaide Botanical and Horticultural Gardens, the South Australia Club, the Board of Aboriginal Protection, the South Australia Savings Bank, and the Adelaide Hospital Board. The family of the Rev. Hussey Macartney, as we have already seen, was connected to the elite "Irish cousinage" of Victoria and, along with other Trinity-educated clergymen, remained at the center of Melbourne's religious, cultural, and public life until the late nineteenth century, a social milieu evocatively reconstructed by historian Penny Russell.[52]

In terms of journalism and political activism, the Reverends Henry Browne, Henry Phibbs Fry, and Thomas Rogers, for example, were at the forefront of journalism and political activism to abolish the convict system in Tasmania.[53] The clergy's influence was felt both in the town and provincial presses, which in some cases propelled them to the forefront of public debate on pressing social and political issues such as relations with Aborigines, exploration, and convict transportation. There is insufficient space here to discuss at length the literary, intellectual, and public contributions of all

49. Atkinson, *Camden*, 98–99; Gladwin, *Anglican Clergy in Australia*, 59–63.

50. Le Couteur, "Brisbane Anglicans," 118. See also Strong, "Reverend John Wollaston," 266–71.

51. See especially Gladwin, "Journalist in the Rectory," and Gladwin, *Anglican Clergy in Australia*, 129–52.

52. For the Rev. Francis Russell and the Melbourne Club, see Holden, *Saints, Sinners and Goalposts*, 32–33; Russell, *Wish of Distinction*.

53. See Gladwin, *Anglican Clergy in Australia*, 125–28; Gladwin, "Flogging Parsons?"

Trinity men in the Australian colonies, so a case study of one clergyman may suffice to provide a picture of their range and influence. The Rev. Henry Phibbs Fry, a law student at Trinity before being ordained as a deacon (expressly for the colonies) in 1838, arrived in Hobart, Tasmania, in 1839. Fry's ship was wrecked off the Cape en route, which *inter alia* delayed patristic scholarship in Australia: Fry lost his library of 600–800 volumes, which included the writings of all the Church Fathers of the first six centuries.[54] A theologian with patristic interests, an inveterate pamphleteer, a newspaper editor, and a penal reformer, he campaigned on a wide range of social and political fronts. And like his theology, which swung from Tractarian to full-blooded evangelicalism during his colonial career, his views on Australian convict transportation swung from initial support of modified transportation to abolition by 1850. He was also prominent in public discussion of education, temperance, and immigration schemes.[55]

During 1845–1846 Fry edited the *Hobart Town Herald*. Pitched at the middle and working classes, its aim was to compel the "spirit of the age" to admit the Church's sacred voice "as authoritatively influencing the feelings and institutions of society." While Fry's *Herald* articles extolled the paternalist social Toryism of Disraeli's Young England, they also welcomed Peel's recent repeal of the Corn Laws because it was "for the good of the labouring classes, regardless of party interests."[56] And although Fry proclaimed the divine origin of the state and man's duty under to God to obey its ministers, he was not afraid to take the government to task, whether the imperial government for its "impartially remorseless" land policy during the current economic depression, or the colonial government for its misguided education policy and its irresponsible attempts to spend itself out of the depression.[57] It was his views on transportation, however, which would have most impact.

Fry's journalism wielded direct influence on imperial policy when in 1846 he forwarded a *Hobart Town Herald* editorial of August 1845 to Lt. Governor Wilmot, who in turn forwarded it to Earl Grey. In Earl Grey's opinion Fry's arguments demonstrated with "great force and clearness" the evils of the transportation system and that the best hope of convict reformation was to remove convicts as exiles and free men after having undergone

---

54. See Candidates' Testimonials 1837-44 (Oxford, RHL, USPG, X-Series, Miscellaneous, X/114), ff 36–37.

55. *Hobart Town Herald* (1845) (became *Tasmanian Southern Reporter* in 1846); Roe, "Fry, Henry Phibbs"; Batt and Roe, "Conflict Within the Church of England," 39–62.

56. *Hobart Town Herald* (23 Jul. 1845).

57. "Prospectus," *Hobart Town Herald* 18 (23 Jul. 1845). An MS copy is held in the State Library of Tasmania, Hobart.

penal imprisonment in the UK. The substance of Fry's views, remarked Earl Grey in his reply to Wilmot, were precisely those of Her Majesty Government, and it was therefore decided that transportation would not be resumed after two years' suspension, as originally planned, but would now be discontinued.[58] In 1850 Fry used a monograph study of the British prison system (*A System of Penal Discipline*, for which he studied fifty British prisons while on leave there during 1849–1850) to launch a powerful assault on the Tasmanian transportation system, condemning it for its practical failure and the government for its vacillation, venality, and "flight from reality."[59] In the event, transportation was abandoned altogether in 1853 as a result of heightened agitation and new Australian economic imperatives after 1850 in the form of the gold rushes. Fry's book was also notable for its anticipation of several post-1850 developments in penology.[60]

These attempts to refine the colonial life of the mind reveal Trinity-educated clergymen as key figures at the heart of a nascent national literary culture, rather than merely agents of a nostalgic literature of exile or what one historian has dubbed the "England-I-love-thee-still" tradition. It is perhaps not surprising that few Irish clergymen fell into the latter camp. When nostalgic at all, Irish Anglican clergy tended to be nostalgic for Ireland. When articulating national identity, they tended to identify as Irish rather than British.[61] As Ronayne has pointed out, these talented, self-confident, and articulate professional men were "generally not the type to disguise their Irishnesss by affecting the manners and mores of the English dominant class."[62] Francis Russell, for example, conceived of mission to the colonies in terms of "the Ancient Church of Ireland, mindful of her St. Columbas and Gaels" and sending "as of old . . . many zealous laborers to the abundant harvest."[63] Marcartney observed after seventy years of ministry that "there is something in Irish Christian love and family affection which you do not meet anywhere else. The Irish not only feel, but show feelings."[64]

58. Earl Grey to Lt. Gov. Sir W. Denison, 5 Feb. 1847, *Convict Discipline and Transportation*, 193.

59. Fry, *System of Penal Discipline*, 160–97.

60. Fry's proposals anticipated several modern developments in penology, including the creation of a professional corps of prison chaplains (resembling military chaplaincy), and separation of the civil and religious departments of prison discipline. See Mannheim, *Pioneers in Criminology*, 53–54.

61. On diasporic Irish identities, see Delaney and MacRaild, "Irish Migration," 130.

62. Ronayne, *Irish in Australia*, 13. So Ridden, "National Identity, Religion, and Liberalism," 7–21.

63. F. T. C. Russell to USPG, 16 Dec. 1846, Canberra, NLA, USPG, Australian Papers, Candidates' Papers, 1821–1898, AJCP Mfm M1223.

64. Curry, "Macartney," 9.

When Fry argued that Australian convicts owed their degradation not just to sin but to "the social sins and evil of Great Britain," he was reflecting a humanitarian posture that was independently critical of the British colonial and imperial project.[65]

PASTORAL AND SOCIAL CONCERN

Many Trinity men were singled out for their genuine pastoral and social concern. The Rev. William Stack, a Co. Cavan native known for his love of kangaroo steaks and itinerating pastoral work in rural NSW, was described in his funeral notice as a clergyman whose "manliness of ... character, combined with his earnestness in the cause of religion, and his frank and genial manners, made him universally respected and beloved."[66] Francis Russell, the Trinity man who traded mission in China for mission in rural Victoria, was described by nineteenth-century Australian historian James Bonwick as "a learned, witty man, vastly popular with all men in his district."[67]

Clergy in each colony were involved in the founding and development of Sunday Schools, asylums, orphanages, hospitals, lying-in institutions, and Magdalen Societies for "fallen" women. In 1844, for example, Stack applied to the government for funding to erect an asylum in Maitland, in rural New South Wales.[68] Rowland Davies, a former student of leading Scottish social thinker and activist Thomas Chalmers, set up savings banks and industrial schools in Tasmania, while his friend and colleague William Browne was a founder and manager of the Launceston Bank of Savings, and a campaigner for savings banks in country post offices.[69] In Hobart the Rev. Frederick Cox introduced evening services in Hobart "chiefly for the sake of the poor," who were ashamed of showing their shabby best clothes in the daylight.[70] Such work ensured the influence of clergy in local communities.

---

65. Henry Fry to John Eardley-Wilmot, 17 Aug. 1846, *Convict Discipline and Transportation*, 186–89. For a broader assessment of the clergy's attitude towards the British Empire, see Gladwin, *Anglican Clergy in Australia*, 217–20. Ronayne, *Irish in Australia*, 6–15, highlights a liberal vision of empire among Anglo-Irish emigrants.

66. William Grant Broughton to William B. Clarke, 24 Jul. 1846 (Mitchell Library, Sydney, William Branwhite Clarke Papers, MSS 139/18/1–45/3).

67. James Bonwick, quoted in "Rev. Dr. Francis Thomas Cusack Russell," n.p.

68. Colonial Secretary to William Stack, 26 Nov. 1844 (State Records of NSW, Sydney, Colonial Secretary Outward Letters, 4/3621).

69. *Hobart Town Courier* (29 Jul. 1847); *Colonial Church Chronicle* (Mar. 1848); *Courier* (Hobart), 27 Jan. 1853; Barrett, "Browne, William Henry."

70. Barrett, "Church, State, and People," 351.

It should be noted, however, that a minority of Trinity men did not live up to the Church's ideals: Matthew Meares, a Co. Westmeath man who graduated in 1822, did penance for adultery; Robert Drought, an elderly Co. Offaly graduate of 1785, had a "servant" who turned out to be his illegitimate daughter; and John Andrewartha, who matriculated in 1823, scandalized his profession when he went into debt as co-owner of a sawmill and tramway in Huon, Tasmania (newspaper reports accused him of being a better engineer than theologian).[71] The independence and self-confidence of several Trinity men led to a number of Trollopean power struggles with bishops, while the "mercurial" John Keane, a Trinity graduate of 1824, faced the courts for slashing the arm of a trespassing convict with a sabre. On another occasion, after he had to be moved to a different parish, his parishioners complained to his bishop of his frequent use of the pulpit "as a vehicle of invective" (Keane had lashed them from the pulpit for attending the local races amid scenes of "riot, drunkenness, gambling, and debauchery").[72] It should be noted, however, that such incidents were rarely the whole story in a clergyman's career. Keane's Australian experience, for example, preceded creative efforts in social reform. After graduating from Trinity in 1824, he spent sixteen years in NSW and three in Glasgow, before being licensed to London's worst slums in Bethnal Green, where he worked for another twenty-five years. He was among the founders and early supporters of the Church of England Self-Supporting Village Society, an effort to ameliorate the effects of "precarious and ill-requited employment" on working people in agricultural and manufacturing districts. Drawing inspiration from Owenite and Moravian settlements (although obviously eschewing Owen's anticlericalism), and supported by the Bishop of Norwich and various members of the aristocracy, the society was founded in 1846, with Keane passing the inaugural meeting's second resolution.[73]

---

71. *Colonial Times* (Tasmania), 26 Mar. 1853; *Tasmanian Church News*, Sep. 1886. Andrewartha and another clergyman, Edward Freeman, defaulted on payments of £500 for a saw mill and steam engine. They were taken to court, where £190 in damages were found against them.

72. Colonial Secretary to John Keane, 21 Mar., 11 Apr. 1831, Sydney (State Records of NSW, Sydney, Colonial Secretary Outward Letters, 4/3616); entry for 17 Aug. 1837 (Sydney Diocesan Archives, Acts and Proceedings of the Bishop of Sydney, vol. 1, fols. 48, 50).

73. An account of the first meeting at Exeter Hall was reprinted from the London papers in the *Sydney Morning Herald* (17 Oct. 1846). See also Harrison, *Robert Owen and the Owenites*, 25–28.

THE THEOLOGICAL SPECTRUM

Pace Anthony Trollope's contention that the typical Church of Ireland clergyman had sucked in "high Protestant principles" with his mother's milk, Trinity men in colonial Australia were not universally ultra-Protestant in their theological commitments. This is in part because, as we have already seen, key colonial recruiters in colony and metropole included high churchmen, Anglo-Catholics, and evangelicals. Moreover, our period also predated the hardening of sectarian division in the wake of the Ulster Revival of 1859 and Gladstone's later proposals for Home Rule.

There is certainly evidence among several Trinity-educated clergy in Australia of both enhanced Protestant commitments and evangelical theological leanings.[74] Fulton, whose evangelical (and indeed Methodist) predilections are evident in the above-mentioned inventory of his library, was also a strident opponent of colonial Catholicism—to the extent that he published three small books on the issue.[75] Several other Irish evangelicals were involved in controversies with Tractarians and Roman Catholics: Peter Beamish, Francis Russell, and John Keane in NSW; Hussey Burgh Macartney in Port Phillip; William Browne and Henry Fry in Tasmania; and George King in Western Australia. It is instructive to compare another historian's finding for Presbyterian clergymen that the greater "evangelical warmth" of Queensland Presbyterianism was "a clear inheritance from the Irish."[76]

Evangelicals' priority for public worship was the provision of access to the pulpit, which they saw as the primary vehicle of Gospel proclamation and subsequent conversion. "The public announcement of God's holy will from our pulpits," declared Stack, "is the highest and most important duty of our ministry." Stack neatly summarized evangelical verities in his declaration that no preaching was worthy of any Christian pulpit that did not first presuppose both minster and congregation as fallen, guilty beings wanting pardon, renewal, and enlightenment. Second, it should vindicate Trinitarian doctrine and the application of that doctrine to the sinner's soul; and third, it should provide:

> full exhibition of the Father's love in sending His Son into the world, of his justice satisfied by his Son's atoning sacrifice ... and of the Spirit in his sanctifying influences upon the disordered

---

74. Gladwin, "Mindful of Her St. Columbas," 307–8.

75. Fulton, *Reasons Why Protestants Think the Worship of the Church*; Fulton, *Strictures Upon a Letter*; Fulton, *Letter to the Rev. W. B. Ullathorne*.

76. Prentis, "Presbyterian Ministry in Australia," 63.

and criminal heart of man. No other foundation than this must any man lay...[77]

At the other end of the spectrum, however, Rowland Davies and William Walsh were key Tractarian exponents in their colonies (as was Henry Fry, who was described by a contemporary as a "red-hot Puseyite" before his evangelical "conversion" in 1851), while at the extreme end Thomas Rogers appears to have converted to Roman Catholicism in later life. Differing opinions on theological and ecclesiological touchstones such as the sacrament of baptism could sometimes lead to internecine conflict. In one of his several books, Fry asserted a Tractarian position in seeing baptism as a channel "of spiritual communion with Christ" and the means by which believers participated in the atonement and righteousness of the body of Christ. Yet Fry also rejected any Rome-ward trend, roundly criticizing John Henry Newman's contemporary defection to Rome as capitulation to heresy.[78] Fellow Hobart Tractarian Frederick Cox rebutted charges that Tractarian clergymen were putting the Church and her ordinances in place of Christ, and the human priesthood in the place of His atonement and intercession. Rather, argued Cox, "the very meaning of all outward ordinances is to help us to approach Him—that for this and for nothing else they are to be used and valued—that communion with Christ is their end and object, and His spiritual presence that which gives them life."[79] In contrast, Launceston evangelical William Browne led six clergymen in petitioning against a statement on "baptismal regeneration" issued by a conference of Australian and New Zealand bishops in 1850.[80]

For Irish colonial clergy the issues at stake appear primarily theological and ecclesiological, in a context of heightened sectarianism and Catholic resurgence, namely the safeguarding of doctrines of salvation and fears among low churchmen that affirmation of doctrines such as baptismal regeneration would hasten the Rome-ward trend of "Puseyites."

CONCLUSIONS

It is clear that Trinity-educated clergymen contributed profoundly to the religious, cultural, intellectual, and public life of the Australian colonies'

77. Stack, *Sermon, Preached in the Church*, 7–8.

78. Fry, *Sermons on the Nature and Design*, 93, 95–96. It should be noted, however, that a sermon on the atonement preceded this sermon in Fry's published collection.

79. See Cox, *Perseverance and Endurance*, 21–22.

80. For a longer discussion of the issues canvassed in this paragraph, see Gladwin, *Anglican Clergy in Australia*, 103. See also Stephens, "Diocese of Tasmania," 53–60.

formative decades between 1788 and 1850. While economic and political push factors contributed to their decisions to emigrate, many nevertheless exhibited a genuine clerical vocation that issued in long colonial service and a reputation for pastoral and social concern.

It is also clear that a Trinity education proved invaluable in many different ways. In the first place, the clergy's liberal classical education qualified them to take their place among the Australian colonies' leading educators, scholars, and professional men. Their training in ancient languages, the classics, and the arts of rhetoric enabled several to be colonial proponents of what Roy Foster has described as the "ascendancy mind": a blend of "wit, satire, rhetoric, and verbal dexterity" that comprised "an Irish style" and had its antecedents in earlier Trinity alumni such as Swift, Burke, and Congreve.[81] The "ascendancy mind" was evident in the colonial clergy's building of cultural institutions and their contributions as scholars, journalists, and controversialists. Here the clergy's writings reveal them as independently critical agents of colony and empire, and men who were proud of their Irish origins. There is also appreciation of this "ascendancy mind" in colonists' encomia, which characterized the ideal Irish clergyman as genial, witty, and urbane. The social and cultural capital that accrued from a Trinity education was also important in establishing the gentility and accompanying social status of these clergymen. In turn, this social cachet helped the clergy to be "all things to all [colonial] men"—whether elite, middle class, or plebeian.

While it should be noted that not all Trinity men would have studied theology or divinity during their university days (the focus on clerical education before 1850 tended to be more on university attendance per se than on a requirement to study divinity while there), there is evidence that Trinity was an important nursery for the theological and ecclesiological formation of several Australian clergymen. Some men, such as Henry Phibbs Fry, wrote theological treatises that were the equal of any written in the metropole, while others were the protégés of Trinity fellows such as Elrington and Todd. It is also clear that while some clergy's theological commitments were "high Protestant" and evangelical, there is evidence of diversity in recruiting networks (evangelical, Anglo-Catholic and high church), and in the tone and content of various clergymen's preaching and writing.

On a broader imperial view, recent scholarship has suggested similar patterns of Irish clerical migration to other settler colonies such as Canada (British North America) and the Cape.[82] Taken together, this suggests the

---

81. Roy Foster, quoted in Ronayne, *First Fleet to Federation*, 5–6.
82. See especially Hardwick, *Anglican British World*, ch. 1.

colonial and imperial significance of Trinity College, Dublin, and its important role in the creation of a nineteenth-century "Greater Ireland."

BIBLIOGRAPHY

Acheson, Alan R. *A History of the Church of Ireland, 1691–2001.* 2nd ed. Dublin: Columbia, 2002.
Atkinson, Alan. *Camden.* 2nd ed. Melbourne: Australian Scholarly, 2008.
Barnard, T. C., and W. G. Neely. *The Clergy of the Church of Ireland, 1000–2000: Messengers, Watchmen and Stewards.* Dublin: Four Courts, 2006.
Barr, Colin, and Hilary M. Carey, eds. *Religion and Greater Ireland: Christianity and Irish Global Networks, 1750–1950.* Montreal: McGill-Queen's University Press, 2015.
Barrett, John. "Church, State, and People in Eastern Australia, 1835–1850." PhD diss., Australian National University, Canberra, 1963.
Barrett, W. R. "Browne, William Henry (1800–1877)." *Australian Dictionary of Biography.* http://adb.anu.edu.au/biography/browne-william-henry-1837.
Batt, Neil, and Michael Roe. "Conflict Within the Church of England in Tasmania, 1850–1858." *Journal of Religious History* 4 (1966–67) 39–62.
Belich, James. *Replenishing the Earth: The Settler Revolution and the Rise of the Anglo-World 1783–1939.* Oxford: Oxford University Press, 2009.
Burtchaell, George Dames, and Thomas Ulick Sadleir, eds. *Alumni Dublinenses. A Register of the Students, Graduates, Professors and Provosts of Trinity College in the University of Dublin.* London: Norgate, 1924.
Cable, K. "Fulton, Henry (1761–1840)." *Australian Dictionary of Biography.* http://adb.anu.edu.au/biography/fulton-henry-2074.
Carey, H. M. *God's Empire: Religion and Colonialism in the British World, c.1801–1908.* Cambridge: Cambridge University Press, 2011.
CCSS. *The Annual Report of the Colonial Church and School Society.* London: Colonial Church and School Society, 1851.
Church of England Quarterly Review 16 (1844) 262–72.
Convict Discipline and Transportation. Correspondence on the Subject of Convict Discipline and Transportation. H. C. and H. L., Parliamentary Papers. London: HMSO, 1847.
Cox, Frederick H. *Perseverance and Endurance, the Duties of This Time. Two Sermons Preached, the One on the Second Sunday in Lent, the Other on the Fifth Sunday after Easter 1851 to the Congregation of St. John Baptist's, Hobart Town.* Hobart, Tasmania: H & C Best, 1851.
Curry, Norman. "Macartney—The Man and His Ministry." In *Victoria's Debt*, edited by James Grant, 9–20. Melbourne: St Paul's Cathedral, Melbourne, 1995.
Delaney, E., and D. MacRaild. "Irish Migration, Networks and Ethnic Identities Since 1750: An Introduction." *Immigrants and Minorities* 23 (2005) 127–42.
"The Form and Manner of Ordering of Deacons." *The Book of Common Prayer*, 732–42. London: Oxford University Press, 1846.
Foster, R. F. *Modern Ireland, 1600–1972.* New York: Penguin, 1989.
Fry, Henry Phibbs. *The Scriptural Evidence of the Apostolic Ministry and Tradition of the Church Catholic.* Hobart, Tasmania: Henry Fry, 1843.

———. *Sermons on the Nature and Design of Heresy; On the Defection of the Rev. J. H. Newman from the Church of England, and Other Subjects*. Hobart, Tasmania: John Moore, 1846.

———. *A System of Penal Discipline*. London: Longman, Brown, Green & Longmans, 1850.

Fulton, Henry. *A Letter to the Rev. W. B. Ullathorne: In Answer to a Few Words to the Rev. Henry Fulton and His Readers*. Sydney: Stephens and Stokes, 1833.

———. *Reasons Why Protestants Think the Worship of the Church of Rome an Idolatrous Worship; to Which are Added Some Allusions, in Answer to the Observations in the Australian Newspaper of 2nd November 1832*. Sydney: Stephens and Stokes, 1833.

———. *Strictures Upon a Letter Lately Written by Roger Thierry, Esquire, Commissioner of the Court of Requests, in New South Wales, to Edward Blount, Esq, M.P*. Sydney: Stephens and Stokes, 1833.

Gladwin, Michael. *Anglican Clergy in Australia, 1788-1850: Building a British World*. Suffolk, UK: Royal Historical Society & Boydell and Brewer, 2015.

———. "Australian Anglican Clergymen in Australia and the British Empire, 1788-1850." PhD diss., Cambridge University, 2011.

———. "Flogging Parsons? Australian Anglican Clergymen, the Magistracy and Convicts, 1788-1850." *Journal of Religious History* 36 (2012) 1-18.

———. "The Journalist in the Rectory: Anglican Clergymen and Australian Intellectual Life, 1788-1850." *History Australia* 6 (Dec 2010) 56.1-56.28.

———. "'Mindful of her St. Columbas and Gaels': Ireland, Empire and Australian Anglicanism, 1788-1850." In *Religion and Greater Ireland*, edited by Colin Barr and Hilary Carey, 297-318. Montreal: McGill-Queen's University Press, 2015.

Grant, James, ed. *Victoria's Debt to the Irish Church: Sermon and Papers Delivered at the Hussey Burgh Macartney Commemoration*. Melbourne: St. Paul's Cathedral, Melbourne, 1995.

Hardwick, Joseph. *An Anglican British World: The Church of England and the Expansion of the Settler Empire, c.1790-1860*. Manchester, UK: Manchester University Press, 2014.

———. "Anglican Church Expansion and the Recruitment of Colonial Clergy for NSW and the Cape Colony, c.1790-1850." *Journal of Imperial and Commonwealth History* 37.3 (2009) 361-81.

Harrison, J. F. C. *Robert Owen and the Owenites in Britain and America. The Quest for the New Moral World*. London: Routledge & Kegan Paul, 1969.

Hart, P. R. "Davies, Robert Rowland (1805-1880)." *Australian Dictionary of Biography*, vol. 1. Melbourne: Melbourne University Press, 1966.

Hassall, J. S. *In Old Australia*. Brisbane: Hews, 1902.

Hempton, David. *Religion and Political Culture in Britain and Ireland*. Cambridge: Cambridge University Press, 1996.

Holden, Colin. *Saints, Sinners and Goalposts: A History of All Saints, East St. Kilda*. Melbourne: Australian Scholarly, 2008.

Le Couteur, Howard. "Brisbane Anglicans: 1842-1875." PhD diss., Macquarie University, Sydney, 2006.

Macintosh, N. *Richard Johnson: Chaplain to the Colony of New South Wales*. Sydney: Library of Australian History, 1978.

Mannheim, Hermann. *Pioneers in Criminology*. London: Stevens & Sons, 1960.

Melbourne, Tom. "The Unexpected Chaplain." *Integrity* 2 (2013) 1-27. integrity.moore.edu.au/article/download/6/5.

Mullins, J. D. *Our Beginnings: Being a Short Sketch of the History of the Colonial and Continental Church Society*. London: Colonial and Continental Church Society, 1923.

Piggin, Stuart. "The Social Background, Motivation, and Training of British Protestant Missionaries to India, 1789–1858." PhD diss., University of London, 1974.

Prentis, Malcolm D. "The Presbyterian Ministry in Australia, 1822–1900: Recruitment and Composition." *Journal of Religious History* 13 (Jun 1984) 46–65.

"Rev. Dr. Francis Thomas Cusack Russell 1823–76." http://www.swvic.org/coleraine/holy_trinity_coleraine.htm.

Ridden, Jennifer. "National Identity, Religion, and Liberalism among the Irish Élite, c.1800–1850." PhD diss., University of London, 1998.

Roe, Michael. "Fry, Henry Phibbs (1807–1874)." *Australian Dictionary of Biography*. http://adb.anu.edu.au/biography/fry-henry-phibbs-2072/text2589.

Ronayne, Jarlath. *First Fleet to Federation: Irish Supremacy in Colonial Australia*. Dublin: Trinity College Dublin Press, 2002.

———. *The Irish in Australia: Rogues and Reformers, First Fleet to Federation*. Camberwell, VIC: Viking, 2003.

———. "Who Was Who among Irish-Australians?" In *The Irish Imprint in Australia*, edited by Reynolds and Pascoe, 33–37. Melbourne: Victoria University of Technology, 1994.

Ronayne, Jarlath, et al. *The Irish Imprint in Australia*. Melbourne: Victoria University of Technology, 1994.

Russell, Penelope A. *Savage or Civilised? Manners in Colonial Australia*. Sydney: University of New South Wales Press, 2010.

———. *A Wish of Distinction: Colonial Gentility and Femininity*. Carlton, VIC: Melbourne University Press, 1994.

Stack, William. *A Sermon, Preached in the Church of St. James*. Sydney: James Tegg, 1837.

Stephens, Geoffrey. "The Diocese of Tasmania." In *Colonial Tractarians*, edited by Brian Porter, 49–62. Melbourne: Joint Board of Christian Education, 1989.

Strong, Rowan. *Anglicanism and the British Empire, c.1700–1850*. Oxford: Oxford University Press, 2007.

———. "Church and State in Western Australia: Implementing New Imperial Paradigms in the Swan River Colony, 1827–1857." *Journal of Ecclesiastical History* 61 (2010) 517–40.

———. "The Reverend John Wollaston and Colonial Christianity in Western Australia, 1840–1863." *Journal of Religious History* 25 (2001) 266–71.

Tompson, Charles. "Retrospect." In *Wild Notes, from the Lyre of a Native Minstrel*. Sydney: Robert Howe, 1826.

Trollope, Anthony. "The Parson of the Parish." *Pall Mall Gazette* (23 January 1866) 58–59.

USPG. *The Annual Report of the USPG*. London: Society for the Propagation of the Gospel, 1849.

Wolffe, John. *God and Greater Britain: Religion and National Life in Britain and Ireland, 1843–1945*. London: Routledge, 1994.

———. *The Protestant Crusade in Great Britain, 1829–1860*. Oxford: Clarendon, 1991.

Yates, Nigel. *The Religious Condition of Ireland, 1770–1850*. Oxford: Oxford University Press, 2006.

13

The Word of God Is Seed
John Wyclif's Evangelical Theology and the Naming of Wycliffe College[1]

SEAN OTTO

JOHN WYCLIF (C.1330–1384) WAS a fiery reformer and outspoken critic of the fourteenth-century church, who placed a special emphasis on the Bible; he wrote a treatise titled *On the Truth of Holy Scripture* in which he elucidated a doctrine of scriptural truth, and in which he makes such claims as "I do not think it is right to admit any science or conclusion to which the Scripture does not bear witness."[2] So when the nineteenth-century founders of Wycliffe College were deciding on that name, they no doubt thought of Wyclif as a shining example of Evangelicalism in an otherwise dark age in which the gospel lay hidden from the eyes of the laity. But was this the case? Who was this man after whom they renamed the Protestant Episcopal Divinity School? What did he stand for? Was he truly evangelical? The short answer is that it is anachronistic to speak of Wyclif as an evangelical in the nineteenth- or twentieth-century understanding of the word. This chapter

---

1. This chapter began life as the Founders' Day Memorial Lecture for 2015. My thanks to Tom Power for the invitation to deliver this lecture, and to include this modified version in this collection, as well as for assistance with materials in the Wycliffe College Archives.

2. Levy, *John Wyclif*, 129; see Wyclif, *De veritate sacre scripture*, I.180/17–18.

will explore a much longer and more nuanced answer, one which explores various aspects of Wyclif's theology, removing "several layers of rich brown Protestant varnish"[3] to unearth something of the real man and his times, and in what ways we can speak about his theology as evangelical.

WHAT IS AN EVANGELICAL?

For our purposes, it is key to define what is meant by "evangelical." In the most straightforward understanding of the word, it simply means "of the gospel," a definition that sits comfortably with the theology of John Wyclif, the *doctor evangelicus* (evangelical doctor),[4] as we shall see. This, however, is not the more common understanding of "evangelical" and only partially describes the group of men who formed the Protestant Episcopal Divinity School, a school whose name was changed to Wycliffe College within the space of a few years. These men were evangelical Anglicans, an identity still embraced by the College, and they espoused evangelical beliefs within the framework of Anglicanism (which we might define as adherence to the Church of England, its Prayer Book, and the Thirty-nine Articles of Religion), a capacious structure populated by various parties with varying degrees of tension. Their Evangelicalism is probably most usefully understood by reference to the definitions of David Bebbington[5] and Timothy Larsen.[6]

Bebbington defines Evangelicalism through four qualities:

> *Conversionism*, the belief that lives need to be changed; *activism*, the expression of the gospel in effort; *biblicism*, a particular regard for the Bible; and . . . *crucicentrism*, a stress on the sacrifice of Christ on the cross. Together they form a quadrilateral of priorities that is the basis of Evangelicalism.[7]

This definition is accepted broadly by those who claim to be evangelical and those who study Evangelicalism.[8] Defined in this manner, there

---

3. MacFarlane, *John Wycliffe and the Beginnings*, 10. See also Crompton, "John Wyclif," 6–34, and Mudroch, *Wyclyf Tradition*.

4. On the use of this cognomen, see Šmahel, "'Doctor evangelicus super omnes evangelistas'" 16–34.

5. Bebbington, *Evangelicalism in Modern Britain*, 11–29.

6. Larsen, "Defining and Locating Evangelicalism," 1–12.

7. Bebbington, *Evangelicalism in Modern Britain*, 2–3.

8. Larsen gives numerous references that bear this observation out; see "Defining and Locating Evangelicalism," 1–2. Several scholars have taken issue with some of the more specific examples that Bebbington used, but in general the quadrilateral

are certain similarities, or what one might call with Wittgenstein "family resemblances,"[9] with Wyclif's theological positions.

Larsen, while seeking not to supplant Bebbington's definition, refines and enhances the "Bebbington quadrilateral" with his own "Pentagon":

An evangelical is:

1. an orthodox Protestant;

2. who stands in the tradition of the global Christian networks arising from the eighteenth-century revival movements associated with John Wesley and George Whitefield;

3. who has a preeminent place for the Bible in her or his Christian life as the divinely inspired, final authority in matters of faith and practice;

4. who stresses reconciliation with God through the atoning work of Jesus Christ on the cross;

5. and who stresses the work of the Holy Spirit in the life of an individual to bring about conversion and an ongoing life of fellowship with God and service to God and others, including the duty of all believers to participate in the task of proclaiming the gospel to all people.[10]

This more refined definition is meant to contextualize what scholars mean by Evangelicalism, and explicitly excludes pre-Reformation Christians, since we do not mean to include people like Francis of Assisi in our definition of Evangelicalism, no matter how well he might fit the mold according to the definition of Bebbington's quadrilateral.[11] This definition, then, excludes Wyclif as well, whatever his relationship to the principles outlined by Bebbington. This is a modern, post-confessional understanding of Evangelicalism, however, and one which rejects claims to any historical continuity. The founders of Wycliffe College, as we shall see, would have rejected such a limitation.

---

has held up to scrutiny. See the various chapters of Haykin and Stewart, *Emergence of Evangelicalism*, 417–32.

9. Wittgenstein, *Philosophical Investigations*, 32e. See also Bambrough, "Universals and Family Resemblances," 207–22. This methodology has been applied to another group almost as amorphous as evangelicals—Lollards—by Hornbeck, *What is a Lollard?*, esp. 1–24.

10. Larsen, "Defining and Locating Evangelicalism," 1.

11. Ibid., 2.

THE FOUNDATION AND NAMING OF WYCLIFFE COLLEGE

From the partisan strife in the Diocese of Toronto and throughout the Church of England in the Dominion of Canada, there arose two associations in the mid-nineteenth century: the Evangelical Association of the United Church of England and Ireland in the Diocese of Toronto (founded 1869) and the Church Association of the Diocese of Toronto (founded 1873), both dominated by evangelical laymen. Out of these two associations grew the impetus for a training college for evangelical churchmen, which grew to fruition with the opening of the Protestant Episcopal Divinity School in 1877.[12]

At first, classes met in a room in the St. James' Schoolhouse, but a building near the corner of College and McCaul streets opened in the fall of 1882.[13] After expansions on the first building, the College moved into its current premises at the corner of Hoskin Avenue and Queen's Park Crescent in 1891, which building has also been expanded several times.[14]

The evangelical principles of the College were clear from the very beginning:[15]

1) The Bible as the Sole Rule of Faith; in opposition to the error that would make the Bible and tradition the *joint* rule of faith . . .

2) Justification by Faith in Christ Alone; in opposition to the sacramentarian system . . .

3) The Sole and Exclusive Priesthood of Christ; in opposition to the sacerdotal assumption which would convert Christ's ministers into an order of sacrificing and mediating priests . . .

4) The Real Presence of Christ by Faith in the Hearts of Worthy Recipients of the Holy Communion; in opposition to the figment of His presence corporeally or spiritually on the communion table . . .

---

12. On the founding of the College, see Hague, "History of Wycliffe College," 1–60; Jocz, "Beginnings," 3–22; for a discussion of Wycliffe's place within Canadian Anglican Evangelicalism, see Katerberg, "Redefining Evangelicalism," 171–88; an account of the founding of the College is found on 171–74.

13. Hague, "History of Wycliffe College," 38–41.

14. Ibid., 56.

15. These principles are listed in the early calendars of Wycliffe College at least as early as 1881; see Wycliffe College Archives (henceforth WCA), *Calendar* (1881) 5–8; see also Hague, "History of Wycliffe College," 18–19.

5) The Church of Christ is "The Holy Catholic Church" . . . "The Holy Church Universal" . . . "The mystical body of Christ, which is the blessed company of all faithful people" . . .

6) The Visible Church (*visibilia ecclesia*) of Christ is a Congregation of Faithful Men, in which *the pure word of God is preached*, and the *sacraments be duly administered* . . .

7) An Historical Episcopate, traceable to Apostolic direction, as conducive to the *well-being*, but *not necessary to the being* of the Church; in opposition to the dogma of a tactual succession . . .

These principles fit fairly neatly with the definitions of Bebbington and Larsen, although closer perhaps to Bebbington, and certainly with a distinctive Anglican flavor, especially since they are founded on the *Book of Common Prayer* and the Thirty-nine Articles of Religion, as their explanatory notes make clear.[16] Note also the decisive way in which the founders of the College state what they are against: the elevation of tradition to equality with Scripture, the "sacramentarian system," Christ's ministers as "sacrificing and mediating priests," transubstantiation, and a "tactual succession"[17] of the episcopate. For these Anglican evangelicals, there can be no standard for faith apart from Scripture (thus the emphasis on "the pure word of God" being preached). There can be no thought that the sacraments of the Church confer salvation *per se*; only faith in Christ can save, and the real presence of Christ in the Eucharist is experienced by those who have this faith. The role and function of the priest is severely curtailed in their view, and they set themselves against what they saw as an overly powerful sacerdotalism in the Church of England. Nor do they recognize any need for each successive bishop to be able to demonstrate his apostolic succession through the laying on of hands through history, and they in fact reject the need for an episcopate, while still recognizing its utility and desirability (they were after all founding a Protestant *Episcopal* Divinity School). Principles 5 and 6 are the only two that are not formulated in overt opposition to some other position, but they are also the most ambiguous. The first is a claim to catholicity and membership in the universal Church of Christ, without any indication of whether or not or how other groups might be part of the universal Church apart from the claim that all faithful people are its members. The second, while emphasizing preaching and sacrament, emphasize also the purity of that preaching and that the sacraments need to be "duly administered."

16. WCA, *Calendar* (1881), 5–8.

17. That is, the idea that legitimate apostolic succession is completed through the laying on of hands at a bishop's consecration.

Again, who is included in the visible Church, and how determinations of the purity of the word and whether or not the sacraments are duly administered are not outlined in much detail. Taken together, however, they demonstrate that the founders were concerned to legitimate Evangelicalism within the Church of England and the wider Christian community, by emphasizing their place within the universal and visible Church.

These unambiguously evangelical principles defined the identity of the Protestant Episcopal Divinity School, but the founders felt the need, at some point, to change the name to better reflect that identity. It seems that the building was referred to as "Wycliffe College" when the Protestant Episcopal Divinity School moved into its premises on College Street in 1882.[18] Yet the corporation did not change its name until sometime after this; it was moved at a meeting of the Board of Management in late 1883 that "application be made to the next session of the Legislature to change the corporate name of the Protestant Episcopal Divinity School Corporation of Toronto to that of Wycliffe College."[19] At a further meeting held in April 1884, the use of "Protestant Episcopal Divinity School" has dropped out, and the meeting is that of the "Council of Wycliffe College."[20] Officially, the corporation's name seems to have been changed to Wycliffe College by a court ruling in 1885,[21] but where exactly the idea for the name came from remains something of a mystery. Dyson Hague in his history of the College suggests the possibility that Montague Burrows's book *Wiclif's Place in History*, published in 1881, might have given inspiration to the College founders.[22] Another possibility is that the founders were caught up in the renewed interest in Wyclif occasioned by the five hundredth anniversary of his death, which was celebrated in 1884, and which gave rise to a number of biographies and the establishment of the Wyclif Society, whose purpose was to publish the reformer's works in their entirety.[23] Whatever the case, the name seems to have struck a chord, and to have been enthusiastically received.[24]

---

18. As indicated in the title of the 1882–3 Calendar: *The Calendar of the Protestant Episcopal Divinity School (Wycliffe College) Toronto*; this calendar was printed in 1882.

19. WCA, Wycliffe College, Council Minute Book #2 1883–1892, fol. 10.

20. Ibid., fol. 20.

21. Hague, "History of Wycliffe College," 38.

22. Ibid., 37.

23. For a sampling of biographies from the period, see the Lollard Society bibliography page: http://lollardsociety.org/?page_id=10. On the founding of the Wyclif Society, see the notice found, *inter alia*, at the back of Buddensieg, *John Wyclif's Polemical Works*.

24. Hague, "History of Wycliffe College," 37–38.

But why this particular name? We get some idea from the works of scholars associated with the College. For instance, Hague characterizes Wyclif as "the first great champion of the principles of the Reformation and the outstanding Reformer of Europe."[25] George M. Wrong, educated at Wycliffe College and the University of Toronto, who was to go on to found the history department at the University,[26] wrote about the Bishop of Norwich's crusade to Flanders in 1383, and mentions Wyclif as "the most striking figure in English history at this period."[27] If it was under the influence of Burrows's book that the opinion of the College founders was formed, then it is easy to see why the name was chosen, for in Burrows's opinion, Wyclif was

> surnamed by his contemporaries "the Evangelical Doctor." The title was prophetic. Long before he became the Reformer of England and Europe, he attained his extraordinary eminence in the Schools by, or at least in connection with, his intimate knowledge of what was then almost a sealed book, the Bible. To what sources he owed the impulse given to his Bible studies is a question involved in too much obscurity to justify treatment in these Lectures. Peter Waldo's followers were Biblemen, not heretics; and the University system was a ready means of intercommunication. Possibly it may have come through that channel.[28]

Wyclif cuts an extremely potent figure here, towering over other scholars of his day, fighting for the liberty to study the Bible, and standing in the tradition of others who would liberate the Bible but were repressed for trying to do so. Of course, it is a Protestant calumny that the Bible "was then almost a sealed book," as more recent research has definitively shown.[29] Certainly this figure of the Bible champion fits well with the evangelical character and principles of the College, especially when to it are added other prominent themes of Burrows's book, such as the Poor Priests,[30] Wyclif's polemics against the papacy and the friars,[31] and the attribution to Wyclif of the Middle English translation of the Bible.[32]

---

25. Ibid., 38. Hague later wrote a biography which characterized Wyclif in much the same way; see Hague, *Life and Works of John Wycliffe*.

26. See Wallace, "Life and Works of George M. Wrong," 229–39.

27. Wrong, *Crusade of 1383*, 46.

28. Burrows, *Wiclif's Place in History*, 48.

29. Among the enormous bibliography on the subject, two classic studies are Smalley, *Study of the Bible*, and De Lubac, *Medieval Exegesis*.

30. See Burrows, *Wiclif's Place in History*, esp. 92–95.

31. Ibid., 85–88.

32. Ibid., 19–23, 88–89.

Charles Venn Pilcher's College Song is likewise effusive in its praise of Wyclif's evangelicalism:

> Victorious Sun of Righteousness,
> At whose supreme command
> Thy Morning Star flamed forth afar
> O'er England's darkened land
> . . .
> Flashed through the night the living light
> Of truth and liberty.
> We, heirs of Wycliffe's glorious name,
> Light-bearers fain would be
> . . .
> Come gain or loss, our pride the Cross,
> Our boast, God's conquering Word.[33]

Little wonder that the College bears Wyclif's name, if this is the image portrayed. How much this characterization is a true reflection of Wyclif and his theological positions is the question to which we now turn.

JOHN WYCLIF'S THEOLOGY

Using Bebbington's quadrilateral, Larsen's expansion, and the founding principles of Wycliffe College as a framework, this section will look at how we might characterize Wyclif's theology in relation to the freight that the founders of the Protestant Episcopal Divinity School wanted his name to carry.

Conversionism

Let us begin with the first of Bebbington's marks of evangelicalism, which corresponds roughly to the second of Larsen's points and the second principle of Wycliffe College. The call to conversion, as Bebbington notes, is central to the gospel, and to turn from sin to faith in Christ has ever been the message of the Christian preacher. Of course, for evangelicals, it is also much more than that; it is a total and complete transformation which changes the sinner into a saint, and is closely linked to the doctrine of justification by faith, and that of assurance.[34] For Anglican evangelicals, there was a tension

---

33. The song, not currently in use to the best of my knowledge at the College, accompanies the frontispiece in Hague's *John Wycliffe*.

34. Bebbington, *Evangelicalism in Modern Britain*, 5–7.

between conversionism and the practice of infant baptism, which the Book of Common Prayer said made those receiving it regenerate. This was the cause of much controversy in the nineteenth century, and was used by other parties within the Church of England to charge evangelicals with disloyalty to the Church.[35] This is likely among the reasons that Wycliffe College was so careful to reassure all and sundry that the College's principles were founded upon the Prayer Book and the Thirty-nine Articles,[36] and conversionism is the least pronounced of the marks of Evangelicalism found there, although this is not untypical of Anglican Evangelicalism.[37]

In desiring his flock to be converted, John Wyclif was no different. In his own preaching, he emphasized the imitation of Christ and the Apostles as exemplars of the Christian life, enumerating the standard tropes of medieval preaching on the virtues and vices, but subverting the virtue ethics popular with Aquinas, Scotus, and the Friars.[38] This, of course, highlights a key difference between Wyclif and the founders of Wycliffe College—Wyclif was living, thinking, and writing in the fourteenth century, and expressed himself within that context; his interlocutors were his fellow scholastic theologians, and his theology reflects that fact.

Another key difference has to do with justification by faith. If conversionism is closely tied to solafideism, then Wyclif cannot be said to hold a position compatible with Evangelicalism in this regard, for he was not a solafideist.[39] For Wyclif, the questions revolved around the relationship between divine omnipotence and omniscience on the one hand, and human freedom on the other. These were questions that much concerned fourteenth-century theologians, who discussed them in terms of necessity. Wyclif wanted to make a distinction between absolute and conditional necessity, whereby all things happen of necessity, but only those things eternally willed by God happen by absolute necessity.[40] A consequence of this is that temporal actions can cause God's eternal volitions; when someone acts meritoriously, God knows this eternally, and can love them because of it.[41] This safeguards human freedom, in that humans are responsible in

---

35. Ibid., 9–10.

36. This is apparent in the elucidations which accompany each principle in the early college calendars, but see also Pilcher, "Principles of Wycliffe College," 103–43.

37. Bebbington, *Evangelicalism in Modern Britain*, 7–8.

38. See Otto, "*Pastoralia* in John Wyclif's *Sermones*," 110–66.

39. For this paragraph, see Levy, "John Wyclif and the Christian Life," 348–54; cf. Conti, "Wyclif's Logic and Metaphysics," 67–126. See also Levy, "Grace and Freedom," 279–337.

40. See Wyclif, *De dominio divino*, vol. 1, ch. 14, esp. 115–16.

41. Levy, "John Wyclif and the Christian Life," 349, gives an example from one

some way for their meriting salvation, and it safeguards God from being implicated in evil, since if all things were absolutely necessary, sin would be the result of God's eternal will. All of this does not, of course, obviate the need for God's grace, which is necessary for people to overcome sin and turn to the good and is the chief actor in a human's doing good, but humans freely choose God's offer of grace according to Wyclif, and they can freely reject it.[42] But—and this is the chief difference between Wyclif and Evangelicalism—despite the essential role of grace in Wyclif's soteriology, he still holds to the system of merit so important to medieval theologians.[43] For Wyclif, no creature can be rewarded with beatitude if it does not first merit beatitude, so it cannot be the passive recipient of beatitude, but must actively cooperate with grace to merit it,[44] though to be sure, this cooperation is the return to God of what God has first offered by His extension of grace to humans.[45]

A third difference has to do with the doctrine of assurance. The sort of assurance so common to Evangelicalism[46] is not only completely absent from Wyclif, but is completely undermined by his ecclesiology. Wyclif held, much like the principles of Wycliffe College, that the universal Church is made up of all those predestined by God to eternal salvation. For Wyclif, the visible church in the here-and-now is made up, following Augustine's teaching, of a mixed body of those predestined and those foreknown to damnation (the *praesciti*). The real difference is that, for Wyclif, one cannot know whether or not one is predestined or foreknown; one cannot know without a special revelation, although one can make a fair guess. Nonetheless, there is a fundamental uncertainty about who is and who is not saved in Wyclif's opinion, and we ought not to act as if our salvation were assured.[47]

There are, then, some rather major differences between Wyclif's theological positions and those of Evangelicalism in regard to conversionism. While both hold a central place for God's grace, essential to how human beings are saved, there is little else in common; Wyclif did not hold a solafideist position, had little time for certitude in his understanding of predestination,

---

of Wyclif's sermons, in which Wyclif illustrates the point from Christ telling the disciples that the Father loves them because they loved Christ; see Wyclif, *Sermones*, I.29, 194/21–5.

42. See Wyclif, *De dominio divino*, vol. 3, ch. 5, 240–41.
43. Levy, "Wyclif and the Christian Life," 352–53.
44. See Wyclif, *De domino divino*, vol. 3, ch. 4, 229–30.
45. See ibid., 226–28.
46. Bebbington, *Evangelicalism in Modern Britain*, 6–7.
47. See Otto, "Predestination and the Two Cities," 145–58.

and worked within a typically medieval frame of reference in working out his exposition of how humans are converted.

Activism

Turning to Bebbington's second mark of Evangelicalism, we find that nineteenth-century evangelicals worked at a nearly impossible pace, preaching, writing letters, teaching Bible classes, visiting, and trying to convert people to Christ.[48] The extensive missionary efforts of Wycliffe College graduates, both within Canada and abroad, is something that was a matter of pride to the officials and supporters of Wycliffe, and well exhibits this characteristic of Evangelicalism.[49] Wyclif for his part was a remarkably productive scholar and preacher, and was adamant that the gospel should be preached and the faith expounded to the whole people, but then again, this was one of the major preoccupations of the medieval Church.

Efforts to improve the education of the clergy and the laity were widespread in the Middle Ages, and preaching was frequent (an entire religious order was founded with the express purpose of preaching far and wide), both in the vernacular (most commonly) and in Latin.[50] Wyclif's own preaching fits this trend, as it certainly took place in both languages.[51] From his pen we have some 245 extant sermons, which were designed for the use of other preachers,[52] and his followers produced an even greater number of Middle English sermons inspired by his thought.[53] For Wyclif, the office of preaching is the highest and most important duty of those in priestly orders. He writes about the power of the word of God, drawing on Luke and Matthew, and compares the word to a seed, and says that the preaching of the word is more important than the preparation of the Eucharist, which makes bread sacramentally Christ's body, but preaching makes the human "in a way, Christ himself."[54]

---

48. Bebbington, *Evangelicalism in Modern Britain*, 10–12.

49. There are two chapters devoted to this aspect of Wycliffe College's work in the *Jubilee Volume of Wycliffe College*, 144–89, and there is a listing of those who have gone on to do missionary work on the wall near the main assembly hall at the College.

50. On catechetical efforts in England, see Reeves, *Religious Education in Thirteenth-Century England*; and for preaching, both in Latin and in the vernacular, see Kienzle, *The Sermon*.

51. Otto, "*Pastoralia* in John Wyclif's *Sermones*," 34–35.

52. Ibid., 38–40.

53. The largest of these collections, 294 sermons, is Gradon and Hudson, *English Wycliffite Sermons*.

54. Wycliffe, *Sermones*, 1.16, 110:16–19, quoted and translated in Otto, "Authority of the Preacher," 80; see ibid., 79–82, for Wyclif's views on the office of preaching.

Something ought to be said about the (in)famous "Poor Priests," who were described by H. B. Workman in his 1926 biography of Wyclif in this way:

> Clad in russet robes of undressed wool reaching to their feet . . . without sandals, purse, or scrip, a long staff in their hand, dependent for food and shelter on the goodwill of their neighbours, their only possession a few pages of Wyclif's Bible . . . , his tracts and sermons, moving constantly from place to place like the early Methodist preachers in the "circuits"—for Wyclif feared as Wesley also feared lest they should become "possessioners," tied to one place like a dog,—given not "to frequenting taverns, hunting, or to chess," but "to the duties which befit the priesthood, studious acquaintance with God's law, plain preaching of the word of God, and devout thankfulness," Wyclif's "poor priests," like the friars before them, soon became a power in the land.[55]

More recent scholarship has moved away from this portrayal, with some scholars going so far as to deny the existence of the movement altogether.[56] Most contemporary scholars believe that there was some sort of movement afoot, centered on Wyclif and his ideas, even if they do not think of it in the same terms as Workman.[57] For our purposes, there are two things that should be noted. First, Workman's description is close to what the founders of Wycliffe College believed, and the comparison with Wesley would be a welcome bolstering of evangelical credibility. Second, it is only reasonable to assume that Wyclif had some sort of following, and that these men, who would be at least initially drawn from the university, would be preachers.[58] For reasons that cannot be gone into here in any detail, these preachers would not be an easily recognizable group, since Wyclif explicitly rejected the idea of religious orders, such as friars and monks, with their *regula* and habits.[59] Nonetheless, that Wyclif was responsible for some sort of gospel-preaching movement does lend itself to positive comparisons with nineteenth-century evangelicals; and in the end, Wyclif acquits himself well

---

55. Workman, *John Wyclif*, II.203–4.

56. Evans, *John Wyclif*, 250–54.

57. Lahey, *John Wyclif*, 165–68; Levy, "Wyclif on the Christian Life," 302–6; Hudson, *Premature Reformation*, 62–81.

58. Lahey, *John Wyclif*, 165–68, is probably the most accessible introduction to the evidence for this.

59. I will discuss this at more length in a forthcoming monograph on Wyclif's anti-fraternal preaching.

in comparison to these industrious men, and there is a certain commonality in regard to this mark of Evangelicalism.

Biblicism

While there were many differences of opinion on the question of biblical inerrancy and the validity of non-literal interpretation of Scripture, it is undoubted that all branches of Evangelicalism fostered a profound respect for the Bible.[60] The founders of Wycliffe College were no different, as the first of their principles makes clear, espousing a view that made no room for extra-biblical tradition in the Church and that grounds all theology in the words of Scripture.

Wyclif's name has long been associated with just this sort of understanding of Scripture; his contemporary opponents viewed him as a dangerous radical in this regard.[61] There is certainly a lot in Wyclif's theology of Scripture to recommend itself to evangelicals, as for instance his emphasis on the centrality of Scripture, and his insistence that human laws need not be added to the divine law of Scripture.[62] However, Wyclif's position on biblical hermeneutics was essentially conservative; that is, it was in line with the Augustinian fourfold sense of Scripture, which posited distinct but interrelated meanings of Scripture.[63] Moreover, Wyclif recognized the Church's role in interpreting Scripture, and placed himself as a trained theologian, a *magister sacrae paginae* (master of the sacred page), within that tradition.[64]

Of course, one of the most famous things about Wyclif is also the one that has been most thoroughly proved to be a myth: that Wyclif translated the Bible from Latin into Middle English.[65] In reality, it is more likely that Wyclif simply acted as an advocate for such a translation, which was undertaken by men associated with him at the University of Oxford.[66] It was, of course, still common belief in the late nineteenth century that Wyclif was

---

60. Bebbington, *Evangelicalism in Modern Britain*, 12–14.

61. On Wyclif and Scripture, see Lahey, *John Wyclif*, 135–68; Levy, *John Wyclif's Theology*; Levy, *Holy Scripture and the Quest*, 54–91; Levy, *On the Truth of Holy Scripture*.

62. A prominent example of this is Wyclif's utter rejection of the decree of the Fourth Lateran Council, *Omnis utriusque sexus*, which legislated annual confession and reception of the Eucharist for all Christians; there are condemnatory passages throughout Wyclif's works, but see Wyclif, *Sermones* 4.6, 49–57.

63. Lahey, *John Wyclif*, 135–36.

64. This is one of Levy's key insights; see Levy, *Holy Scripture and the Quest*, 54–91.

65. See Deanesly, *Lollard Bible*.

66. See Dove, "Wyclif and the English Bible," 365–406.

responsible for the translation, and it is still a persistent myth today, as a simple internet search will amply illustrate. Nor, it should be recognized, does the fact that Wyclif's part in the translation was limited mean that the recognition of Wyclif's biblicism was misplaced, as he was certainly an advocate for Scripture (as interpreted by the Church) as the basis for faith and doctrine.

Wyclif's understanding of Scripture, while not that of nineteenth-century evangelicals, marked as it was by the fourfold understanding of Scripture and more emphasis on tradition than is usually recognized, was certainly one that placed great emphasis on its role in Christian life and the formation of doctrine. At least in this regard, Wyclif (and medieval theologians in general) bears resemblance to Evangelicalism.

Crucicentrism

Several of the principles of Wycliffe College have to do with the centrality of Christ's cross to the Christian faith, as the principles oppose systems that would see the sacraments as mediating salvation, or that would have a mediating priesthood between individuals and the Father apart from Jesus Christ. These are soundly evangelical principles, as the centrality of Christ's death on the cross and the doctrine of (substitutionary) atonement are and were of utmost importance to the various forms of Evangelicalism.[67]

Wyclif likewise placed the cross at the center of Christianity. He writes in *Trialogus*, in his discussion of baptism, that satisfaction for sin can only be accomplished through the death of Christ, where he refers to Romans 6:3: "However we have been baptized in Christ Jesus, we have been baptized into his death."[68] But Wyclif actually argues very little about the atonement, writing in an aside that because man had sinned, a man must make satisfaction for sin, in which he followed Anselm.[69] He does argue against indulgences, since this practice places another mediator between God and the sinner, and it is God alone who can forgive sin.[70] But he also retained a belief in Purgatory,[71] a doctrine rejected by the founders of Wycliffe College,

---

67. Bebbington, *Evangelicalism in Modern Britain*, 14–17.

68. Lahey, *John Wyclif: Trialogus*, 224–29, at 225.

69. Lahey, "Wyclif's Trinitarian and Christological Theology," 127–98, at 170. The aside is made in Wyclif, *De benedicta incarnacione*, 90.

70. See Hudson, "Dangerous Fictions," 197–214. Wyclif discusses indulgences in milder tones in *De ecclesia*, chapter 23, and in harsher tones in *John Wyclif: Trialogus*, 283–85.

71. Levy, "Wyclif on the Christian Life," 336–41.

following the Articles of Religion, which read concerning Purgatory: "The Romish Doctrine concerning Purgatory... is a fond thing, vainly invented, and grounded upon no warranty of Scripture, but rather repugnant to the Word of God."[72] In this, Wyclif was a man of his times, and differed rather markedly from his nineteenth-century admirers, at least in particulars about the function of the Cross and the doctrine of the atonement.

CONCLUSION

The emphases of Wyclif's theology might be seen in some ways to reflect the ethos and priorities of the founders of Wycliffe College; but in other ways, he seems as distant as one might imagine given the four intervening centuries between his death and the founding of the College. There are, without doubt, strong similarities between the theology of Wyclif and that of the founders of Wycliffe College, just as there are undoubtedly important and strong dissimilarities. Here it might be helpful to bring in once again the idea of family resemblance. The markers of resemblance are a profound respect for the Bible as the basis of Christian life and doctrine; an unflagging energy for the gospel and conversion; and a central place for the Cross of Christ in the redemption of sinners. Wyclif and nineteenth-century Anglican evangelicals are certainly in the same family tree; there are unmistakable family traits. Yet Wyclif might be thought of as a great-uncle rather than a great-grandfather, for there are unmistakable differences as well, most importantly the incompatibility of Wyclif's soteriology with a solafideist position, including his espousal of the doctrine of Purgatory, his unmistakable skepticism about certainty regarding who is and who is not saved, and his entirely medieval worldview, including a thoroughly medieval understanding of Scripture. There was much for the founders of Wycliffe College to admire about the man they thought of as the Morning Star of the Reformation, but much of what they thought of him was founded in misunderstanding and Protestant myth. Nonetheless, even when we strip away the varnish, there is much to which evangelical Anglicans can aspire, and if the truest mark of an evangelical is a love of the gospel, then John Wyclif would put the most ardent evangelical to shame.

72. *The Book of Common Prayer* (1962), 707.

BIBLIOGRAPHY

Bambrough, Renford. "Universals and Family Resemblances." *Proceedings of the Aristotelian Society* 61 (1960–61) 207–22.

Bebbington, David W. *Evangelicalism in Modern Britain: A History from the 1730s to the 1980s.* London: Routledge, 2002.

The Book of Common Prayer. Toronto: Anglican Book Centre, 1962.

Buddensieg, Rudolf, ed. *John Wyclif's Polemical Works in Latin.* London: Wyclif Society, 1883.

Burrows, Montagu. *Wiclif's Place in History.* London: Isbister, 1884.

Conti, Alessandro D. "Wyclif's Logic and Metaphysics." In *A Companion to John Wyclif: Late Medieval Theologian,* edited by Ian C. Levy, 67–126. Leiden, The Netherlands: Brill, 2008.

Crompton, James. "John Wyclif: A Study in Mythology." *Transactions of the Leicestershire Archaeological and Historical Society* 42 (1966–67) 6–34.

Deanesly, Margaret. *The Lollard Bible and Other Medieval Biblical Versions.* Cambridge: Cambridge University Press, 1920.

De Lubac, Henri. *Medieval Exegesis: The Four Senses of Scripture.* 3 vols. Grand Rapids, MI: Eerdmans, 1998–2009.

Dove, Mary. "Wyclif and the English Bible." In *A Companion to John Wyclif: Late Medieval Theologian,* edited by Ian C. Levy, 365–406. Leiden, The Netherlands: Brill, 2008.

Evans, G. R. *John Wyclif: Myth and Reality.* Downers Grove, IL: IVP Academic, 2005.

Gradon, Pamela, and Anne Hudson, eds. *English Wycliffite Sermons.* 5 vols. Oxford: Oxford University Press, 1983–1986.

Hague, Dyson. "The History of Wycliffe College." In *The Jubilee Volume of Wycliffe College,* 1–60. Toronto: University of Toronto Press, 1927.

———. *The Life and Works of John Wycliffe.* 2nd ed. London: The Church Book Room, 1935.

Hague, Dyson, et al. *The Jubilee Volume of Wycliffe College 1877–1927–1937.* Toronto: Wycliffe College, 1938.

Haykin, Michael A. G., and Kenneth Stewart, eds. *The Emergence of Evangelicalism: Exploring Historical Continuities.* Nottingham, UK: Apollos, 2008.

Hornbeck, J. Patrick. *What is a Lollard? Dissent and Belief in Late Medieval England.* Oxford: Oxford University Press, 2010.

Hudson, Anne. "Dangerous Fictions: Indulgences in the Thought of Wyclif and his Followers." In *Promissory Notes on the Treasury of Merits: Indulgences in Late Medieval Europe,* edited by R. N. Swanson, 197–214. Leiden, The Netherlands: Brill, 2006.

———. *The Premature Reformation: Wycliffite Texts and Lollard History.* Oxford: Oxford University Press, 1988.

Jocz, Jakob. "*Beginnings*: The Principleship of James Paterson Sheraton." In *The Enduring Word: A Centennial History of Wycliffe College,* edited by Arnold Edinborough, 3–22. Toronto: University of Toronto Press, 1977.

Katerburg, William H. "Redefining Evangelicalism in the Canadian Anglican Church: Wycliffe College and the Evangelical Party, 1867–1995." In *Aspects of the Canadian Evangelical Experience,* edited by George A. Rawlyk, 171–88. Montreal: McGill-Queen's University Press, 1997.

Kienzle, Beverly Mayne, ed. *The Sermon.* Typologies des source du moyen age occidental, fasc. 81–83. Turnhout: Brepols, 2000.

Lahey, Stephen E. *John Wyclif.* Oxford: Oxford University Press, 2009.

———. "Wyclif's Trinitarian and Christological Theology." In *A Companion to John Wyclif: Late Medieval Theologian,* edited by Ian C. Levy, 127–98. Leiden, The Netherlands: Brill, 2008.

Lahey, Stephen E, ed. and trans. *John Wyclif: Trialogus.* Cambridge: Cambridge University Press, 2013.

Larsen, Timothy. "Defining and Locating Evangelicalism." In *The Cambridge Companion to Evangelical Theology,* edited by Timothy Larsen and Daniel J. Treier, 1–12. Cambridge: Cambridge University Press, 2007.

Levy, Ian C. "Grace and Freedom in the Soteriology of John Wyclif." *Traditio* 60 (2005) 279–337.

———. *Holy Scripture and the Quest for Authority at the End of the Middle Ages.* Notre Dame, IN: University of Notre Dame Press, 2012.

———. "John Wyclif and the Christian Life." In *A Companion to John Wyclif: Late Medieval Theologian,* edited by Ian C. Levy. Leiden, The Netherlands: Brill, 2008.

———. *John Wyclif's Theology of the Eucharist in Its Medieval Context: Revised and Expanded Edition of Scriptural Logic, Real Presence, and the Parameters of Orthodoxy.* Milwaukee, WI: Marquette University Press, 2015.

Levy, Ian C., ed. *A Companion to John Wyclif: Late Medieval Theologian.* Leiden, The Netherlands: Brill, 2008.

Levy, Ian C., ed. and trans. *John Wyclif: On the Truth of Holy Scripture.* Kalamazoo, MI: MIP, 2001.

MacFarlane, K. B. *John Wycliffe and the Beginnings of English Non-Conformity.* London: English University Press, 1952.

Mudroch, Vaclav. *The Wyclyf Tradition.* Edited by Albert Compton Reeves. Athens, OH: Ohio University Press, 1979.

Otto, Sean A. "The Authority of the Preacher in a Sermon of John Wyclif." *Mirator* 12 (2011) 77–93.

———. "*Pastoralia* in John Wyclif's *Sermones*: Controversial Preaching in Later Medieval England." PhD diss., University of St. Michael's College, Toronto, 2013.

———. "Predestination and the Two Cities: The Authority of Augustine and the Nature of the Church in Giles of Rome and John Wyclif." In *Authorities in the Middle Ages: Influence, Legitimacy and Power in Medieval Society,* edited by Tuija Ainonen et al., 145–58. Berlin: DeGruyter, 2013.

Pilcher, C. Venn. "The Principles of Wycliffe College." In *The Jubilee Volume of Wycliffe College,* 103–43. Toronto: University of Toronto Press, 1927.

Reeves, Andrew. *Religious Education in Thirteenth-Century England: The Creed and Articles of Faith.* Leiden, The Netherlands: Brill, 2015.

Šmahel, Frantisek. "'*Doctor evangelicus super omnes evangelistas*': Wyclif's Fortune in Hussite Bohemia," *Historical Research* 43.107 (1970) 16–34.

Smalley, Beryl. *The Study of the Bible in the Middle Ages.* 3rd ed. Notre Dame, IN: University of Notre Dame Press, 1989.

Wallace, W. S. "The Life and Works of George M. Wrong." *The Canadian Historical Review* 39.3 (1948) 229–39.

Wittgenstein, Ludwig. *Philosophical Investigations.* Translated by G. E. M. Anscombe. 2nd ed. Oxford: Oxford University Press, 1997.

Workman, H. B. *John Wyclif: A Study of the Late Medieval English Church*. 2 vols. Oxford: Clarendon, 1926.

Wrong, George M. *The Crusade of 1383: Known as That of the Bishop of Norwich*. London: James Parker, 1892.

Wyclif, John. *De benedicta incarnacione*. Edited by E. Harris. London: Wyclif Society, 1886.

———. *De dominio divino*. Edited by Reginald Lane Poole, 4 vols. London: Wyclif Society, 1890–.

———. *De ecclesia*. London: Wyclif Society, 1886.

———. *De veritate sacre scripture*. Edited by Rudolph Buddensieg, 3 vols. London: Wyclif Society, 1905–6.

———. *Sermones*. Edited by Johann Loserth, 4 vols. London: Wyclif Society, 1887–90

Wycliffe College Archives. *The Calendar of the Protestant Episcopal Divinity School*. Toronto: [n.p.], 1881.

Index

Africa, 8, 14, 25, 27, 99, 133, 134, 250, 277
Alderwood, H., 257
Alexander, Sarah Ann (Sadie), 256
Alexander, William, 13, 16
Allman, Margaret, 257
Alvery, Henry (Toronto), 93
Andrewartha, John, 293
Anglican Women's Training College, 213, 228, 241, 243–47, 249–52, 260, 262–64, 267–68
Annesley, William Richard, 3rd earl of Annesley, 35
Apocalypticism, 5, 6, 113–14, 119, 125, 167–68
Aquinas, Thomas, 308
Ardagh, diocese of, 30, 172
Armagh, diocese of, 15, 17, 19, 32, 43, 87, 110, 122
Arminianism, 48, 54, 56, 72, 97, 98, 202
Armitage, Ramsay, 245
Armour, Samuel, 176
Armstrong, John, 154
Armstrong, Nicholas, 50
Armstrong, William Chambers, 134
Ashley-Cooper, Anthony, 7th earl of Shaftesbury, 154
Asia, 8, 246, 253, 254, 257
Association of Discountenancing Vice, 8
Atkins, Walter, 153
Atonement, 7, 60, 62, 63, 65, 69–75, 99, 187, 214, 295, 313–14

Australia
    clergy recruitment, 278–84
    clergy influence, 284–89
    cultural influence, 289–92
    pastoral role, 292–93
    theological diversity, 294–95

Bagot, Sir Charles, 204
Bailey, Edna Cecilia, 257
Baker, Hugh Ryves, 157
Baldry, Gertrude, 257
Baldwin, Maurice S., 235, 236
Baldwin, Robert, 206
Balfour, Andrew, 192
Bandinel, Bulkeley, 91
Bandon, 172
Barker, Frederic, 28
Barrett, Jackie, 52
Barry, Redmond, 280
Baylee, Joseph, 31, 149, 150, 156–57
Bayly, Mary, 257
Beamish, Peter, 282, 283, 285, 294
Bedell, William, 93, 98, 134, 140
Belfast, 32, 36, 37
Bell-Cox, James, 153
Bellett, George, 50, 54
Bellett, John, 50, 54
Belsham, Thomas, 62
Bennett, Verna, 257
Benson, Christopher, 106
Benwell, Rosemary Anne, 249, 271
Beresford, George, 135
Beresford, John George, 22–23, 82, 110–12

Bernard, James, 2nd earl of Bandon, 172
Bernard, Nicholas, 92
Bethesda Chapel, 7, 18–20, 23, 26, 52
Bethune, A. N., 190–91, 208, 210–11
Bible
  higher criticism, 202, 217
Bickersteth, Edward, 25, 155
Bickersteth, Robert, 155
Biddle, Mary, 262, 271
Birkenhead, 8, 31, 146, 147, 148, 149, 150
Birmingham, 151, 152
Bishop Strachan School, 212
Black, Charles Ingham, 153
Blacker, Miss L, 134
Blacker, Lucinda, 134
Blair, Robert, 88, 89
Blake, Dominick Edward Jr. 8, 30, 172, 176, 182, 185, 192, 203
Blake, Dominick Edward Sr., 8
Blake, Edward, 30, 176
Blake, Frances, 30
Blake, Samuel Hume, 9, 10, 176, 191, 192, 201–23, 242
Blake, Sophia (Sophy), 176
Blake, William, 30
Blake, William Hume, 176, 203, 207
Blakeney, Richard Paul, 148
Blest, Albert, 137
Blomfield, Charles James, bishop of London, 154
Blosse, Francis Lynch, 91–92
Board of First Fruits, 32
Boldrewood, Rolf, 287
Bond, William, bishop of Montreal, 29
Book of Common Prayer, 189, 232, 245, 304, 308
Boyd, Archibald, 146
Boyd, David, 287
Boyton, Charles, 5
Bradley, June, 246, 251, 258, 260, 263, 271
Bradley, Dorothy, 257
Bramhall, John, 84, 93, 95, 96
Brandon, diocese of, 251, 252, 261

Britain, 1, 62, 75, 86, 131, 144, 170, 177, 183, 191, 202, 210, 277, 279, 283, 292
British and Foreign Bible Society, 133, 134, 230
Brough, Charles, 8, 30, 176, 182, 192, 194
Broughton, William Grant, 285
Browne, Henry, 289
Browne, William, 281, 292, 294, 295
Bryan, Bernard, 261
Bucer, Martin, 56
Bulteel, Henry, 55, 56
Burgess, Henry, 192
Burgh, Walter Hussey, 28, 280
Burke, Edmund, 18, 27, 296
Bushe, William, 22
Butcher, Samuel, 35
Butler, Joseph, 63, 64, 65, 67, 70–72, 75–77
Butler, William Archer, 33

Calvin, John, 54, 89, 92–93, 286
Calvinism, 48, 54, 56, 68–69, 72, 74, 81–82, 84–85, 89, 91–95, 97–98, 163, 191, 202–4, 207, 222
Cambridge University, 8, 17, 23, 29, 43, 46, 108, 115, 122, 143, 145, 157, 164, 165, 169, 178, 179, 180, 193, 196, 203
Campbell, John McLeod, 74
Canada, 1, 3, 5, 8–11, 13, 27, 29–30, 39, 81, 123–24, 141, 166–68, 170–73, 175, 177, 180, 182, 185–86, 190, 192, 194–95, 201, 204–7, 209–10, 215–16, 219, 221–22, 226–73, 277, 296, 303, 310
Canterbury
  Convocation, 232–34
Carleton, William, 15
Carmichael, James, 30, 180, 190
Carruthers, Ruth, 248
Catholic Association, 2
Caton, Ina, 252
Caulfield, Charles, 32
Cayley, John D'Arcy, 217–18
Centre for Christian Studies, 213, 228, 268

Ceylon, 133, 140
Chabot, Rev, 257
Chalmers, Thomas, 292
Chapels of Ease Act, 32
Chappell, William, 96, 98
Charlesworth, Hector, 210
Chester, diocese of, 30, 31, 146, 151
Cheyne, John, 280, 285
Chile, 250
China, 27, 250, 253, 256, 283, 292
cholera, 3, 33
Christian and Missionary Alliance, 215
Christology, 61
Church Army, 229
Church Association, 148, 158, 191, 209–11, 303
Church Education Society, 139
Church Home Mission, 23, 25–26, 35
Church Missionary Society, 8, 14, 23, 139, 219, 230, 283
  Hibernian, 8, 21, 25, 133
Church of England, 8, 13, 14, 29, 30, 31, 35, 72, 82, 93, 94, 95, 103, 118, 121, 122, 125, 143, 144, 146, 149, 153, 156, 163, 177, 193, 195, 202–5, 208–9, 212, 215–16, 219, 220, 227–28, 231–34, 238, 241–43, 252, 293, 301, 303–5, 308
Church of England Deaconess and Training Missionary House (Toronto), 228
Church of England Self-Supporting Village Society, 293
Church of Ireland
  articles (1615), 20, 84, 92, 94–95, 98
  clergy, 3–4, 14, 28, 99, 167, 173, 279, 296
  emigrants, 3–4, 6, 8–9, 28–30, 35, 99, 167–68, 176–77, 180, 193, 195, 279, 296
  evangelical, 2, 5, 7–8, 10–11, 13–39, 41, 48–56, 63, 72–73, 75, 83–85, 99, 103, 106, 110, 121, 130–32, 141, 144–56, 158, 162–64, 170–73, 179, 190–93, 195, 201, 204–18, 222–23, 278, 282, 284–86, 294–96
  general synod, 13
  historiography, 80, 99, 104, 106, 122–23
  laity, 4, 6, 17, 35, 99, 103, 164–65, 167, 191–92, 204, 208
  parishes, 2, 19, 26, 27, 30, 34, 36, 38, 50, 103, 108, 129, 132–36, 138, 188, 195, 205
  population, 1, 9, 29, 168, 177–78, 190, 204, 279
Church Temporalities Act (1833), 2, 3, 80, 109, 144, 279
Clark, Howard, 244
Clarke, Samuel, 67, 71
Clute, Frances, 257
Cody, Henry, 207, 212, 214, 216, 218, 223, 245
Coleridge, Samuel Taylor, 27, 61, 72–73
Coleman, F. J., 257
Collins, Ida, 262
Conyngham, William, 35
Connacht, 32, 33
Connell, Thomasina, 242, 244–45, 247
Connor, diocese of, 36, 80, 88
Cooke, Henry, 16, 85
Coolen, Betty, 257
Cooper, Anthony Ashley, 7th earl of Shaftesbury, 154
Cooper, Edward Synge, 135
Copleston, Edward, 110, 120
Cork, 28, 32, 33, 34, 81, 154
Cotton, Henry, 86, 105
Cox, Betty, 258, 261
Cox, Frederick, 292, 295
Crabtree, Dora Ann, 257
Cranmer, Thomas, 117
Crookes, Anne, 240
Cronyn, Benjamin, 5, 9, 10, 30, 170, 171, 176, 179, 180, 182, 183–84, 190, 192–95, 205, 208
Cronyn, Margaret, 176, 207
Cronyn, Rebecca, 176, 207
Cronyn, Verschoyle, 176, 207
Cross, Frances (Fanny), 242
Cullen, Paul, Cardinal, 102

Cumberland, Ernest Augustus, duke of, 110
Curwood, Helen, 257
Cusack, Margaret, 113

Dale, Thomas Pelham, 233
Daley, Dorothy, 271
Dallas, Alexander, 35
Dalton, Henry, 50
Daly, Robert, 14–15, 50
Darby, Anne, 42
Darby, Christopher, 43
Darby, John, 42
Darby, John Nelson, 4–5, 8, 10, 21, 41–56
Davies, Rowland, 281, 292, 295
Dawson, John, 136
Day, Maurice F., 24, 36
Deaconesses
  ministries, 249–66
  office, 233–41
  origins, 229–33
  sources, 227–29
  training, 242–49
  end, 266–73
Deaconess School, 9, 213
de Blaquière, Peter, 207
deism, 62, 63, 65–66, 70, 73, 114
Denroche, Edward, 187, 192
Dickinson, Charles, 110
Digby family, 5
Digby, William, 20, 21, 28
Dixon, H. C., 218
Donegal, 19, 33, 282
Donovan, Daniel, 155
Down, diocese of, 36, 80, 88
Draper, Rosemary, 269
Driscoll, John, 193
Dromore Clerical Society, 19
Dromore, diocese of, 17
Drought, Robert, 293
Drummond, Henry, 147
Dublin, 4, 7, 10, 15, 16, 17
du Moulin, John Philip, 30, 180, 190

Echlin, Robert, 88, 89
Edgar, Annie, 242, 267
Egypt, 250

Elphin, diocese of, 20, 21, 35, 135
Elrington, Charles Richard, 4, 23, 80–87, 90–99, 111, 122, 144, 149, 191, 281, 283, 296
Elrington, Thomas, 45, 49, 91
Emancipation Act (1829), 6, 29, 49, 80, 109, 131, 144, 167
Emerson, Norman, 26
Emery, Harriet, 242, 243, 244, 256, 261–62
Enraght, Richard William, 151
eschatology, 56
Evangelical Alliance, 214
Evangelical Association, 191, 303
evangelical/evangelicalism, 2, 5, 7–8, 10–11, 13–32, 36, 38–39, 41, 48–56, 72–73, 75, 83–85, 99, 103, 106, 110, 121, 130–32, 141, 144–58, 162–64, 170–73, 179, 190–95, 201, 203–18, 222–23, 230–37, 240, 243–48, 278, 281–86, 290, 294–96, 300–314
  definition, 301
  activism, 301, 310–12
  biblicism, 301, 312–13
  conversionism, 301, 307–10
  crucicentrism, 301, 313–14
Evans, Francis, 172, 185, 192
Exham, Beth Ann, 244, 256, 258, 263

Falloon, William Marcus, 148, 150, 156–57
famine, 29, 31–34, 39, 141, 144, 150, 205, 279, 280
Farrell, James, 28, 282
Faulkner, Gwyneth, 257
Faussett, Miss, 133
Ferard, Elizabeth, 232
Ferns and Leighlin, diocese of, 3, 109, 121
Ffrench, Edmond, 34
First Nations see Indigenous
Fitzgerald, William, 106
Flanagan, John, 187
Fleury, Dr. Charles, 30
Flood, Richard, 30, 171, 176, 182, 186, 189, 192
Forster, Audrey, 262, 271

Foster, Margaret, 254
Fowler, Marguerita, 251–52
Fowler, Robert, 18
Frame, John, 270
France, 42, 114, 137
Freke, James, 32
French Revolution, 5, 49, 114
Froude, Richard Hurrell, 115
Fry, Henry Phibbs, 280–81, 284, 289–92, 294–96
Fry, Oliver, 281
Fulton, Henry, 16, 28–29, 285–87, 294

Gandier, Ruby-Maude, 257
Gardiner, Elias William, 257
Gardner, Ruth, 257
Garratt, Samuel, 154
Garrett, John, 136
Gibbs, F. H., 257
Gibson, William, 37
Gladstone, William Ewart, 153, 294
Glasgow, 293
Godley, John, 82
Gooderham, Margaret, 246
Gore, Norman, 257
Gore, William, 282
Grace, Thomas, 20
Grant, Charles, 22
Graves, James, 86
Graves, Richard, 22, 49, 55, 56
Gray, Frances, 252, 257
Gray, Robert, 67
Green, Brian, 264
Green(e), Thomas, 171, 175, 184, 188, 195
Gregg, John, 26–27
Gregg, Robert Samuel, 26–27
Grey, Charles, 2nd earl Grey, 110, 145, 290–91
Griffith, Charles, 280
Guinness, Arthur, 19, 172
Guinness, Hosea, 22

Hains, Philip, 150
Hales, Francis, 282, 285
Hamilton, Charles, 212
Hamilton, George, 14, 22
Hamilton, Hugh, 14, 21

Hamilton, William Rowan, 111
Hannah, Helene, 251
Hannan, Rev, 139
Hardinge, William, 86
Harris, Elmore, 213
Harrison, Mary Elizabeth, 257
Harte, Henry, 47
Hasell, Eva, 248
Havergal College, 202, 203, 212, 236
Havergal, Frances Ridley, 212
Hawkins, Frances, 254
Hay, Dorothy, 257
Hellaby, Hilda, 254, 255, 263, 270
Hewitt, Sir George, 22
Hewitt, James, 2nd viscount Lifford, 17, 22
Heylin, Peter, 94–95
Hibernian Bible Society, 9, 20–21, 33, 130, 134, 139
  Sligo branch, 9
Hibernian Church Missionary Society, 21, 22, 133, 134, 138
Hibernian Sunday School Society, 130
Hill, Bold Cudmore, 172
Hill, G. A., 174
Hincks, Edward, 14, 37
Hinds, Samuel, 281, 283
Hinton, Harold, 257
Hobart, 282, 290, 292, 295
Hobson, Richard, 150, 155–57
Hodgins, J. G., 209
Hodgkinson, Francis, 111
Holtby, Mary, 257
home rule, 112, 157, 294
Horobin, Hattie, 254
Howard, Charles, 28, 289
Howard, George William Frederick, 7th earl of Carlisle, 26
Howard Society, 19
Howland, W. H., 214–15
Howson, John Saul, 231–32
Hoyles, Norman Wright, 236
Hume, Abraham, 150
Hume, Catherine, 203
Huron College, 10, 180, 184, 208
Huron, diocese of, 9, 29, 30, 182, 184, 190–92, 193, 195–96, 205, 207, 210, 235

324 Index

hymnody, 15, 27, 113, 189, 209, 216–17

India, 14, 25, 27, 75, 133, 137, 250, 253, 277
Indigenous, 30, 35, 133–34, 138, 171, 182, 184, 186, 189, 196–99, 219–21, 227, 229, 246, 248, 253, 255, 259, 269, 272, 279
International Sunday School Committee, 215
Irish Church Missions, 35, 155
Irish Protestant Benevolent Society, 221
Irish Society, 21, 22, 33, 35, 130, 136, 137, 139, 140
Irving, Edward, 147
Irwin, Frederick, 282
Irwin, Henry, 21, 22
Isherwood, T. W., 257
Island and Coast Society, 21, 32

Jacob, Mary Nameria, 235
Jacobs, Peter, 189
Jamaica, 42, 139
Japan, 250, 253, 254
Jebb, John, 16, 17, 20, 21, 31, 33, 51, 110, 121
Jewell, John, 56, 117
Jews, 125, 139, 147, 246, 250, 253
Jocelyn, Robert, 3rd earl of Roden, 20, 154, 172
Johnson, William, 192
Jones, David, 265
Jones, Mabel, 240, 247
Jones, Trever, 246

Keane, John, 293–94
Kearney, Henry, 50, 54
Keble, John, 118, 124
Keewatin, diocese of, 216
Kelly, Thomas, 4, 7, 18
Kelly, Thomas snr, judge, 18
Kentucky, 37
Kenya, 27
Kilkenny, 21, 30, 32, 171, 187, 280, 288
Killala and Achonry, diocese of, 34

Killaloe, diocese of, 28, 106
King, George, 294
King, Sir Robert, Viscount Lorton, 22
King, Robert, 82, 86
King's Inns, 15, 44
Kingsmill, Joseph, 154
Kirkpatrick, Richard Carr, 152–53
Knox, Alexander, 51, 110, 121
Knox College, Toronto, 217
Knox, Edmund, 212
Knox, Ellen, 212
Knox, John, 89
Knox, Robert, 36–37
Knox, William, 28
Kyle, Samuel, 49, 82, 110

Lambeth Articles, 95
Lambeth Conference, 190, 238–39, 269–70
Lancashire, 8, 146, 151
La Touche, J. D., 21
Laud, William, 93, 95–98, 100, 202
Lecky, W.E.H., 13
Lefroy, Thomas, 15, 21, 32
Lefroy, William, 146
Leo XII, 35
Lew, Joan, 246, 253
Lewis, John Travers, 4–5, 81, 184–85, 190–91, 194–95, 203
Liberal Party (Canada), 206
Lightbourn, Frances Gray, 271
Lightbourn, Gilbert, 257
Littledale, Richard, 153
Liverpool, 8, 30, 31, 146–48, 150, 153, 158
Lloyd, Bartholomew, 23, 110, 111, 144
Lloyd, George Exton, 240
Locke, John, 45, 49, 68
Loftus, Adam, 93
London City Mission, 230
London Hibernian Society, 130, 137
Long, William, 154

Macartney, Hussey Burgh, 28, 280, 285, 287, 289, 294
Macdonnell, Sir Richard Graves, 28
Mack, Frederick, 171, 172
MacNeece (McNeece), Thomas, 38

Magee, William, 7, 22–23, 35, 49, 52, 60–77, 110, 187
Magee, William Connor, 146, 193
Magrath, James, 173–74
Magrath, Thomas William, 173
Maguire, Robert, 154
Mahaffy, J. P., 26
Maitland, Samuel Roffey, 83, 105, 114–17, 292
Manchester, 30, 53, 151, 158, 212
Mansel, H. L., 61, 76–77
Mant, Richard, 4, 80–81, 83, 85–89, 92, 99, 122
Marsden, Samuel, 28–29
Martin, Clara Brett, 211
Martyr, Peter, 56, 151
Mason, Henry Monck, 15, 19
Masters, Daisy, 256
Mathias, Benjamin, 7, 19–20, 22–23, 26, 35
Matthews, Ruth, 271
Maturin, C. R., 15
Maturin, Henry, 18–20, 22, 50
Maude, F., 172
Maunsell, George
Maurice, F. D., 61, 72–77
Maynooth College, 115, 276
McCalmont, Hugh, 15
McCaul, John, 204, 207, 303
McFarlane, Lloyd George, 257
McGee, Elsie, 257
McGee, Robert, 195
McIlvaine, Charles, 28, 36–37
McMurray, William, 171, 186
McNeile, Hugh, 22–23, 31, 146–48, 150, 156
Meares, Matthew, 293
Medley, John, 216, 226, 235
Mennonites, 187
Methodism, 14, 18, 73, 102, 168, 177, 181, 187–88, 196, 232, 294, 311
Mildmay Conference Centre, 155
Mildmay Institute, 10, 31, 247, 248, 252
Mildmay Deaconess House, 10, 31, 233, 237, 242, 247
Mill, John Stuart, 55
millennialism, 56, 90, 132, 147, 214

mission, 2, 8, 9, 10,11, 14, 15, 21, 23, 25, 27, 30, 35, 75–76, 129–35, 137–41, 147, 149, 150, 152–55, 162,166–68, 170–75, 178, 180–89, 192, 194–95, 201, 209, 212–14, 216, 218, 220–21, 228–33, 235–36, 242–43, 247–51, 253–60, 262, 264, 273, 277–78, 281–83, 291–92, 310
Missionary Society (MSCC), 219, 242, 252
Monsell, William, Lord Emly, 112
Montagu, William, duke of Manchester, 154
Montgomery, Henry, 16
Montreal, 29, 180, 182, 190, 215
Moody, D.L., 10
Moore, Stephen, 3rd earl of Mountcashel, 172
Moravian, 293
Morton, Thomas, 75
Mostyn, George, 136
Muncey [Monsee], 30
Munster, 15, 31, 32
Murray, Richard, 45, 172

Naftel, Emma, 242
Nangle, Edward, 149
Napier, Sir Joseph, 15
Nash, Richard, 49
National education, 2
Nathanael Institute (Toronto), 253, 262
Nelson, Isaac, 37
New Brunswick, 216, 226, 234, 235, 237, 261
Newfoundland, 134, 259, 267
Newman, Francis, 55
Newman, John Henry, 54, 64, 103, 106, 109, 110, 114–22, 124–25, 152, 295
New South Wales, 28, 281, 283, 285, 292
New Westminster, 240, 254, 263
New York, 140, 242
New Zealand, 8, 13, 27, 277, 280, 286, 295
Nightingale, Florence, 231, 232

326　Index

Niblock, Rev., 257
Niven, Marion, 242, 249, 262
Nixon, Francis Russell, 285
nominalism, 65, 68
Norfolk Island, 29
Norton, John, 134

Oakley, Frederick, 154
O'Brien, James Thomas, 14, 16, 24, 39, 109, 121
O'Connell, Daniel, 2
O'Conor, Charles, 92
O'Curry, Eugene, 112
O'Donovan, John, 112
O'Hara, Charles, 135
Ojibwa, 171, 182, 188, 189, 194, 197
O'Meara, Frederick Augustus, 172, 179, 181–82, 185–86, 188–89, 191–95, 197
O'Neill, Henry H., 172, 181, 187
Ontario, see Upper Canada
Ontario, diocese of, 4, 81, 185, 190, 191–92, 194, 196, 203, 234
Orange Order/Orangeism, 5, 115, 120, 121, 125, 144, 148, 149, 150, 278
Osler, F. L., 181, 193, 194
Ossory Clerical Association, 8, 21
Ossory, diocese of, 14, 16, 21, 22, 24, 32, 109, 121
Otway, Caesar, 15, 25–26, 84
Owen, Derwyn, 240, 262
Owen, Robert, 293
Oxford Movement, 4, 102, 109, 114, 116, 121–22, 124–26, 151
Oxford University, 46, 55, 108, 115, 169, 178, 193, 203, 312
　Bodleian, 107

Parr, Richard, 96–97
Palmer, Arthur, 30, 172, 182, 185
Palmer, William, 115
Pastorini, Signor, 5, 131
Patrick, St., 48, 93, 113, 145
Paul, St., 20, 45, 227
Pearson, J. L., 152
Peers, Michael, 257
Pennefather, Catherine, 31

Pennefather, Edward, 10, 15, 44,
Pennefather, William, 10, 24, 25, 31, 32, 155, 233
Perceval, Robert, 19, 22
Perry, Charles, 28, 283, 285
Peters, Miss, 244
Pezzack, Margery, 271
Phear, J. B., 157
Philadelphia, 42, 242
Phillips, L., 257
Philpott, Henry, 151–52
Phipps, Robert, 111
Pilcher, Charles Venn, 307
Plymouth Brethren, 4, 41
Pogson, Ruth, 260, 261, 266
Pollock, James S, 151–52
Pollock, Thomas, 151–52
Ponsonby, John, 172
Potter, Lewis, 137
Powerscourt, Theodosia Lady, 4
Pratt, Josiah, 50
Presbyterian, 2, 4, 19, 81–85, 88, 99, 102, 204, 294
　Church, 14, 16, 37, 126
Priestley, Joseph, 62
Prior, Thomas, 52, 111
Prisoners Aid Society, 214
Prophecies, 4–5, 56, 113, 119, 131,165, 214
Protestant Churchman's Union and Tract Society, 214
Protestant Episcopal Divinity School, 10, 191, 300, 301, 303–5, 307
Public Worship Act (1874), 153
Purdon, Richard, 46
puritan/puritanism, 92–93, 95, 97, 102, 105, 113, 122, 125, 202
Pye-Smith, John, 71

Quarry, John, 20
Quebec, 133, 167, 171, 172, 175, 189, 193, 215, 234, 253
Quirt, Bessie, 253

Radcliff, Arthur, 174
Radcliff, Thomas, 174, 176, 191
Radcliff, William, 174
Rae (Ray), Annie, 238, 256

Rainsford, William, 209
Raphoe, diocese of, 17, 20, 22, 50, 60
Reeves, William, 82, 86
Reform act (1832), 109,
Reformed Episcopal Church, 215
Reformed theology, 23, 37, 62, 71–72, 75, 103, 115, 118
Reid, James Seaton, 84, 88–89, 94–95, 97–98
Rendell, Mary, 252, 271
residential schools, 208, 219–21, 229, 246, 248, 253, 259
Ridley College, 202, 203, 212, 236
Ritualism, 122, 148, 153–54, 201, 215
Robinson, Margaret E., 251
Robinson, Pamela, 257
Robinson, Thomas, 47
Roe, Peter, 8, 21, 22, 30, 171
Rogers, Thomas, 289, 295
Roman Catholic, 1–4, 29, 31–32, 34–36, 48, 51, 81, 83–84, 102, 108, 113–15, 120, 122, 125, 131, 136, 139–40, 146, 148, 151, 154–55, 158, 165–66, 177–78, 203–4, 215, 232, 234, 279, 294–95
romantic movement, 7, 15, 50
Rose, Hugh James, 115, 116, 117
Row, Thora Wade, 271
Rowan, Arthur, 15
Rowan, Robert S., 151
Rowe, Lionel, 257
Royal Irish Academy, 14, 19, 111
Rupert's Land, diocese of, 189, 216
Russell, Francis, 281, 283, 285, 287, 291–92, 294

Sadleir, Franc, 107, 111
St. Aidan's College, 31, 147, 150, 157–58
Salmon, George, 15, 24, 35, 38, 39
Sandys, Suzanne Lucinda, 238
Saskatchewan, diocese of, 240, 247, 252
Sayle, Iris, 248
Schoales, John Whitelaw, 282
Scotland, 36, 46, 72, 88–89, 112, 126, 140, 177, 179, 292
Scott, Ruth, 242, 250, 253, 256
Scotus, Duns, 308
Scovil, Coster, 257
Scripture Readers Society, 21, 130
Scriven, Elizabeth, 134
Scriven, Samuel, 134
Seaborn, Robert L., 267
Seaver, George, 32, 36
Secretan, Muriel, 251
Sedgwick, J. E., 158
Seychelles, The, 76
Shanley, Bev, 271
Shaw, George Bernard, 15
Shaw, Robert, 32
Shedd, William G. T., 62
Sheraton, J.P., 212, 214
Shore, Edith, 263–64, 271
Sierra Leone, 27
Simpson, William, 257
Sinclair, Rev, 257
Singer, Joseph H, 7, 8, 23–26, 53–54, 56, 84, 144
Singleton, William, 280, 285
Sisters of St. John the Divine, 235, 244
Skey, Lawrence, 218
Sligo and Western Evangelical Society, 137
Smith, William, 62
Smithurst, J., 138
Smyly, Josiah, 19
Smyth, Arthur, 18
Smyth, Edward, 18
Smyth, William, 18–19
Snake, James, 186
Snell, George, 270–71
Snuggs, Ruth, 253
Society for Converting and Civilizing the Indians and Propagating the Gospel Among Destitute Settlers, 170, 173
Society for the Propagation of the Gospel, 8, 27, 30, 169, 220, 281
socinianism, 23–24, 63
Soules, Norma, 263
souperism, 34
South Africa, 27, 250, 277
Soward, Reg, 241, 243–45
Soward, Ruth Cornish, 241, 243–45
Stack, William, 292, 294

Index

Stackhouse, Reg, 257
Stanley, Muriel, 257
Stawell, William, 280
Steel, Margaret, 244, 262
Stewart, Charles, 167, 171, 172, 175, 193
Stewart Travelling Mission Fund, 186
Stock, Joseph, 45
Stokes, Whitley, 49, 111
Stone, William, 280, 288
Stopford, Edward, 35, 37, 83
Stopford, Joseph, 20, 22, 24, 49, 51
Strachan, John, 163–69, 171–73, 175–76, 179–80, 182, 185–86, 189–91, 193, 196, 204, 206–8, 212
Stringer, Isaac, 256
Sullivan, Edward, 30, 179–80, 190
Sumner, John Bird, 31, 146–47, 154
Sunday School by Post, 229, 258
Sunday School Society, 21, 130, 139
Surdivall, H., 257
Suzuki, Aya, 254
Sweatman, Arthur, 211, 216, 256
Sydney, 16, 28, 280, 282, 285, 287
Synge family, 5, 15

Tamkin, Mary Alice, 264
Tasmania, 276, 281, 284, 285, 289–94
Taylor, Henry, 62
Taylor, Letitia Jane, 152
Taylor, W. E., 257
Thirty-nine Articles, 56, 95–96, 301, 304, 308
Thompson, Gilbert, 249
Thorpe, Dr., 140
Tighe, Thomas, 17, 19
Tithe, 3–4, 6, 29, 80, 136, 144, 167, 279
Todd, James Henthorn, 4, 82–83, 85–86, 89–90, 93, 102–26, 151, 191, 281, 296
Todd, Robert Bentley, 103, 115
Todd, William Gowan, 86
Toleration Act, 18,
Tompson, Charles, 286
Tone, Wolfe, 28
Tonna, Charlotte Elizabeth, 230

Toplady, A. M., 14
Toronto Bible Training School, 213
Toronto, diocese of, 169, 174, 178, 182, 184, 185, 189, 191, 204, 210–11, 216, 218, 236, 238, 241, 247–48, 260, 264, 266, 270–71, 303
Toronto Mission Union, 214
Toronto Willard Tract Depository, 214
tory, 109–10, 123, 147, 202, 206, 290
Traill, Anthony, 32
Traill, Robert, 32
Tractaranism
Trafford, Mrs, 133
Travers, Walter, 93
Treadwell, Margaret, 259
Trench, Power Le Poer, archbishop of Tuam, 20–21, 23, 30, 33–35
Trench, Richard Chenevix, 32
Trench, Richard Le Poer, 2nd earl of Clancarty, 20
Trinity College Dublin
board, 81, 83, 87, 90, 108–11
chapel, 7, 23–26, 48, 165
College Theological Society, 26, 35
curriculum, 5–7, 23, 25, 44–47, 53, 61, 67, 72, 108, 164–66, 188, 191, 203
divinity school, 7, 14, 20, 22–26, 29, 36, 38, 62–63, 103, 107–8, 114, 123, 125, 144–45, 157, 164–66, 179, 193, 203, 296
Dublin University Magazine, 29, 112, 195
examinations, 24, 43–44, 46, 123, 145, 164–66
fellows, 8, 14, 17–20, 24, 42, 45–46, 48–50, 52–53, 56, 60, 82, 84, 86, 105, 108–11, 113, 115, 144, 151, 281, 296
library, 107, 114, 118
livings, 17, 19, 20, 22, 33, 38
tutors, 14, 25, 43, 53–54, 56, 105, 108, 111, 144, 166
Trinity College, Melbourne, 287
Trinity College, Toronto, 191, 196
Trollope, Anthony, 288, 293, 294

Tuam, diocese of, 21, 30, 31, 33
Tucker, Grace, 254
Tyndale College and Seminary, 213

Uganda, 27
Ulster, 82, 88
  plantation, 88–89, 122
  revival, 32, 36–38, 294
Union, Act of, 30, 42, 81, 117, 124, 130, 144
Unitarians, 7, 61–62, 69, 73
United Church of Canada, 268–69
United Irishmen, 28, 285
United States, 14, 28, 177, 184, 210, 227, 228, 230, 277, 279
University College, Toronto, 217
University of Toronto, 9, 30, 206–7, 217, 237, 242–43, 257, 306
Upper Canada, 29, 163, 177, 203, 206, 209, 215, 236, 238, 252, 259, 264, 271
Upper Canada Clergy Society, 171–73, 181–83
Upper Canada College, 180, 206
Upper Canadian Travelling Missionary Fund, 171
Ussher, Henry, 22
Ussher, James, 10, 80–81, 83–84, 87–98, 107, 114, 122, 202
Ussher, John, 22

Vancouver, 242, 246, 250, 251, 254, 262, 268, 271
Vaughan, Samuel, 42
Victoria College, Toronto, 217
Voltaire, 49

Waddilove, W. J. D., 171, 175, 195
Wade, Nugent, 153
Waldo, Peter, 306
Wales, 13, 177
Walker, John, 4, 7, 18, 19, 21, 28, 45, 49
Walker, Mae, 254
Wall, Charles William, 111
Walmesley, Charles see Pastorini, Signor

Walsh, William, 295
Watson, Joshua, 281
Watts, May, 242
Way, Wilbur, 257
Wells, George, 251
Wentworth, Thomas, 1st earl of Strafford, 84, 95–98
Wesley, John, 16, 17, 18, 48, 51, 72, 232, 286, 302, 311
West, John, 138
Western Australian Missionary Society, 282
Westminster School, 42, 47
Weymouth, Florence (Flossie), 257
Whately, Richard, 106, 110–11, 119–21, 125, 145, 163, 167, 175
whig, 2, 48, 106, 109–11, 123, 144, 145, 157, 170, 206
Whitaker, George, 207
White, Jane, 179, 180
Wilberforce, William, 63, 73
William III, king
Wilmot, John Eardley, 290–91
Wilson, Daniel Sir, 237
Wilson, Sybil, 237–38, 242
Wiseman, Nicholas, 155
Wolfe, Charles, 15
Wollstonecraft, Mary, 230
Women's Aid Association, 235
Women's Auxiliary, 219, 228, 229, 235
Woodward, Thomas, 33
Worcester College, 115
Wray, Henry, 111
Wrong, George M., 306
Wyclif/Wycliffe, John, 10–11, 114, 300–328
Wyclif Society, 305
Wycliffe College (Toronto), 10, 191, 202, 210–14, 235–36, 242–43, 245, 247, 300–328
Wyndham-Quin, Edwin (Lord Adare), 112

Yukon, diocese of, 189, 254, 255, 256, 263, 270
YMCA, 214, 215

www.ingramcontent.com/pod-product-compliance
Lightning Source LLC
Chambersburg PA
CBHW052145300426
44115CB00011B/1530